Red Legacies in China

HARVARD CONTEMPORARY CHINA SERIES 18

Red Legacies in China

CULTURAL AFTERLIVES OF THE COMMUNIST REVOLUTION

Edited by
Jie Li and Enhua Zhang

Published by the Harvard University Asia Center
Distributed by Harvard University Press
Cambridge (Massachusetts) and London 2016

Printed in the United States of America

The Harvard Contemporary China Series is designed to present new research that deals with present-day issues against the background of Chinese history and society. The focus is on interdisciplinary research intended to convey the significance of the rapidly changing Chinese scene.

The Harvard University Asia Center publishes a monograph series and, in coordination with the Fairbank Center for Chinese Studies, the Korea Institute, the Reischauer Institute of Japanese Studies, and other faculties and institutes, administers research projects designed to further scholarly understanding of China, Japan, Vietnam, Korea, and other Asian countries. The Center also sponsors projects addressing multidisciplinary and regional issues in Asia.

Library of Congress Cataloging-in-Publication Data

Red legacies in China : cultural afterlives of the Communist Revolution / edited by Jie Li and Enhua Zhang.

pages cm—(Harvard contemporary China series ; 18)

Includes bibliographical references and index.

ISBN 978-0-674-73718-1 (pbk. : alk. paper)

1. Politics and culture—China. 2. Decommunization—China. 3. Art—Political aspects—China. 4. China—Civilization—1949– I. Li, Jie, 1979– editor. II. Zhang, Enhua, 1974– editor. III. Series: Harvard contemporary China series ; 18.

DS777.6.R43 2016

951.05—dc23

2015019170

Index by Mary Mortensen

♾ Printed on acid-free paper

Last figure below indicates year of this printing

20 19 18 17 16

Contents

Plates and Figures

Plates

Following page 220

Figures

Acknowledgments

This edited volume originated from the conference "Red Legacy in China," held at Harvard University in April 2010 and sponsored by the Chiang Ching-Kuo Foundation Inter-University Center for Sinology, the Harvard-Yenching Institute, and the Fairbank Center for Chinese Studies. We thank all the participants and discussants at the conference for their thoughtful and stimulating contributions. A conference report is available online at *China Heritage Quarterly*, No. 22, June 2010.

We are deeply grateful to Elizabeth J. Perry and David Der-wei Wang for their continuous support and critical inquiry of this project from conception to completion. We also very much appreciate the editorial expertise and patient help from Kristen Wanner and Robert Graham at the Harvard Asia Center Publications Program through the long process of manuscript preparation and production. The two anonymous external reviewers gave encouraging and illuminating comments that helped to make this a better book. Julie Hagen's meticulous copyediting and Nancy Hearst's proofreading made many wonderful stylistic improvements. We also thank the Harvard-Yenching Institute and the Fairbank Center for their subventions toward the book's publication costs.

Chapter 2, "Building Big, with No Regret," was first published in the architectural journal *AA Files* 63 (2011), and Chapter 4, "Socialist Visual Experience as Cultural Identity," appeared as "What Does Socialist Visual Culture Mean to Contemporary Art" in Xiaobing Tang's *Visual Culture in Contemporary China: Paradigms and Shifts* (Cambridge University Press, 2015). We thank *AA Files* and Cambridge University Press for permitting us to republish these pieces.

—Jie Li and Enhua Zhang

INTRODUCTION

Discerning Red Legacies in China

Jie Li

> We are the heirs of communism
> Inheriting the glorious tradition of the forebearers of the Revolution.
>
> —"Song of the Young Pioneers"

> In this absurd time, they encourage you to sing revolutionary songs, but they do not encourage you to wage a revolution.
>
> —He Bing 何兵, China University of Political Science and Law, 2011

As Chinese schoolchildren continue to sing the revolutionary anthem "Song of the Young Pioneers," what *are* the legacies of the Communist Revolution in today's China?[1] The celebrations of the sixtieth anniversary of the founding of the People's Republic of China (PRC) in 2009 and the ninetieth anniversary of the founding of the Chinese Communist Party (CCP) in 2011 seemed to be culminations of a recent official and popular revival of so-called red culture, wherein cultural artifacts associated with the Communist Revolution received makeovers as "red classics," "red songs," "red art," "red collections," "red restaurants," and "red tourism." Yet after nearly four decades of market reform and social transformation, to what extent are the ideas, realities, and memories of the Mao era still relevant? How have the notions and practices of "revolution," "communism," and "socialism" changed over time? Which aspects and layers of the revolutionary past have been glorified, contested, or disavowed since the end of the Cultural Revolution—and by whom, how, when, and why?

The contributors to this volume examine "red legacies" in China—remainders and reminders of the Communist Revolution in the post-Mao era. Evoking at once utopian ideals and traumatic catastrophes, red legacies may be found in the remnants of public culture from the 1950s to the 1970s and contemporary representations and reinventions of the revolutionary past, as well as in inherited aesthetic forms, practices, and mindsets. Mediated by monuments and artifacts, texts and images, bodies and places, red legacies pose critical questions for the continuity and transformation of Chinese identity from the socialist to the postsocialist eras. At stake is not only how the present remembers the past but also how the past might shape the present—how the ideas, symbols, and sacrifices on the revolutionary path might serve as resources or liabilities for Chinese society, in both material and spiritual terms. The chapters in this volume revisit, analyze, and critique red legacies in their various cultural forms.

How are we to periodize red legacies? China's red culture can be traced back to the 1921 founding of the CCP and the establishment of Communist base areas from Jinggangshan to Yan'an, but it was only after the CCP's political victory in 1949 that those early decades of revolutionary mobilization entered mainstream culture as myths, legends, and monuments; these in turn played a great role in "continuing" the revolution until Mao's death in 1976. In other words, the revolutionary struggles that took place prior to 1949 were already important legacies for the first three decades of the PRC. Although our definition of the revolutionary past includes the pre-1949 period, this volume treats such early Communist history mostly in terms of its post-1949 *representation* and *mediation* in museums, art, theater, literature, and film. The post-Mao reverberations of the public culture of the Mao era remain the primary focus of this collection.

Unlike post-Communist countries in the former Soviet bloc, China never underwent an explicit regime transition—neither after Mao's death in 1976 nor later, after the nationwide protests in 1989. The CCP has continued its authoritarian rule, but since Deng Xiaoping's market reforms, "socialism with Chinese characteristics" can barely mask China's abandonment of Communist ideals and its entrance into the global capitalist economy. The ideologies, cultures, and institutions from the Mao era have either faded away entirely or persisted in residual forms, meeting with erasure or revival at various times and places. In recent years, red culture made a localized official comeback under former Chongqing party secretary Bo Xilai, who promoted the dissemination of Maoist slogans and the singing of red songs to tap into popular sentiment, before he fell spectacularly from power in the spring of 2012. Meanwhile, the central government has juggled selective memories of pre-1949 revolutionary struggles with a willing amnesia about the Mao era. Although the party officially repudiated the Cultural Revolution as catastrophic turmoil in a 1981 resolution, textbooks, museums, and official mass media circumvent any mention of this traumatic decade and of other sensitive histories like the post–Great Leap Famine and the Anti-Rightist Movement. The Maoist past thus remains a volatile site of contestations that can both bolster and threaten the current government's legitimacy. China's contradictory, even schizophrenic, relationship to its red legacies is best expressed in the epigraph by He Bing of China University of Political Science and Law: "they encourage you to sing revolutionary songs, but they do not encourage you to wage a revolution."[2]

In intellectual discourse and popular culture, red legacies are also riddled with paradoxical and ambiguous meanings. In the decade after Mao's death in 1976, the Cultural Revolution became a major subject in literature, art, and cinema, giving rise to such literary and cultural movements as the "Scar" (伤痕) and "Searching for Roots" (寻根) movements.[3] However, the plethora of unofficial historiographies giving a cathartic outlet to past sufferings remained in the shadows of censorship and never dealt with crucial issues of collective guilt and responsibility. In the late 1980s and early 1990s, a posthumous cult of Mao flourished throughout the country. Historical ignorance, folk beliefs, and disillusionment with market reforms all contributed to a mass commodification of Maoist memorabilia, the rerelease of Cultural Revolution songs set to rock beats, a recycling of red art into the Political Pop of commercial advertisements, and various red-themed restaurants and tourist destinations.[4] The 1990s also saw the emergence of "New Leftist" public intellectuals who criticized the government's market-oriented policies for creating inequality and sought to resuscitate Maoist ideals. Their arguments and those of their liberal opponents have garnered passionate supporters and strident critics in cyberspace since the turn of the twenty-first century.[5]

Cultural Sites of Memory

As generations born *after* the Cultural Revolution come of age, memories based on personal, lived experiences of the Chinese Communist Revolution and the Mao era are giving way to mediated cultural forms. In highlighting the term "red legacies," this volume focuses less on the reminiscences of the middle-aged and elderly generations than on what theorists of collective memory have labeled "sites of memory" and "cultural memory." The French historian Pierre Nora coined the term "sites of memory" (*lieux de mémoire*) to designate a collection of geographical places, historical figures, literary or artistic objects, emblems, and symbols that constitute French national identity. He argues that these sites of memory exist because there are no longer "milieus of memory" (*milieux de mémoire*), or settings in which memory is a real part of everyday experience.[6] In a similar juxtaposition, the German scholar Jan Assmann distinguishes between "communicative memory," constituted through informal everyday interactions, and "cultural memory," which is written into sacred texts and crystallized in symbols, rituals, and narratives.[7] Applying Assmann's distinction to contemporary China, Susanne Weigelin-Schwiedrzik points out that official historiography in the People's Republic of China has been based on those "sacred texts" edited and published as Mao Zedong's *Selected Works*, and thus not only remote history but also recent history has been treated as part of the nation's cultural memory.[8] Also applying Nora and Assmann to a Chinese context, the recent collection *Places of Memory in Modern China* examines a few significant sites of memory in modern and contemporary China, ranging from the First Emperor's Terracotta Warriors to the Chiang Kai-shek Memorial Hall.[9]

While the concepts of cultural memory and sites of memory are indispensable grids from which to consider what the past means in the present, these terms also connote a convergence toward a single cultural tradition, national identity, and historical master narrative, putting less weight on controversy and multiplicity. Thus we propose *red legacies* to provide a new critical framework and interpretive strategy within which to examine the profusion of official and unofficial cultural artifacts associated with the Chinese Communist Revolution. We submit that red legacies are outcomes of agency and practice, not "a vague wave of associations which supposedly come over an entire population when a set of past events is mentioned."[10] Hence this volume investigates the commerce between past and present, and reconstructs the palimpsests of red legacies as they have accrued over time.

In the field of contemporary Chinese studies, this volume builds on—but is to be distinguished from—related scholarship that aims at three goals: to uncover or set straight historical facts; to show how different social groups remember the Chinese Revolution and the Mao era; and to examine contemporary *representations* of that past in film, fiction, or art.[11] Rather than excavating "what really happened" in China's "revolutionary decades," we examine the meanings of the past in the present, or what the past does *for* and *to* the present.[12] Instead of remembrances of firsthand experiences, we ask what is transmittable across generations, as well as what has been repressed but continues to exert influence.[13] We seek to go beyond analyses of cultural artifacts as disembodied texts to trace the processes of their production and reception as well as their status as symbolic capital and cultural assets.[14] Finally, discussions of Chinese "post-socialism" have to this point been more concerned with the expansion of global capitalism and its discontents than with examining both the inheritances and the debts, and the vitalities and the sequelae that "revolutionary history" might have left behind.[15]

The chapters in this volume emphasize the indebtedness of the present to the past as well as the resurrections of the past in the present. Instead of capturing the zeitgeist of a given period or accounting for how historical epochs succeed one another in a monumental, teleological fashion, we share a layered approach that borrows from Michel Foucault's archaeological and genealogical methods.[16] This approach elucidates the relations between what Raymond Williams calls "dominant," "residual," and "emergent" forms.[17] Rather than treating red legacies as transhistorical constants, the authors of this book excavate the layered strata of cultural memory sites to trace how given revolutionary symbols and myths were created in the first place, how their forms and meanings changed in specific historical contexts, and how they have been mobilized by different agents during the past few decades. As residual forms that remain alive—as opposed to dead, "archaic" ones—red legacies can serve to bolster the dominant culture or provide resources for an alternative or opposition to it.

Besides more obvious red legacies, like the "red classics" and Cultural

Revolution posters, we also seek to detect "invisible" red legacies, such as totalitarian aesthetics and habits of thinking, as well as the revolution's human costs—both voluntary and involuntary sacrifices that beg the questions of whether, what, and how we can learn from disjunctions between theory and practice, between ideology and experience. Sometimes the very censorship of certain memories constitutes a legacy in its own right, showing that the past is not quite passé. It is also worth keeping in mind that, while the Chinese government and dominant political and economic interest groups play key roles to shape the meanings of the past in the present, red legacies also reside in alternative realms that resist or lie beyond official repressions and representations.

Instead of China's political, economic, and institutional heritage, this book focuses on red legacies in the cultural realm, with chapters on the visual and performing arts, literature, and cinema, as well as architecture, museums, and memorials. Apart from engaging with critical theory and writing new cultural historiographies, the authors use diverse methods, including archival research, art-historical interviews, and close readings of images and texts, as well as ethnographic thick description. By focusing on the cultural afterlives of the Communist Revolution, this book distinguishes itself from the recent volume edited by Sebastian Heilmann and Elizabeth Perry that examines the influences of Chinese revolutionary experiences and legacies on contemporary political institutions and policy styles, explaining the Communist Party's regime resilience through "adaptive authoritarianism" and drawing attention to "Mao's invisible hand."[18] Whereas social scientists have approached revolutionary memories by defining models that can explain (and possibly predict) larger political and social patterns, the authors of this volume offer critical interpretations of the nuances and complexities of cultural phenomena and intellectual currents. And whereas social scientists privilege taxonomies, statistics, and scientific periodizations, we attend more to the media and genres, the poetics and aesthetics of red legacies that not only "channel and constrain the articulation of memory" but also participate in shaping present and future social practices.[19] The chapters in this volume are organized in five parts—"Red Foundations," "Red Art," Red Classics," "Red Bodies," and "Red Shadows." Following are introductions to each part, along with synopses of the individual chapters.

Red Foundations

Before this collection turns to discussing the cultural afterlives of the Chinese Revolution or state socialism, Part 1 attends to how red legacies came to be created in the first place. Time and again summoned into being through mass political campaigns and commemorative occasions, the texts, images, artifacts, and monuments that would later become red legacies were often meticulous and grandiose constructions in the socialist era that projected the future as much as they mythologized the past. The first two chapters of this volume take us behind the scenes to trace the construction of some of socialist China's most iconic self-representations. They show that political leaders oversaw major projects, such as the excavation and "museumification" of the First Party Congress site in the early 1950s (Chapter 1) and the construction of the Ten Great Buildings in the late 1950s (Chapter 2). In turn, "cultural officials" and "cultural workers"—ranging from museum staff to architects—implemented their visions, often working as collaborating collectives rather than individually. Following careful negotiations and multiple revisions, the makers of red legacies manipulated texts, artifacts, and visual images from the past to accord with contemporary political agendas and to fashion history into myth.

As Denise Y. Ho shows in Chapter 1, the task of preserving and memorializing sites of China's pre-1949 revolutionary history was an important part of the Communist Party's propaganda effort from the founding of the People's Republic, drawing inspiration from Republican-era and Soviet precedents. One of the key locations was the site of the First Party Congress, the first *place* in the party's foundation narrative and one that would be identified and restored as a revolutionary relic and a symbolic place for pilgrimage. This chapter chronicles the search for and authentication of the site after the founding of the People's Republic, as well as the subsequent construction and presentation of its exhibitions. Drawing on records in the Shanghai Municipal Archives, periodicals, and more recent official history and memoir, Ho traces the revisions to the First Party Congress exhibition—both what was on display and the oral scripts followed by the docents—from the 1950s to the present. She argues that there was a persistent tension between authenticity and interpretation, between reproducing the site (as artifact) as it was, originally, and revising history (as narrative) to cope with the changing politics of the Maoist and post-Mao eras. In the early 1960s, museum officials created an authoritative "mask" of official history, a construct "carefully designed to cover uncertainties, contradictions, and uncomfortable truths." During the Cultural Revolution, the museum changed from a political textbook to a political broadside, promoting the cult of Mao and providing a critique of the latest Cultural Revolution enemies. This chapter concludes by examining how the First Party Congress site has been renovated and its exhibits created anew in the reform period, and how—despite new trends in museology and the presentation of objects—it remains a center for "red tourism" and a memorial to revolution within Shanghai's rapidly changing cityscape.

Whereas the First Party Congress site was excavated, reinvented, and commemorated as a revolutionary symbol from the Republican era, the "founding fathers" of the PRC were also eager to create brand new monuments to represent the new socialist state to the world and for posterity. In Chapter 2, "Building Big, with No Regret," Zhu Tao traces the construction of Beijing's Ten Great Buildings project during the Great Leap Forward as a new architectural milestone that triggered a nationwide building boom in the Mao era. Politicians, city planners, and architects struggled to devise a style suitable for a Chinese *and* socialist regime. Consuming enormous resources and labor, the Ten Great Buildings were constructed within twelve months, between 1958 and 1959, to meet the government's deadline to commemorate the tenth anniversary of the "New China" at the same time that the country was experiencing one of its most dire socioeconomic crises. Through comparisons with Republican-era precedents and today's megaprojects in what Zhu calls a state-capitalist style, this chapter identifies a long-standing tradition in China wherein an obsession with the projection of power through architectural style takes precedence over civic structures, like schools and homes. Zhu further argues that the tradition of "building big," regardless of exorbitant costs and devastating social consequences, still exerts a powerful influence over China's architectural, urban, and social development today. Especially in the 2000s, central and local governments have employed brand-name international architects for grand architectural projects and staged spectacular events to gloss over social contradictions and boost national pride. Finally,

Zhu suggests that China's very capacity to "embrace change, unburdened with regret" is indebted to the revolutionary tradition of creating a tabula rasa at breakneck speed without qualms over the "brutal erasure of past conditions."

Red Art

Apart from architectural monuments and symbols, the medium of propaganda posters played an important role in the construction of red iconography in the Mao era. In quantitative and spatial terms, as Harriet Evans points out in Chapter 3, posters were the most important visual means through which the Cultural Revolution was created and played out. While artists had little choice but to follow the prescribed messages and aesthetic standards from central and local propaganda departments, their oral histories reveal ideas and aspirations that transgressed the posters' explicit themes. Likewise, readers and audiences could also "poach" texts to overturn official interpretations, thereby endowing the images with nuances, polysemy, and ambiguity. Evans argues that these "ambiguities of address"—present in the structure, composition, and sometimes even the color of the posters—go a long way toward explaining how they simultaneously evoke complex, contradictory memories of horror *and* pleasure among their contemporary audiences. After the Cultural Revolution, the once-omnipresent posters gradually disappeared from the spaces of everyday life in the 1980s, only to return, starting in the 1990s, as popular collectibles. The images have been widely revisited in popular commercial advertising, red tourism, and contemporary art, suggesting a complex subjectivity that defies both condemnation of and nostalgia for the Maoist past.

While various contemporary Chinese artists have appropriated the striking imagery of Cultural Revolution posters, none has created works as successful, provocative, or complex as Wang Guangyi. In Chapter 4, Xiaobing Tang focuses on the notion of "socialist visual experience" first articulated by the artist around the year 2000 in order to reconstruct the conceptual evolution in his art, observing three successive stages in Wang's mature work to date. A first stage of "visual critique," in which Wang Guangyi juxtaposed Cultural Revolution–style political images with prevalent logos of global consumerism, was followed, Tang observes, by a stage of "cultural critique." In this second stage, the artist turned the socialist legacy into an intellectual resource as well as a cultural identity and voiced critical opposition to the contemporary state of affairs. His effort to "restore" or "return to" a socialist visual experience therefore amounts not so much to a political statement as to a cultural rediscovery. The more challenging move, however, is Wang Guangyi's critique of contemporary art as an institution. This "institutional critique," Tang argues, is a logical extension of the artist's work. In claiming that his art is but a result of what the people have created and that his objective is to make art dissimilar from commercialized art objects, the artist poses challenges to the very system of contemporary art that he helped legitimize in the 1980s and 1990s. Tang suggests that this most recent stage in Wang Guangyi's development hearkens back to some of the anti-institutional, antiestablishment politics of earlier avant-garde movements, such as the Red Guard art movement of the mid-1960s.

Red Classics

In a 1963 speech, Mao Zedong warned against a "counterrevolutionary restoration" on a national scale that would "change the color" of "the whole of China."[20] Fear of a possible Chinese evolution toward capitalism was spread through the socialist education campaign known as "Never forget class struggle," which helped pave the way for the Cultural Revolution. After Mao's death, however, his successors reversed China's revolutionary path and enacted a "capitalist restoration." Comparing texts that span the Maoist and the post-Mao eras, the three chapters in this part of the book provide genealogies of red legacies in theatrical, literary, and cinematic productions. Their authors read such post-Mao cultural artifacts as new historiographies that challenge and critique the authoritative narratives of canonical red classics, making claims to greater authenticity in their historical content and greater realism in their formal expressions. The first decade after Mao's death in 1976 brought the official repudiation of the Cultural Revolution, the rehabilitation of previously purged or maligned figures, and more humanized versions of revolutionary historiography. As the party relinquished its monopoly over all cultural spheres, writers and filmmakers engaged in a sustained reflection on and critique of the revolutionary narratives while subverting the genre conventions of socialist realism. With temporal distance and the deepening of market reforms in the 1990s, however, traumatic memories of the revolutionary past have also given way to discontent with China's growing inequality, corruption, and social insecurity. Not only the Communist teleology but also the capitalist teleology of economic development came into question in their invocation of red legacies, which became a resource for critiquing the status quo.[21] Yet the market itself quickly absorbed the red nostalgia that arose out of disillusionment with economic reforms, making commodities out of all red cultural artifacts.[22] The government has similarly exploited the complex alchemy of red legacies for the new ideological purposes of nationalism and state capitalism, even when the color "red" has been emptied of its revolutionary connotations.

In Chapter 5, "Performing the 'Red Classics,'" Xiaomei Chen examines three revolutionary music and dance epics produced in the PRC between 1964 and 2009. Instrumental in promoting the cult of Mao, the 1964 performance of *The East Is Red* showcased some of the best talents in voice, music, dance, poetry recitation, and drama, meanwhile distorting actual historical events, effacing the roles of other revolutionary leaders, and eliminating post-1949 acts. In the post-Mao era, signature songs from *The East Is Red* continued to be featured in annual concerts celebrating the birth of the party, the army, and the nation, as well as in amateur performances put on by retirees and ordinary citizens. Taking *The East Is Red* as a model and "sister performance," *The Song of the Chinese Revolution*, which premiered in 1984, revised the historical narrative of the Communist Revolution by restoring the roles of formerly erased revolutionary leaders and restaging old revolutionary legends from a personal angle, presenting pathos-ridden sacrifices of mothers and children rather than heroic male martyrs. Its only act on the Mao era skipped from the 1949 founding of the PRC to the 1976 fall of the Gang of Four as a triumphant new beginning. Finally, the 2009 production *The Road to Revival*, performed in celebration of the sixtieth anniversary of the founding of the PRC, departed from its two precursor texts by highlighting post-Mao political regimes and the capitalist approach to rescuing China from national disasters and moving toward prosperity. In serving the new ideology of state capitalism, Chen suggests that the aestheticization of politics persisted, demonstrating once again the "enduring power of revolutionary epic performances" to manipulate "historical narrative, political orientation, star and popular culture, and nationalistic sentiments."

As much as the state has continued to exercise control over cultural production in the post-Mao era, there has nevertheless been ample room for polyphony among new generations of writers. As David Wang argues in Chapter 6, "Red Legacies in Fiction," a cornucopia of literary works in the new millennium have been more daring in critiquing the status quo and more polemical in presenting historical plotting and political platforms than the discursive fervor surrounding "China's Rise." First, Wang sketches a modern genealogy of literature and revolution, showing that the "red legacy" of using fiction as a vehicle to reform politics, to enlighten the nation's youth, and to "speak for the insulted and wounded" can be traced back to the early twentieth century, the May Fourth cultural movement, and the Yan'an period, when Mao called on all literature and arts to serve revolutionary politics. Wang further classifies literary fiction of the Mao era into two main genres: the revolutionary history-romance on the period leading up to the People's Republic of China and the peasant novel. Both forms sought to engage the dialectic of revolution and history, to fashion progressive subjectivity, and to project a utopian vision. In the New Era after the Cultural Revolution, when history had collapsed and the revolution had lost its mandate, root-seeking and avant-garde writers of the 1980s rewrote revolutionary narratives, going "from the sublime to the ironic, from a surplus of meaning to a hollowing out of meaning." By the turn of the century, seasoned writers, such as Mo Yan and Yu Hua, as well as newer voices, like Yan Lianke and Hu Fayun, produced a new literary canon by teasing out the fictitious traces in historical accounts and political propaganda, and demonstrating the wide spectrum of lived experiences in the People's Republic over the past six decades.

Following this survey of red legacies in fiction, Jason McGrath discusses the formal and thematic links between the cinema of the Mao era and post-Mao films, in Chapter 7, "Post-Socialist Realism in Chinese Cinema." Like its literary counterpart, Mao-era cinema combined revolutionary romanticism and revolutionary realism in depicting socialist heroes who "propel history forward" while "modeling the ideal Communist citizen of the future." In showing that "Communists have more fun," McGrath points out the variety of Mao-era genres—war epics, spy thrillers, musicals, and comedies—that served the single master narrative of Communist liberation and called for "ongoing vigilance against reactionary forces." Cinema in the post-Mao era, however, manifested a "loss of historical certainty" and actively invoked Mao-era genre conventions only to empty them of heroism and to subvert their narratives of progress, thus revealing the conventionality of socialist realism while implicitly claiming a realism of its own. McGrath uses the term "post–socialist realism" both to define these new films against the influence of socialist realism and to draw attention to their realist portrayals of the postsocialist economic and social condition. This new realism makes use of techniques such as on-location shooting, natural lighting and sound, naturalistic performances, long shots, and long takes, as well as giving attention to seemingly irrelevant or contingent details. McGrath explores transgenerational interactions with Mao-era cinema through comparative close readings of films by China's so-called Fourth-, Fifth-, and Sixth-Generation filmmakers, concluding with a discussion of how digital cinema might both complicate and extend these tendencies.

Red Bodies

Having examined the red legacies found in China's monuments, visual art, theater, literature, and film, Part 4 of this volume examines the mediation of red legacies through the *bodies* of the leaders and the masses—both in a corporeal sense and as representations. In discussions of Mao's "two bodies" through his posthumous impersonators, the body of the crowd used in national spectacles, and the commodified bodies of Lenin and the subaltern in Yan Lianke's fiction, the three chapters in this section show that human bodies are not just the subjects and objects of representation but also serve as a significant *medium* through which the revolution could be carried out and transmitted.[23] At the height of the Mao cult in the 1960s, the "live encounters" between the Great Helmsman and the millions of young Red Guards at Tiananmen Square were instrumental for launching the Cultural Revolution. Equally significant were the many mass rallies and parades that accompanied every anniversary and political campaign throughout the Mao era.[24] Reproduced *ad infinitum* through photography, painting, and sculpture, Mao's ubiquitous face and body, on display in public and private spaces, retained a sacred aura that inspired worship by the masses.

In the three and half decades since his death, Mao's body and image have continued to dominate the center of political power. In Chapter 8, Haiyan Lee investigates how the political-theological idea of Mao's "two bodies" lives on in the performative art of Mao impersonation in contemporary China. She argues that the party's greatest ideological achievement after the Cultural Revolution has been its bifurcation of Mao into the mortal "body natural" and the immortal "body politic"—Mao the fallible human being and Mao the anchor of regime legitimacy—as he embodies both popular sovereignty and one-party autocracy. Despite what Lee calls the "overtly nationalist and covertly capitalist makeover," the party retooled Mao's immortal body "to sanction developmental goals rather than class struggles." Lee goes on to examine both the institutionalized practice of using "special actors" to portray Mao (and other political leaders) in PRC "main-melody" film and television and the emerging phenomenon of freelance impersonators reenacting Mao's speeches and calligraphy at tourist sites and entertainment venues. Framing this discussion is a close reading of Chinese American author Yiyun Li's short story "Immortality," about the fate of a man born with Mao's face and groomed to be Mao's official impersonator. By situating Mao impersonation on the spectrum of performative practices from spirit mediumship, at one end, to satirical art, at the other, Lee aims to make sense of the fraught relationship between the aura of Mao's image and its aesthetic and commercial appropriations. This chapter also addresses the question commonly raised by Western journalists: why are the Mao impersonators determinedly unfunny?

Not only has Mao's body been redeployed for contemporary political and commercial purposes, but also the bodies of the people—the masses—have remained at the beck and call of contemporary nationalist spectacles. In Chapter 9, "Human Wave Tactics," Andy Rodekohr examines the use of the crowd image in more than three decades of Zhang Yimou's work as both a director and cinematographer, which he argues engages the legacies of Chinese revolutionary visual culture. Considering Zhang's use of crowds in terms of ritual and technological visuality, this chapter shows how his direction of the Opening Ceremony for the 2008 Olympic Games in Beijing resorted to "human wave tactics" and the mass-reproducible forms of propaganda. A legacy from China's civil war and the Korean War, the "human wave" describes a massive headlong attack from the front line of a battle force, favoring overwhelming scale over strategic maneuvering. China continued to deploy the tactic in peacetime to create a "state of emergency" (or ecstasy) when individual interests had to be sacrificed to the collective good—such was the case during the Great Leap Forward and the construction of the so-called Ten Great Buildings, which Zhu Tao writes about in Chapter 2. The bodies of the masses were collectively mobilized in a similar fashion for the 2008 Olympics, even while the Opening Ceremony carefully expunged all explicit references to the Mao era. At once complicit in and critical of such human wave tactics, Zhang's historical costume films, such as *Hero* (2002) and *Curse of the Golden Flower* (2006), subordinate maximalist images of crowds to the more qualified drama between the main actors, thus interrogating the problematic relationship between leaders and masses and exposing how political-aesthetic spectacles mask the violence and sacrifice that contribute to their formation. Finally, Rodekohr analyzes Zhang Yimou's cinematography of crowds in early Fifth-Generation films from the 1980s as a "hollow gesture" toward the utopia they once promised, pointing out that his crowds on screen generated consumerist and nationalist crowds off-screen, instead of revolutionary masses.

In Chapter 10, "Time Out of Joint: Commemoration and Commodification of Socialism in Yan Lianke's *Lenin's Kisses*," Carlos Rojas reads contemporary China's transition from communism to capitalism through the prism of subaltern subjects who appear to fall through the cracks of history. In Yan Lianke's 2004 novel *Lenin's Kisses*, a local leader in Hunan fabricates an elaborate scheme to purchase Lenin's preserved corpse from Russia and install it in a newly constructed mausoleum to attract tourists from China and around the world, thereby bringing the county so much revenue that its residents would not know how to spend all the money. As Rojas points out, this novel explores a set of structural tensions inherent in contemporary China's transition from communism to capitalism by deploying a dialectic of bare life and living death, focusing in particular on the way in which the two intersect around the figure of the commodity. If Marxism arose originally in response to the pernicious workings of capital and profit-driven development, here we find a perverse capitalistic drive emerging out of a preserved emblem of the

Marxist legacy. Rojas argues that the dialectic of communism and capitalism embodied by Lenin's corpse symbolizes the death of Cold War Communist regimes as well as the continuing force of capitalist development and the corrective critiques that it inspires.

Red Shadows

The first four parts of this volume focus on cultural appropriations of red legacies for symbolic capital in the present and ironic commentary on the status quo. Part 5 emphasizes darker red legacies that have been disavowed, edited out, or otherwise subjected to state-sponsored amnesia. Although the human costs and failures of the Communist Revolution remain on the margins of what may be represented, the Maoist past continues to exert an influence and cast a shadow on today's People's Republic of China in linguistic, cultural, intellectual, and institutional realms. Chapters 11 and 12 argue for the necessity of acknowledging and coming to terms with red legacies as both appealing ideals and tragic realities—both theories and practices. Meanwhile, the last two chapters also call for the *renewal* of certain red legacies, such as the guerrilla spirit of rebellion against hegemonic power as well as Maoist cultural practices that purport to give voice to subaltern memories.

Despite sustained echoes of Ba Jin's 1986 call for a Cultural Revolution museum, as Chapter 11 shows, the traumatic catastrophes of the Great Leap Famine and the Cultural Revolution have been practically eliminated from official public culture. Nevertheless, there have emerged fragmentary local initiatives to construct peripheral, small-scale "memory places" to commemorate the excesses of the Mao era. Apart from such prominent structures as the Red Era museum series in Sichuan and the Cultural Revolution Museum in Guangdong, "Museums and Memorials of the Mao Era" also discusses derelict cemeteries and mass graves, former sites of commune headquarters or labor reform camps, and contemporary art galleries. Some of these places were constructed during the Mao era, such as the local museum hosting the famous Rent Collection Courtyard that promoted class struggle in the mid-1960s, and the grandiose tombs that Red Guards built for their dead comrades during the Cultural Revolution's factional violence. After showing how the meanings of such sites have changed over time, the chapter proceeds to make a number of curatorial proposals for memorials and museums seeking to pass on memories of the Mao era to future generations. Drawing inspiration from institutions and memorials around the world that commemorate totalitarian pasts, victims of manmade catastrophes, and failed utopian projects, this chapter argues for a plurality of local memorial projects that would bring together trauma and nostalgia, subjective remembrances and objective documents, major historical events and everyday artifacts, scholars and artists, sympathetic identification and critical reflection. It highlights four related paradigms: "stumbling stones," or small memorials of specific victims erected where they once lived; documentation centers that feature oral history collections; monumental ruins that have been preserved and transformed; and community museums that invite contributions from the local population.

In the volume's final chapter, Geremie Barmé considers a few areas in which we can detect traces of what he calls the "abiding, and beguiling, heritage of the Maoist era and state socialism." Taking as his starting point the precipitous fall of Bo Xilai in March 2012, Barmé shows that red bloodlines and family connections have continued to play a significant role in turning red symbolic capital into economic and political capital.[25] While thinkers labor to salvage Marxism, this chapter argues that red legacies constitute a body of cultural, intellectual, and linguistic practices that are profoundly ingrained in institutional behavior in China. Meanwhile, the fictionalization of revolutionary history has proliferated in popular culture, and it is in these "remakings, spoofs, and recountings of High Maoist policies, cultural styles and forms," writes Barmé, that "we can detect ways in which the impotent, powerless, and dispossessed find a way to express opposition" to the "party's theory-led monopoly on discourse, ideas, and everyday politics." While resistance from within may be the most trenchant of red legacies, "the spirit of rebellion, the active involvement with a politics of agitation, action and danger, is one legacy that seems safe to contemplate only at a distance." Finally, Barmé pinpoints the necessity of historical remembrance and warns against the "crimson blindfold" that deletes or discounts the frustrations and failures of the past in order to formulate coherent narratives that serve as scholastic and cultural legitimations of an authoritarian regime.

Legacies: Inheritance or Debt

The contributors to this volume are all concerned with the *value* of red cultural legacies, but we do not believe in any simplistic and totalistic affirmation or negation of a red legacy as a whole (hence the multiplicity of legacies as opposed to the singular legacy). We attend to a variety of meanings and implications—positive or negative, nostalgic or traumatic, serious or playful—that cultural artifacts associated with the revolutionary past might have in present contexts. We also examine the fraught relationship between red cultural legacies and the current regime's legitimacy, asking how the revolutionary past has served as both asset and liability for the state. Beyond state appropriation, might individuals also turn the symbolic capital of red legacies into economic capital or tactics of resistance? Finally, we ask whether the revolutionary past might provide alternatives for a better future. Can the revolution's successors receive past blessings while dispelling its curses, or must debts be settled before inheritances can be paid out?

Apart from Marxist ideology, revolutionary history, and the trauma and nostalgia that constitute collective memories of the Mao era, we show that totalitarian aesthetics, language, habits, and tactics—as well as an absent regard for humans' sacrifices—continue to exert their influence in hidden and potentially more powerful ways. Instead of reckoning with either the Mao era's manmade catastrophes or revolutionary ideals, today's government has continued to construct a spectacular façade of power by tapping into the red legacies in performance art, discursive practice, public architecture, and mobilization strategies. Zhu Tao (Chapter 2), Xiaomei Chen (Chapter 5), and Andy Rodekohr (Chapter 9) discern red legacies in the scale, speed, and cost of grandiose state-sponsored projects that deploy and employ impressive numbers of people. Whether during the Great Leap Forward or in preparation for the 2008 Olympic Games, whether in celebration of the tenth or the sixtieth anniversary of the People's Republic, the logic of numbers and speed determined everything in the "total mobilization" of people and resources. In other words, red totalitarian aesthetics turned out to be highly resilient and versatile in transcending and absorbing ideological contradictions.

It is important simultaneously to appreciate the revolution's utopian ideals and to reckon with its enormous human sacrifices—as well as to see how "positive" and "negative" red legacies may be inextricably intertwined. As much as we tease out distinctions and nuances among different red legacies, we are wary of—as Barmé puts it—"a 'strategic disaggregation' of the ideological/theoretical from the historical/lived" in order that abstract ideas may be championed "clear of the bloody and tragic realities of the past." The continued appeal, relevance, and salience of red legacies lie in the interstices between unfulfilled longings for community and social justice that motivated past revolutionaries and unmourned traumas that accompanied the revolutionary experience. While serving as a conduit for these desires and memories, red cultural artifacts can be mobilized to both support and criticize the status quo.

Instead of creating a single master narrative that subsumes red legacies under the dominant culture of the present, cultural producers in the new millennium have begun to fashion multiple alternative understandings of the past and visions of the future. As I show in Chapter 11, even without official sanctioning, local civil societies have begun to create memory places that mediate—and mediate *between*—the collective trauma and the nostalgia associated with the Mao era, thereby opening up horizons for reconciliation and for transgenerational transmissions of the past. David Wang argues that the "small talk" of contemporary Chinese fiction teases out the complex traces underneath historical dynamics, thereby serving as a remedy for a society inundated with "big talk," from theories to criticisms, doctrines, and manifestos (Chapter 6). And as China's state socialism gives way to global capitalism, it is worth considering—and critiquing, as Zhu Tao does—the suggestion made by international architects to build for the public good rather than private interests in a country that remains Communist at least in name (Chapter 2). Ultimately, the fate of China's red legacies is far from sealed. Much as they have been instrumentally appropriated or hijacked by those in power, there is yet the possibility to turn them into a shared heritage and lessons for future generations.

Notes

1. For the complete lyrics with an English translation, see http://www.chinese-tools.com/songs/song/68/shaonian-xianfengdui.html (accessed June 20, 2014).
2. From an informal graduation speech given by Vice Dean He Bing in 2011. The

comment circulated widely in China and was also quoted by Western journalists. For a video of this speech, see https://www.youtube.com/watch?v=wu2tlRMs1BU (accessed June 20, 2014).

3. Michael Berry, *A History of Pain: Trauma in Modern Chinese Literature and Film* (New York: Columbia University Press, 2008), chap. 4; Sabina Knight, *The Heart of Time: Moral Agency in Twentieth-Century Chinese Fiction* (Cambridge, MA: Harvard University Asia Center, 2006), chaps. 6 and 7; Yomi Braester, *Witness against History: Literature, Film, and Public Discourse in Twentieth-Century China* (Stanford, CA: Stanford University Press, 2003), chaps. 5, 6, and 9.

4. Geremie Barmé, *Shades of Mao: The Posthumous Cult of the Great Leader* (Armonk, NY: M. E. Sharpe, 1996); Jennifer Hubbert, "Revolution Is a Dinner Party: Cultural Revolution Restaurants in Contemporary China," *China Review* 5, no. 2 (2005): 125–50.

5. Merle Goldman, *From Comrade to Citizen: The Struggle for Political Rights in China* (Cambridge, MA: Harvard University Press, 2005); Gloria Davis, *Worrying about China: The Language of Chinese Critical Inquiry* (Cambridge, MA: Harvard University Press, 2007); Wang Hui, *The End of the Revolution: China and the Limits of Modernity* (New York: Verso, 2009).

6. See Pierre Nora, "Between Memory and History: *Les Lieux de Mémoire*," *Representations* 26 (1989): 7–25.

7. Jan Assmann, "Communicative and Cultural Memory," in *Cultural Memory Studies: An International and Interdisciplinary Handbook*, eds. Astrid Erll and Ansgar Nünning (New York: de Gruyter, 2008), pp. 109–18.

8. See Susanne Weigelin-Schwiedrzik, "In Search of a Master Narrative for 20th-Century Chinese History," *China Quarterly* 188 (2006): 1070–91. In contrast to official historiography as a form of cultural memory, she considers the contested unofficial historiographies—such as memoirs and historical documentaries—as "communicative memory" that is "finally becoming visible and is claiming its due."

9. Marc Andre Matten, ed., *Places of Memory in Modern China* (Leiden: Brill, 2012).

10. Jay Winter and Emmanuel Sivan, eds., *War and Remembrance in the Twentieth Century* (Cambridge: Press Syndicate of the University of Cambridge, 1999), p. 9.

11. A number of collected volumes have brought together all three approaches: Ching Kwan Lee and Guobin Yang, *Re-envisioning the Chinese Revolution: The Politics and Poetics of Collective Memories in Reform China* (Stanford, CA: Stanford University Press, 2007); Song Yongyi, ed., *Wenhua dageming: Lishi zhenxiang he jiti jiyi* 文化大革命: 历史真相和集体记忆 (The Cultural Revolution: Historical truth and collective memories) (Hong Kong: Tianyuan shuwu, 2007); William C. Kirby, *The People's Republic of China at 60: An International Assessment* (Cambridge, MA: Harvard University Asia Center, 2011).

12. Exemplary works in this area include Joseph W. Esherick, Paul G. Pickowicz, and Andrew G. Walder, eds., *The Chinese Cultural Revolution as History* (Stanford, CA: Stanford University Press, 2006); Roderick MacFarquhar, *Mao's Last Revolution* (Cambridge, MA: Harvard University Press, 2006); Paul Clark, *The Chinese*

Cultural Revolution: A History (New York: Cambridge University Press, 2008); and Chang-tai Hung, *Mao's New World: Political Culture in the Early People's Republic* (Ithaca, NY: Cornell University Press, 2011).

13. Two extensive studies of social memory are Lisa Rofel, *Other Modernities: Gendered Yearnings in China after Socialism* (Berkeley: University of California Press, 1999), and Gail Hershatter, *The Gender of Memory: Rural Women and China's Collective Past* (Berkeley: University of California Press, 2011). Another study that combines oral histories with close readings of Mao-era cultural artifacts is Barbara Mittler's *A Continuous Revolution: Making Sense of Cultural Revolution Culture* (Cambridge, MA: Harvard University Asia Center, 2012).

14. Studies of postsocialist cultural representations of the revolutionary past include selected chapters in Ban Wang, *Illuminations from the Past: Trauma, Memory, and History in Modern China* (Stanford, CA: Stanford University Press, 2004); Braester, *Witness against History*; Jiang Jiehong, ed., *Burden or Legacy: From the Chinese Cultural Revolution to Contemporary Art* (Hong Kong: Hong Kong University Press, 2007).

15. See, e.g., Sheldon Lu, *Chinese Modernity and Global Biopolitics: Studies in Literature and Visual Culture* (Honolulu: University of Hawai'i Press, 2007); Jason McGrath, *Postsocialist Modernity: Chinese Cinema, Literature, and Criticism in the Market Age* (Stanford, CA: Stanford University Press, 2008); Xudong Zhang, *Postsocialism and Cultural Politics: China in the Last Decade of the Twentieth Century* (Durham, NC: Duke University Press, 2008).

16. Michel Foucault, *The Archaeology of Knowledge* (New York: Pantheon Books, 1972), and "Nietzsche, Genealogy, History," in *The Foucault Reader*, ed. Paul Rabinow (New York: Pantheon, 1984), pp. 76–100.

17. Raymond Williams, *Marxism and Literature* (Oxford: Oxford University Press, 1977), pp. 121–27.

18. Sebastian Heilmann and Elizabeth Perry, eds., *Mao's Invisible Hand: The Political Foundations of Adaptive Governance in China* (Cambridge, MA: Harvard University Asia Center, 2011).

19. Quotation is in Lee and Yang, *Re-envisioning the Chinese Revolution*, p. 11.

20. Mao Zedong, note on "The Seven Well-Written Documents of Chekiang Province concerning Cadres' Participation in Physical Labour" (May 9, 1963), quoted in *On Khrushchov's Phoney Communism and Its Historical Lessons for the World* (Peking: Foreign Languages Press, 1964), pp. 71–72.

21. See, e.g., Qin Shao, "Waving the Red Flag: Cultural Memory and Grass-roots Protest in Housing Disputes in China," *Modern Chinese Literature and Culture* 22, no. 1 (Spring 2010): 197–232.

22. Jennifer Hubbert's study of two different museums that display Mao buttons shows that there are also nuances and distinctions among commodified artifacts. See "(Re)collecting Mao: Memory and Fetish in Contemporary China," *American Ethnologist* 33, no. 2 (2006): 145–61.

23. This insight is indebted to William Schaefer's reading of Mao's saying that the Chinese people are "poor and blank." See Schaefer, "Poor and Blank: History's

Marks and the Photographies of Displacement," *Representations* 109, no. 1 (Winter 2010): 5.

24. Hung, "Parades," in *Mao's New World*, pp. 92–108.

25. David Apter and Tony Saich, *Revolutionary Discourse in Mao's Republic* (Cambridge, MA: Harvard University Press, 1994).

PART 1

Red Foundations

ONE

MAKING A REVOLUTIONARY MONUMENT

The Site of the First National Congress of the Chinese Communist Party

Denise Y. Ho

In July 1976, the monthly periodical *People's Liberation Army Pictorial* published a four-page photo spread depicting soldiers visiting the historic sites of the Chinese Communist Revolution. Beginning with the site of the First Party Congress in Shanghai (*yida huizhi* 一大会址) and ending with Tiananmen Square in Beijing, the eight photographs gave readers a virtual tour of Chinese Communist Party (CCP) history. Designed to celebrate the party's July anniversary, the images were paired with eight poems in the format of a traditional tourist's itinerary of eight vistas. Yet this kind of tour was different: the eight places were official revolutionary sites, and the content of the poems was political and didactic, with metered couplets that took on a military cadence. The poem accompanying the site of the First Party Congress, for example, concluded with the lines, "The Party is the mother, and I am the child / Visiting the Party in person is to express love for the Party / Soldiers will always be loyal to the Party / Following the Party to build a new era!"[1] Though the lines emphasized that personally undertaking a political pilgrimage was the best expression of a soldier's devotion, the format of the article suggests that simply through studying the pictures and reciting the songs, readers could engage in revolutionary tourism.

The *People's Liberation Army Pictorial*'s framing of revolutionary sites demonstrates how such places and buildings—revolutionary sites, revolutionary traces, or revolutionary relics (*geming wenwu* 革命文物)—were constructed and interpreted for contemporary purposes. These sites of the revolutionary past were props in the narrative of party history, preserved as sites of political indoctrination. Even if one did not have the opportunity to make the pilgrimage, a virtual tour was possible through the images that existed in the popular imagination. Each year on the anniversary of the party's founding, the First Party Congress site was described in newspapers. The staff of the First Party Congress museum organized traveling exhibitions to be shown at workers' palaces and communes in the countryside. Images of revolutionary relics even circulated in small handbooks for children; one publication reproduced photographs of artifacts, instructing readers to "look at revolutionary relics and study the revolutionary tradition."[2] Thus revolutionary pilgrimage—both real and imagined—has its own history in the Maoist period.

This chapter examines the making of a revolutionary monument through the history of the First Party Congress site. By studying both the creation of the physical site and the ways in which it was presented to visitors over time, one can explore how the narrative of the party's founding was used to serve contemporary politics. Underlying this process was a fundamental tension between authenticity and interpretation. On the one hand, cultural officials were charged with reproducing the original site; the authenticity of the revolutionary relics would reflect the party's legitimacy and, in turn, inspire appropriate reverence. The goal of authenticity was even more important given the Communist Party's relationship with history; the party's rise to power, after all, was attributed to correct historical understanding. On the other hand, faced with the changing politics of the Maoist period, curators continuously rewrote history for the exhibition. This tension between authenticity and interpretation is a red legacy that persists into the post-Mao era.

This study, based on documents from the Shanghai Municipal Archives, begins with the designation of the First Party Congress site as a revolutionary monument. It shows how revolutionary relics were marshaled to create a foundation narrative for the party, arguing that authentication of the site was a way both to authenticate the revolution itself and to provide political legitimacy for the CCP. Next, turning to the politics of display, the chapter traces the revisions to the First Party

Congress exhibition from the 1950s to the beginning of the Cultural Revolution. Uncovering the ways in which museum officials attempted to follow the "red line" (*hongxian* 红线) reveals how the authoritative mask of official history was carefully designed to cover uncertainties, contradictions, and uncomfortable truths. Finally, I examine the site's history during the Cultural Revolution, when the museum's audience shifted from cadres and foreigners to a broader public. At the same time, its content changed from that of a political textbook to a political broadside, promoting the cult of Mao and critiquing the latest enemies of the Cultural Revolution. While the First Party Congress site remains a place for CCP pilgrimages today, it has adapted its exhibitions to modern museum practice and expanded its public role by becoming a patriotic education site. Today, the site's ability to be relevant to contemporary society rests on the party's legitimacy; the authenticity of the revolutionary monument depends on the authenticity of the party whose founding it tells.

Authenticating Revolution and the Construction of the First Party Congress Site

Today's First Party Congress site—at once historic site, memorial, and museum—is carefully distinguished from its surroundings in the high-end entertainment area of Shanghai's Xintiandi neighborhood (fig. 1.1). A brown street marker, standard for historic sites in Shanghai, directs visitors to a neatly preserved block of five residences that in 1921 housed the First Party Congress meeting. The two-story houses are a modest gray and red brick, framed by the plane trees of the former French Concession. A marble placard identifies the site as a National Cultural Relic, and the Chinese flag waves at one corner.

Of course, when the Communist Party took power in 1949, the site did not exist as such. While the new state sought to preserve the revolutionary relics of its own rise to power, identifying them presented two difficulties: artifacts of the revolution were not immediately recognized as such, and sites of the party's clandestine organization were hidden in neighborhoods transformed by war and occupation. To take up the task of excavating the revolution, the Shanghai Party Committee Propaganda Department dispatched Shen Zhiyu, then a thirty-four-year-old cadre

FIGURE 1.1. Tour groups pose outside the First Party Congress site in Shanghai, 2010. Photo by the author.

from the Shanghai Museum. The Party Committee, following an idea proposed by Mayor Chen Yi, was determined to locate the site of the First Party Congress and establish a memorial museum.[3] To search for the party's birthplace, Shen was instructed, was an important political responsibility.[4]

The use of monuments and museums to serve revolution was not new to this period. In the Republican era (1912–49), monuments to revolution were built and incorporated into political rituals; the Sun Yat-sen Mausoleum is perhaps the most prominent example of a revolutionary monument that the Communist Party inherited. There were national and local revolutionary relics; in 1929, the Shanghai Bureau of Education designated as historic sites the tomb of the Guomindang revolutionary Song Jiaoren and the tomb to the May Fourth martyrs, who died in patriotic protest.[5] Likewise, the revolutionary history museum also had Republican-era precedents. In 1929 the Jiangsu Provincial Government issued orders to collect revolutionary objects, and in 1945 Sun Yat-sen's widow donated his Shanghai residence to the state as a place where people might study the Three Principles of the People.[6] Even in the base areas, the Communist Party used small-scale exhibitions to propagandize its revolution.[7]

The idea of commemorating the revolution in the People's Republic was also directly influenced by the Soviet experience. Chinese cultural officials went on study tours to learn from Soviet museums, and the pages of the museum trade journal *Wenwu cankao ziliao* 文物参考资料 (Cultural relics reference materials) are filled with articles on Soviet museums and methods of display.[8] In 1950, as Shanghai officials searched for the First Party Congress site, vice director of the Bureau of Cultural Relics Wang Yeqiu (1909–87) presented a description of the Soviet Museum of the Revolution to his colleagues.[9] Showing an explicit admiration for the Soviet model, Wang wrote that such a revolutionary museum would be continually added to until the arrival of communism. Chinese museums in this period widely adopted the display techniques that Wang observed: large oil paintings, charts comparing past to present, artifacts, and the extensive use of historical materials. Particularly impressive to Wang in the Soviet museum's collection was a set of torture instruments, including a leather whip that caused him to reflect, "This was familiar to me, because I also survived the leather whip of China's reactionary rulers."[10] The didactic and affective way in which Wang Yeqiu experienced the Soviet Museum of the Revolution was as its designers intended. The museum in the Soviet context was meant to be a living textbook for mass education.[11]

Following the Soviet example, the Chinese built the Museum of the Chinese Revolution in Beijing. Its task of collecting artifacts began in 1949, and the museum was one of the "Ten Great Buildings" constructed to celebrate the tenth anniversary of the People's Republic in 1959.[12] The Museum of the Chinese Revolution, as Chang-tai Hung has shown, affirmed the "red line," using its exhibitions to frame modern Chinese history in terms of Mao Zedong Thought.[13] For the purposes of studying the First Party Congress site, the Museum of the Chinese Revolution is important because it served as the central authority and Shanghai officials would study from Beijing's exhibitions. But the First Party Congress site was both different and unique. Instead of being a new building, a blank slate for a living textbook, the site itself was centered around a revolutionary relic, a unique site that signified the party's origins and was to become a place of pilgrimage. Its authenticity was central to its "important political responsibility."

Recounted in reform-era articles, the tale of discovery and authentication demonstrates the political seriousness and exactitude of the task of excavation. In September 1950, when Shanghai Museum cadre Shen Zhiyu was given the mission of finding the First Party Congress site, the Propaganda Department did not know anything about the site except that it was somewhere in the former French Concession. That the history of the site was politically sensitive is demonstrated in Shen's pursuit of the address: both of his initial leads were linked to a political traitor. The first was Yang Chuhui, the wife of the late Zhou Fohai, an original participant in the Party Congress meeting who later became a prominent member of the Wang Jingwei puppet government. In an ironic twist, the Propaganda Department convinced the Public Security Bureau (PSB) to release Yang from prison so she could participate in Shen's revolutionary project.[14] Shen Zhiyu's second lead was found in the writings of the late Zhou himself, closed to the public as the writings of a traitor.[15] Granted special approval to read them, Shen learned only that the First Party Congress had met in the home of a Li Hanjun, on Bei Le Road.[16]

Together with another official, Shen's colleague Yang Zhongguang, Shen and Yang Chuhui scoured the streets of the French Concession. Yang Chuhui led them to Chen Duxiu's former home, locating his meeting room and an editorial office of *New Youth* magazine.[17] But the landscape of the neighborhood had changed dramatically in the decades since the First Party Congress, and Yang Chuhui would seize upon a house and then realize that it was not the Li residence. At the same time, Yang Zhongguang followed up on a lead that the meeting might have taken place at the Bowen Girls' School. In 1951, photographs of the school were sent to Mao and to Dong Biwu, another original participant, who examined the photographs and reported that the school had provided dormitory space for the participants, but—contrary to the memoir—the actual meeting had taken place at the home of Li Hanjun's brother, Li Shucheng. Yang then went to Beijing to visit Li Shucheng, now minister of agriculture, and was given the address 78 Wangzhi Road, French Concession.[18] Returning to their search, Shen and Yang Chuhui found at that address a small whitewashed noodle shop called Hengfuchang Noodles, with two families living upstairs. As Shen later remembered, when he informed them that their building was the birthplace of the

Chinese Communist Party, "everybody clapped their hands and smilingly exclaimed, 'So it turns out that the place we live in is a precious place!' [*yi kuai baodi* 一块宝地]." Shen declared that the site would become a memorial museum and that the families would have to leave, and in the narrative the families gladly assented, saying, "That is as it should be! [*shi yinggai de* 是应该的]."[19]

If the narrative of finding the site reveals the problems of memory and memoir, the story of its verification underscores the importance of authenticity in its restoration. The creation of the monument was by no means assured, and it actually took several more years for the property to be authenticated. After the Shanghai Party Committee's Department of Propaganda reported its finding to the Central Committee's Department of Propaganda, central propaganda officials determined that if the sites—the *New Youth* office, the Bowen Girls' School, and the First Party Congress site—were indeed reliable, they could be preserved and made into memorials.[20] While it was still verifying the site, the Shanghai Party Committee rented the houses in September 1951, bought the property in May of the following year, and began to submit it for inspection.

On taking over the First Party Congress site, the Shanghai Party Committee decorated the rooms with paintings of Marx and Lenin and with pieces of Mao Zedong's calligraphy. In the winter of 1952, when Wang Yeqiu of the Cultural Relics Bureau came to inspect the site, he ordered that the buildings be restored to their original condition (*yuanzhuang* 原装), explaining that "a memorial museum to revolutionary history should be decorated exactly as it was originally; in this way you may allow visitors to imagine the original scene and inspire feelings of deep veneration."[21] In 1953, three miniature replicas were sent to the Department of Propaganda in Beijing for approval. Mao also inspected the models and dispatched Bao Huiseng, another contemporary participant and an adviser to the State Council, to Shanghai. In March 1954 Bao Huiseng and Xue Wenchu (the wife of Li Shucheng) confirmed the location of the meeting; Xue gave instructions on how to restore the interior and later donated artifacts, including a tea service and a chair.[22] Still, Shanghai officials were not able to complete the restoration, as researchers could not confirm whether the meeting took place upstairs or downstairs. The arrangement of the house was finally settled in 1956 when Dong Biwu came to inspect the site. In those days, Dong explained, the delegates would have met downstairs because there were women in the family of the household. Officials placed a rectangular table downstairs, as the meeting room remains arranged to this day.[23] Wang Yeqiu's direction that the site be restored to its original condition and the care with which the Shanghai officials attempted to recreate it indicate how important authenticity was to the revolutionary monument. This even extended to the exterior of the building; officials wishing to preserve the original atmosphere (*qifen* 气氛) of the area later decided to preserve the adjacent buildings as well.[24]

Once the First Party Congress site was authenticated and its original aspect restored, Shanghai officials turned to the project of creating a museum. Originally, in October 1951, the Shanghai Party Committee had planned a revolutionary history museum with three branches; one branch would exhibit party history and Mao's writings, the second would display the history of the labor movement, and the third would exhibit Mao Zedong's personal effects.[25] In 1955 the Memorial Museum Preparatory Committee began to draft plans for creating a whole new museum. Its initial proposal to the Ministry of Culture in 1956 was to clear a huge block surrounding the site, and to include a museum and a garden. Because of the financial hardships following the Great Leap Forward, however, the plan for a large museum complex had to be abandoned.[26] Though the exhibition attached to the First Party Congress site would remain in the original buildings, it is still worth remembering this original plan for a greater revolutionary history museum, whose outlines are at least partly responsible for the scope of the Xintiandi district in Shanghai today.

Thus restored in the 1950s, the First Party Congress site became Shanghai's most politically significant cultural relic. The ways in which the state recognized revolutionary relics and the efforts local officials made in identifying them demonstrate the political value of the sites of revolution. In 1961, for example, the First Party Congress site was named a national cultural relic under state protection (*quanguo zhongdian wenwu baohu danwei* 全国重点文物保护单位), a designation given to only three other Shanghai sites, all of them connected with the revolution.[27] On the national list, the site of the First Party Congress was first among the Shanghai sites. Thus in the bureaucracy of cultural heritage, the revolution gave Shanghai political and cultural cachet.[28] Local cultural preservation efforts reflected this priority; the Shanghai Bureau of Culture went to great lengths to track revolutionary footprints, especially places where Mao might have been. In the 1960s the bureau interviewed old cadres to determine where Mao had lived in Shanghai.[29] In another case, the Bureau of Culture convened a conference to determine whether Mao had ever visited a garden that was slated for destruction.[30] Shanghai's claim to history was revolution.

The People's Republic made revolutionary monuments by uncovering and elevating revolutionary relics, placing them at the center of the revolution's history, and imprinting them on contemporary memory. These created artifacts, such as the First Party Congress site, were used to support the state's revolutionary narrative and were employed to frame historical, national, and revolutionary understanding. Attention to authenticity was paramount; it was necessary to return the sites to their original condition, detailed restorations followed the meticulous cross-checking of participants' memories, and the sites themselves were open to internal inspection only after all the particulars could be ascertained. A revolutionary relic had to be authentic in order to lend its authenticity to the party's revolutionary narrative. The party, having attributed its rise to power to a correct interpretation of history, could not be seen to be inaccurate. The First Party Congress site, the first station in the pilgrim's tour of revolutionary history, thus had to be "exactly as it was originally" so that visitors could "imagine the original scene." The site itself proved relatively easy to authenticate and restore. In the years that followed, however, officials would struggle with the difficulties of writing the texts for the exhibitions and narrating the display for the public. The interpretation of the First Party Congress site reveals the tensions inherent in portraying a revolution that was still in the making.

The Politics of Display

The First Party Congress site was at once monument, historic site, and museum, with the site itself playing the role of the central artifact on display. In the exhibition, centered on the restored meeting room, officials retold the narrative of the party's founding and interpreted its significance for the revolution. Revolutionary history was told through two texts—a physical text displayed on the walls and an oral script recited by the docents. The physical text included a narrative, illustrations, and captions, a textbook history come to life. And as visitors were guided through the site, museum staff recited a script—one prepared for Chinese guests and one delivered to foreign visitors. These texts, and how they changed over time, demonstrate the tension between authenticity and interpretation in the politics of display. Officials were pulled between myth and reality, what was known and what was "still being researched," what could be presented and what was taboo, and what could be told to a domestic visitor versus what was related to a foreign guest.

These dilemmas were observed by the Sinologist Pierre Ryckmans when he visited the First Party Congress site in 1972, during the Cultural Revolution. Though archival records of foreign visitors usually relate polite responses, and the press reported great enthusiasm from foreign friends, Ryckmans experienced the site as a museum of the absurd, rife with confusion and contradictions. Disputed facts were glossed with authority, the meeting room was displayed with twelve chairs, and Ryckmans was told that the First Congress met on July 1, 1921. Uncomfortable facts—the presence of foreigners at the meeting, the participants who later defected, and the actual decisions made—were omitted. But while Ryckmans astutely highlighted the disconnect he found between authenticity and interpretation, he misunderstood the museum officials at the site. Ryckmans suggested that they had put together the display haphazardly, choosing "arbitrarily from among the various contradictory accounts of the event." His guide and the curator were portrayed as fools in his recounting, the thinness of the short lecture was attributed to the guide's ignorance, and he described a stammering curator who was unable to recommend a book on party history.[31]

Using archival documents, we can reconstruct the politics of Mao-era museology and see that—to the contrary—museum officials knew exactly what they were doing. Behind the scenes of the museum, officials were fully aware of the contradictions in the narrative, they were often purposefully ambiguous, and they were actually instructed to feign ignorance or to reply to certain questions with non sequiturs. By exploring the politics of the museum display through three texts—the physical text on the walls, the oral texts, and the scripted answers to questions—I argue that the revolutionary history textbook was continuously revised to suit contemporary politics. The tension between authenticity and interpretation was masked behind an authoritative telling of the revolution that mythologized the significance of the party's founding and placed Mao at its center.

The route through the exhibition began in the downstairs meeting room, was followed by a three-room supplementary display, and concluded in a reception room for discussion and for leaving comments.[32] Like the Soviet-style revolutionary textbook, official Chinese Communist Party history unfolded chronologically through the display, supported by pictures, photographs, and replicas of documents presented on the walls and in glass cases. Though the time frame of the text sometimes shifted—officials in the late 1950s planned to extend the exhibition's content up to 1949—the exhibit always focused around the party's founding in 1921. Paralleling the state's instructions for collecting revolutionary relics, the First Party Congress site began with the Opium War, the Taiping Rebellion, and the 1911 Revolution, focusing on the New Democratic Revolution since May Fourth.[33] Three titles, supported by Mao quotations, marked the division of the display: "The Great Wall of the Chinese Working Class," "Marxism-Leninism Spreads to China," and "The Establishment of the Chinese Communist Party."[34] Local stories were integrated with the national narrative. For example, curators took care to depict Shanghai people opposing the Mixed Court of the International Settlement, and Shanghai workers participating in the May Fourth Movement.[35]

Despite the authoritative narrative that accompanied the exhibition, the text was repeatedly revised. The most significant changes were made to the First Party Congress exhibition between the years 1960 and 1964, during which time museum officials struggled to follow the "red line." In August 1960, First Party Congress authorities wrote a report explaining that they had carefully studied the Museum of the Chinese Revolution's red line and summarized the policy as using Mao's analysis of revolution to frame the exhibition's contents, emphasizing Mao's role in party activities and using Mao's writings to highlight the influence of his thought.[36]

To emphasize Mao's role in the revolution, the red line stressed actions, ideology, and leadership. At the time of the party's founding, the report explained, Mao's interpretation represented the correct direction of the combination of Marxism-Leninism with the realities of the Chinese Revolution. To highlight Mao's ideas and actions, museum officials pledged to elevate his activities throughout the exhibit, interpreting the May Fourth Movement according to Mao's own analysis and emphasizing his organization of the Hunan workers' movement. Mao's writings were to be prominently displayed in order to demonstrate that Mao had recognized the importance of cultivating workers' consciousness, that his ideas were victorious over Chen Duxiu's.[37] Reflecting on their earlier work, First Party Congress officials admitted that they had failed because they had merely put one event after another. To follow the red line, each peasant movement had to be larger than the previous one, and should also demonstrate some kind of ideological breakthrough. Officials learned much from touring the Museum of the Chinese Revolution in Beijing. In portraying revolutionary history, they determined that each event should represent some aspect of Mao Zedong Thought, and that historical events and crucial issues (*guanjian wenti* 关键问题) were to reflect (*tixian* 体现) Mao's correct policies.[38]

To follow the red line was also to explicitly serve the present (*wei dangqian zhengzhi fuwu* 为当前政治服务). One could serve the present, the report suggested, by integrating the proper quotations, by referring to the present in the narration, and by organizing the content to allude to contemporary politics. For example, curators were to emphasize (*cezhong* 侧重) struggle in addressing the history of the United Front. In discussing New Democracy, it was decided, one should refer to the ideas of continuous revolution and revolution occurring in stages, to emphasize that the revolution was not yet over. Proper quotations should be chosen to serve "present-day socialist construction."[39] Finally, aesthetics could be used to serve the red line: important images physically enlarged, significant points highlighted in red, visuals used to support the red line, and quotations literally decorated with red flags.[40]

The demands of the red line can be traced in the revisions to the museum's exhibition in the following years. In 1964, for example, the First Party Congress officials revised their exhibition to accord with the contemporary goal to "strengthen anti-imperialist, antirevisionist struggle." To illustrate the historical roots of anti-imperialist struggle, curators edited captions depicting the protests at Shanghai's Mixed Court of the International Settlement and the May Fourth demonstrations. A new document, a 1920 Chinese gazette explaining Lenin's repeal of the unequal treaties, continued the anti-imperialist theme. To emphasize continuous struggle and warn against revisionism, the First Party Congress followed the Museum of the Chinese Revolution in including Li Dazhao's essay "On Question and Theory" to explain the triumph of an emphasis on theory over Hu Shi's pragmatism. The reference to the present was clear; pragmatism and revisionism were threats to the revolution.[41] Indeed, the emphasis and contours of this exhibition echoed its 1964 contemporary, the song-and-dance epic *The East Is Red*. As Xiaomei Chen explains in Chapter 5 of this volume, under Zhou Enlai's leadership *The East Is Red* made Mao the founding father of the Communist Party, blamed Chen Duxiu for the failure of 1927, and celebrated Mao's "correct line" as a guide to the revolution's victory. Just as *The East Is Red* became the standard revolutionary history textbook, the First Party Congress site presented artifacts to support the same text.

In addition to artifacts, visual images could also be manipulated. During the same revision of the site in 1964, several pictures were replaced, including a drawing of Taiping soldiers showing a small group of uninspired-looking men, seen from behind. Instead a new illustration was commissioned that depicted Hong Xiuquan pumping his fist in the air, "leading the peasant masses." In this picture, the peasant masses wear suitably fierce expressions, turning to rally around Hong Xiuquan with upturned faces and feet planted apart, surrounded by waving flags.[42] Rejected images also reveal the demands of the red line. In 1962, for example, the Department of Propaganda rejected an oil painting depicting a meeting scene from the First Congress. In the painting a young Mao stands in the center right of the scene, one arm outstretched, as he addresses participants listening raptly around the table. On the walls of the room are portraits of Lenin and Marx and a calendar dated July 1; a simple light fixture illuminates Mao like a spotlight. In his comments, Wang Chaowen of the Department of Propaganda harshly criticized his Shanghai colleagues for the image. He explained that all of the representatives could not be portrayed, because some later left the party and, regarding the two foreigners, one had become a Trotskyite and the other's history was unknown. Therefore, the painting should include only Mao Zedong, Dong Biwu, Chen Tanqiu, He Shuheng, and Wang Jinmei "having a conversation during the meeting." Depicting all the delegates, he emphasized, would lead to "adverse side effects," and the circulation of images of the painting through the press or other media would bring up questions that could not be answered.[43] At least one way to solve the problem of this mise-en-scène was not to portray any people at all, which is how the meeting room was itself re-created.

In addition to the malleable texts of the exhibition, First Party Congress officials also prepared two scripts for the docents who accompanied visitors through the museum. To introduce the meeting room, the docents would explain that twelve representatives—naming only those permitted in the above-mentioned painting—convened the First Party Congress on July 1, 1921. The narrators continued by explaining that the meeting was interrupted by French Concession police and later reconvened at a lake in nearby Jiaxing County, interpreting this anecdote as evidence that the party had struggled with counterrevolutionary forces from its inception. The views of the representatives were analyzed as "right" and "left"—the former, mistaken for thinking the party should focus on encouraging the study of Marxism among intellectuals, and the latter, incorrect for advocating a separate working-class struggle. In contrast, the docents explained, Mao and his supporters advocated fighting for the development of a proletarian class, and with that, the party was set upon its proper path. The meeting room, restored to its original condition, was the revolutionary trace (*geming shiji* 革命史迹) of that moment.[44]

A different text was prepared for foreigners. This narrative was more complete, giving the historical context for the study of Marxism in China, listing the origins of the congress's representatives and including the two foreign participants sent by the Communist International (Comintern). But though this text was created for foreign consumption, it adhered no less to the red line. Mao's activities in Hunan were highlighted, the encounter with the French Concession police was still interpreted as a baptism by enemy struggle, and the First Party Congress was still identified as the turning point in the Chinese Communist Revolution.[45] What is more revealing about the "foreigners' text" is that many more pages were devoted to questions and answers. This suggests that foreigners—unlike domestic visitors—often asked questions, as Pierre Ryckmans did, and these questions had answers that had to be scripted as well.

In fact, First Party Congress site officials had an entire list of problematic questions (*yinan wenti* 疑难问题), grouped into three categories: questions about who owned the house in which the meeting took place, about the Comintern representatives, and about the other, unnamed Chinese representatives at the Congress. The ownership of the house was problematic because Li Hanjun had left the party in 1924. Originally, the docents' answer was that it had been borrowed from a representative, then the answer was amended to "borrowed from a resident," and finally the answer was reduced to "it is unclear" (*bu qingchu* 不清楚). The names of the Comintern representatives underwent a similar process of erasure; first, docents mentioned the presence of the two foreigners—"Maring" and "Nikolsky"—and even gave their names, then they did not mention them at all.[46] Finally, the staff concluded that since most foreigners already knew about the Comintern representatives, they would mention their presence. But if visitors asked their names, the docents' proper answer was "it is unclear." The most problematic of the questions had to do with the unnamed Chinese representatives. The first prescribed response was to list only the five approved members. Museum officials also tried saying, "Those who are now party and state leaders include Comrade Mao Zedong and Comrade Dong Biwu." If visitors pursued their line of questioning, asking if any other participants were still living or if the docents would talk about the other representatives, the docents were given two choices for their response: "There is also Comrade Li Da, who is president of Wuhan University. Other participants died of illness, or others changed political affiliations," or "it is unclear."[47]

Museum officials clearly understood and were frustrated by the tension between authenticity and interpretation. They were also aware that the foreign visitors were dissatisfied with the answers; although some would stop asking questions, the docents reported that the foreigners' "facial expressions were unhappy."[48] However, even though they worried that *not* providing answers would harm friendships with the foreigners—who, after all, were all socialist friends—they persisted in their subterfuge. In addition to the nonanswers, docents were instructed on how to change the subject swiftly. If asked who owned the house, the docents should respond quickly that the rooms were borrowed and then launch into the story of the French police, "turning the foreign visitor's attention in another direction." If the visitor persisted, the docents were ordered not to give any specific answer.[49] Another solution to the number-of-delegates problem was just to put out *more* chairs than there were participants.[50] The fact that the answer to every question eventually devolved into "it is unclear" demonstrates that official answers were not the result of confusion or ignorance but were carefully calculated deflections.

The outward tension between questions and answers and between historical facts and official interpretation was mirrored behind the scenes in the kind of research that the staff carried out as part of their work. Despite outwardly feigning ignorance or insisting "it is unclear," the museum's officials worked hard to gather information, to seek truth from facts, and to restore authenticity to the narrative. Their carefully documented search for information provides us with a case study of one particularly difficult question: What was Mao's actual role in the First Party Congress? The way officials researched their answer reveals a number of problems with following the red line: contradictions between memoirs and official history, the ghostwriting of memoirs and missing official histories, and bureaucratic barriers between First Party Congress researchers and Central Archives authorities.

In November 1964, First Party Congress officials set out to find the answer to a question sometimes posed by foreign visitors: "Comrade Dong Biwu recalls that Chairman Mao was elected a Central Committee member at the First Congress; this appears in 1961 in your reports in the media; is this [fact] verified?" Museum researchers questioned Dong's secretary when he visited the site, and the secretary responded that Dong was not relying on his personal memory but rather on materials from the Soviet Union in the party archives. However, when museum officials requested the materials from the Central Archives, they were told that the matter had not yet been researched and the archivists could not make a conclusion. The First Party Congress site researchers persisted, going to Beijing to consult their colleagues at the Museum of the Chinese Revolution. There they received the same answer that the archives had given. So Shanghai officials scripted the following answer: "At the time, Chairman Mao was the leader of the Hunan small group. After the First Party Congress, he did leadership work in the Hunan party. In the early years of the Communist Party, Chairman Mao combined Marxism-Leninism with the practical reality of the Chinese Revolution. He is the representative of the birth of the party on the proper path."[51]

Like many of the answers in the script, the uniform answer docents could offer did not address the questions. Despite their meticulously documented research—including interviews, attempts to access party archives, and seeking help from the Museum of the Chinese Revolution—the Shanghai officials' determination to find the truth was thwarted. In addition to the issue of gaining archival access, there was the question of the sources themselves. Dong Biwu's memoir, which appeared in the press and was cited by the visitor, wasn't actually written by Dong, and museum officials eventually realized this.[52] When they confronted the secretary ghostwriter, researchers pointed out that there were discrepancies between the memoir (from 1961) and earlier party histories. They also had no updated party history to turn to; museum officials could rely on neither a ghostwritten memoir nor an out-of-date party history. The second problem with sources was that documentation on the First Party Congress was limited. Perhaps the scant documentation was embarrassing, or perhaps, in the wake of the Sino-Soviet split, the Soviet role in convening the First Party Congress was an undesirable detail; either of these reasons might have closed the doors in the faces of the researchers from the First Party Congress site. They had no way to seek truth from facts.

But the issue was probably more significant. The uncomfortable silence researchers encountered came from the suggestion that Mao was less important at the First Party Congress than he had been made to appear. The relevant document from the Comintern archives that the Chinese held in the Central Archives did not include names.[53] There were no sources to affirm that Mao was made a Central Committee member at the First Party Congress. Beyond the embarrassment that Dong Biwu and the media had been wrong was the inconsistency about the early political influence of Chairman Mao—at precisely the time when the museum was being asked to highlight the role of the paramount leader and the influence of Mao Zedong Thought. The truth was that Mao was not central to the First Party Congress, nor was the First Party Congress meeting an important moment in the history of the Communist Party. As Hans Van de Ven has shown, the early years of the CCP were marked by weak central leadership, conflicts between central and local branches, and failed attempts to organize mass movements. The party was organized along Leninist lines in 1925, became a mass political party with a centralized organization in 1925–7, and absorbed a much larger and diverse membership in the wake of the May Thirtieth Movement of 1925.[54] At the moment of its founding and throughout the period of the First United Front, the CCP was subordinate to the Nationalists and subject to the factionalism of the Comintern.[55] The First Party Congress was not the turning point that the exhibition made it seem.[56]

Perhaps, just as the First Party Congress museum staff knew that Dong Biwu did not write his own memoir, they also may have surmised that the Central Archives were closed to them because the answer it contained was not the right one. Unfortunately, the museum staff thus had to tiptoe around this historical uncertainty, hope that "further research" would resolve the problem, and tell visitors that Mao was "the representative of the birth of the party," rather than actually answer their questions.[57] A seemingly trivial question posed to the tour guides at the First Party Congress site brings the problem of history-telling in the Mao years into sharp relief. History was supposed to be authentic and authoritative. The party's view of history was, after all, a reflection of its mastery. But behind the scenes of the museum, the red line fashioned history into myth, even as the revolutionary narrative was continuously revised to accord with contemporary politics.

Cultural Revolution and Aftermath

During the first three years of the Cultural Revolution, which extended from 1966 to 1976, the First Party Congress site was closed to the public and the displays in the three supplementary exhibition rooms were removed.[58] In 1969 the Shanghai Revolutionary Committee directed the site to reopen its doors, and staff began receiving visitors from the worker-peasant-soldier categories, as well as foreigners. Over the years, the museum repeatedly proposed making a new exhibition, but Zhang Chunqiao and Yao Wenyuan of the Shanghai Revolutionary Committee rejected such requests as both impractical and too politically sensitive.[59] Though this decade is portrayed in official museum history as a period of closed doors, First Party Congress museum officials remained at work, organizing traveling exhibits, actively collecting revolutionary relics, and reporting to the Bureau of Culture.[60] Museum staff also collected artifacts from the Cultural Revolution itself, working with the Shanghai Museum to collect such relics (*wenwu* 文物), with a focus on Shanghai's January Revolution.[61] In the midst of the Cultural Revolution, the aim of the revolutionary history museum—to collect artifacts for the narrative—remained intact.

Even without the supplementary exhibits, the First Party Congress site continued to receive domestic visitors and foreign tourists in great numbers.[62] In contrast to the 100,000 cadres and foreigners received from 1952 to 1965, the estimated number of visitors between 1966 and 1976 was more than four million (plate 1).[63] Instead of being given a lecture by a docent, a carefully crafted tape recording was played for Chinese visitors. And this narrative was shortened: rather than beginning with the Opium War, the new lecture began with the October Revolution.

Like the previous narrative, the lecture strictly followed the red line. Mao's actions and Mao's interpretation of revolutionary history guided the story; his quotations were woven in seamlessly, often accompanied by "Chairman Mao says" or "Chairman Mao teaches us," but in some places the quotations were not attributed to the chairman at all, suggesting either that his words were already well known, or that following the red line to its extreme had erased any boundaries between Mao's words and the party's.[64]

The revisions to the recorded text were mostly a matter of degree—the red line was followed more strictly, binding historical events more tightly with a stream of Mao quotations, and the tape recording concluded with the obligatory choruses of long life to Chairman Mao. But in its final few paragraphs the narrative included criticisms of all of Mao's perceived enemies within the party.[65] Critiquing figures from Chen Duxiu to recent adversaries—such as purged officials like Defense Minister Peng Dehuai and President Liu Shaoqi—the recorded text for the First Party Congress site shifted from an official history to a political broadside. Archival memos suggest that the text was frequently updated: the next version of the recording added Lin Biao to the list of people taking the opportunist road (*jihui zhuyi luxian* 机会主义路线), and in the next year the museum organized a special exhibit on his crimes.[66] Further, this editorializing was not limited to the recording's final paragraphs; during the "Criticize Confucius—Criticize Lin Biao" campaign, Mao's role at the party's founding was rewritten to include his opposition to Confucius and Mencius.[67] Thus the medium of the audiotape provided the First Party Congress site with a technology suited to an era of tumultuous politics—one could make a new tape immediately, no individual docent could be faulted for misspeaking, and no one could ask any questions.[68]

While the exhibition rooms were shuttered, traveling exhibitions presented museum staff with a different kind of opportunity. In line with Cultural Revolution rhetoric, the First Party Congress brought revolutionary relics to the masses. For example, a 1975–6 exhibition that traveled to the Shanghai Museum, the Shanghai Youth Palace, and the Pudong Workers' Palace, among other places, reached an estimated 360,000 visitors over eight months.[69] Not all visitors were part of organized groups; on one day at the Shanghai Youth Palace a quarter of the four thousand visitors were individuals who had come on their own.[70]

Bringing their work to the countryside, the First Party Congress officials also organized small portable displays that they carried to suburban factories and countryside communes, reaching many thousands who would not otherwise have come to Shanghai.[71] While official reports of an exhibition's universally glowing reception must be read with some caution, it seems that museum officials truly felt less constrained away from the First Party Congress site. The archival record suggests that staff listened to viewer feedback and took it seriously. In the weeks following Zhou Enlai's death, for example, viewers requested pictures from his life. Accordingly, the Bureau of Culture's Revolutionary Committee approved the addition of eight photographs, representing a brief acknowledgment of the people's ability—albeit limited—to memorialize their own history.[72]

When Mao's death brought an end to the Cultural Revolution in 1976, the First Party Congress took on two new roles: a site of political pilgrimage and a site of political rectification. In the days following his death, waves of people made mourning pilgrimages to Shanghai.[73] In the following year, mourning gave way to celebration as the First Party Congress site was featured in national and local papers on the anniversary of Mao's death. The press reiterated that this was the site where the Great Helmsman had personally (*qinshou* 亲手) raised the first red flag, this was where Chairman Mao had lit the shining beacon of China's revolution, and this was the sacred birthplace of the party.[74] Descriptions of the site included accounts of exemplary pilgrims, and in the same way that people "reported" to images of Mao during the Cultural Revolution, now visitors at the site made pledges of duty and sacrifice—sisters building the socialist countryside, students off to Xinjiang, soldiers being deployed. Newspapers depicted foreign visitors in the same manner of a pilgrimage, going out of their way to visit the site, copying Mao quotations from the walls, and leaving hyperbolic comments in the guestbook about China as a revolutionary fortress for the world.[75] Memorialization at the site, domestic and foreign, was highly performative. It remains a red legacy to this day.

In keeping with the memorialization of Mao, the First Party Congress site also served as a stage on which to criticize the Cultural Revolution. Museum officials themselves blamed the Gang of Four for obstructing their work, and instead praised Zhou Enlai for encouraging the exhibition of revolutionary relics. Individuals also used the site to perform their own rectification. *Liberation Daily* described one such example: Huang Chibo, a veteran and former PSB official imprisoned during the Cultural Revolution, rushed to the First Party Congress site on his release. Gazing at the chairs and tea service in the meeting room, Huang told the museum officials, "This is the place where Chairman Mao created the party, it must be preserved!"[76] Huang's visit was both a personal and public performance of loyalty to the chairman, to the party, and to its revolutionary ideals.

A more complete rectification of names came with the thorough renovation of the First Party Congress site's buildings and a new exhibition in 1980. Though Mao was still listed first among the participants at the First Party Congress, all thirteen names were included from then on. Photographs of party founders Li Dazhao and Chen Duxiu, and their essays, were placed on display. Liu Shaoqi, who had been vilified in the taped recording from the Cultural Revolution, was incorporated into a section on labor-organizing activities and depicted leading a strike at Anyuan. Museum officials stressed the use of historical materials (*lishi ziliao* 历史资料), especially memoirs and essays by the participants, and highlighted the need for a "scientific attitude that [sought] truth from facts." To this end, they prominently displayed the documents "created" at the First Party Congress, the materials that museum officials had been denied in 1964.[77] The new exhibition itself followed the narrative of the official history, and photographs and historical materials took center stage. And as if to demonstrate that the scientific attitude that placed historical materials at the center also extended to the authenticity of the site, the final artifact in the exhibition was Dong Biwu's inscription from when he verified the site in 1956.[78] Authenticating party history became itself part of history.

The call for a "scientific attitude to seek truth from facts" reflected a serious change in party history research in the post-Mao period. In the pages of *Party History Research Materials*, a journal established in 1979, historians debated the questions of who had attended the meeting, when it had taken place, and what the meeting had concluded. In the journal's first issue, for example, historians compared nine memoirs claiming that there had been either twelve or thirteen participants. They concluded that Bao Huiseng was there—contradictions in Mao Zedong's memory notwithstanding—and that if he was a delegate, there would have been thirteen representatives.[79] Today's First Party Congress site reflects these findings of party historians; the agenda is carefully reconstructed with the opening date on July 23, 1921, and the closing session in Jiaxing is the meeting at which the Central Bureau (Zhongyang lingdao jiguan 中央领导机关) was elected.[80]

The display of party history reflected changed attitudes toward historical research. As the Museum of the Chinese Revolution's curators explained in 1979, "seeking truth from facts" had to be applied to the display of party history: "the *wenwu*, documents, and photographs that reflect historical reality could not be willfully edited [*renyi xiugai* 任意修改]."[81] The curators argued that one could not revise history (*xiugai lishi* 修改历史), using the example of a ballad from the Anyuan strikes that had been doctored to include Mao's name. Maoist-era principles of exhibition, Museum of the Chinese Revolution officials argued, had been wrong. They overturned the idea of the red line—one could not write party history from start to finish according to Mao Zedong Thought, portray Mao Zedong Thought as an ideology completely formed, or use Mao quotations to stand in for historical events. The curators explained that one could not read the past according to the present, exaggerate the role of individuals (including Mao himself), or use the museum to judge individual mistakes without accounting for their overall contribution to history. And finally, one could not take artifacts and photographs and modify them or make them up (*weizao* 伪造).[82] The curators of the Museum of the Chinese Revolution thoroughly rejected the red line, arguing for authenticity instead of Mao-era interpretation.

Rejecting the red line, however, did not mean that ideology was erased from museum work in the post-Mao period. Official history still frames the presentation of the revolutionary narrative, and indeed another ideology—that of the Four Modernizations—came to influence the culture of exhibitions in the era of reform. With improved livelihoods, a new kind of consumer required more cultural diversions. As Yu Lebin of the First Party Congress site explained to colleagues in 1987, "modern people" wanted to educate their children, expand their minds in their free time, and learn about the latest discoveries. To appeal to these new consumers, he suggested, the exhibition had to be modernized and the displays made more high-tech, so that visitors could have a more personal experience (*shenli* 身历). As the demands of the modern consumer expanded to include tourism, First Party Congress officials planned package tours based on revolutionary sites (*geming shiji lüyouxian*

革命史迹旅游线), a precursor to what has come to be known as "red tourism." The post-Mao reform era thus brought many changes to the First Party Congress site: the building was renovated, its exhibition was rewritten according to a "scientific attitude," and its new audience became the modern Chinese consumer who demanded entertainment and leisure. But despite the "scientific attitude" toward party history, politics have never left center stage, and the tension between authenticity and interpretation remains to this day.

Conclusion: The First Party Congress Site Today

Since the beginning of the reform era, both the format and the display at the First Party Congress site have changed. Gone are the Soviet-style narratives and epic paintings, the red line of the Maoist era, and the political erasures that omitted names and removed chairs from the meeting room. Today, the modernized exhibition, nestled in the Xintiandi district of Shanghai, prides itself on following the latest trends in global museology. For the latest expansion of the permanent exhibition, for example, officials stressed the need to "use objects to represent history" (*yiwu daishi* 以物代史). This new principle of display reverses the Maoist-era use of objects as props for the revolutionary narrative. Indeed, writing in 2009, First Party Congress site curator Ni Xingxiang criticized the long tradition of emphasizing history and neglecting objects. The current exhibition is centered around artifacts, fulfilling the museum's duty to use contextualization and new technologies to "bring the *wenwu* and viewers closer together, to allow viewers and the *wenwu* to have a face-to-face conversation and interaction."[83]

But despite this emphasis on artifacts and technology, the purpose of the exhibition is still didactic. Now the revolutionary history narrative is part of China's patriotic education, and the viewers that Ni and his colleagues have in mind are, increasingly, groups of young people (see fig. 1.2). At the Museum of the Chinese Revolution in 1990—one year after Tiananmen—Jiang Zemin, then CCP general secretary, stressed that because young people had no understanding of history, the task of the museum was to "strengthen patriotic education, patriotism, and socialist education."[84] "Patriotic education" for schoolchildren is the new

FIGURE 1.2. A girl poses in the lobby of the First Party Congress memorial site, 2011. Photo by the author.

watchword, and to that end museum officials see youth organizations as the primary audience for revolutionary memorial museums.[85] For the new generation of Chinese youth, the revolution is an increasingly distant memory. The curators of the First Party Congress site identify educating these youth as their central mission.[86]

Does the First Party Congress site mean something different in the post-Mao era? Has it been depoliticized, and is it even an anachronism in the consumer culture of Xintiandi? Some observers have suggested that it is; the architectural historian Samuel Liang calls the site, juxtaposed with theme park–like Xintiandi, a "reinvented veneer," "a false preservation and false revolution," and a place frozen in time. Liang argues that the restored site of the First Party Congress suffers from amnesia because it obscures the revolutionary nature of the historic meeting and because developers have demolished the working-class neighborhood that once surrounded it. By replacing revolution with a story of glory and progress, Liang explains, "the regime has thus installed a hegemonic power structure, which the memorial symbolizes, to prevent any further revolutions."[87] If one agrees with this interpretation, then the emphasis on cultural relics, or *wenwu,* and the removal of the narrative renders the First Party Congress site simply a collection of objects. Understood in this way, the site is itself an antique curiosity, dwarfed and swallowed up by the cosmopolitan consumer landscape that surrounds it.

But inside the museum, and in the text of the revolution that the party continues to present to the Chinese people, official history and revolutionary narrative still shape the interpretation of history. Though the permanent exhibition has changed, it is still structured by official history, divided into sections entitled, "The establishment of Chinese Communist Party is the inevitable outcome of Chinese historical development," "The establishment of Chinese Communist Party is the product of the integration of Marxist-Leninist thought and the Chinese workers' movement," and "The establishment of the Chinese Communist Party is the great event that opened a new era."[88] As these categories indicate, party historiography continues to shape how history is presented. And the party's founding is still celebrated on July 1, a fact that the journalist Sang Ye uses to challenge the "real history" of the Chinese Revolution.[89]

As for the objects themselves, they remain classified as revolutionary relics. Although they are sometimes referred to simply as relics, and some museum officials prefer modern relics (*jinxiandai wenwu* 近现代文物) as being more "scientific," it is the objects' association with the revolution that makes them worth preserving.[90] Curator Ni Xingxiang asks his colleagues, if those working in a revolutionary memorial museum do not respect revolutionary relics, how would they expect to move an audience?[91] The authenticity of the revolutionary relics is paramount, and previous eras are criticized for replacing originals with replicas, or for displaying replicas and originals together without distinguishing real from fake. As Curator Ni argues, if an exhibition does not make clear the authenticity and provenance of the revolutionary relic, then it "cannot truly move the hearts of the viewer, and the audience will be suspicious of the authenticity of the revolutionary relic . . . and this will seriously influence the social position of the revolutionary memorial museum, directly influencing the effect of the revolutionary memorial museum on society."[92] In other words, if the relics are not authentic, neither is the revolution.

The legitimacy of the Communist Party in the post-Mao era has lost much of its foundation. Political scientists and China watchers debate the sources of the regime's resilience, offering economic development or nationalism as possible alternatives to Communist ideology. In this context, the tension between authenticity and interpretation at the First Party Congress site remains, but it has undergone a curious inversion. When Shanghai officials first established the revolutionary monument, the authenticity of the site lent legitimacy to the party and its revolution. Today, in contrast, the importance of the site depends on the legitimacy of the party and the revolutionary narrative it tells. Now the party's revolution must be contextualized for the commercialized China of Shanghai's Xintiandi. In this context, museum curators have employed the latest technology and museum expertise, preferring to "let the artifacts tell the story." But the text that remains in the memorial hall still tells a triumphal narrative, and a diorama of wax figures illustrates the continued centrality of Mao in the myth of the CCP's founding—red legacies for our own times.

Notes

1. Nie Bing 聂兵 and Qiao Yan 峭岩, "Renmin zhanshi xin xiang dang" 人民战士心向党 (The people's soldiers turn their hearts toward the party), *Jiefangjun huabao* 解放军画报 (People's Liberation Army Pictorial), July 1976, p. 2.

2. *Kan geming wenwu, xue geming chuantong* 看革命文物, 学革命传统 (View revolutionary relics and study the revolutionary tradition) (Shanghai: Shanghai renmin chubanshe, 1976).

3. Shen Zhiyu 沈之瑜, "Yida huizhi shi zenme zhaodao de" 一大会址是怎么找到的 (How the First Party Congress site was found), in Shen Zhiyu, *Shen Zhiyu wenbo lunji* 沈之瑜文博论集 (Collected writings of Shen Zhiyu on cultural relics and museums), ed. Chen Qiuhui 陈秋辉 (Shanghai: Shanghai guji chubanshe, 2003), pp. 353–57.

4. Ye Yonglie 葉永烈, "Zhonggong zhi chu de zhuixun: Fang Shen Zhiyu tongzhi" 中共之初的追寻: 访沈之瑜同志 (Searching for the origins of the Chinese Communist Party: Interviews with Comrade Shen Zhiyu), in Shen Zhiyu, *Shen Zhiyu wenbo lunji*, ed. Chen Qiuhui, pp. 412–20.

5. Ma Chengyuan 马承源, Huang Xuanfeng 黄宣佩, and Li Junjie 李俊杰, eds., *Shanghai wenwu bowuguanzhi* 上海文物博物馆志 (Gazetteer of Shanghai's cultural relics and museums) (Shanghai: Shanghai shehui kexueyuan chubanshe, 1997), p. 379.

6. "Jiangsu geming bowuguan choubeichu zhengji xize" 江苏革命博物馆筹备处征集细则 (Collection of regulations for the Jiangsu Revolutionary Museum Preparatory Committee), *Shanghai tebieshi jiaoyuju jiaoyu zhoubao* 上海特别市教育局教育周报 (Shanghai Municipal Bureau of Education Weekly) 4 (1929): 7–8. See also Shanghai Municipal Archives 上海市档案馆 (hereafter SMA), no. Q1-6-676.

7. *Jiefangqu zhanlanhui ziliao* 解放区展览会资料 (Materials on exhibitions in the liberated areas), ed. Zhongguo geming bowuguan (Beijing: Wenwu chubanshe, 1988).

8. For more on Soviet museums, see Lü Jimin 吕济民, *Zoujin qian Sulian bowuguan* 走进前苏联博物馆 (Approaching the museums of the former Soviet Union) (Beijing: Wenwu chubanshe, 2008). In 1957, to celebrate the October Revolution, *Wenwu cankao ziliao* 文物参考资料 (Cultural relics reference materials) devoted several issues to museums in the Soviet Union.

9. Wang Yeqiu 王冶秋, "Sulian guoli geming bowuguan" 苏联国立革命博物馆 (Soviet Museum of the Revolution), *Wenwu cankao ziliao* 10 (1950): 66–76.

10. Ibid., p. 71. As a member of the underground, Wang was twice imprisoned.

11. For a contemporaenous account of museums in the Soviet Union, see O. Leonova, *Museums of the USSR* (Moscow: Foreign Languages Publishing House, 1939). For a historical study of the ways in which the October Revolution was narrated over time, see Frederick C. Corney, *Telling October: Memory and the Making of the Bolshevik Revolution* (Ithaca, NY: Cornell University Press, 2004). For the politics of writing history in the Soviet Union, see Karen Petrone, *Life Has Become More Joyous, Comrades: Celebrations in the Time of Stalin* (Bloomington: Indiana University Press, 2000).

12. On the Ten Great Buildings, see Chapter 2.

13. Chang-tai Hung, "The Red Line: Creating a Museum of the Chinese Revolution," *China Quarterly* 184 (2005): 914–33.

14. Ye Yonglie, "Zhonggong zhi chu de zhuixun," p. 413.

15. Ibid., p. 414. This lead actually came from Zhou Zhiyou, a son of Zhou Fohai and Yang Chuhui who had joined the CCP underground. At this time, Zhou Zhiyou was a subordinate of Yang Fan, the Public Security Bureau chief.

16. The relevant excerpt that Shen Zhiyu read in the library is reproduced in *Shanghai geming shi yanjiu ziliao: Jinian jiandang 70 zhou nian* 上海革命史研究资料: 纪念建党70 周年 (Research materials on Shanghai revolutionary history: Commemorating the seventieth anniversary of the founding of the party) (Shanghai: Shanghai sanlian shudian, 1991), pp. 321–24.

17. Shen Zhiyu, "Yida huizhi shi zenme zhaodao de," p. 353.

18. Ibid., pp. 354–55.

19. Ibid., p. 355.

20. "Zhongyang guanyu dang de diyici daibiao dahui de dizhi baocun wenti gei Shanghai shi wei de zhishi" 中央关于党的第一次代表大会的地址保存问题给上海市委的指示 (Central directive to the Shanghai Party Committee regarding the preservation of the First Party Congress site) (July 3, 1951), in *Zhongguo gongchandang xuanchuan gongzuo wenxian xuanbian: 1949–1956* 中国共产党宣传工作献选 编: 1949–1956 (Selected documents on the propaganda work of the Chinese Communist Party: 1949–1956), vol. 3 (Beijing: Xuexi chubanshe, 1996), p. 249.

21. Ye Yonglie, "Zhonggong zhi chu de zhuixun," p. 419.

22. Shen Zhiyu, "Yida huizhi shi zenme zhaodao de," p. 356. See also SMA, no. B172-4-313, pp. 5–6.

23. For an institutional account of some of these events, see Chen Peicun 陈沛存 and Ren Rui 任锐, "Sishi nian zhi huigu" 四十年之回顾 (Looking back forty years), in *Shanghai geming shiliao yu yanjiu* 上海革命史料与研究 (Materials and research on Shanghai revolutionary history), vol. 1 (Beijing: Kaiming chubanshe, 1992), pp. 236–38. The archival record shows that careful accounts were made of these visits, the questions asked, and the answers. One such account, of a visit by Comrade Dong's wife in 1964, refers back to Dong's earlier comments and includes summaries of telephone conversations. SMA, no. B172-1-477, pp. 95–97.

24. SMA, no. B172-1-477, pp. 26–31.

25. Chen and Ren, "Sishi nian zhi huigu," p. 237.

26. Ibid., p. 240.

27. The others were Sun Yat-sen's residence, the headquarters of the Chinese Socialist Youth League, and the tomb of the writer Lu Xun (Zhou Shuren, 1881–1936). Ma, Huang, and Li, *Shanghai wenwu bowuguanzhi,* p. 387.

28. *Quanguo gesheng, zizhiqu, zhixiashi diyipi wenwu baohu danwei mingdan huibian* 全国各省，自治区，直辖市 第一批文物保护单位名单汇编 (The first group of national cultural relic work units in each province, autonomous region, and municipalities under the central government) (Beijing: Wenwu chubanshe, 1958), p. 10.

29. SMA, no. B172-1-477, pp. 107–15.

30. Ibid., pp. 134–39.

31. Simon Leys [Pierre Ryckmans], *Chinese Shadows* (New York: Penguin Books, 1978), pp. 90–92. First published in French (*Ombres Chinoises*), in 1974.

32. SMA, no. B172-5-240, p. 20.

33. SMA, no. B1-2-770, p. 4, and no. B172-5-521, p. 17.

34. SMA, no. B172-5-240, pp. 5–9.

35. SMA, no. B172-1-477, pp. 72–75.

36. SMA, no. B172-5-240, p. 104.

37. Ibid., pp. 98–100.

38. Ibid., pp. 100–102. Later in the report, its authors suggested that things should be ordered by importance, not necessarily by chronological order (*bu anzhao lishi chengxu lai ba* 不按照历史程序来摆), p. 103.

39. Ibid., p. 102.

40. Ibid., p. 103.

41. SMA, no. B172-1-477, p. 73.

42. Ibid., p. 79.

43. SMA, no. A22-1-66, pp. 36–39. Wang Chaowen warned that even portraying those five in conversation was potentially dangerous and that the individuals should be carefully investigated. I do not know what happened to this painting, and I was prohibited from photocopying an image of it in the archives. It does appear that Wang's instructions were followed, as a painting with five figures—Mao at the center—appears in a newspaper photograph in 1977. *Jiefang ribao* 解放日报 (Liberation daily), August 29, 1977, p. 2.

44. SMA, no. B172-5-240, pp. 18–19.

45. Ibid., pp. 22–23.

46. Maring was the Comintern pseudonym of Hendricus Sneevliet, a Dutch activist. Nikolsky was Vladimir Neiman, an agent of the Comintern's Far Eastern Secretariat. See Alexander V. Pantsov and Steven I. Levine, *Mao: The Real Story* (New York: Simon & Schuster, 2012), pp. 100–106.

47. SMA, no. B172-5-240, p. 24.

48. Ibid.

49. Ibid., p. 23.

50. In response to a Soviet trade delegation's questions about why there were only twelve chairs in the room, the museum staff put out sixteen chairs. Ibid., pp. 15–16.

51. SMA, no. B172-1-477, p. 80. This statement was approved by the Bureau of Propaganda in February 1965.

52. Ibid., p. 96.

53. Hans van de Ven explains that the report to the Comintern stated that three men were elected to a secretariat, and that other published sources and party histories agree that the three men were Chen Duxiu (appointed to head the secretariat), Zhang Guotao (in charge of organization), and Li Da (propaganda). Hans J. van de Ven, *From Friend to Comrade: The Founding of the Chinese Communist Party, 1920–1927* (Berkeley: University of California Press, 1991), p. 88. The document from the Comintern archives is reproduced in *Zhongguo gongchandang xuanchuan gongzuo wenxian xuanbian: 1915–1937* 中国共产党宣传工作文献选编：1915–1937 (Selected documents on the propaganda work of the Chinese Communist Party: 1915–1937), vol. 1 (Beijing: Xuexi chubanshe, 1996), pp. 323–26.

54. On this point of early party history, see van de Ven, *From Friend to Comrade*, pp. 240–41.

55. Bruce A. Elleman, *Diplomacy and Deception: The Secret History of Sino-Soviet Diplomatic Relations, 1917–1927* (Armonk, NY: M. E. Sharpe, 1997), and *Moscow and the Emergence of Communist Power in China, 1925–30: The Nanchang Uprising and the Birth of the Red Army* (New York: Routledge, 2009).

56. May Thirtieth is also identified as the turning point in literature; see John Fitzgerald, *Awakening China: Politics, Culture, and Class in the Nationalist Revolution* (Stanford, CA: Stanford University Press, 1996), pp. 336–37. On how the First Party Congress is portrayed as a turning point in popular culture, see Huang Xiaoyan 黄晓彦, *Shanghai hongse lüyou* 上海红色旅游 (Shanghai red tourism) (Shanghai: Shanghai daxue chubanshe, 2005), pp. 1–2. Mao himself immortalized the moment by writing that the founding was "a great incident that opened the heavens and earth" (中国产生了共产党, 这是开天辟地的大事变), a 1949 quotation that is cited in contemporary popular histories. Zhang Wenqing 张文清, *Mao Zedong zai Shanghai* 毛泽东在上海 (Mao Zedong in Shanghai) (Shanghai: Shanghai shudian chubanshe, 2003), p. 14.

57. A reform-era article published by the official Party School is similarly sanguine, though more direct. It cites Li Weihan's memoirs and explains, "Although Mao Zedong was not one of the CCP's initiators [*faqi ren* 发起人] . . . in thinking and in organization he made a contribution to the building [*jianli* 建立] of the

Chinese Communist Party." Hua Xing 华幸, "Mao Zedong he Zhongguo gongchandang de chuangli" 毛泽东和中国共产党的创立 (Mao Zedong and the establishment of the Chinese Communist Party), in *Mao Zedong zai Shanghai*, p. 256. A more recent history of the individuals at the First Party Congress acknowledges that Mao Zedong was "an ordinary representative" at the meeting, that at the time he was not yet a great personage and was a young student of Marxism-Leninism. Meng Xing 孟醒, *Shui zhu chenfu: Zhonggong yida daibiao chenfulu* 谁主沉浮: 中共一大代表沉浮录 Who is in control? The ups and downs of the representatives to the First Party Congress) (Beijing: Renmin chubanshe, 2009), pp. 150–51.

58. In 1966 the First Party Congress site, previously official called the Shanghai Revolutionary History Memorial Museum Preparatory Office, was renamed the First Party Congress Memorial Hall (*yida jinianguan* 一大纪念馆). SMA, no. B172-3-85, p. 2.

59. SMA, no. B172-3-127, p. 41.

60. Chen and Ren, "Sishi nian zhi huigu," pp. 236–38.

61. SMA, no. B172-3-127, pp. 9 and 12–14. For a report on the activities of this group, see SMA, no. B172-3-176.

62. For the full text of museum transcripts used in 1969, see SMA, no. B244-3-143.

63. SMA, no. B172-3-221, p. 30.

64. SMA, no. B172-3-85, pp. 35–39.

65. Ibid., p. 38.

66. Ibid., pp. 34 and 39, and SMA, no. B172-3-127, p. 7. Earlier in the Cultural Revolution, Lin Biao had featured prominently in the exhibition's narrative; see SMA, no. B244-3-143, p. 19.

67. SMA, no. B172-3-127, p. 29.

68. Foreigners were the exception; it appears that foreign visitors were still received in person and an extensive list of appropriate answers was supplied to the docents, explaining the purpose of the Cultural Revolution, the meaning of revisionism, Liu Shaoqi's crimes, and so on. SMA, no. B244-3-143, pp. 22–30.

69. SMA, no. B172-3-221, p. 31.

70. Ibid., p. 25.

71. Ibid., pp. 30–38.

72. Ibid., pp. 2–3.

73. Wang Jinyou 王金友, "Huainian Mao zhuxi jianchi xue Dazhai" 怀念毛主席坚持学大寨 (Remembering Chairman Mao, pursuing the study of Dazhai), *Zhejiang ribao* 浙江日报 (Zhejiang daily), September 21, 1976, p. 3.

74. "Hongqi juchu zhanzheng cheng" 红旗举出战争成 (Journey from the site where we raised the red flag), *Jiefang ribao*, August 29, 1977, p. 2. "Guanghui qizhi zhi zhengcheng" 光辉旗帜指征程 (Glorious flag directs our journey), *Wenhui bao* 文汇报 (Wenhui daily), September 7, 1977, p. 2.

75. "Mao zhuxi de guanghui zhao huanyu" 毛主席的光辉照寰宇 (Chairman Mao's glory shines upon the whole world), *Jiefang ribao*, October 18, 1977, p. 3. For an example of museum records of foreigners' questions and comments, see SMA, no. B172-3-85, pp. 46–47.

76. *Jiefang ribao*, August 29, 1977, p. 2.

77. "Zhonggong yida huizhi jinianguan tiaozheng chenlie neirong" 中共一大会址纪念馆调整陈列内容 (The contents of the First Party Congress Memorial Museum's revised exhibition), *Wenhui bao*, July 1, 1980, p. 1.

78. "Dangshi shang guanghui yi ye" 党史上光辉一页 (A glorious page from party history), *Wenhui bao*, June 21, 1981, p. 2.

79. "Guanyu Zhonggong 'yida' daibiao renshu de jizhong shuofa" 关于中共一大代表人数的集中说法 (Several ways of explaining the number of representatives at the First Party Congress), *Dangshi yanjiu ziliao* 党史研究资料 (Party history research materials) 1 (1979): 7–11.

80. *Zhongguo gongchandang diyici quanguo daibiao dahui huizhi* 中国共产党第一次全国代表大会会址 (The Chinese Communist Party First Party Congress site), ed. Zhongguo gongchandang diyici quanguo daibiao dahui huizhi jinianguan 中国共产党第一次全国代表大会会址纪念馆 (The memorial site of the First Chinese Communist Party Congress) (Shanghai: Shanghai renmin meishu chubanshe, 2001), p. 103.

81. "Dangshi chenlie de jige wenti" 党史陈列的几个问题 (A few issues on exhibiting party history), *Dangshi yanjiu ziliao* 6 (1979): 123.

82. Ibid., pp. 122–29.

83. Ni Xingxiang 倪兴祥, "Chedi 'yiwu daishi' chenlie zhidao sixiang de tihui" 彻底以物代史陈列指导思想的体会 (The experience of thoroughly carrying out the exhibition principle of "using objects to represent history"), *Zhongguo bowuguan tongxun* 中国博物馆通讯 (Chinese museums newsletter) 9 (2009): 6–8.

84. Jiang Zemin 江泽民, "Canguan 'Zhongguo gemingshi chenlie' jieshushi de jianghua" 参观中国革命史陈列结束时的讲话 (Speech upon viewing the "Exhibition of Chinese revolutionary history"), *Dangshi yanjiu ziliao* 9 (1990): 2–3.

85. Ni Xingxiang, "Chedi 'yiwu daishi' chenlie zhidao sixiang de tihui," p. 8.

86 Interview with Xin Honglin 信洪林, vice director of exhibitions, First National Congress of the Communist Party of China Memorial Museum, June 13, 2007.

87. Samuel Y. Liang, "Amnesiac Monument, Nostalgic Fashion," *Wasafiri* 23, no. 3 (2008): 47–55.

88. For the full text, see *Zhongguo gongchandang diyici quanguo daibiao dahui huizhi jinianguan*, p. 27.

89. Sang Ye, *China Candid: The People on the People's Republic* (Berkeley: University of California Press, 2006), p. 7.

90. Interview with Xin Honglin, June 13, 2007.

91. Ni Xingxiang, "Chedi 'yiwu daishi' chenlie zhidao sixiang de tihui," p. 7.

92. Ibid., p. 8.

TWO

BUILDING BIG, WITH NO REGRET

From Beijing's "Ten Great Buildings" in the 1950s to China's Megaprojects Today

Zhu Tao

> Aren't there certain people who believe we are incapable of constructing a modern country? We must save face by answering them with actions and facts.
>
> —Wan Li 万里, Mobilization Conference for Beijing's National Day Projects, 1958

After a tour of Beijing's latest crop of megabuildings—including the National Grand Theater, the "Bird's Nest" Olympic Stadium, the "Water Cube" National Aquatics Center, and the China Central Television (CCTV) headquarters—an American friend described his experience: "When you saw the first one, it felt unreal—you couldn't believe such a gigantic building could ever be built, but once you'd seen ten of them in a row and realized that there were still many others, it felt *surreal*."[1] China has long been obsessed with constructing monumental buildings; however, but, the magnitude of its current boom is unprecedented. Not just in the major cities, but also in many small and medium-size towns, new stadiums, opera houses, museums, and government complexes—all of immense size and grandeur—are being erected with the full approval of the authorities. This sweeping mania for building big, fueled by the continuing economic boom, is the impetus drawing many international architects to work in China.

"But why does it have to be *that* big?" Foreign architects working on megaprojects in China are often asked this question when presenting their designs outside of China. The most convenient answer is, of course, "That's none of my business—it's strictly the client's decision." However, some architects have made more of an effort, most notably Rem Koolhaas and Ole Scheeren, the two chief architects of the massive CCTV headquarters building, who attempted to contextualize the project's *bigness* through their own social and formal arguments as well as their particular expectations of China.

According to Koolhaas, CCTV embodies his "optimism about the intentions of the Chinese state," which he believes will be able to develop an ingenious system that will take care of the public interest far better than the systems of Western capitalism.[2] CCTV, with its manifold programs compressed into a single gigantic "continuous loop," is intended to encompass the concepts of collectivity, continuity, integration, and communication—as opposed to the privatization, decentralization, and fragmentation increasingly found in capitalist institutions driven by market forces and information technology.[3] Clearly, Koolhaas's conception is very much in alignment with the 1920s Russian constructivist ideal of the "social condenser."

In addition to Koolhaas's social and formal argument, Scheeren has also attempted a historical justification. In 2006, during a lecture at Columbia University, he tried to convince his audience that CCTV's bigness was not a unique contemporary phenomenon at all, but rather part of the "brilliant tradition" that evolved during China's long journey toward modernity. Highlighting an image of Beijing's vast Ten Great Buildings project of 1958–9, he explained that in little more than a year China's capital had been radically transformed, remade as a modern city—"an utterly inconceivable task for us foreigners" (fig. 2.1).

He elaborated further, suggesting that China had "a fascinating ability to embrace change," and appeared to be "somewhat unburdened by a characteristic all too common in the West—that of regret. The western spirit has long practiced sentimental and dramatic thoughts about the past. In contrast, China appears to have a willingness and an ability to courageously face up to new situations and work enthusiastically towards an idea of progress—even if these radical changes imply the sometimes brutal erasure of past conditions."[4]

It is not my aim to judge whether these statements are a sincere and passionate declaration of an architect's utopian vision of China or merely

FIGURE 2.1. The Ten Great Buildings in Beijing, 1959. Courtesy Beijing Municipal Archives.

self-serving rhetoric in support of a particular piece of work. They are, however, certainly provocative, and they spurred me to look more closely at the history of Beijing's Ten Great Buildings and, in particular, at its core project, the Great Hall of the People (figs. 2.2 and 2.3). An analysis of how that project was planned, designed, constructed, and culturally represented illuminates the role of the megabuilding in relation to China's politics, economy, and society. In turn, such an examination makes it possible to confront questions that Koolhaas and Scheeren barely touch on, such as why, throughout its modern history, has China been obsessed with building big, regardless of the exorbitant costs and often-devastating social consequences? If China's practice of building big in the 1950s helped constitute a socialist legacy, then how does this legacy relate to the proliferation of megaprojects in China's cities today?

FIGURE 2.2. Panorama of the newly expanded Tiananmen Square, with the Museum of the Chinese Revolution (*left*) and the Great Hall of the People (*center*), 1959. Anonymous photographer.

FIGURE 2.3. The East Gate of the Great Hall of the People, 1981. Photo by Wu Yinxian. Courtesy Taikang Space, Beijing.

The Complex of the Character *Wan* 万

The first question to be asked about the Great Hall of the People is a simple one: Why did it have to be so big? It was designed as a meeting place for the annual National People's Congress (NPC), which usually draws about three thousand delegates, along with an equal number of auditors, meaning that about six thousand people attend each year. That has been the case for the past fifty years, and it is not expected to change in the future. Why, therefore, did the brief require a "great conference hall for ten thousand people"? One explanation is that Chairman Mao simply loved the character 万 (*wan*, 10,000). In Chinese literature, *wan* does not always signify a specific number; rather, it may symbolize something huge and plentiful.[5] You can find many *wans* in Mao's "romantic-revolutionary" poems: 看万山红遍 (I see ten thousand crimsoned hills), 万里雪飘 (Ten thousand miles of whirling snow), 万类霜天竞自由 (Under the freezing sky ten thousand creatures contend in freedom).

In fact, Mao's dream of a great conference hall can be traced as far back as the early 1940s. Standing in the party's ramshackle conference room in Yan'an, Mao vowed that after the revolution succeeded, he would build a conference hall "for ten thousand," where the party leaders would come together with the Chinese people to discuss all the great issues facing the country. In Mao's thinking, the usually abstract and symbolic character *wan* could be literally translated into a concrete quota for a megabuilding project. Soon after the founding of the People's Republic in 1949, Mao raised the idea again as he stood on the Tiananmen Rostrum 天安门城楼 and looked out across the square.[6] His dream would be realized at the end of the following decade.

"Go all out, aim high, and achieve greater, faster, better, and more economical results in building socialism!"—Mao's slogan was adopted as the "general line" for China's development at the Second Session of the Eighth NPC, held in May 1958. The Great Leap Forward had officially begun. Following on the heels of the First Five-Year Plan, completed in 1956, this was a far more ambitious plan for the radical collectivization of the country's resources, designed to eradicate the "right-deviation and conservative tendency" of China's socioeconomic development.

A plenary session of the Politburo of the Chinese Communist Party

Central Committee (CCPCC) in August 1958 established two significant goals for the Great Leap Forward: the mass mobilization of labor, with the aim of doubling the nation's annual steel output to 10.7 million tons by the end of the year, and the setting up of people's communes to boost agricultural production and to accelerate socialist development. This economic and social restructuring was to be accompanied by an architectural and urban initiative: the construction of a massive array of public buildings in Beijing and the enlargement of Tiananmen Square to create the biggest public space in the world, able to accommodate a million people. Furthermore, the CCPCC decreed that all of these projects had to be completed before National Day (October 1) the following year, in time for the commemoration of the tenth anniversary of the founding of the "New China."[7]

Total Mobilization of Design

On September 5, 1958, Wan Li, secretary-general of the Communist Party's Beijing Committee and deputy mayor of Beijing, formally communicated the CCPCC's decision to Beijing's municipal government: ten public buildings, under the label of the National Day Projects (NDP), were to be completed by October 1, 1959. Besides the Great Hall of the People, these included the Museum of the Chinese Revolution, the Museum of Chinese History, the National Theater, the Military Museum, the Science and Technology Hall, the Art Museum, the Cultural Palace of Nationalities, the National Agricultural Exhibition Hall, and an expansion of the existing Industrial Exhibition Hall.[8] A mobilization conference for the National Day Projects was quickly convened and telegrams were wired to senior architects in the provinces, inviting them to come to Beijing to participate in the design of the buildings. Meanwhile, the Building Construction Bureau and the Civil Engineering Bureau were instructed to prepare building materials and organize construction teams to ensure that ground could be broken for all of the projects within a month's time.

Three days later, on September 8, approximately one thousand experts from Beijing's design institutes and construction units gathered for the mobilization conference. Wan Li stood before the assembly and delivered a speech in which he made it clear that the purpose of the projects was "to reflect the great achievements in industrial and agricultural production, as well as in many other areas, after ten years of development of the New China."[9] But this was not to be a mechanical exercise. Rather, he said:

> We must carry out the task with high quality, a high artistic level, and high speed. High quality requires exceptional design and construction, which will guarantee that the buildings will endure and be utilized through the end of this century and still function into the next one; high artistic level means to make the buildings noble, elegant, gracious, and beautiful, so far as conditions permit; high speed means to finish the construction in a brief time span.[10]

"In short," Wan said, referring to Mao's general line, "our achievements need to be greater, faster, better, and more economical." Architects also had to "carry forward the spirit of collectivism and carry out a socialist collaboration. . . . Chinese intellectuals are great talents; they are also very patriotic and proud of their nation. I hope," Wan continued, "the architects who design these projects are not participating for their own individual fame but for the honor of the 600 million Chinese people that these buildings represent—each of us is only one of those 600 million."[11]

Collective Creation

After Wan Li's speech, the delegates from Beijing's design institutes immediately dispersed to their home bases and mobilized their most talented professionals. Traveling in the opposite direction, more than thirty senior architectural experts from all over China arrived at Beijing's Peace Hotel on the evening of September 10. They were warmly welcomed and informed that they were expected to hand in their first drafts in five days' time. The experts were very excited and some of them started to work on their designs that very night.[12]

The National Day Projects Committee employed a unique process for the design competition. Strict deadlines were imposed for the submission of each stage of the work, at the end of which the participants—who could work individually or in groups—would come together to review and discuss each other's work under the supervision of the leaders. The idea was that they would learn from each other—"to compensate for shortcomings" (*quchang buduan* 取长补短). Once opinions coalesced into a kind of consensus, the designers went back to work on the next round, and the process would repeat. Through a series of reviews, synthetic summarizations, and modifications, the concept then gradually moved toward "centralization"—"integrating all the different parties' strengths" (*bocai zhongchang* 博采众长), as a Chinese idiom so aptly states. The final schematic design was expected to "reach the best effect" at its "most ideal stage" 在"最理想的阶段"达到"最佳效果." This competition mechanism was devised to ensure that individual talents converged with maximum efficiency into a collective solution. At the time, it was called a "semi-open collective schematic design competition" 半开放式的集体创作方案竞赛.[13] Obviously, individual intellectual property rights were never a consideration.[14]

At the outset of the process, "to fully liberate the designers' minds" (or because there was no time for rational planning), the committee issued design briefs with no content apart from the name, size, and location of each project. There were no specific requirements regarding their functions, which were left to the interpretation of the individual architects. Of the Ten Great Buildings, three were tentatively earmarked for Tiananmen Square: the Museum of the Chinese Revolution, the Museum of Chinese History, and the Great Hall of the People. Again, for each of the three only the figures for the floor area, or the total building area, were provided; there was no information about specific functional requirements or the exact site location, or even a clearly defined boundary for the square itself. The architects, therefore, had to wade through a morass of unknown criteria while simultaneously grappling with issues ranging from the urban planning of the square to the architectural design of the individual buildings.

While most of the projects moved swiftly during the first three rounds of the design competition, the three most prestigious projects on Tiananmen Square got stuck. According to the biography of Liu Ren, second secretary of the CCP's Beijing Municipal Committee, "These experts [had] never designed buildings on such a grand scale, and after many efforts, their schemes were still banal. Moreover, the senior experts were uncomfortable with criticizing each other, so the design work did not proceed smoothly."[15] Premier Zhou Enlai was gravely concerned. To further "liberate minds" and encourage innovation, he commanded that members of the general public, and especially young students, be mobilized to participate in the design process.

The concept for the expansion of Tiananmen Square and the three projects located on it gradually emerged during the fourth and sixth rounds of the competition. Through the collective process, a decision was made that the square would be widened by 500 meters and that one building would be placed on each side in a symmetrical layout—with a now-combined Museum of the Chinese Revolution and Museum of Chinese History on the east and the Great Hall of the People on the west. The Great Hall could be higher than the Tiananmen Rostrum, it was agreed, but it had to be in harmony with it aesthetically.

After reviewing the schemes produced from the sixth round, Premier Zhou added his own recommendations, and on October 9, 1958, the committee instructed the architects to prepare a seventh draft based on Zhou's assessment. Wan Li selected eight schemes and sent photographs of them to architectural experts around the country, requesting their feedback. When all of their responses had been assembled, the "semi-open collective design competition" started to draw to a close: the committee contacted three Beijing institutes—Tsinghua University, the Beijing Institute of Architectural Design (BIAD), and the Beijing Urban Planning Bureau—and asked each of them to submit a "synthesized scheme," based on the eight short-listed projects, to help Zhou make the final decision (fig. 2.4).

The "Growth" of a New Style

In the course of the competition, various "citizen architects," both amateur and professional, submitted more than 400 schemes for the National Day Projects, including 84 floor plans and 189 elevations for the Great Hall. Some of these were highly innovative, but none survived the collective design process.[16] One of the proposals envisioned Tiananmen Square not only as an arena in which crowds could congregate, wave banners, and shout slogans, but also as a public space where people could socialize and relax: only a small portion of the ground surface was to be covered over with concrete, and the remaining vast open space was to form a "Central Park" in the heart of Beijing. Another scheme, in the spirit of what we would today call "cross programming," suggested adding a programmatically "energetic" Youth Palace alongside the stiff Great Hall, with an open corridor linking the two together.

For the Great Conference Hall for Ten Thousand People—the Great Hall—most schemes adopted a model based on classical theaters, reflecting the general understanding of how NPC meetings were conducted. The space and participants were separated into two parts: the rostrum to be occupied by the leaders and speakers, and the auditorium for delegates and listeners. Only two sketches, submitted by Yang Tingbao 杨廷宝, presented a fundamentally different concept. As opposed to the theater model, Yang proposed a parliamentary assembly hall with a single unified space in which the delegates would be able to see not only the speakers on the rostrum but also one another. But how, exactly, could Yang's plan accommodate a mass of ten thousand attendees while at the same time enabling clear lines of sight across the space? There was no precedent for such an architectural feat in human history, and Yang's sketches did not provide any details about how the dilemma might be resolved.

In the fluctuating political climate of China in the mid-1950s, discussions of architectural style were highly politicized, and various formal languages were capriciously attacked. Apprehensive about the country's unpredictable politics, and disillusioned by the growing realization that the link between formal expression and political content was totally arbitrary, Chinese architects developed an eclectic attitude toward architectural form, freely moving between styles and sometimes combining a few together—their choices guided solely by the particular political and economic circumstances of the moment. In 1958, the euphoria of the beginning of the Great Leap brought with it a brief interlude of aesthetic relaxation, which left its mark on the design of the Ten Great Buildings.

The submitted proposals for the Great Hall represented a miscellany of styles, from modernist to Soviet-inspired socialist-realist to the new "National Form," and everything in between. The scheme that was ultimately selected was in the Western neoclassical style, with gigantic colonnades. One cannot but wonder about the logic of the choice: just why would a fledgling socialist state, fully determined to catch up with the West and "sprint toward communism," think that a Western neoclassical idiom was best for its Great Hall of the People? It seems bewildering. Yet neoclassical architecture evidently has an appeal that crosses ideological boundaries: it was part of Jefferson's vision for U.S. government buildings, part of Hitler's vision for buildings of the Third Reich, and part of Stalin's vision for buildings of the Soviet Union (Stalin infamously declared: "People have the right to pillars!").

In 1960 Zhao Dongri 赵冬日, director of the Technology Office of the Beijing Urban Planning Bureau 北京市规划局技术室 and one of the chief architects who worked on the Great Hall, tried to justify the selected scheme: "[For] a great building with such a huge political significance, what kind of style should be adopted? . . . Obviously, we cannot and should not accept capitalist modern forms; likewise, the reformed National Form is essentially backward-looking rather than forward-looking. It has no sense of class, and does not express the Communist ideology."[17] So, what constituted the "politically correct style," "the New Socialist Form for Chinese architecture"? Zhao elaborated:

> The use and scale of the Great Hall of the People are the concrete determining factors of architectural art. The building should be large, and its shape magnificent. Moreover, since it is built on Tiananmen Square, it must have a certain relationship with China's ancient buildings. It should be harmonious with them, but it must also supersede them, triumph over them. The architectural style should be joyful and clear so as to become the symbol of our new era.[18]

Zhao's statement points to how the size of the building—its sheer bigness—had actually predetermined its architectural characteristics. In fact, besides the Western neoclassical colonnades on its façade, the most prominent feature of the selected scheme was that it was double the size stipulated by the competition brief.

Greater

In the original design program, the site for the Great Hall was 37,800 square meters and the total floor area 50,000 square meters. During the design process many architects complained that this was too small to successfully contain Mao's ten thousand, and the NDP Committee quickly decided to expand the floor area to 70,000 square meters. Despite this, the first few rounds failed to yield any satisfactory schemes for consideration by senior officials.

From today's perspective, the fact that the competition was eventually won by the team from the Beijing Urban Planning Bureau appears highly irregular, if not scandalous, since this team was led by the very same people who were administering the Ten Great Buildings project as a whole. The team's general supervisor was Liu Ren 刘仁, the second secretary of the Beijing Municipal Committee of the CCP (BMCCCP), and one of the top directors of the NDP Committee. The team's two chief architects, Zhao Dongri and Shen Qi 沈其, were both commissioned by the BMCCCP to oversee the entire design for the NDP. Just as the issue of an individual designer's intellectual property rights was not addressed, it seems that "conflict of interest" was not considered to be a problem either.

Liu Ren knew the design process and its circumstances inside out. After many schemes were submitted without any satisfactory results, he personally went to Tiananmen Square and paced off the designated site for the Great Hall. He concluded that the expanded floor area of 70,000 square meters was still not grand enough to express the spirit of Mao and Zhou's vision, and he directed Zhao and Shen to be bold and start over without space constraints. Zhao and Shen went back to the Planning Bureau and told an assembled group of young architects, "This project is a test of the architect. Are you up to it, or not? Do you dare to spend money, or are you scared?" Forty years later, Tao Zongzhen 陶宗震, one of those young architects, recalled that he "became fearless," launching into his schematic design without taking the site or floor area into account, and instead "only considering how to highlight the grandeur of the Great Hall of the People as a monument of the era."[19] Tao's scheme was selected by Premier Zhou on October 14, 1958, thirty-six days after Wan Li delivered his speech to the mobilization conference.

Tao was then immediately asked to make a set of design development drawings and to deliver them to the BIAD, which was responsible for creating the construction documents. (Design development drawings were usually done on a scale of 1:200, but Tao had to create his on a 1:400 scale because no drafting board could be found that was large enough to accommodate the plan for the Great Hall.) Tao did not have time to calculate the total floor area until after he had finished the drawings. The result came as a shock—170,000 square meters, more than two times the area required by the initial brief. The dimensions of the site were also greatly expanded. But Tao's scheme proved impossible to change, for two reasons. First, his plan had a strict symmetrical layout, with the Great Conference Hall for ten thousand in the center and the Banquet Hall for five thousand to the north. Both of these were required by Mao. The size of the office building for the NPC Standing Committee, on the south side of the building complex, could have been reduced somewhat, but at the expense of destroying the symmetry.[20] The second reason was even more critical: the tenth anniversary was only eleven months away, leaving no time for a major modification of the design.

Better

Many architectural experts were unhappy with the way the design competition had been conducted, and were especially dissatisfied with the design of the winning entry. They conveyed their concerns to Premier Zhou. In Beijing, the two main critics of the winning design were Liang Sicheng 梁思成 and Wang Huabin 王华彬. Liang communicated a clear ranking of preferred architectural styles: (1) Chinese and new, (2) Western and new, (3) Chinese and old, (4) Western and old. The style of the chosen scheme undeniably belonged to the fourth category, which he considered the least desirable. As for scale, Liang said that the winning entry made the same fundamental mistake as St. Peter's in Rome, which was to double the size of all components, making people feel as if they had entered a world of giants. Wang Huabin also criticized the project for being oversized and for creating numerous dark interior spaces that would require a great deal of artificial lighting and ventilation. In another letter to Zhou, six professors and experts in Shanghai argued against the widening of Tiananmen Square to 500 meters, which they considered excessive in relation to its surroundings. In addition, they considered the selected Great Hall scheme similar to the winning entry for the League of Nations in Geneva, which was neoclassical in style and not at all innovative. In the words of Tan Yuan 谭垣, "The Great Hall of the People is big, but not great."[21]

On January 20, 1959, Premier Zhou and Beijing's mayor Peng Zhen 彭真 invited a group of architectural and structural experts and artists to a symposium to discuss the design of the Great Hall. At this juncture, the BIAD had completed the working drawings for the foundations and the construction teams had already started to dig. After listening to the various critiques, Zhou concluded that the first priority was to ensure the structural safety of the Great Hall. In terms of the scale, he began by quoting the words Mao always used to rebut those intellectuals who criticized him for "craving bigness and achievement" 好大喜功: "We crave socialism's greatness and achievement, which is far from purposeless."[22] But he also added that, in contrast to St. Peter's—which was the product of a theocracy, built to glorify God—the Great Hall was "people-oriented," so the architects had to articulate the building details to make the scale friendly to the human body. Concerning the building's style, Zhou cautioned the experts not to be constrained by narrow, nationalist sentiments but instead strive to emulate "the broad mind of a proletarian and the all-encompassing spirit of an internationalist." Zhou stressed that ultimately the most important issue was not whether the building design was old or new, Western or Chinese, but rather that in eight months it should be ready to provide a place "for ten thousand people to meet and five thousand people to eat together." The scheme had to be fixed without further delay, so that construction above the foundation could begin immediately.[23]

Faster

The core spirit of the Great Leap Forward was speed, just as the propaganda of the time promulgated: "High speed is the soul of the General Line."[24] After the one-month design charette, the "high speed" of the Great Hall's construction was first manifested in what Scheeren has referred to as a "brutal erasure of past conditions." Within a single month, a total of 2,170 residential buildings (housing 684 families) and 1,823 business and industrial buildings (containing 67 work units) on the 137,300-square-meter site were demolished and all of the families and work units removed.

The required "high speed" was also demonstrated in the population's fervent embrace of the new. One of the methods invented during the Great Leap Forward for managing architectural projects was the so-called Three Simultaneities (*sanbian* 三边) approach, a process that involved simultaneously designing, preparing materials, and carrying out construction. The construction teams had already begun to prepare materials and equipment after Wan Li's mobilization speech in September 1958. On October 16, when the scheme was approved, they immediately started to level the site and test the soil pressure: "Workers just can't wait for the signal to start to work."[25] Following the approval of the schematic design, the BIAD had just four days to produce the design development drawings and seven days to do the working drawings for the foundation. By October 28, work had started on the foundation, and the site of the Great Hall was swarming with activity. With only ten months remaining to complete the construction, more than ten thousand people worked three shifts a day.

The construction headquarters set up four branch offices to supervise the four parts of the construction: the Banquet Hall, the Great Conference Hall, the Central Hall, and the Office Building for the Standing Committee of the NPC. On December 6, the BIAD dispatched teams of architects to each branch office to ensure the fullest implementation of the Three Simultaneities. Many military tactics developed by the Chinese Communist Party during the civil war were redeployed in the construction process. More than a thousand campaigns were launched to resolve the myriad problems that arose as construction progressed. The CCP was also masterful at controlling the ideological and political aspects of the work. A broad array of propaganda and educational programs—with constantly evolving motivational slogans—were devised for the workers by political organizations, workers' unions, and youth leagues on the site. Cultural interests also boost productivity—the CCP was well versed in this regard. The Ministry of Culture sent a team of more than thirty artists to the site to direct the "cultural life" of the workers. They established an amateur art school to train interested individuals in music, performing arts, and literature. All of the significant themes driving the construction of the Great Hall—heroic struggle, revolution and production, an iron will, and a burning passion to construct a monument for eternity at a dazzling, ultramodern speed—can be found in "Battle on the Crossbeams," a poem written by one of the workers:

> The Banquet Hall, and the crossbeams
> are all densely wrapped up with steel.
> The plaster workers are more fervent than fire,
> with a will as strong as steel.
> The iron carts flying, and compactors vibrating,
> we are fighting for speed and sure quality.
> After battling for two days and one night,
> we heroes conquer the crossbeams.
> The red flag is fluttering.

宴会厅, 井字梁,
密密麻麻全是钢。
洋灰工人赛烈火,
强像钢梁。
铁车飞, 振捣忙,
争取速度保质量。
大战两天又一夜,
英雄战胜井字梁,
红旗飘扬。[26]

More Economical

Recent historical research has begun to reveal that the main feature of the Great Leap Forward was the astonishing waste generated through the extraordinarily irrational actions propelled by the slogan "Greater and faster!" The most notorious example of this profligacy relates to steel production. The national mobilization effort of 1958 achieved its target of 10.7 million tons of steel, but more than 3 million tons of this total—the output of small backyard steel furnaces—turned out to be unusable and ended up in landfills.[27] Even in the official records of the Ten Great Buildings project, Wan Li admitted that "in less than one year, designing, preparing materials, and carrying out construction simultaneously had resulted in a lot of difficulties and wasteful acts."[28] The high speed of development and the low level of technology, combined with the blind zealotry of the political leaders and the "human wave tactics" of construction, frequently contradicted the fourth principle of Mao's general line: "Greater, faster, better, and more economical."[29]

The Anshan Steel Company 鞍钢 was assigned the task of producing the steel for the Great Hall's banquet and conference halls—all four million tons of it. Production was completed by December 1958 and the steel was shipped to factories in Beijing, Shenyang, Tangshan, and Taiyuan, where the steel frames were to be fabricated. However, when samples were tested, serious problems became apparent. On January 23, 1959, the Ministry of Metallurgical Industry sent a group of experts to assess the quality of the steel: they concluded that it did not meet the required standards. Anshan Steel blamed the poor quality on the fact that "the old regulations have been destroyed by the Ideological Rectification Campaign and new ones have not yet been established, so there are loopholes in quality control." The NDP Committee decided to discard the whole shipment and asked Anshan Steel to start all over again.[30]

With the frenzied leap of 1958 and 1959, China suffered from the consequences of unbalanced economic development. The prioritizing of steel production resulted in a dramatic reduction in agricultural land, but peasants were still forced to hand in more grain to the government than they could spare, based on false production figures fabricated by local officials. Cases of edema and starvation became rampant in rural areas. Other sectors of development were obstructed too, especially light industry. The production of daily commodities fell rapidly, and many cities began to suffer a severe shortage of food and other basic necessities.[31]

On February 28, 1959, in the face of a deteriorating economy, a scarcity of materials and workers, and serious difficulties in removing and relocating former inhabitants of the construction site, Premier Zhou held a conference in Zhongnanhai 中南海 to discuss how to scale back the National Day Projects. As a result of this meeting, it was decided that of the Ten Great Buildings announced in September 1958, two were to be combined into one building (the Museum of the Chinese Revolution and the Museum of Chinese History); two were to be reduced in scale (the Military Museum and the Agricultural Exhibition Hall); one was to be eliminated from the list (the Industrial Exhibition Hall); and three (the National Theater, the Science and Technology Museum, and the Art Museum) were to be replaced by more modest buildings (the Diaoyutai State Guesthouse, Minzu Hotel, and the Overseas Chinese Building). The Great Hall remained untouched.

Even after this huge cutback in scale and repeated "antiwaste campaigns" on the construction sites, the Ten Great Buildings project still exceeded the initial budget by a large margin. The estimate of 1958 had anticipated a total construction area of 372,000 square meters and an expenditure of 140 million yuan. In 1959, according to "An Analysis of the Ration of Materials Used for the National Day Projects," official data revealed that the total construction area was in fact 639,000 square meters and the cost was 438 million yuan. The cost of the Great Hall alone rose from 36 million to 101 million yuan—not so far removed from the initial budget for all ten projects.[32]

It should be noted that this huge investment in the National Day Projects was going on while major disasters—political, economic, and environmental—were also unfolding in the wake of the Great Leap Forward. Foremost among them was the outbreak of the Great Famine in China's countryside, which peaked in 1960 and did not end until 1962, by which time it had claimed the lives of 36 to 45 million people.[33]

In the short space of ten months, China stumbled from its frenzied leap into a dire crisis, but the construction of the Great Hall of the People did not falter. Driven by a single blind will, it carried with it countless spatio-political ideals and the technological talents of its people. In official propaganda, the Great Hall is always portrayed as a singular and incomparable accomplishment, and on a superficial level it appears to be a "great, glorious, and correct"—as well as rational—construction. However, on closer inspection one realizes that, far from being rational, almost every chain in its process was forged by blind and arbitrary decisions. Viewing the Great Hall from a critical distance, we might ask whether it could be considered an extreme example of a long-standing building tradition that still exerts a powerful influence on China today.

In this tradition, an obsession with architectural style and symbolic expression—the projection of power—transcends the greater social purposes of spatial planning and practice. Grandiose events and rituals take precedence over the basic elements required for people's daily life. The capricious decisions of political leaders often circumvent any fair or just decision-making process. All available social and natural resources are mobilized—regardless of the cost—to build, at breakneck speed, a monument that is supposed to endure forever. No matter how modern the technology employed, these impulses are emblematic of a deep-rooted antimodern way of thinking. And the Great Hall of the People stands as a towering testament to this Chinese building tradition.

Megabuildings: Dinosaurs of What Movement(s)?

When examining the legacy of "building big" from a larger historical perspective, one might jump to two overly broad generalizations. The first view is that throughout history dictators have felt impelled to construct monumental buildings as a way of materializing their megalomaniac visions and inspiring shock and awe. In this respect, Mao's Ten Great

Buildings in Beijing in the 1950s are no different from those planned and built in the 1930s by Hitler in Berlin, Mussolini in Rome, or Stalin in Moscow. The second view connects the red legacy of the 1950s to China's long history of dynastic rule: since the first emperor, Qin Shihuang 秦始皇, united China more than two thousand years ago, all great Chinese emperors have been obsessed with destroying the palaces of the previous dynasty and replacing them with new ones of unprecedented grandeur, on the principle that "one cannot demonstrate majesty without [architecture's] magnificence 非壮丽无以重威."[34] In other words, Beijing's Ten Great Buildings were in essence an extension of the imperial heritage of vast building projects that began with Emperor Qin's Royal Palace and the construction of the Great Wall and continued up to the Forbidden City of the Ming and Qing dynasties. To a large degree, these two views are valid, but they fail to acknowledge the legacy of building big in the context of modern China, and specifically its relation to China's nationalism, its contemporary politics, and its conception of architecture's role in society.

BIGNESS AS A NATIONAL IDENTITY

China is a big, strong, unitary nation-state with a long and glorious history, and to reflect this, its buildings should be grand, robust, and imbued with a "national character." These two beliefs, now taken for granted by most Chinese people, are in fact cultural and political constructs of the Chinese nationalism that started to develop in the nineteenth century. Two crises helped shape this nationalism during the transition from the late Qing empire to the Republican state: the humiliating clash with Western imperialism and the uprising of the so-called frontier barbarians (the indigenous ethnic peoples who lived on the margins of the Qing territory). In response to this upheaval—which shook traditional certainties about the preeminence of Chinese civilization—many intellectuals sought to produce a discourse of "national unity" to support the creation of a homogeneous, Han-dominated nation-state.[35]

The search for China's architectural identity was one component of the efforts to forge a cohesive national polity and culture. After the period of the May Fourth Movement in the 1910s and 1920s, the debate between the rival strands of radical antitraditionalism and neotraditionalism found expression in China's architectural development in the 1930s: one form opted for an unreserved adaptation of Western modernism, and the other, a combination of Chinese traditional form with modern materials and construction. Within the second camp, many architects pursued a national style through ad hoc design experiments, while a group of architectural historians, led by Liang Sicheng, believed that an "authentic" Chinese style could be distilled through historical study.

Liang's field studies of the traditional buildings that remained mostly in North China in the 1930s, and his two survey books on Chinese classical architecture, established the foundations of Chinese architectural historiography.[36] They also defined a cultural and aesthetic orthodoxy: that one dominant architectural style best represented the "official" national style—namely, the Buddhist temples of North China built during periods of "vigor" and "elegance" (ca. 850–1400, from the Tang to the Jin dynasty), which he praised as "grand and robust." The court buildings constructed later were deemed by Liang to be "rigid and pretentious," while the diversity of China's architectural culture—the vernacular buildings of different regions—was also roundly dismissed.

Among the many design explorations of the national style in this period, two vast projects, envisioned and partially constructed during the 1930s, can be seen as foreshadowing the Ten Great Buildings: the Nationalist government complexes of the Nanjing Capital Plan and the Shanghai City Center Plan. During a crucial period when the nation was suffering from great poverty and social disorder, these two "plans" were distinguished by their ostentation and excessive cost. The Sino-Japanese War of 1937–45 and the civil war of 1945–9 put a halt to their construction.

Both formally and technologically, Chinese architecture from 1950 to 1976 owed a considerable debt to the first half of the twentieth century. In the years 1952–4, in addition to modernism and the National Form (the latest official name for the national style), Soviet-style socialist-realism was imported as a new element in China's architecture. Beijing's Ten Great Buildings project, built with extraordinary speed, on huge dimensions, and with great political zeal, marked a new milestone in the nation's history. It also triggered a nationwide boom in building, inspiring other National Day projects in 1958–9 as well as many other monumental buildings during the Cultural Revolution, from 1966 to 1976.

Similarly, a new phase of modernization took place in China in the post-Mao era, in concert with a fundamental shift in focus from waging radical political campaigns to striving for economic empowerment. From the 1990s, in particular, the extended bipolar opposition between modernism and the National Form began to morph into a more complex configuration as a consequence of four major forces: the acceleration of the culture of consumption in China's new urban environment; the eclectic stylistic approach adopted by Chinese government officials; the emergence of young architects with independent professional practices; and the influx of large numbers of foreign architects that came with globalization. However, despite the new variation in formal expression and the seemingly diverse, almost ad hoc, modes of practice, nationalism continues to serve as the dominant ideological foundation for a major portion of China's architectural output. This is especially apparent in the government's obsessive reliance on grand architectural projects and spectacular events, such as the Beijing Olympics and the Shanghai World Expo, to gloss over social contradictions, boost national pride, and "save face"—in other words, gain the respect and approbation of the outside world.

In 2008 two significant events raised profound questions about the function of architecture in China and its relation to society. One, the Beijing Olympics, produced a massive array of glitzy, awe-inspiring architectural icons, and the other, the Sichuan earthquake, destroyed tens of thousands of substandard civic structures, including more than ten thousand school buildings, and some five million people lost their homes. While the megabuildings erected for the Olympics, in Beijing and many other cities, were staged to represent China's "coming out" as a giant superpower, the collapsed schools revealed, with painful acuity, the still-fragile state of the country's infrastructure. Juxtaposed images from these two events constitute a striking iconography that signifies the deep-rooted contradictions in today's China.

BIGNESS AS A LOCAL CHARACTERISTIC

China's contemporary "building-big syndrome" extends beyond Beijing and the country's major cities to the countless megabuildings that have proliferated across the country with the acquiescence of the different tiers of government. Within China's current system of governance, each level is accountable not to its local constituency but to a higher echelon of authority. The construction of lavish buildings has become one of the most effective ways for local party members to demonstrate their "good" governance to their superiors.[37] Whereas in feudal China strictly hierarchical building codes kept local officials in check, in Mao's China, as well as in the current regime, every local cadre acts as a "little Mao" with his own megalomaniacal vision of building big, no matter how remote or abjectly poor the district. Whereas in the 1950s and during the Cultural Revolution, all local cadres were fully committed to imitating Beijing's megabuildings, in today's era of globalization, they are free to produce all kinds of astonishing constructions, from literal duplicates of the Tiananmen Rostrum or the U.S. Capitol to ultramodern work designed by international "starchitects."

BIGNESS AS A SOCIALIST MANIFESTO

As noted earlier, the CCTV headquarters architect Ole Scheeren has remarked on China's "fascinating ability to embrace change," unburdened by "regret." Scheeren apparently considers that an absence of regret is a good quality, allowing China to cast off its burdens and, in the style of the futurists, run to catch up with the fast pace of modernization. "Embracing change" also makes it possible to fully exploit the transient and ephemeral aspects of modernity—and this, to a great extent, is exactly what China has been doing. From the Great Leap Forward of the 1950s to the current economic boom, China has frequently fallen into a "state of emergency" (or ecstasy), to which it has responded with a "total mobilization" in which everything is determined by the logic of numbers and speed. But, following the extreme logic of French cultural theorist Paul Virilio, if speed reigns, then the constant increase in acceleration will lead to nothing more than the annihilation of space and matter—the "liquidation of the world."[38] Why, then, does the constantly accelerating China, a country so obsessed with bigness, continue to construct colossal buildings in its longing for permanence and timelessness?

This phenomenon might be readily dismissed as a symptom of retrogressive, antimodern thinking. Although in many ways China has undoubtedly evolved into a modern country, one might postulate that the megabuilding boom, encouraged by the various levels of officialdom, reveals that the Chinese government is still mired in a chimerical vision—an admixture of the mindsets of a feudal emperor, a Communist dictator and a nationalist zealot. Indeed, it is here that Koolhaas and Scheeren's

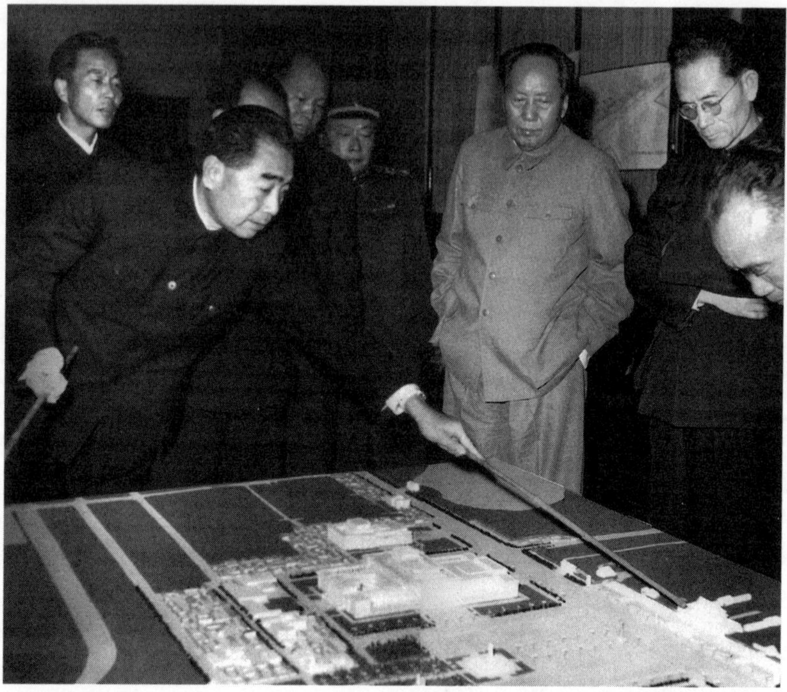

FIGURE 2.4. Mao Zedong (*center right*), Zhou Enlai (*left*), and other central-government leaders inspecting the design for the Ten Great Buildings and Tiananmen Square, October 14, 1958. Anonymous photographer.

social and formal argument for the CCTV building tries to add another layer of meaning, which appears truly intriguing.

As mentioned at the outset, Koolhaas made it clear that his design for the CCTV headquarters was based on a social critique of the capitalist system and his high hopes for socialist development in China:

> Because we felt that in capitalist countries the effect of capitalism and the effect of the market . . . have been largely negative, in the sense that there's no more public but every operation is being undertaken by the privates. And therefore, the status of architects has fundamentally changed and you're no longer doing something for public good but for private interests. In that sense, there was an attempt by us to see whether the more traditional work of the architect—somebody working for public good—would still be possible in a communist context.[39]

FIGURE 2.5. Mao Zedong, Zhou Enlai, and other central-government leaders in the 1950s "inspecting" Rem Koolhaas and Ole Scheeren's 2002 design for the CCTV headquarters building. Photo collage by Zhu Tao.

According to Koolhaas's "Beijing Manifesto," the capitalist system also leads to architectural failure because it tends to decentralize large organizations, discouraging communication between people: "In the market, architecture = real estate. Any complex organization is dismantled—each part put in its place for the least amount of money. All media companies suffer the subsequent paranoia: each sector talks about the others as 'them,' distrust is rife, motives questioned. There is no whole."[40] By contrast, Koolhaas argues that the CCTV design, with its extraordinary joining of programs into one gigantic "continuous loop," demonstrates a critical alternative: "In China, money does not have the last word (yet). There is a conceptual space that could accommodate the construction of the CCTV as a whole—a single entity in which all parts are housed permanently—aware of each other's presence. A collective."[41]

Among the many ironies in this situation, the most striking one is that Koolhaas's client, China Central Television, could not be further removed from his assumed socialist predisposition to "work for the public good." Not only is it one of the state's most powerful propaganda machines, currently under the direct control of the CCP's Central Propaganda Department, but CCTV is also a gigantic money-making machine that monopolizes TV broadcasting across the entire country.

In 1958–9, the Chinese architects who worked on Beijing's Ten Great Buildings became embroiled in a continuing struggle to devise a style that would express the ethos of the new socialist regime. Half a century on, Koolhaas, one of the world's leading architects, proposed that the CCTV headquarters, with its daunting architectural form, could be the progenitor for developing a kind of "collectivity" for the welfare of the public. Even Koolhaas himself was aware—retrospectively—of a certain paradox here. His "Beijing Manifesto" asks, rhetorically, "Was [CCTV] merely a landmark, one in an endless sequence of alien proposals of meaningless boldness? Were its structural complexities simply irresponsible?"[42]

With the continuing proliferation of megabuildings in China, has the country finally managed, more than sixty years later, to "save face," as Wan Li originally hoped, through Beijing's Ten Great Buildings of the 1950s? And in the process, has a powerful clientele of international "starchitects" now collectively created the new National Form for China—a State-Capitalist style promoted with great pride and exuberance, but also with no little arbitrariness? Will the "progressive" form of some of these megabuildings also be able to trigger some positive changes in the sociocultural agenda, and even the mentality of the Chinese government? Or will the ultimate virtue of the buildings' bigness be to outlast a flawed regime and eventually assume its ideal role as a "social condenser" for the public good? These are the most perplexing questions at a time when China's revolutionary sentiments and nationalist zeal are mixing with the currents of globalization (fig. 2.5).

Notes

1. This chapter was developed from a paper presented at "Red Legacy in China: An International Conference," held by the Harvard-Yenching Institute and the Fairbank Center for Chinese Studies, Harvard University, in 2010. It was first published

in the journal *AA Files* (2011): 104–10. My thanks to Thomas Weaver for editing that article. I also acknowledge with gratitude the General Research Fund 752513 from the Research Grants Council, Hong Kong, which allowed me to further develop my research into this chapter.

2. Ma Weidong, "Interview with Rem Koolhaas," *A + U*, special issue: "CCTV by OMA" (July 2005): 16.

3. Rem Koolhaas, *Content* (Cologne: Taschen, 2004), pp. 486–89.

4. In his 2006 lecture, Ole Scheeren reiterated what he had written in his essay "Made in China," in *A + U*, special issue: "CCTV by OMA" (July 2005).

5. Wang Jun 王军, *Cheng j* 城记 (City record) (Beijing: SDX Joint Publishing Company, 2003), pp. 271–72.

6. Wang Zhengming 王争鸣, *Qiji shi zenyang chuangzao de: Renmin dahuitang jianshe shihua* 奇迹是怎样创造的—人民大会堂建设史话 (How the miracle was created: A historical account of the construction of the Great Hall of the People) (Beijing: Cathay Book Shop, 2001), p. 13.

7. Ibid.

8. This list differs from the final list of Ten Great Buildings mentioned later in this chapter.

9. Wan Li 万里, "Zai Beijing shi guoqing gongcheng dongyuan dahui shang de jianghua" 在北京市国庆工程动员大会上的讲话 (Speech at the Mobilization Conference for the National Day Projects of Beijing), *Wan Li Wenxuan* 万里文选 (Selected writings of Wan Li) (Beijing: People's Publishing House, 1995), p. 48.

10. Ibid., p. 49.

11. Ibid., p. 50.

12. Jin Shengji 金圣基, *Renmin dahuitang jianwenlu* 人民大会堂见闻录 (Memoirs of the Great Hall of the People), vol. 1 (Beijing: Chinese Communist Party History Publishing House, 1988), p. 13.

13. Ruan Zhida 阮志大, "Renmin dahuitang yinian nei jiancheng zhi mi" 人民大会堂一年内建成之谜 (The mystery of the completion of the Great Hall of the People in one year), *Jianzhu xuebao* 建筑学报 (Architectural journal) 3 (2000): 7.

14. The Chinese "semi-open collective competition," in various modified forms, continues to be employed today. Chinese officials sometimes arrange the schematic design competitions not to select a winner but to assign an affiliated architect (or design institute) to "integrate the strengths of all the different parties," which often causes great bafflement and frustration among the international participants

15. Beijing shiwei *Liu Ren zhuan* bianxiezu 北京市委《刘仁传》编写组 (Beijing Municipal Committee of the CCP editorial and writing group of *The Biography of Liu Ren*), *Liu Ren zhuan* 刘仁传 (The biography of Liu Ren) (Beijing: Beijing Press, 2000), p. 429.

16. The following introduction to the various design-scheme entries is drawn mainly from an article by Zhao Dongri 赵冬日, "Cong renmin dahuitang de sheji fang'an pingxuan lai tan xin jianzhu fengge de chengzhang" 从人民大会堂的设计方案评选来谈新建筑风格的成长 (On the growth of a new architecture style through the selection of the schematic design for the Great Hall of the People), *Jianzhu xuebao* 建筑学报 2 (1960): 13–16.

17. Ibid.

18. Ibid.

19. Tao Zongzhen 陶宗震, "Tian'anmen guangchang guihua ji renmin dahuitang sheji jishi" 天安门广场规划及人民大会堂设计纪实 (A record of the planning of Tiananmen Square and the design of the Great Hall of the People), *Zhongwai jianzhu* 中外建筑 (Chinese and foreign architecture) 5 (1997): 7.

20. Ibid.

21. Yang Yongsheng 杨永生, ed., *Jianzhu baijia yishi* 建筑百家轶事 (A hundred architects' anecdotes) (Beijing: China Architecture and Building Press, 2000), p. 22.

22. Mao first used this slogan during his Hundred Flowers Campaign, when Chen Mingshu 陈铭枢, the former governor of Guangdong Province under the Nationalist government, criticized him as "overambitious, biased, moody, and with no respect for tradition" 好大喜功, 偏听偏信, 轻视古典, 喜怒无常; Zhang Xiruo 张奚若, the minister of education at that time, also criticized Mao as "overambitious, eager for quick success, despising the past, and having a blind faith in the future" 好大喜功, 急功近利, 否定过去, 迷信将来. Mao took these criticisms to heart and refuted them on many occasions. For example, on January 11, 1958, during the Nanning Conference, his response was: "I am craving the bigness of 600 million people and the achievement of socialism—what's wrong with that?" During the Second Session of the Eighth National People's Conference, Liu Shaoqi delivered a report on behalf of the Central Committee and spoke in the same tone as Mao: "Some people are criticizing us as 'craving bigness and achievement, eager for quick success.' Exactly! Should we not crave the bigness of 600 million people and the achievement of socialism? Should we seek instead smallness and mistakes? Should we be overly conservative and content with the present?" See Li Rui 李锐, *Dayuejin Qinli Ji* "大跃进"亲历记 (Witness of the Great Leap Forward) (Haikou: Nanfang chubanshe, 1999), p. 170.

23. Zhang Bo 张镈, *Wo de jianzhu chuangzuo daolu* 我的建筑创作道路 (My journey of architectural design) (Beijing: Zhongguo jianzhu gongye chubanshe, 1994), pp. 155–58; Wang Zhengming, *Qiji*, pp. 27–28.

24. "Lizheng gao sudu" 力争高速度 (Endeavor to achieve high speed), editorial in *People's Daily*, June 21, 1958.

25. Beijing shi guihua guanlichu sheji yuan Renmin dahuitang sheji zu 北京市规划管理处设计院人民大会堂设计组 (The design team of the Great Hall of the People, Beijing Urban Planning Department), "Renmin dahuitang" 人民大会堂 (The Great Hall of the People), *Jianzhu xuebao* 9/10 (1959): 10, 23.

26. Wang Zhengming, *Qiji*, p. 108.

27. Ding Shu 丁抒, "Cong dayuejin dao dajihuang" 从"大跃进"到大饥荒 (From the Great Leap Forward to the Great Famine), at http://blog.boxun.com/hero/dangshi/23_1.shtml (accessed October 15, 2015).

28. "Guoqing shizheng gongcheng ganbu huiyi zongjie tigang" 国庆市政工程干部会议总结提纲 (A summary report for the concluding meeting with the National Day Projects cadres), June 20, 1959, Beijing Municipal Archives, 125-1-1228.

29. For an extensive discussion of the "human wave tactics," see Chapter 9.

30. "Guanyu renmin dahuitang wujia gangcai zhiliang bu he yaoqiu yanzhong yingxiang shigong jindu de baogao" 关于人民大会堂屋架钢材质量不合要求严重影响施工进度的报告 (A report on the faulty quality of the steel for the roof frame in the construction of the Great Hall of the People and its serious impact on the progress of the construction), February 2, 1959, Beijing Municipal Archives, 2-11-128.

31. Yang Jisheng 杨继绳, *Mubei: Zhongguo liushi niandai dajihuang jishi* 墓碑—中国六十年代大饥荒纪实 (Tombstone: Record of China's Great Famine in the sixties) (Hong Kong: Cosmos Books, 2008), p. 1050.

32. "Guoqing gongcheng wuzi shiyong ding'e fenxi" 国庆工程物资使用定额分析 (An analysis of the ration of materials used for the National Day Projects), Beijing Municipal Archives, 125-1-1386.

33. Yang Jisheng, *Mubei*, pp. 1050–52; Yang Jisheng, "Dajihuang qijian Zhongguo de renkou sunshi" 大饥荒期间中国的人口损失 (The loss of population in the Great Famine of China), in *Dayuejin, dajihuang: Lishi he bijiao shiye xia de shishi he sibian* 大跃进、大饥荒: 历史和比较视野下的史实和思辨 (Great Leap Forward, Great Famine: Historical facts and speculations from the historical and comparative perspectives), ed. Song Yongyi 宋永毅 and Ding Shu 丁抒, vol. 1 (Hong Kong: Green House Book Store, 2009), pp. 2–33; Ding Shu, "Dayuejin, dajihuang qijian feizhengchang siwangshu de xiaxian" 大跃进、大饥荒期间非正常死亡数的下限 (The lower limit of the number of unnatural deaths during the Great Leap Forward and the Great Famine), in ibid., p. 34; Frank Dikötter, *Mao's Great Famine: The History of China's Most Devastating Catastrophe, 1958–62* (London: Bloomsbury, 2010), p. 333.

34. According to *Shi ji* 史记 (Records of the grand historian) by Sima Qian 司马迁, in 206 BCE Liu Bang 刘邦, the Han emperor, questioned his prime minister, Xiao He 萧何, about the rationale for building an extravagant royal palace during the uncertainty of wartime. Xiao replied: "It is precisely because the war is not settled yet that the palace should be built. You, son of heaven, occupy the whole world as your home. One cannot demonstrate majesty without [architecture's] magnificence. We should also make sure that [the palace's architectural grandeur] will never be superseded by the future generations." See *Shi ji jin zhu* 史记今注, ed. Ma Chi-ying 马持盈, vol.1 (Taipei: Taiwan shangwu yinshuguan, 1979), pp. 339–40.

35. James Leibold, *Reconfiguring Chinese Nationalism: How the Qing Frontier and Its Indigenes Became Chinese* (New York: Palgrave Macmillan, 2007).

36. Liang completed his manuscripts for *Zhongguo jianzhu shi* 中国建筑史 (History of Chinese architecture) in 1944 and *Chinese Architecture: A Pictorial History* (in English) in 1946. *Zhongguo jianzhu shi* was formally published by Baihua Wenyi Publishing House (Tianjin) in 1998; *Chinese Architecture: A Pictorial History*, edited by Wilma Fairbank, was published by MIT Press (Cambridge, MA) in 1984.

37. On this issue I am indebted to Frank Dikötter, who suggested that I look beyond Chinese nationalism and investigate more closely contemporary Chinese politics and governance.

38. Paul Virilio, *L'Horizon négatif* (Paris: Galilée, 1984), p. 59, quoted in *High-Speed Society: Social Acceleration, Power, and Modernity*, ed. Hartmut Rosa and William E. Scheuerman (University Park: Pennsylvania State University Press, 2009), p. 216; Paul Virilio, *Speed and Politics*, trans. Mark Polizzotti (New York: Semiotext[e], 1986), pp. 149–50.

39. Ma Weidong, "Interview with Rem Koolhaas," p. 12.

40. Koolhaas, *Content*, p. 486.

41. Ibid.

42. Ibid., p. 487.

PART 2

Red Art

THREE

AMBIGUITIES OF ADDRESS

Cultural Revolution Posters and Their Post-Mao Appeal

Harriet Evans

Posters of China's Cultural Revolution occupy a prominent but paradoxical place in the memory and imaginary of Mao's China; they elicit complex and contradictory responses among diverse audiences, Chinese and global. Some, particularly those who experienced the political persecution and physical violence of the era, see them as unwelcome reminders of an oppressive and brutal regime. For others, they recall lost dreams of youth, and yearnings for a socialist future of justice and equality.[1] For yet others, they represent the imagined certainties of a past structured by order and stability. In the decades since their production, their images have been repeatedly reworked for popular consumption in commercial publicity and design, art, "red tourism," and political satire. Their contradictory associations—revolution and commodification, propaganda and subversion, global capitalism and the Chinese Communist Party's self-legitimizing—beg perplexing questions about their appeal. Is it plausible to suggest that their contemporary reworking in global advertising, for example, is guided simply by commercial profit, or that their appearance in Political Pop art is a form of cultural dissidence? Is there any substance to the argument that propaganda subverts its own messages through absenting from its images the very events, experiences, and subjectivities it sets out to condemn? Does the nostalgic pleasure of collecting the posters erase their original political sentiments and their potential contribution to a contemporary critique of embedded structures of power? How does the new life of Cultural Revolution posters—now reproduced in huge numbers and sold in Beijing's markets and street stalls—correspond to the recanonization of classic films of the Mao era in the past decade or so? Or, to echo Susan Sontag's argument about fascist art, does their power, and therefore their danger, lie in their combination of ostensibly benign aesthetics, utopian longings, and universal appeal?[2]

In a review of a 1999 volume titled *Political Posters in Central and Eastern Europe*, Gale Stokes suggests that few who experienced life in Central Europe or the Soviet Union during the Communist era would not find themselves "morbidly" nostalgic when faced with the book's images of "the simultaneous enthusiasm and falsity of the promise, the fatuousness of the claims, the wit of the opposition, and the sly presence of western modes of expression."[3] Nostalgia, though not necessarily morbid, certainly characterizes many retrospective responses to China's Cultural Revolution posters. A "totalitarian nostalgia," Geremie Barmé has argued, lies behind much of the post-1980s popular consumer passion for red memorabilia as symbols of the supposed fixities of an ordered past, in contrast to the insecurities of the present.[4] At the same time, the "Mao craze" (*Mao re* 毛热) of the early 1990s spawned a new genre of avant-garde art that famously included Wang Guangyi's appropriation of Cultural Revolution poster images in his *Great Criticism: Coca-Cola* (1993) that satirized politics by parodying its revolutionary icons.[5] Arif Dirlik and Xudong Zhang have argued that the retro chic of the commodification of revolution is part of a postmodern trend to "eliminate [the] teleology" of the party-state's neoliberal ideology.[6] Wang Guangyi's work, in particular, as Xiaobing Tang persuasively argues elsewhere in this volume, recalls the powerful "socialist visual culture" of the Cultural Revolution, in a politics of vision that makes a critical intervention in contemporary ways of seeing and affirms the "inevitability of dissensus." However, as the global "celebritization" of avant-garde artists of the 1990s dulled their critical edge and they were absorbed into the commercial mainstream, and as the government turned to sponsoring red tourism in the early years of the new century, such arguments could tell only part of the story.[7] In a commercial and ideological environment in which postmodern revolutionary images shore up official projects of "patriotic education," the revolutionary theme parks and red restaurants that are now standard features of China's commercial landscape offer forceful evidence of a global capitalist logic wedded to a neutralizing political critique.[8]

Satire and parody, political critique, commercial appropriation, and government sponsorship of so-called red tourism for patriotic education: poster imagery is selectively present in all such contemporary takes on China's revolutionary past. However, these different uses of and responses to poster images are not discrete, and they do not, in my view, adequately explain the fascination the posters hold for collectors, curators, scholars, and "lay" viewers, in China and elsewhere. In China, they are appropriated, displayed, and collected in a political and cultural context that still prohibits public critical reflection on the Cultural Revolution. As reworked in contemporary art and commercial advertising, they reappear in an environment that, on the one hand, condemns the Cultural Revolution as "ten years of chaos" and a "tragedy for the Chinese people" and, on the other, still hails its main instigator—Mao Zedong—as a great revolutionary leader. The posters' appeal is inseparable from the paradoxical manipulations of power—both at the time of their initial production and now, under the market's absorption of them—that establishes the parameters of their display and the visual grammar of their content.

Today, the posters present another paradox, one overlooked by the argument that the nostalgia behind the celebration of Mao-era films in the 1990s served consumerism by blanking out the ruptures of the recent past.[9] Nostalgia, as Nicholas Dames has argued, represents a form of knowledge that can transform catastrophe into longing. First described in Homer's *Odyssey* as a shared "delight in grief," nostalgia is always about loss, but this loss may function not just as a condition to be lamented but as "a medium in its own right" that "can be its own cure."[10] Members of a younger generation, unacquainted with the moment or object of catastrophe and denied access to information about it or memories of it, can experience the sense of loss felt by their parents only at an evident remove. Their parents, in turn, may transfer their sense of loss to their children in the form of diverse demands and expectations, as various scholars have suggested.[11] Loss might not even be an issue for many young people; indeed, for them the posters' powerful appeal, seen in the numbers of young Chinese people who have visited recent displays of Cultural Revolution posters at exhibitions in Australia and the United Kingdom, may reside in their fascination with the "exotic" unknown of their parents' lives.[12] As visual reminders of a past that cannot be explored, Cultural Revolution posters may beckon to young people not for the moral or political position they depict, and much less for their celebration of a body politic mediated by worship of an all-powerful leader, but for their quality in symbolizing hidden stories of their parents' past. They may also beckon through their vibrant depictions of youthful revolt against established structures of power; it is noticeably these images that stand out in the ironic commentaries about much post-Mao popular art. Between nostalgia's erasures of past "authenticities" and the appropriations by the market, the posters may inure people to the truth of the past by closing down the visual avenues of memory and imagination. However, this may also obscure the posters' productive significance for young people as ways into imagining and critiquing their parents' pasts, however implausible that imagination or anodyne that critique might appear to be.

In what follows, I argue that the enduring appeal of Cultural Revolution posters for diverse audiences across place and time lies in their ambiguities in a visual hierarchy that not uncommonly subordinated Mao's figurative and symbolic status to other themes and interests. Indeed, the broad visual repertoire of the posters contains modes of address and appeal only tenuously linked, if at all, to Mao's iconic authority. Barbara Mittler has suggested that ambiguities of reception go some way toward explaining the pleasure that Cultural Revolution objects now produce, both for those who view them with a nostalgia for their youth and for those who are too young to have experienced the movement.[13] Their ambiguities lie not only in their viewers' reception but also in their different registers of address, both then and now. A private collector and curator of Cultural Revolution posters in Shanghai noted that posters of the period are rich aesthetic repositories of the complex desires and pleasures that inspired a generation of young people.[14] Interviews with poster artists and collectors, and documentary films on the Hu County peasant painters (*Hu xian nongmin hua*, 户县农民画) and collecting red art, similarly suggest the interplay of diverse interests and longings in the creation of the posters.[15] For example, they could depict women in domestic settings and in feminized colors and forms that addressed experiences and desires that could not be publicly articulated.[16] Notwithstanding their overt messages, designed and fine-tuned by the party authorities, many poster images, including well-known if not iconic ones, were visualizations of ideas—"dreams, emotions, desires, and life experiences," as one of the Hu County painters in Ai Xiaoming and Hu

Jie's documentary film *Painting for the Revolution* put it—that transcended the explicit message.[17] Moreover, the aesthetic and stylistic diversity of China's propaganda posters (*xuanchuan hua* 宣传画) defies their characterization as a single genre. Effective posters set up not a single linear relationship with their audience, as the notion of the "propaganda" poster is widely understood to indicate, but a more negotiated—if far from open-ended—relationship that invited diverse, inconsistent, and unauthorized readings, corresponding with aspirations and desires that did not fit into the official temporality of revolution.[18] Political constraints prevented articulation of these aspirations at the time, but this chapter attempts to excavate them through interviews with poster artists. Their reflections on their work and their focus on images of youth help explain the posters' ambiguous appeal to their audiences.

Any analysis of Cultural Revolution posters has to take into account crucial differences of generation, political ideology, and experience among their intended audiences. Now, nearly half a century after their production and translated into the political, economic, and cultural space of global capitalism, their commercial and aesthetic appeal corresponds with ideological and cultural impulses that differ from those of their initial production. The individual who comes across their images as an outside observer or foreign collector, or the young Chinese designer who appropriates their images for contemporary purposes, does not draw on the lived experience of the violence and political persecution of their moment of production. For them, the pleasure of their response is facilitated by their detachment from the events to which the posters allude. The same may be said of recent commentaries celebrating Mao Zedong as, for example, a "great leader who will live in our hearts forever."[19] The playful and commercial uses to which the propaganda posters are often put in advertising and design are highly selective; their focus on youthful dynamism excludes references to hard manual labor or the trials of sickness and old age, even though these not infrequently appeared in the originals. The pleasure they invoke does not "redeem" them as innocent of political meaning; for many, the pleasure in collecting, displaying, painting, and writing about these posters is not inconsistent with the painful memories of the past. The posters neither simply validate an inauthentic memory of the past nor simply reaffirm nostalgia's function as a cure for unspeakable loss. Across their differences in style, composition, and theme and the relationships they set up with their audiences across space and time, they evince different and disquieting responses, including memories of pain *and* pleasure, associated simultaneously with the events of the time, aspirations and desires that were silenced by Cultural Revolution politics, and a critique of the present.

Western and Chinese interest in posters since the formal end of the Cultural Revolution has led to their widespread commercial reproduction and a number of exhibitions and auctions, in Hong Kong, the United States, and Europe.[20] A few relevant articles have recently been published, most notably by Chinese scholars, some of which go beyond the standard "propaganda" framework and interpretations of their style as a reflection of the political and social campaigns of the time.[21] In contrast to the attention given to the commodification of Mao's iconic image and, more recently, red tourism, this interest has not been matched by much critical analysis of how posters "worked" on their publics as visual tools designed to inspire certain behaviors and to appeal to different interests and desires.[22] The following, then, is an attempt to open up discussion about the different registers of address and the appeal of poster imagery from the Cultural Revolution as a specific instance of the complexity of China's red legacy.

The Changing Power of Posters

Posters were, at least in quantitative terms, the most important visual means through which the Cultural Revolution was created and played out. Their massive print runs ensured that they were seen in every work unit and production brigade, school classroom and home. On the posters hanging in schools, shops, and homes, work-unit dormitories, factory workshops, and government offices, Mao's iconic authority was a dominant—though far from exclusive—theme; he bathed his followers in rays of light and in the reds and yellows of the Eastern sun, inspired them with the slogans of the "Little Red Book," and led them, under seas of red banners, to undertake miraculous feats of socialist farming, industrial production, and military training.

The process of "de-Maoification" that began with economic reform after 1978 did not lead to the total disappearance of Mao imagery from spaces of display. While monumental statues of Mao were brought crashing to the ground and big red wall slogans were whitewashed over, posters of the previous decade still adorned many small offices and homes, though often more as wallpaper or decorations than as icons. Mao's historical contribution as a revolutionary leader was revised in the 1981 document "Resolution on Certain Questions in the History of Our Party," which condemned his role in inspiring the events that led to the Great Leap Famine of 1959–61 and the Cultural Revolution. However, Mao was not officially repudiated, as Stalin was by Soviet premier Nikita Khrushchev in his famous "secret" speech to the Twentieth Party Congress in 1956, and Mao's role as national savior has been upheld in official documents, celebrations, and media extravaganzas as well as in the popular imagination. Since the 1980s, the popular awe his figure and name inspires has been evident in the talismanic use of his image—hung, for example, from the rearview mirrors of taxis and buses to protect their drivers from harm—just as wearing the Mao badge during the Cultural Revolution was considered to offer a form of protection against the multiple "ill winds" of that time.[23] By the mid-1990s, the combination of the rapid marketization of the economy and the wave of nostalgic longing, or "Mao fever," converged in a new commodification of red culture in street stalls, restaurants, and bars throughout China's large cities. Cultural Revolution images now appeared on T-shirts, cigarette lighters, playing cards, placemats, and more, alongside new editions of Mao's collected writings and hagiographic films and celebratory displays of his life. In recent years, red tourism has mushroomed at major revolutionary sites, as the government has attempted to cash in on the popular reverence for Mao to promote patriotic education.[24] The discursive and commercial prevalence of Mao's iconic image boosts his status for the large numbers of the disadvantaged who associate him with a spiritual hope denied them by market competition.[25]

Alongside Mao's image, propaganda posters continue to be familiar components of the everyday visual landscape, despite the enormous transformations that landscape has undergone in the past few decades. Indeed, their presence for sale in street stalls and their continued display on the walls of ordinary homes are, it might be conjectured, obliquely sustained by their association with Mao's authority. The long-term public presence of the posters' images in China, now reworked for new purposes, is echoed by their iconic status worldwide. Well before the end of the Cultural Revolution, posters were collected by Western visitors for what John Gittings has described as their "emphatic and exuberant" depictions of the political campaigns of the time.[26] They were also widely exported by the government to Europe, Latin America, and Africa. Their "red, bright, and shiny" (*hong, guang, liang* 红光亮) images are embedded in the contemporary visual habitus framing Chinese and foreign imaginaries of the Cultural Revolution, including those of people who have no direct experience of the events of those years. Indeed, Western fads for Cultural Revolution memorabilia help sustain their commercial presence on the Chinese market.[27] Across time and place, the creators and consumers of such imagery combine a mesh of different interests, blurring the boundaries between the revulsion, nostalgic longing, political critique, and youthful exhilaration it inspires in viewers.

The appeal to youth was arguably just as prominent a theme in poster imagery of the Cultural Revolution as was the adulation of Mao. The Red Guard posters of the first years of the Cultural Revolution, with their striking reds and blacks, explicitly encouraged youthful challenges to authority. Various accounts shed light on the different motivations behind young Red Guards' enthusiasm for going "up to the mountains and down to the countryside" (*shangshan xiaxiang* 上山下乡), as the slogan of the time put it. Alongside the excitement of rebelling against established power were desires to get away from parents, to take advantage of free train travel to traverse the country during the "Great Linkup" (*da chuanlian* 大串联) of the late 1960s, and to experience something different from urban life. The visual prominence of youth in the posters of the time thus appealed to interests and desires that corresponded with the official ideology as well as with the individual motivations produced by family and personal circumstances. As the Shanghai poster collector and curator Yang Peiming put it, posters of the time were a visual expression of the complex emotions of a generation of young people.[28] Their ambiguities of address spoke of experiences and aspirations encapsulated but not entirely explained by the canonical interpretation of young people's enthusiasm for spreading the word of revolution.

Artistic Ambiguities

Pan Jiajun's *Wo shi haiyan* 我是海燕 (I am a petrel) was one of the most popular and influential paintings of the Cultural Revolution (plate 2). Created in 1972, it earned the artist numerous awards and much publicity in the national press, and it was widely disseminated as a poster. It features a young woman soldier braving a storm to repair telegraph cables and was hailed as a "classic" (*dianxing* 典型) depiction of a revolutionary heroine who represented the aspirations and longings of a generation. "I want to be a soldier like her," an engineering technician who worked in the correspondence department of the People's Liberation Army's central command is reported to have said.[29] The painting inspired a series of similar paintings by other artists, including *Kuangshan xin bing* 矿山新兵 (New recruit at the mine) by Yang Zhiguang 杨之光, *Nü weiyuan* 女委员 (Woman committee member) by Tang Xiaoming 汤小铭, and *Yugang xinyi* 渔港新医 (New doctor at the fishing port) by Chen Yanning 陈衍宁 (plate 3), all of which were reproduced and circulated as posters.

The heroic idealism of their images resonated with passionate young students brought up to believe in the dignity of revolutionary self-sacrifice. Li Gongming 李公明, dean of fine arts at Guangzhou's Academy of Arts, has further suggested that the appeal of *Petrel* also lay in its implicitly erotic qualities. The young woman's round face was utterly unlike the fine features of popular film stars of the time, he writes, but the positioning and shape of her body, drenched by the pouring rain, were enough to elicit an avalanche of letters addressed to the painter from admiring young men.[30] Beckoning to different aspirations and desires, her figure offered several possible interpretations.

The following discussion draws on recorded interviews conducted in the summer of 2008 with Guangzhou-based artists who started their careers as poster artists in the 1960s.[31] My initial aim in talking with them was to discuss the interests and aspirations that motivated poster artists working for local government and party propaganda organs, and through this to think about the poster as an aesthetic frame for diverse narratives of the Cultural Revolution. The artists' comments revealed many insights, including some that explained the spaces of interpretation set up between artist and viewer that Pan Jiajun's *Petrel* exemplifies. They spoke in animated tones and seemed to welcome the opportunity to recollect personal experiences of artistic projects undertaken at a time that is still closed to serious public debate. I will describe parts of my conversations with three of those whom I met.

Wu Haiying 吴海鹰 became a well-known artist on the Canton art scene in the 1990s, and her works were frequently on exhibit in the city's main art galleries. When she graduated from Canton's Academy of Fine

Arts in 1965, she was appointed, together with one of her peers, to work with the Guangdong Art Corporation Studio under the Guangzhou Cultural Bureau. Throughout the Cultural Revolution, the studio was responsible for the design and production of film and opera advertisements as well as posters and artworks. During her time there, Wu painted a number of works that became famous posters, including *The Red Lantern* (*Hongdeng ji* 红灯记), and portraits of Gorky and Madame Curie. The themes she painted were assigned by the Municipal Committee, and her posters were often displayed in major venues such as Canton's Haizhu Square and the Memorial Museum to the Martyrs, but, as Wu explained, "the specific issues of how to create the image and what aesthetic means and expressions to combine this with were up to us. For example, the theme could be singing the praises of Daqing 大庆, or learning from Dazhai 大寨, but how to organize the topic into a painting was up to us." She and her fellow artists had to follow the established stylistic devices of *hong, guang, liang* (red, bright, and light) and *gao, da, quan* 高大全 (tall, large, and full), yet, she asserted, "each [painting] had an individual style" (*dou shi ge ren de fengge* 都是个人的风格) and displayed the individual painter's ideas about aesthetic beauty.

From time to time, aesthetic choices could cause not inconsiderable problems. Canton was home to China's trade exhibitions throughout the Cultural Revolution years, and many of the posters Wu and her contemporaries were involved in producing were specifically commissioned for the trade fairs. They were often enormous in size and were displayed in some of Canton's most prominent public sites. As the official body responsible for presenting China's cultural face to the Western world, the Art Corporation's work was closely vetted for possible ideological idiosyncrasies. Paintings were carefully examined by the leaders of the propaganda departments of the Municipal Committee and the Cultural Bureau to assess the clarity of the main theme and the editorial and aesthetic standards of artistic expression or design. They might be criticized for being too bright, or not bright enough, or for not giving enough prominence to the main theme. According to Wu's account, she and her peers were generally quiescent in the face of such comments, but on one occasion not long after the curtain had closed on the Cultural Revolution, she had an argument with one of her "leaders." Her boss, in her terms "an old cadre with a soldier background, a nice guy but not well-educated," criticized her for a painting she had done for the eastern side of Haizhu Square during the trade fair of 1979. The theme she used was based on a quotation from Marx that she reworked into the slogan "The road to science is not flat, climb the mountain of technology for the country." She decided to include Marx's portrait in the center background, but the director of the Propaganda Department insisted that she replace it with an image of Chairman Mao. Why, she wondered, since, as she put it, "Mao never said much about technology, and his head would change the entire effect of the poster?" The director was "not happy" and hung up the phone on her, but she stuck to her guns, earning the reputation in the Cultural Bureau of belonging to an "abnormal K blood group." Wu explained her refusal to cooperate with her "leader": she did not want to offend him, but as a professional artist she felt she should be the one to decide. Her refusal to cooperate, coinciding with the early relaxation of the constraints on individual creativity of the Cultural Revolution years, allowed Wu to protect her choice on the grounds of her professional leverage over her "uneducated" boss.

Zhang Shaocheng 张绍城 was one of Wu's contemporaries, known during the Cultural Revolution years as one of Guangzhou's "heavenly kings" (*tianwang* 天王) of poster art. Now a well-known artist in the region, he has been a key figure in Canton's art world since the 1960s, when his posters, drawings, and designs were regularly publicized in the local and national press. He paid also involved in painting the enormous posters and murals that welcomed the "outside world" to Canton during the trade exhibitions. He gave particular attention to what he considered the aesthetic requirements of physical beauty in his work. "Long necks were a must," he said; "a person with a high nose, flat lips, long chin—that was beautiful." He was also very clear about the qualities posters needed to appeal to their public: an element of surprise, good use of aesthetic proportions and composition, and an appeal to the main trends of the time. To illustrate his ideas, during our interview he opened a published collection of his earlier works to show me his *New Saplings of the Vast Universe* (*Guangkuo tiandi xin miaozhuang*, 广阔天地新苗壮), a poster painted in 1973 to widespread acclaim, which continues to feature in contemporary references to representative works of the period (plate 4).[32] The painting features three educated youths sent down to the countryside: in the foreground is a smiling young woman looking ahead and beyond the frame to the left. Behind her stand two young men in a similar pose, but the main focus is on the woman. "Why did everyone think this poster of mine was good? Because there were no beauties at the time. You certainly won't think it's good-looking now. We now have lots of advertisements, but then there were no beauties." When I asked him if he had deliberately painted a beautiful woman to appeal to his audience, he responded, "Look, the painting has no political content, there are no poor and lower-middle peasants, no soldiers. . . . It [exemplifies] Zhou Enlai's instructions. He said, 'Not only do we need revolutionary passion, we also need revolutionary emotion.'" Zhang suggested that his use of lyrical greens and blues rather than the usual bright reds of the time were significant in explaining the appeal of *New Saplings.* Without the oppressive strong lines and bright colors of the standard posters of the time, his audience could read into the image fantasies and longings that were not explicit in the poster's theme, but which Zhang clearly intended to feed.

Zhang's companion at lunch when we initially met in Canton in July 2008 was Chen Bingchong 陈炳冲, head of the art department at one of Canton's largest secondary schools. He spoke little at the lunch, except to respectfully agree with Zhang's comments. As we left the restaurant after lunch, he invited me to his school to see his collection of Cultural Revolution art. Zhang had already mentioned that Chen had collected many of the draft drawings for his Cultural Revolution posters, but I did not anticipate the vast number of impeccably ordered cuttings, drawings, sketches, and photographs that Chen had kept since the Cultural Revolution. The son of a poor working-class family, Chen's parents could not afford to send him to art school, so as a young boy keen on art in the 1960s, he used to hang around Zhang's studios, where Zhang often gave him odd jobs and helped him with his art.

Chen's Cultural Revolution materials were in dark blue file boxes of different sizes, stored in an enormous dresser at the back of a room. From one of them he took out two small scrapbooks he had made out of newspaper, both full of drawings he had done when he was fourteen or fifteen. The drawings were sketches of people, individually and in groups, that he had copied from posters. The pages of the scrapbooks were worn and thin; they had seen considerable use. His ink line drawings were of familiar Cultural Revolution faces, fists, raised arms, and sturdy figures, resembling those of the teaching manuals of the time. He had a small collection of Zhang Shaocheng's draft drawings, bound together in another homemade scrapbook, and two books of cuttings from local Red Guard publications and newspapers, many of which featured examples of work by the painters Chen really admired—including Zhang Shaocheng. He also showed us some of his own artwork, including a painting that he had painted for the Red Guard organization to which he had belonged. It had been used on flyers he and his peers distributed in the streets. The pinnacle of his career as a public artist came in 1979 when he was responsible for designing the enormous backdrop for the opening ceremony of a national sports meeting in Canton. His zeal, however, was not first of all for the ideological or political message that any of these images contained, but for how they had helped him develop his technical and creative skills as an artist. He recalled how, during one long day in May 1973, he had copied out by hand an entire book, translated from its original English into Chinese, on the physical and muscular structure of the body. He had been unable to realize his ambition to become an artist like his mentor but had encapsulated the aspirations and dreams of his youth in his small scrapbooks.

Interviews with peasant artists of Hu County similarly revealed a range of motivations and aspirations that had inspired local farmers to sign up to become artists. The field-site training programs, set up by the Xi'an Academy of Fine Arts during the Cultural Revolution, offered farmers-turned-painters the chance to earn work points and to have time off from farming, and they also bestowed upon participants the cultural and political honor of being selected to "meet Chairman Mao" in Beijing. But the scenes of idyllic prosperity in the Hu County paintings were explained in different terms by the artists themselves. "Peasants did not care much about politics," one of the artists interviewed in Ai Xiaoming and Hu Jie's documentary film *Painting for the Revolution* commented. In a place that had suffered during the famine, he said, "we were painting our dreams, our emotions, and our inner desires."[33] Fan Zhihua 樊志华, one of Hu County's better-known artists, referred to the famous *Earth Ramming* painting as an example of this.

As these few examples indicate, the desires, pleasures, and frustrations that poster painters could inscribe in their work at the time included erotic enjoyment, the exercise of personal choice and skill, adolescent dreams of becoming an artist, and longings for prosperity. They demonstrate that diverse interests were at work in the aesthetic choices and compositions the artists made, despite the editorial strictures of the time. These interests resonated with Chen Bingchong, for example, because he recognized in them what he called a "representative" quality onto which he could transfer his artistic aspirations. His and his mentor's sketches belong to a specific historical moment when, between training and ideological space, there were clear constraints on what they could paint. However, neither he nor Zhang ascribed the pejorative notion of "propaganda" to their work, despite its widespread use for mass political education. Though clearly aware of and indeed instrumental in the political uses to which their paintings had been put, the Hu County artists interviewed by Ai Xiaoming and Hu Jie for their documentary painted their longing for a better life into their work. The potentially fluid relationship between poster art and viewer that such motivations suggest may in part be explained by the selective character of memories dating back half a century or so. Nevertheless, their accounts contrast with the generic reduction of Cultural Revolution posters to the status of propaganda deceptions of a totalitarian order.[34]

Another Look at the "Iron Girl"

Among the numerous erasures in memories of China's Cultural Revolution are those associated with the image of the "new socialist woman." In the form of the iconic "iron girl," women of the 1960s and 1970s are widely represented in academic commentary on the art and literature of the time as masculinized or gender-neutral figures, competing with men for equal status in spaces and activities associated with male authority.[35] The iron girl was the emblem of a system of political control that denied women their "natural" femininity, as media commentators and academics have repeatedly pointed out since the early 1980s. However, recent scholarship on women in the Mao era has begun to explore alternative readings of the iron girl through the memories of women of the time. An analysis of the All China Women's Federation journal *Women of China* (Zhongguo funü 中国妇女) that includes interviews with representatives of the Federation has revealed that women's engagement with the state's policies of gender equality suggests their considerable identification with the new opportunities offered to them.[36] Autobiographical accounts give evidence of how women's often enthusiastic participation in the political campaigns of the time cannot be read as docile responses to political commands.[37] At first glance, and across differences of style and composition, images of women in the posters of the Cultural Revolution appear to correspond with all the dominant features of the stereotypical iron maiden.[38] Women appear doing things conventionally associated with masculine occupations and activities, in line with the ideological commitment to enabling women to engage in social labor as the condition of their liberation. Their demeanor and activities testify to their new status as equals to men; they are militia trainees, inspired Red Guards, barefoot doctors, and rural cadres. They are young, healthy, and strong, with sturdy features, robust faces, and eyes shining with revolutionary zeal. Dressed in more or less the same clothing designs and colors as men, their images denote commitment, hard work, physical strength, and youthful determination to fight for the collective cause. Though often more colorful than the photographic images featured on the cover of *Women of China* in the preceding decade, the posters give evidence of the same message celebrating women's newly empowered and independent status in domains hitherto dominated by men. The form of the female subject in these posters positions women at the vanguard of China's progress toward a socialist modernity in which women are men's equals in creating history.

At the same time, in contrast to the cover images of *Women of China*, posters of the early 1970s frequently positioned women in domestic contexts that tempered the rhetoric of "male-female equality"; depictions of women at home, as "tea ladies," or as grannies looking after small children, made frequent appearances.[39] In *New Family* (1973) a young mother crosses the threshold of her rural home, accompanied by an elder woman, probably her mother-in-law, and a younger woman, possibly her sister-in-law. The latter is being pulled into the space of the home by one of two small children. In the background, a smiling farmer, the husband of the central woman, looks on as his womenfolk take up their role as principal actors in the domestic domain. *Awake Late into the Night* (1975) features a young mother sitting at a small table writing notes as her young child sleeps at her side (plate 5). On the wall behind her is a poster displaying the image of the lead character of *Azalea Mountain,* one of the "model" operas, in symbolic confirmation of the young mother's determination to burn the midnight oil to complete her studies. One of the different interpretations these posters invite is that women are the guardians of the home and children, authoritative in spaces that do not threaten the male prerogative in the public world.

For some women, at least, such images were seen as an unwelcome reminder of women's subordinate status.[40]

Other visual cues—patterned blouses and tight belts, pink and red hair ribbons—could remind viewers of desires that could not be easily articulated in the constrained language of Cultural Revolution discourse. In an interview in the summer of 2008, Li Gongming explained the appeal of posters of the time with reference to their promise of the "beautiful world" (*meihao shijie* 美好世界) of the future and to the imaginative space for erotic fantasy they offered young people in an ideological and moral environment that condemned such interest as bourgeois degeneration. Zhang Shaocheng's attention to feminine appeal in his *New Saplings* resonated with the desires of many viewers, and, though anecdotal, many conversations I have had with men and women who grew up under Mao's banner attest to the erotic allure of images of women such as Wu Qinghua, the revolutionary heroine of the model ballet, *Red Detachment of Women* (plate 6).[41] Barbara Mittler similarly refers to her interviewees' comments about the sexiness of the Red Detachment's beautiful women dressed in tight, and very short, shorts.[42] Such appeal may have addressed men and women in different ways; the erotic allure of women in the images of Wu Qinghua may have empowered women's desire for beauty at the same time that it may have "objectified" the female body for the male gaze. Poster images of women during the Cultural Revolution thus addressed their audiences through ambiguous possibilities of meaning that departed from, but could be contained by, their overt ideological message. So long as they respected their given ideological guidelines, poster artists, Wu Haiying and Zhang Shaocheng included, could paint intentions into their work that resonated with the desires and fantasies of their publics. The apparent inconsistencies in their appeal converged in images that could accommodate the posters' overt message while simultaneously channeling other desires.

Iconic Consumer Pleasures

The reproduction of China's revolutionary icons since the late 1980s has taken many forms, in restaurant settings, avant-garde art, talismanic memorabilia, and commercial advertising as well as poster copies, as I have noted and others have written about at length. With the late 1980s explosion of the "Mao craze," Mao's image was appropriated for more critical ends by avant-garde artists. The critic Li Xianting was the first to provide a framework for new uses of the iconic symbols of the socialist past in coining the term "Political Pop" in 1991, in an essay titled "Apathy and Deconstructive Consciousness in Post-1989 Art." Li argues that Political Pop started out from acknowledgment of an everyday existence that under Mao was "saturated with politics [as] the accustomed state of being" to "satirize politics, providing an effective (but by no means heroic) means of neutralizing the hold of a politically saturated mentality on the inner mind." For him, the consumerist impulses of the Mao craze and Political Pop art were "linked in that there is inherent in both the use of past icons or 'gods' to criticize, or in the case of the latter, to satirize, current reality."[43]

While the Mao craze, much avant-garde art, and Political Pop were initially inspired by social, political, and cultural impulses outside and, in some cases, hostile to party ideological controls, the popular interests with which they corresponded were increasingly used by the government to promote patriotism.[44] Epic films on Mao's life were released around the centenary anniversary of Mao's birth in 1993, and Central Television screened a gala performance on December 26 from Shaoshan, Mao's birthplace. A wave of government-sponsored attempts to boost red tourism followed, with the official designation of a network of red sites, including red-tourism "bases," "cities," and "classic sites" targeted to attract 30 million tourists by the end of an initial five-year period (2005–10).[45] Red tourism emerged as an economic strategy, an offshoot of the state's promotion of domestic tourism as a key growth area in the national economy. But, as Kirk Denton argues, red tourism is also a pedagogical strategy, a state response to the recognition that museums, in and of themselves, are inadequate as a medium for patriotic education.[46] Jie Li and Enhua Zhang have shown, in a fascinating documentary film, *Shaoshan Pilgrims*, that Mao's iconic image continues to exercise extraordinary authority, even if many of the "pilgrims" to Shaoshan are marshaled by work units and packaged tourism.[47] A focused ethnographic analysis of the forces at work in encouraging tourists to Shaoshan to bow in synchronized obeisance to Mao's image would reveal singular interests at work; the different uses his image serves makes it a visual site of multiple hopes, dreams, beliefs, critiques, and aspirations.

While official interests inscribe the physical landscape with a linear narrative of revolution and national development, as Denton points out, the popular interests of red pilgrims doubtless correspond with diverse temporalities. The iconic images of revolution, including those in posters re-reproduced between the Mao craze and red tourism, are not susceptible to a single or unitary interpretation.

One morning in October 1999 as I was pulling my suitcase through Heathrow Airport's Terminal 3—ironically, on my way to a symposium on Cultural Revolution posters at Indiana University to celebrate the fiftieth anniversary of the founding of the People's Republic—I was startled to find myself facing an enormous advertisement for *Forbes International* magazine. The image was a rough version of one of the most common "crowd" scenes in Cultural Revolution art, featuring workers, peasants, and soldiers marching in unison toward the viewer, all waving Little Red Books.[48] The caption above read "Capitalists of the world unite," replacing the famous slogan from the *Communist Manifesto* that appeared on Chinese posters of the early 1970s. Following the height of the Mao craze and the global dissemination of Mao-era poster images in the work of avant-garde artists, the Western public was already used to the postsocialist reassembly of such images. However, in contrast to most I had seen, the *Forbes* advertisement appropriated almost wholesale the entire structure and composition of a Cultural Revolution poster. By the winter of the same year, I had come across more commercialized evocations of such imagery in London's fashionable interior design shop Conran, which had published a glossy catalogue advertising a forthcoming collection of reproductions of Cultural Revolution porcelain figurines. Stalls in the Camden Lock market in North London were selling khaki bags and caps adorned with red stars, large hot-water thermoses like those that were a household staple during the Mao years, and enamel mugs with revolutionary slogans, as well as Cultural Revolution poster reproductions.[49]

Much of the commerce in revolutionary items that flourished on the streets of Beijing at the same time, and that in part catered to Western tourists' interests, similarly focused on the youthful exuberance of poster imagery. Postcards advertising new music venues and nightclubs were distributed free of charge in areas catering to the young *nouveaux riches*, such as Nanluoguxiang and Sanlitun. Street stalls in more popular commercial districts, such as Dashilanr, sold packs of cards printed with poster images, reproductions of the Hu County works and other posters, along with cigarette lighters that opened to the tune of *The East Is Red*. By the early 2000s, Cultural Revolution theme restaurants had taken off in a number of cities, some with considerable commercial success. The Red Classics Restaurant (Hongse jingdian 红色经典) in the suburbs of Beijing was one such business to which customers reportedly flocked. One visitor reporting on his experience at the restaurant in 2004 noted how revolutionary slogans and posters adorned the walls, and facsimiles of *People's Daily* headlines covered the ceiling.[50] For customers who paid several hundred yuan per person, waiters dressed in Cultural Revolution garb danced and sang to Cultural Revolution tunes on a small stage, the backdrop for which was a giant reproduction of a famous Cultural Revolution poster. Audience participation was encouraged and to urge them along, each diner was given a little triangular red flag to wave along to the rousing tones of the loud revolutionary songs praising the chairman, denouncing landlords, and celebrating the power of youth to forge a bright new future. There seemed to be a "palpable atmosphere of glee—a frisson of excitement (even hilarity) at participating in something still officially regarded as somewhat taboo and excessive. Older audience members, in particular, stood up to sing (and dance), reliving memories of their youth, while their younger compatriots clapped along, exchanging knowing smiles and laughter."[51]

Discussion about the impulses that sustain the appeal of Mao's iconic image among contemporary consumers is, of course, distinct from discussion about the appeal of the broader repertoire of Cultural Revolution poster imagery. The two are linked through the legitimating authority Mao's image and the market give to the current consumerist play with Cultural Revolution poster imagery, as I have noted. However, in contrast to the central theme of the commodification of Mao during the Mao craze and more recently in the commercially filtered narratives of revolution targeted at red tourists, contemporary uses of poster imagery appropriate and rework their original themes in modes of address and appeal that are little concerned with the nostalgic "sanctity" of Mao's iconic portrait. Parodic, satirical, nostalgic, and politically anodyne though much of this commodification may be, it also operates through setting up relationships of mutual recognition, even of identification, as well as antipathy and critique, between image and audience. These are necessarily fluid, since they appeal to memories—also nostalgic—and experiences of youth across different generations. So a party secretary of Shangri-La Prefecture in Yunnan Province may delight in singing revolutionary songs in a karaoke bar and marching in front of videos of the youthful film celebrities of the Cultural Revolution.[52] A different generation takes delight in blogs spoofing poster images of the same stars with slogans corresponding to the gender politics of contemporary China. The young triumvirate of the worker, peasant, and soldier announce, "You'll come a cropper if you don't listen to what your wife says." The Eighth Route Army soldier brandishes a gun as he indignantly demands, "Well, do you love me or not?"[53] The celebration of a consumerist present and future, apparent in many contemporary renderings of revolutionary posters, may be inseparable from the logic of capitalism, but the appeal of such renderings is not transparently explained by it.

Between nostalgia for a lost past and claims that such commodification shores up an official ideology of patriotism, such "macro" arguments seem inadequate to explain the appeal of contemporary evocations of revolutionary imagery. Produced by and for consumers in China and the West whose experience of the Cultural Revolution rests in large part on their familiarity with its contemporary images, the appeal of these images corresponds with other factors deriving from their capacity to speak to complex and seemingly paradoxical emotional and political yearnings.

Cultural Revolution posters contain countless images that can be reproduced for the contemporary market: grannies teaching children to sew, peasant elders teaching youths about China's traditional medical arts, festive scenes of family reunions at the Spring Festival, village audiences enraptured by the performances of traveling cultural troupes, sports competitions, militia training, the export of tractors to African countries, and many more. Many such poster themes make little explicit reference to Mao, even if he is invariably present in symbolic form.[54] Few, however, fail to picture young people, whether rebelling against authority, scaling telegraph poles, buying goods in a village shop, or attempting to block the powerful flow of a riverine flood. These themes are all visually framed to reflect the ideals of the time: bravery, commitment to learning, frugality, collective spirit, and revolt against the established structures of authority. Intersecting these themes are other, less prominent ones, apparent in the curves and colors of the female body, the figures' pensive or angry expressions, the muscles of the male torso, the delight portrayed in shared experiences of freedom, and the hardships depicted for manual labor.

Mao's iconic presence aside, current reproductions of Cultural Revolution posters indicate an even more selective focus on youth. The reworked lines of Red Guards in the nightclubs' publicity cards, for example, may be a vulgar derivative of Wang Guangyi's *Coca-Cola,* but the image shares with its 1968 original a similar delight in youthful authority. Similarly, the *Forbes* ad celebrates the collective power of youth to forge a new world. The future that today's young generation in China looks toward is associated with opportunities and obstacles that their rebellious predecessors could not have imagined; today's young generation enjoys an economic and cultural independence from their parents that is, arguably, unprecedented in China. Creative play with revolutionary images calls to mind the assertive rebelliousness of youth. It may, as Xiaobing Tang argues in the next chapter, draw on a shared visual culture of past revolution to channel a political critique of the present.[55] One might also conjecture that young people's sense of indebtedness to their elders, widely evidenced in the anthropological literature on the changing forms of filiality in China, is also present in such images. Thus the image of the young revolutionary in the Red Classics restaurant, for example, may draw customers in by holding out a range of meanings that assert a continuity with the parental past, both for those who grew up in it and for those born since, at the same time that it celebrates youthful claims to a new world. The visual appeal of the commercially filtered revolutionary image works not through a single narrative but offers its viewers a multiple temporality in which nostalgia for a lost past is the flip side of competitive success in forging the future. From this perspective, the relationships that contemporary evocations of revolutionary images set up with their viewers simultaneously address ambiguous memories and longings, fears, pleasures, and excitements that denote different aspects of the past, present, and future.

However, the structures of political power in China, during the Mao era and since, bring us back to the difficult and unsettling question of the politics addressed by these ambiguities. The political and ideological interests framing the collective nostalgia the posters evoke are served by political and social critique, but also by nostalgia's silent acknowledgment of past suffering and loss. Furthermore, echoing Susan Sontag's argument, the longings they evoke continue to make them effective because many are still attached to the romantic ideals of youth, expressed by successive post-Mao generations in "diverse modes of cultural dissidence and celebrations of new forms of community" that do not "preclude the search for absolute leadership."[56] As we are constantly reminded by cultural critics and ordinary urban citizens alike, the spiritual emptiness of contemporary life feeds into a redemptive desire for new forms of worship in China, whether it takes the shape of the Falungong, the Christian revival, or the adulation of Mao. The youthful dynamism of Cultural Revolution posters addresses diverse audiences that invest different interests in those images. But in a political environment that limits the possibilities of critical political debate, the charms of such images cannot be separated from the structures of power that benefit from them.

Conclusion

Writing about China's posters now, in an ideological and cultural context far removed from the Cultural Revolution, is complicated by the multiple erasures of mainstream narratives of the "ten years of chaos." These erasures are sustained by complex interests and are by no means the simple effect of official constraints on public discussion about the Cultural Revolution. Indeed, it can be argued that the reappearance of revolutionary posters in the contemporary cultural and political landscape contributes to the general amnesia about the period's darker aspects.[57] As Jie Li discusses later in this volume, calls by Ba Jin and others to construct a Cultural Revolution museum were, and continue to be, precisely directed toward retrieving memories of the past in order to prevent a repetition of history.[58] Following Sontag's thesis, the charms of these posters may also mask their danger by appealing to new forms of community that, however parodic or "dissident" they might seem, are not inconsistent with longings for national power under strong leadership.

At the same time, the homogenizing pejorative of "propaganda" has played its own part in obscuring diverse memories and experiences of the period, including the pleasures derived from producing and collecting. That the posters at the time of the Cultural Revolution could become the means through which individuals exercised choice—limited though it was—suggest some small ways in which the Cultural Revolution was not the cultural desert of mainstream accounts. Paul Clark has detailed the themes, technical devices, and productions that in his view resulted in much greater innovation, experimentation, and diversity during the period than is generally acknowledged.[59] Within the ideological and aesthetic constraints of the time, artists could exercise a certain degree of choice and agency in what they painted; their paintings could become the receptacle for desires and aspirations that, though muted so as not to cross ideological boundaries, could in some cases resonate with their audiences' desires along lines that had little to do with their explicit message. As we have seen, the colors and composition in a poster such as *New Saplings* indicate how concessions can be made to the dominant discourse at the same time that the exclusion of some of its key symbols—the color red, the sun, the inspirational word—could address other interests. "Effective" posters established an ambiguous space of interpretation between poster and viewer that contemporary designers, artists, and collectors recognize in their own aesthetic choices.

Some might read a dangerous fascination into the introduction of pleasure in an analysis of images that shored up an oppressive regime. My point is not that posters of this period were or are unalloyed objects of pleasure, or even principally objects of pleasure. Pleasure—including the pleasure of nostalgia—cannot be construed as an emotion removed from sensations of pain and melancholy, or from a desire for rebellion. The paradox is that in a political environment that constrains critical inquiry into the Cultural Revolution, an analysis of the way propaganda posters addressed their audiences contributes to the historical project of excavating memories of the Cultural Revolution and political critiques that mainstream narratives obscure, and at the same time it reveals memories and imaginaries of the recent past that cancel out its ruptures. To acknowledge the tensions within the posters' ambiguities of address and appeal is to acknowledge this paradox—and to acknowledge the unsettling complexities of China's red legacies.

Notes

1. The transnational circulation of the posters of the period is a fascinating topic in its own right, and one that has not to date received the scholarly attention it deserves. One possible line of inquiry about their international influence at the time was indicated by the writer and politician Miklós Haraszti at the opening in

Budapest of *East Is Red*, an exhibition of Chinese posters and memorabilia sponsored by the Open Society Archives and the University of Westminster, in February 2000. Haraszti spoke about how the exhibits reminded him of the hopes he had invested in China's revolution after the Soviet suppression of the Hungarian uprising in 1956. Another line of inquiry emerges from a comment made by a former Ugandan student of mine, whose interest in the University of Westminster's Chinese poster collection was motivated by his own memory of the Chinese posters that were displayed on the walls of his high school classroom in a small town outside Kampala.

2. Susan Sontag, "Fascinating Fascism," *New York Review of Books*, February 6, 1975, reprinted in Sontag, *Under the Sign of Saturn* (New York: Farrar, Straus & Giroux, 1980), pp. 73–105.

3. Gale Stokes, review of *Political Posters in Central and Eastern Europe, 1945–95: Signs of the Times by James Aulich and Marta Sylvestrová, Slavic Review* 60, no. 2 (Summer 2001): 400–401.

4. Geremie Barmé, *In the Red: On Contemporary Chinese Culture* (New York: Columbia University Press, 1999), pp. 316–19.

5. For relevant discussion about other artists in the early 1990s, see Francesca Dal Lago, "Personal Mao: Reshaping an Icon in Contemporary Chinese Art," *Art Journal* 58, no. 2 (Summer 1999): 46–59.

6. Arif Dirlik and Xudong Zhang, "Introduction: Postmodernism and China," in "Postmodernism and China," special issue, *boundary 2* 24, no. 3 (Autumn 1997): 1–18.

7. Julian Stallabrass sees a global tendency, in his general critique of the consumerist devaluation of art's independent critical capacity, resulting in the prevalence of artwork that reproduces well on magazine pages, the rise of the celebrity artist, and work that "cosies up" to commodity culture and the fashion industry. Julian Stallabrass, *Art Incorporated: The Story of Contemporary Art* (Oxford: Oxford University Press, 2004), p. 136.

8. Rebecca Karl, "Joining Tracks with the World: The Impossibility of Politics in China," *Radical Philosophy* 131 (May/June 2005): 20–27.

9. Dai Jinhua, "Imagine Nostalgia," trans. Judy T. H. Chen, in "Postmodernism and China," special issue, *boundary 2* 24, no. 3 (Autumn 1997): 143–61.

10. Nicholas Dames, "Nostalgia and Its Disciplines: A Response," *Memory Studies* 3 (2010): 273.

11. Vanessa Fong, *Only Hope: Coming of Age under China's One-Child Policy* (Stanford, CA: Stanford University Press, 2004); Harriet Evans, *The Subject of Gender: Daughters and Mothers in Urban China* (Lanham, MD: Rowman & Littlefield, 2008), chap. 7.

12. The exhibition *China and Revolution: History, Parody and Memory in Contemporary Art*, was part of an Australian Research Council–funded project led by Stephanie Hemelryk Donald and cocurated by Stephanie Hemelryk Donald and Harriet Evans at the University Gallery, Sydney, and then at RMIT, Melbourne, January 21–March 19, 2011. The exhibit was visited by 14,000 people, and newspaper reviews of the exhibition noted the large number of young people among the visitors.

13. Barbara Mittler, *A Continuous Revolution: Making Sense of Cultural Revolution Culture* (Cambridge, MA: Harvard University Asia Center, 2013), p. 22.

14. Interview with the collector Yang Peiming, conducted by Jie Li and Harriet Evans on July 6, 2009, in Shanghai.

15. Ai Xiaoming 艾晓明 and Hu Jie 胡杰, directors of *Wei geming huahua* 为革命画画 (Painting for the revolution: Peasant paintings from Hu County, China), 2006; Hu Jie and Ai Xiaoming, directors of *Hongse meishu* 红色美术 (Red art), 2007. The interviews to which I refer were conducted in Guangzhou in 2008 with Li Gongming, Dean of Fine Arts, Guangzhou Fine Arts Academy, and with Jie Li in Shanghai in 2009.

16. Xiaomei Chen, "Growing Up with Posters in the Maoist Era," in *Picturing Power in the People's Republic of China: Posters of the Cultural Revolution*, ed. Harriet Evans and Stephanie Donald (Lanham, MD: Rowman & Littlefield, 1999), pp. 101–22.

17. Ai Xiaoming and Hu Jie, *Wei geming huahua.*

18. Toby Clark, *Art and Propaganda in the Twentieth Century: The Political Image in the Age of Mass Culture* (New York: Harry N. Abrams, 1997), pp. 7–15.

19. See the blog entitled "Forgeries of Cultural Revolution Propaganda Posters and the Appreciating Value of Revolutionary Posters" ("文革"宣传画的辨伪和革命宣传画升值空间有多大), at http://hi.baidu.com/xinyuanbao168/item/f1c31fa95ca664fe15329bcc, initially posted online February 7, 2011 (accessed May 29, 2014).

20. In the United Kingdom, Bloomsbury Auctions has held two auctions in recent years, one solely of posters in 2007, and another, in 2009, of Cultural Revolution porcelain. An exhibition titled *Art for the Masses* was held in Edinburgh in 2004, based on the private collection of Peter Wain. According to a recent online report, the average domestic price for a poster that first sold in China at 20 cents has increased to more than 4,000 times that amount), at http://hi.baidu.com/xinyuanbao168/item/f1c31fa95ca664fe15329bcc (accessed June 10, 2014).

21. See, e.g., Li Mei 李媚, "Dangdai yujing xia: Xuanchuanhua zai gonggong lingyu de wenhua jiazhi zhi fansi" 当代语境下: 宣传画在公共领域的文化价值之反思 (In contemporary context: Reflections on the cultural value of propaganda posters in the public domain), *Yishu jie* (艺术界 Art Circle) 3 (2004): 148–49. Wu Yibo 吴轶博, "Mao Zedong shidai xuanchuanhua" 毛泽东时代宣传画 (Propaganda posters of the Mao era), *Jilin yishu xueyuan xuebao* (吉林艺术学院学报 Journal of Jilin College of Arts) 6 (2007): 3–22. The most serious treatment given posters of the period by Chinese scholars is Wang Mingxian and Yan Shanchun, *Xin Zhongguo meishu tushi 1966–1976* 新中国美术图志 史 1966–1976 (Art history of New China 1966–1976) (Beijing: Zhongguo qingnian chubanshe, 2000).

22. Paul Clark, *The Chinese Cultural Revolution: A History* (Cambridge: Cambridge University Press, 2008), and Richard King, ed., *Art in Turmoil: The Chinese Cultural Revolution 1966–76* (Hong Kong: Hong Kong University Press, 2010), give detailed attention to cultural production and the art of the Cultural Revolution but little specific attention to posters. Wang Mingxian and Yan Shanchun, *Xin Zhongguo meishu tushi 1966–1976*, pp. 216–40, devotes a chapter to posters of the Mao years and the early 1980s, but only a cursory reference to the "extremes" of poster art during the Cultural

Revolution. Victoria Bonnell's rich study of Soviet political posters explores important aspects of the posters' appeal to their audiences within the context of Russian traditions of folk and religious art, but this is not matched, to date, by any equivalent study of posters of the Mao era. See Victoria E. Bonnell, *Iconography of Power: Soviet Political Posters under Lenin and Stalin* (Berkeley: University of California Press, 1997).

23. Melissa Schrift, *Biography of a Chairman Mao Badge: The Creation and Consumption of a Personality Cult* (New Brunswick, NJ: Rutgers University Press, 2001), pp. 120–54; see also Robert Benewick, "Icons of Power: Mao Zedong and the Cultural Revolution," in *Picturing Power in the People's Republic of China: Posters of the Cultural Revolution*, ed. Harriet Evans and Stephanie Donald (Lanham, MD: Rowman & Littlefield, 1999), pp. 134–37.

24. Kirk Denton, "Revolutionary Memory and National Landscape: Red Tourism," in *Exhibiting the Past: Historical Memory and the Politics of Museums in Postsocialist China* (Honolulu: University of Hawai'i Press, 2014), pp. 214–42.

25. My recent research on the everyday life of local residents of Beijing's Dashilanr reveals considerable nostalgia in their views about Mao. However, I interpret this not so much as "totalitarian nostalgia," as Barmé might put it, nor as a desire to recuperate the certainties of the past, but as an implicit critique of the present. As one local resident put it, "We may be better off materially now, but we are not better off spiritually and emotionally." Recorded interview, July 8, 2007.

26. John Gittings, "Excess and Enthusiasm," in *Picturing Power in the People's Republic of China: Posters of the Cultural Revolution*, ed. Harriet Evans and Stephanie Donald (Lanham, MD: Rowman & Littlefield, 1999), p. 27. Scholars from Colombia, Tanzania, and Uganda have given me anecdotal evidence of their presence in schools and Maoist political training camps at the time in Africa and South America.

27. For comments on the correspondence between poster imagery and Western views of Mao's China, see Zhu Fugui 朱富贵, "Wen'ge xuanchuanhua: Yige shidai de qiba" 文革宣传画: 一个时代的奇芭 (Posters of the Cultural Revolution: Miracle of an Era), *Qingnian zuojia* (青年作家 Young Writers) 2 (2006): 59–62. A detailed analysis of the part that Western interest has played in sustaining market interest in Cultural Revolution posters awaits further research, but Western interest in collecting and selling posters has certainly contributed to their continued presence on the market and probably the increasing prices they fetch; one poster vendor in Beijing's Hongqiao antiques market regularly sends his international buyers reproduced poster images on postcards at Christmastime.

28. Interview with Yang Peiming, conducted by Jie Li and Harriet Evans, on July 6, 2009, in Shanghai.

29. Li Gongming 李公明, "Er shi shiji liu qishi niandai Guangdong meishu jianlun" 二十世纪六七十年代广东美术简论 (A brief essay on Guangdong art in the 1960s and 1970s), in Guangdong meishuguan 广东美术馆, ed., *Licheng: Guangdong xin Zhongguo yidai meishujia* 历程: 广东新中国一代美术家 (Course of the past: A generation of Guangdong artists in New China) (Guangdong: Lingnan meishu chubanshe, 2002), p. 16.

30. Ibid.

31. My thanks to Professor Li Gongming of the Guangzhou Academy of Arts, who introduced me to these artists and was present at my interviews with them.

32. Wang Mingxian and Yan Shanchun, *Xin Zhongguo meishu tushi 1966–1976*.

33. Quoted in the film *Painting for the Revolution* (2006).

34. Igor Golomstock, *Totalitarian Art in the Soviet Union, the Third Reich, Fascist Italy, and the People's Republic of China* (London: Collins Harvell, 1990).

35. Wang Mingxian and Yan Shanchun, *Xin Zhongguo meishu tushi 1966–1976*, p. 53.

36. Wang Zheng, "Creating a Socialist Feminist Cultural Front: *Women of China* (1949–1966)," in "Gender in Flux: Agency and its Limits on Contemporary China," special issue, *China Quarterly* 204 (December 2010): 827–49. See also Kimberley Ens Manning, "Embodied Activisms: The Case of the Mu Guiying Brigade," in ibid., pp. 850–69.

37. Zhong Xueping, Wang Zheng, and Bai Di, eds., *Some of Us: Women Growing Up under Mao* (New Brunswick, NJ: Rutgers University Press, 2001); Evans, *The Subject of Gender*; Gail Hershatter, *The Gender of Memory* (Berkeley: University of California Press, 2011).

38. For a fuller analysis of the semiotic possibilities of these posters, see Harriet Evans, "Comrade Sisters," in *Picturing Power in the People's Republic of China: Posters of the Cultural Revolution*, ed. Harriet Evans and Stephanie Donald (Lanham, MD: Rowman & Littlefield, 1999), pp. 68–78.

39. Wang Zheng relates how, in response to a question she asked about why the cover images of *Women of China* did not show women in their domestic life, Hou Di 侯狄, formerly editor of *Women of China*, replied instantly that "at that time we never thought about that. It is hard to imagine how low women's status was at that time." Hou Di and her sisters were faced with male readers' and officials' attempts to bar women's entrance into the public domain. With only limited space to pursue their commitment to women's equal recognition in the public arena, they did not want to use it to consolidate the prejudice Hou Di described when recalling the male reader who challenged the journal's platform of gender equality by saying "women are flying a kite under the bed" (meaning, that is as high as they can go). Wang Zheng, "Creating a Socialist Feminist Cultural Front," pp. 843–44.

40. Ibid.

41. Chen, "Growing Up with Posters in the Mao Era," pp. 111–12.

42. Mittler, *A Continuous Revolution*, p. 23.

43. Geremie R. Barmé, *Shades of Mao: The Posthumous Cult of the Great Leader* (Armonk, NY: M. E. Sharpe, 1996). Li Xianting, "Political Pop," in *Encyclopedia of Contemporary Chinese Culture*, ed. Edward Davis (New York: Routledge, 2005), pp. 658–59. See also Francesca Dal Lago, "Il realismo critico della giovane arte cinese" (The critical realism of young Chinese art), in *Punti Cardinali dell'Arte: XLV Esposizione Internationale d'Arte 1993: La Biennale di Venezia*, exhibition catalogue (Venice: Edizioni La Biennale di Venezia, 1993), p. 538.

44. Wu Hung, *Remaking Beijing: Tiananmen Square and the Creation of a Political Space* (London: Reaktion Books, 2005), chap. 5.

45. Denton, "Revolutionary Memory and National Landscape," p. 220.

46. Ibid., p. 242.

47. Jie Li and Enhua Zhang's documentary film *Shaoshan Pilgrims* was presented to a panel on "Memory of the Past, Capital of the Present: Red Legacy in China" at the Annual Meeting of the Association for Asian Studies, Philadelphia, March 2010.

48. For more on the use of such crowd imagery during the Cultural Revolution, see the discussion by Andy Rodekohr in Chapter 9, "Human Wave Tactics."

49. A small exhibition in Edinburgh of fine porcelain artifacts from the Cultural Revolution similarly testified to the global appeal of such images. *Revolutionary Art of the Mao Zedong Era, 1950–1976,* National Museums of Scotland, Edinburgh, May 1, 2003 to March 2004. For a review of this exhibit, see Harriet Evans, "Mao: Art for the Masses," *Orientations* 34, no. 9 (November 2003): 64–65.

50. Magnus Wilson, "China's Cultural Evolution: Canon-mockery, E'gao and Red Dining," *Telos* 151 (Summer 2010): 151–72. The popularity of Cultural Revolution images among the young is evidenced more widely by their use as downloadable, often humorous, graphics and animations for mobile phones. For a detailed discussion of this, see Siulam Natalie Wong, "On the (Re)Emergence of Cultural Revolution Imagery in China, Hong Kong and Singapore in the 21st Century," PhD diss., University of Westminster, 2010.

51. Ibid.

52. Personal observation made when I accompanied the party secretary in question to dinner and a karaoke bar while conducting research for another project in Shangri-La, Yunnan, in July 2010.

53. See http://zrb50.blog.163.com/blog/static/4796349320093821334400/ (accessed May 29, 2014).

54. Stefan Landsberger, "Mao as the Kitchen God: Religious Aspects of the Mao Cult during the Cultural Revolution," *China Information* 11, no. 2/3 (1996): 196–214. For a chronological description of the posters' changing aesthetics, see also Landsberger, *Chinese Propaganda Posters: From Revolution to Modernization* (Amsterdam: Pepin Press, 1995).

55. See Chapter 4, "Socialist Visual Experience as Cultural Identity."

56. Sontag, "Fascinating Fascism," p. 96.

57. Ba Jin, *Suixiang lu* (Random thoughts) (Beijing: Sanlian, 1987).

58. See Chapter 11, "Museums and Memorials of the Mao Era."

59. Clark, *The Chinese Cultural Revolution.*

FOUR

SOCIALIST VISUAL EXPERIENCE AS CULTURAL IDENTITY

On Wang Guangyi and Contemporary Art

Xiaobing Tang

> An artist may not be able to solve any problems, but it is his basic professional duty to raise questions by means of his art and to endow his work with signs of intellectual reflection.
>
> —Wang Guangyi, 1990

A central figure in the fast-moving and globally connected story of contemporary art from China, a story often narrated in close parallel to the growing prominence of the Chinese economy since the early 1990s, is no doubt Wang Guangyi 王广义 (1957–).[1] Best known since the early 1990s for his *Great Criticism* series, Wang is in many a survey and art-historical account described as the defining Political Pop artist, a Chinese Andy Warhol with a poignant political thrust. His bold, poster-like images of Chinese socialist subjects, be they workers or Red Guards, charging at Western consumer brand names such as Coca-Cola and Louis Vuitton, splice together disparate visual icons and logos and often provoke bemused, if also confused, responses.

International excitement over this refreshing turn in Chinese art was first registered by *Flash Art: The Leading European Art Magazine*, when it featured on the cover of its January/February 1992 issue Wang's *Great Criticism: Coca-Cola*, the first mature work in what was to become a seemingly endless series. Almost overnight, Wang Guangyi himself became a hot brand name and a poster child for the spectacular success of Chinese contemporary art. In 2007, Howard Farber, a New York art collector who a decade before had paid $25,000 for Wang's *Coca-Cola*, raked in $1.59 million when he sold it at an auction in London. Aware that this particular work had become "the most reproduced image of Chinese contemporary art," the collector remarked that "every story in any magazine or book about Chinese art would probably use this image."[2] He seems to have been proved right about Wang's work becoming an icon of Chinese art, the latest example being the dust jacket for *A History of Art in 20th-Century China*, a lavishly illustrated and monumental tome published by Charta in 2010. The same collector had also famously described *Great Criticism: Coca-Cola* as "the Mona Lisa of Chinese contemporary art" (plate 7).[3]

Indeed, any narrative of the development of Chinese art from the mid-1980s to the twenty-first century would be incomplete without discussing or reproducing one or more works by Wang Guangyi. Yet the artist maintains his relevance through far more than a paradigmatic image such as his *Coca-Cola*. By extending his *Great Criticism* series to target a wide range of objects, from consumer goods to institutions, Wang single-handedly popularized a playful and fractured way of looking that allows a society caught in the midst of rapid transformation to see itself with a sense of humor, estrangement, and maybe unsettled resignation. His work, as art critic Li Xianting 栗宪庭 observed early on, has not only influenced many other artists but also has spawned a unique Chinese manner of speaking in the postideological era.[4] In recent years, spin-offs of *Great Criticism* would frequently pop up in Internet graphic designs or on advertising billboards. What Wang Guangyi initiated and popularized is indeed a distinct and capacious visual pattern and code.

As an artist with considerable popular appeal and tremendous market success, Wang Guangyi enjoys much critical acclaim as well, especially after a November 2002 retrospective exhibition. The retrospective was held at the government-funded He Xiangning Art Museum in Shenzhen and amounted to an official recognition of Wang, along with fellow artists Zhang Xiaogang 张晓刚 (1958–) and Fang Lijun 方力钧 (1963–), as a pioneer who, working outside the established system of support for artists, has made a deep impact on contemporary Chinese art and visual culture. Titled *Image Is Power*, the exhibition was presented as part of a research project on the history of contemporary art. It signaled a forceful assertion of contemporary art, up until then largely regarded as independent or even dissident, as well as a new critical discourse in the increasingly diversified field of cultural production. It was also clear that the curators sought to appreciate these prominent artists in the context of contemporary Chinese art and cultural history. Images created by Wang Guangyi, Zhang Xiaogang, and Fang Lijun are particularly powerful because, in the words of the curators, their highly sensitive, original artwork "has infused contemporary Chinese art with a steady tension between reality and idealism." What the three featured artists have in common, furthermore, is "the provocative means and historicist approach that they employ in their reflections on the profound changes in our lives and experiences."[5]

Provocative Wang Guangyi continues to be, as he keeps a keen eye on the changing cultural landscape and responds to it by turning to look ever more deeply into historical experiences, both personal and global. He is also known for his bold and intriguing, if sometimes enigmatic, remarks in interviews, and not infrequently he finds himself caught up in debates and controversies. In 2008, art critic Huang Zhuan 黄专, who was a cocurator of the *Image Is Power* exhibition, organized a comprehensive retrospective devoted entirely to Wang Guangyi. A close observer of Wang's work, Huang Zhuan intended to examine through the new exhibition Wang Guangyi's "visual politics" and to uncover a different artist than the mythologized "father of Chinese Political Pop." He evidently wished to counter a simplistic reading of Wang Guangyi as either a belated Andy Warhol or a provocateur for a given cause.[6] To resist a facile endorsement or rejection of Wang's work based on a narrow view of what constitutes politicality, the art critic called for a firm grasp of the internal logic and conceptual operations underlying the artist's creativity. This is clearly a sensible and productive approach. Yet in portraying the artist as a masterful strategist who, with no specific position or commitment of his own, takes pleasure in triggering new visual sensations at opportune moments, Huang runs the risk of neutralizing Wang Guangyi's politics altogether.

Insightful as his study is about a commercialized Wang Guangyi, Huang Zhuan may have difficulty in accounting for the continuing relevance of such a pivotal notion as "socialist visual experience" to Wang's work. With this notion, which he began elaborating around 2000, the artist claimed not only a historical memory and artistic resource, but also a cultural identity. It is a theoretical concept that compels him to regard the present historically and to position himself in a critical relationship with other visual practices and regimes. Through the concept of a socialist visual experience, Wang Guangyi voices a pluralistic understanding of history and eventually arrives at a critique of the institution of contemporary art. The concept, in other words, helps us recognize successive stages in the artist's development.

Beginnings

More directly than any contemporaries, Wang Guangyi has since 2000 expressed a desire to reexamine the socialist visual experience. He has also stated repeatedly that his goal is to revive, or to return to, a "socialist spirit." It is tempting, as some commentators have readily found, to regard Wang's claims as a gimmick or an eccentricity, just as it is hard for many others to believe that the market-savvy and best-selling artist of *Great Criticism* fame should be at all interested in a disavowed mode of cultural production that was organized around a systemic rejection of market mechanisms and the exchange value of art. Wang himself is acutely aware of the seemingly disingenuous contradictions between his professional success and his beliefs. In a 2008 interview he lamented that, regardless what he had to say nowadays, most people would probably think of only one phrase when they thought of him: "Show off." He could even hear their unspoken retort: "With all the money under your belt, what business do you have talking about what you are talking about?"[7] Wang's frustration was profound. He accused a mercantile society of treating works of art as nothing but objects for possession, and vowed, through his work, to restore dignity to art.

Yet the "socialist turn" in Wang Guangyi was far from either an abrupt departure or a pretense. The fact is that a critical moment in his evolution as a contemporary artist pivoted on the discovery of visual materials from the socialist era. This rich resource has, ever since the late 1980s, served as a key element in Wang's artistic vision and conceptual explorations. We should therefore view his call for revisiting the socialist visual experience at the turn of the new century as an acknowledgment of a latent but enduring search. As we will also see, "socialist visual experience" was the artist's thoughtful response to a rapidly changing world.

We may locate the moment when Wang Guangyi discovered the critical potential of visual materials from the socialist era in a work that he made in 1988. On a black-and-white photograph of Chairman Mao waving at Red Guards from the Tiananmen Rostrum during the Cultural Revolution, Wang drew with a marker six thick horizontal lines over five equally steady parallel vertical lines and called it *Waving Mao Zedong: Black Grid.* Not unlike graffiti, the neat grid of dark lines converted the magazine photograph into a ready-made. As art historian Lü Peng 吕澎 comments, the artist accomplished, in a Duchamp-esque manner, a calculated remaking of a once-sacred printed image and effectively—in fact playfully—altered our relationship to it (fig. 4.1).[8]

In the preceding few years leading to this moment, Wang Guangyi had dedicated himself to creating three series, called *Post-Classical, Red Rationality,* and *Black Rationality,* respectively. In those experimental works, he would subject iconic images in Western art history, such as the *Pietà*, the *Mona Lisa*, and *The Death of Marat*, to a stoic, systematic revision and recodification. One source of inspiration for this analytical approach was E. H. J. Gombrich's theory of inherited "schemata" in perception and their revisions by succeeding artists in the course of history. Gombrich's work on art and illusion was introduced to Chinese art circles in the mid-1980s, and the thirty-year-old Wang Guangyi quickly absorbed the gist of the theory justifying continual revisions. "It is Gombrich who has given me notions about schema/culture revisions as well as continuity," he remarked in 1987.[9] Another source of exciting new ideas for Wang and his generation was their exposure to American Pop artists such as Andy Warhol, Robert Rauschenberg, and Jasper Johns. A November 1985 Rauschenberg exhibition in Beijing, funded by the American artist himself, was an exhilarating eye-opener for many and sparked widespread interest. After seeing the show twice at the China Art Gallery, Yu Feng 郁风 (1916–2007), an esteemed seventy-year-old artist and art critic, said she fell in love with the American "daredevil" and admired his ingenuity for "making the ordinary extraordinary."[10]

Waving Mao Zedong: Black Grid continued the rigorous and impassive analytical approach that Wang Guangyi employed in his *Red* and *Black Rationality* series, but it also signaled a departure. With this

FIGURE 4.1. Wang Guangyi, *Waving Mao Zedong: Black Grid* 招手的毛泽东—黑格, 1988, mixed media, 22 × 21 cm. Courtesy of the artist.

seemingly accidental but inspired work, the artist brought himself much closer to the spirit of Pop art and experienced the thrill of making the contemporary world an object of his artistic revision. He began to look away from the hallowed but remote European masterpieces, and directed his gaze at his own lived visual environment. Soon enough, the conceptual implications of *Waving Mao Zedong: Black Grid* were played out on a large scale in *Mao Zedong: Red Grid No. 1*, a triptych in oil that won Wang unprecedented attention in the landmark and eventful exhibition *China/Avant-Garde*, which took place at the China Art Gallery in February 1989. The emotionless grid is there again and is evenly spread over the standard portrait of Mao, one of the most recognizable visual icons in the twentieth century (plate 8).

According to Wang Guangyi, the grid was a reference to a device widely used for properly transferring portraits of Mao to supersize canvases for public display during the Cultural Revolution years. By foregrounding a device that is meant to remain invisible, he laid bare the pictorial nature of a powerful political icon and compelled us to view the image differently, as assembled fragments. Both the image and its construction are presented as a deliberate process, and our viewing habits and assumptions are put to the test. Some twenty years later, Wang Guangyi in an interview would reject the suggestion that the grid was either American or a nod to the art of Mondrian, and he insisted that his action "was a gesture of deep respect toward Chairman Mao, meant to make him human."[11]

Indeed, Wang Guangyi would look back and consider the "Mao under the grid" series (altogether, five oil paintings) that he finished in 1988 a major turning point in his career. In a 2004 interview with Li Xianting, the charismatic art critic instrumental in promoting Political Pop and contemporary art in general, Wang recalled his excitement at coming up with the idea of applying his analytical method to the image of Mao. The reason that he stopped reassembling Western classics and turned his grid to Mao, he said, was because he had been "unconsciously looking for something related to my own life." Critics may have had complex things to say about his *Post-Classical* series imagery, but the artist never felt truly excited about it. Through *Mao Zedong: Red Grid No. 1*, however, Wang gained a new confidence as well as a new understanding: "One reason for the existence of contemporary art is that it must be related to your life experience." He reached a meaningful maturity, he later believed, when he brought Mao Zedong onto his canvas, because it made him better see what to do next. Portraits of Mao had been an intimate part of his upbringing, and they also pointed to a potent and far-reaching visual order and mode of image making. "Had I not made the 'Mao under the grid' series, I could not have gone very far with my art," reflected Wang in 2004.[12] What this early series ignited was an enduring interest in revisiting and reimagining the socialist visual culture produced in twentieth-century China.

By 1990 Wang Guangyi was already publicly announcing a reorientation in his art. With sweeping generalizations that were part of the earnest style of intellectual discourse of the 1980s, he sought to give contemporary art a distinctive identity and mission. Contemporary art differs from classical art, on the one hand, and from modern art, on the other, he asserted, because a contemporary artist no longer subscribes to either the classical myth of "depiction" or the modern myth of "creation." Instead, a contemporary artist regards existing visual images and cultural artifacts with a dispassionate, analytical eye and studies such materials as if in an academic discipline. Wang conceded that such a rational approach to "cultural remnants" could be a demanding affair, which explains why even a prominent contemporary artist such as Joseph Beuys would occasionally retreat to the realm of mythologies. Yet if one did not dispense with ontological myths about art, which Wang attributed to "humanistic passions," one would not be able to acquire a "language that experiments with logic," he said. Nor could one hope "to enter into a problem-solving relationship with art." Wang then declared that his calling as a contemporary artist was to "provide a logical solution to mythological problems."[13]

The language of this seminal 1990 essay by Wang Guangyi is occasionally opaque, even impenetrable, but his embrace of contemporary art is loud and clear. For him, contemporary art is to be driven primarily by conceptual innovations, by methodical analyses and revisions of prevalent artistic conventions. It demands a mode of abstract thinking that enables a discerning and disciplined view, which in turn transforms an artist's relationship to "cultural artifacts from the past." It is this perceptual realignment that opens up an opportunity for the artist to assert his presence, and to make his art speak to his contemporary world.[14] "Contemporary" therefore designates more than a temporal awareness; it prescribes a present intervention that reorders existing forms and hierarchies. The compelling force behind contemporary art, Wang observes in conclusion, is the cultural condition in which an artist finds himself. An artist may not be able to solve any problems, but he ought to raise questions by means of his art and charge his work with critical intelligence.

In the same essay, Wang Guangyi also introduces several of his recent works as evidence of his commitment to the concept of contemporary art. One of them is the *Great Criticism* series, which he began creating in 1990.

Double Vision

His distaste for myth making in art notwithstanding, the moment that brought forth Wang Guangyi's *Great Criticism: Coca-Cola* is often mythologized in various accounts that he himself proffered over time. One story has it that the artist was inspired when, working in his studio one day, he caught sight of a pack of cigarettes lying on top of an old political poster.[15] Wang would also recall drinking from a can of Coke as the epiphanic moment.[16] Regardless of its genesis, the series of medium-size oil paintings collectively called *Great Criticism* quickly got people's attention at its appearance in 1990, because the images were both familiar to Chinese viewers and yet entirely unexpected. By 1992, these works would be hailed as Political Pop par excellence, and Wang Guangyi would be anointed for good as the father of Pop art with Chinese characteristics.

The initial discussion of *Great Criticism* that Wang Guangyi provided in his 1990 essay would serve as a basic interpretive framework for many commentators over the next few years. Wang explained: "I combine images of workers, peasants, and soldiers from the 'Cultural Revolution' with those imported commercial graphics that have filtered into the everyday life of the public today. Cultural elements from two different time periods therein cancel out each other's essential content in a relationship of irony and deconstruction, and an absurd but total emptiness emerges."[17] Variations on this reading would follow, and most commentators would note the effect of irony and a comical mismatch. Art critic Li Xianting, for instance, agreed that by willfully directing Cultural Revolution–style mass criticism against Western commercial culture, Wang achieves "a humorous and absurd effect that yet carries with it an implied cultural criticism."[18]

A more developed reading came from art critic and historian Lü Peng when he sought to explain why *Great Criticism* was both unsettling and amusing to a Chinese viewer. Well acquainted with Wang Guangyi's work and interests, Lü Peng sees the series as an exemplary case in which the artist acted on Gombrich's theory and elevated revisions of visual schemata to the level of cultural critique. At the heart of the composition, he observes, is a striking monochromatic "historical visual schema"—a familiar image that triggers involuntary and painful memories of a recent past. Yet working with the rhetoric of Pop art, the artist nonchalantly replaces the objects of deadly mass criticism, which used to be either political enemies or symbols of traditional culture, with familiar commercial logos. A viewer therefore is first disoriented and then startled when he or she realizes the targets of denunciation are signs and logos ubiquitous in contemporary everyday life, and that "mass criticism" of the past turns into a "great criticism" of the present. It is as if criticism conducted in a bygone era were extended and deferred to the current moment. At the same time, the once richly symbolic figures in *Great Criticism* appear helplessly ridiculous as they are cut off from their historical context. And the ideas they embody also appear hopelessly outlandish. Through an operation akin to what Jacques Derrida calls "différance," Lü Peng claims, Wang Guangyi gains a "genuine critical dimension," a dimension not seen in American Pop artists such as Warhol, Lichtenstein, or Rosenquist.[19]

Insightful and endorsing as his reading may be, Lü Peng nonetheless does not fully explain where the critical dimension of Wang Guangyi's work resides or comes from. He asserts that *Great Criticism* confronts current political issues, but he does not address the question of which political issues or what the artist's politics may be. In addition, there is an evident unease with the striking monochromatic image at the center of Wang's canvas. The formulaic rendition of workers, peasants, and soldiers (the socialist trinity) is in the critic's eye a past instrument of political oppression, a symbol of proletarian dictatorship. And the contemporary viewer is expediently presumed to be a victim in the previous political culture, an object of mass criticism rather than an active agent or subject. What startles this hypothetical viewer/victim, in Lü Peng's reading, is first of all the spectral return of a nightmare, which the critic refers to as "an unbearable history." But there is another shock in store, as the viewer realizes his contemporary surrogates in this nightmarish vision are nothing but Western commercial logos. Maybe this is why the viewer/victim in Lü Peng's account desperately needs to find the spectral figures ridiculous and laughable. He cannot bear to see himself ridiculed or struggled against once again.

At the heart of Lü Peng's critical insights lies a blindness attributable to a reactive and consensual negation of the Cultural Revolution, a negation mandated by a disavowal of the complexity and aspirations of the recent past. It is a blind spot that lets the art critic see only reduced aspects of images retrieved from the Mao era, and keeps him from fully grasping what constitutes Wang Guangyi's cultural critique.

An even more one-dimensional reading of *Great Criticism* may be found in the accusation that "most Political Pop artists are ambivalent about the Cultural Revolution and Mao's ideology." By "ambivalence," Gao Minglu 高名潞, another influential art critic and historian active since the 1980s, meant a lack of resolute rejection of, or even an inexcusable flirtation with, the terrifying Mao era. Those Political Pop artists, he complained, "glorify the persuasive power and unique aesthetic of Mao's propagandist art," and Wang Guangyi's placing of propagandist art next to consumer mass culture epitomizes the "double kitsch" that is Political Pop. Writing in 1998, Gao Minglu was critical of a strategy that marketed Political Pop as an independent, avant-garde art form in order to cater to an international art community still clinging to a Cold War geopolitical imagination. His point was that Political Pop and Cynical Realism, the other best-selling brand of Chinese art in the early 1990s, were neither independent nor avant-garde but an odious "combination of ideological and commercial practices." However, in portraying Wang Guangyi and other Political Pop artists as money-grabbing "career artists" in cahoots not only with the current regime but also with Maoist legacies, Gao Minglu seemed to be urging the international art community to renew its Cold War anti-Communist vigilance and commitment.[20] And his dismissal of *Great Criticism* as "a kitsch advertisement of an advertisement" hardly addresses the complex reactions that Lü Peng began to describe.[21]

The label of "double kitsch" coined by Gao Minglu was used by another critic in discussing various avant-garde positions in Chinese contemporary art. Norman Bryson saw in *Great Criticism* an exceptional pessimism: "The aspirations active in the social field on each side of the dual system (modified socialism, modified capitalism) are mocked and negated by reducing both to a level of kitsch design: each system is treated as a set of debased signifiers and formulae, as though both systems were already essentially dead."[22] This observation may remind us of Wang Guangyi's own remark about "an absurd but total emptiness" with regard to *Great Criticism*. Yet what Wang juxtaposes on his canvas are not two contemporaneous, or equally dead, sign systems. Rather, he retrieves a vanished image and pits it against a contemporary state of affairs that is self-evident and writ large (plate 9).

The nonsynchronicity of the two visual systems that Wang Guangyi brings together on a flat surface is of critical importance. The two systems may share the same background of loud primary colors, but the present tense belongs to Western brand names, and the Chinese political subjects are an afterimage of a once strident but now muted era. Those pervasive commercial logos are at once abstract and concrete, distant and yet tangible, and they form a contemporary hieroglyphics of desire and consumption that claims to be a universal language. By contrast, the afterimages of the socialist trinity are formulaic and faded, but they still possess sharp and robust lines and movements, and they exude a purposeful if now apparently misplaced and spectral self-confidence.

The compositional device of *Great Criticism* is juxtaposition, which foregrounds the distance between two contrasting systems by holding them in intimate proximity. It is a device that effectively reveals a structural incompleteness, because only fragments of different systems, instead of totalities, can be presented in juxtaposition. This is how the most powerful and emblematic symbol of a given system, be it socialist or capitalist, is exposed as but a sign of a limited and parochial vision or reach. This is also why Wang Guangyi believes his work establishes a relationship of irony and deconstruction, which in turn allows the truth claims of two disparate time periods to cancel each other out. When we see both belief systems as inherently incomplete, as Wang observes perceptively, we find ourselves looking over an "absurd and total emptiness." The absurdity is complete because there is no positive term or value for us to embrace wholeheartedly, and because our desire to identify with or hold onto either of the two debunked systems is itself shown to be absurd.

This is evidently the effect that many critics, including the artist himself, appreciate and associate with deconstruction and a Derridean differance. Li Xianting, for instance, sees in "the seemingly arbitrary combination" a "humorous and absurd effect" mixed with a biting satire. Yet while juxtaposition serves as an expedient deconstructive device, the real conceptual breakthrough occurs at the moment when the artist decides *what* to juxtapose, or simply what to see. It is a breakthrough informed by Wang Guangyi's commitment to methodically examine "cultural artifacts from the past," and to find a "language that experiments with logic" through his art. In the visual materials of an era that was universally believed to be bankrupt and passé, he found a new resource, a way of seeing beyond the current visual regime. His innovation consisted, therefore, in bringing the remnants of a past imagination back into view and inserting them as a stubborn, unresolved reminder in the contemporary system of meaning or visual order.

The *Great Criticism* series therefore introduces a new way of seeing, through which we are enabled to see not only incongruous signs and fragments but also different historical formations and subjectivities. Amid the rising consumerist landscape, Wang Guangyi reactivates the spectral afterimage of a socialist past and splits our vision. Refracted through his canvas, the desiring gaze that we direct at a consumer product such as a can of Coca-Cola or a Nikon camera becomes distracted and perverted by a peripheral object. Our gaze is led through a distant scene that is at once outlandish and familiar, at once inexplicable and vaguely exciting. No longer in full possession of our gaze, we begin to see ourselves mirrored in the afterimage, or rather to see ourselves misrecognized, and as we lose our concentration momentarily, the commodity in front of us also loses its allure and promissory power. At this point, we may seek relief in laughing out aloud or in bemoaning a general absurdity, but the fact is that our gaze has been rent asunder and made incoherent.

The cultural critique of *Great Criticism,* therefore, stems not from a past critical gesture being transposed onto the present, but from a fragmentation of the current visual order. Wang Guangyi's work at this stage concerns not so much different political visions as it does the politics of vision. Or, as Jacques Rancière would say, it enables a redistribution of the sensible, a practice that will be discussed later in the chapter.

Socialist Visuality

Soon after the *Great Criticism* series began appearing, *Beijing Youth Daily* devoted a special section to "the Wang Guangyi phenomenon" in March 1991. Presenting the artist as a leading figure as well as a "complex entity filled with contradictions," the editors called attention to Wang Guangyi's statement that society always selects its artists for either success or failure. They were happy to take Wang's latest work as a sign that contemporary art was becoming more accessible, since *Great Criticism* seemed to exemplify the idea of art "from the masses and to the masses."

In his interview with the newspaper, Wang remarked: "So far as contemporary art is concerned, it ought to be, it seems to me, a reorganization of shared public experiences. It affects everyone, is a large-scale 'game,' and compels the public to participate in it."[23]

Wang's statement on the public nature of contemporary art underlines the exciting possibilities that came with his new self-positioning with regard to the object of his art. He put much emphasis on a shared public visual environment or culture, and suggested that the artist's task was to enable the public to relate to it anew and differently. Given the context of his recent work, it was clear that he believed the Cultural Revolution had generated a public, shared visual experience. Yet in the interview he chose not to dwell on this important source of his latest work, lest his treatment of visual material from the Cultural Revolution should raise troublesome questions given the current mainstream consensus, which was to dismiss the decade of 1966–76 as an unprecedented and unmitigated catastrophe willfully inflicted on Chinese society and culture by Mao himself.

On this occasion, Wang's decision was to let the images speak for themselves. A viewer with either experience or knowledge of modern Chinese visual culture will recognize that those resurrected images of workers, peasants, and soldiers engaged in "great criticism" are tokens of a socialist mass culture—specifically, a strident visual culture produced and broadly disseminated through much of the Cultural Revolution. It was a resolutely public and vociferous visual culture, sustained by artistic practices that had no precedents comparable in scope or scale. A distinct visual grammar and vocabulary emerged from the Cultural Revolution, as did radical understandings of art and innovative methods of making art. Mobilized as a vital instrument in a grassroots revolt against the old world and existing power structures, art was itself subjected to far-reaching critiques and reclaimed as a necessary part of the collective effort to implement a socialist transformation in the visual sphere and experience.

The most concentrated and most radical expression of this desire to create a revolutionary visual culture was the Red Guard art movement that reached its explosive peak in 1967, hardly a year into the violent *Sturm und Drang* of the Cultural Revolution. The onset of the Great Proletarian Cultural Revolution is usually dated to May 1966, when the Central Committee of the ruling Communist Party issued a circular to the party and the entire nation. The document exposed deep ideological divisions within the leadership, and called on party members and general citizens faithful to Mao Zedong's program to rise up and seize power from the reactionary capitalist authorities then dominating various cultural institutions, such as education, academia, the press, literature, and the arts.[24] Within weeks, posters aggressively denouncing school administrators for political insidiousness appeared on a university campus in Beijing. When Mao hailed them a few weeks later as "the first Marxist-Leninist big-character posters in the nation," the fury of a youthful revolt was fully unleashed.

Many complex factors, from political infighting to geopolitical pressures, from philosophical disagreements to demographic shifts, led Mao to launch a grassroots revolution against the social order and cultural establishment of the very New China that he had envisioned, brought forth, and presided over. It was far from a whimsical or deranged decision. On the contrary, Mao, a true revolutionary, had long believed in a constant revolution in culture and consciousness as a necessary antidote to the Soviet-style ossification of the spirit of socialism in the form of bureaucratic institutions and compartmentalization. Through a cultural revolution, he sought to address, as the historian Arif Dirlik puts it succinctly, "a basic problem of socialism in power: that socialist societies are as vulnerable as any other to producing structures of power that attenuate the revolutionary vision of freedom and equality."[25]

Sensing that few in the leadership were as committed to fighting revisionist inertia and deviation, Mao placed his hopes in idealistic youths to revitalize the revolution independently of the system. Red Guards, consisting of members of the generation born after the Communist victory in 1949, thereby emerged in the summer of 1966 as the "earnest vanguard of the Cultural Revolution." They were college and high school students who had organized themselves into paramilitary units, and who viewed it as their grand historic mission to defend Chairman Mao and eradicate his enemies, which consisted of the current power structure and traditional values and practices. Their youthful faith was expressed in a popular battle cry: "Revolution is not a crime; to rebel is justified!" Ardent in their desire to reclaim the revolutionary heritage, millions of Red Guards took pride in methodically plunging first Beijing, then the entire country, into a "Red Terror," resorting with pious passion to the theatrics of violence that the young Mao Zedong had eloquently endorsed with regard to the peasant movement in Hunan in the late 1920s.[26]

Integral to the passionate antiestablishment revolt of the Red Guard movement was a futuristic imagination that had bestirred different generations across the continents. The destruction of museums, libraries, and everything else redolent of *passatismo* that an ebullient F. T. Marinetti had urged in his "Futurist Manifesto" in 1909, for instance, turned into an antitradition ritual, which the Red Guards performed repeatedly in many variations and on a staggering scale. Unaware of such spiritual connections, the young Chinese revolutionaries took to heart the futurist slogan, "Except in struggle, there is no more beauty!" At the same time, Vladimir Mayakovsky's constructivist vision of city streets becoming brushes, and public squares spreading out as palettes for artists engaged in building a new socialist life in Russia in the 1920s, was taken as an inspiring blueprint for action. A group of Red Guards from the Beijing Aeronautics Institute undertook an intense project over the summer of 1966 to paint every wall, gate, storefront, and other public surface in the country so that a "red ocean" would arise and inundate the world as people knew it. The campaign to paint China red was short-lived, but it loudly proclaimed the symbolic value of the primary color in a revolutionary visuality. Ever since the second decade of the twentieth century, futurist visions of modernity had held a fascination for Chinese poets and artists, but for the Red Guard generation, life in the present was nothing but the future in the making. This future-present life was to be lived creatively, as a work of art, just as art was to be a vital part of a fulfilling life (plate 10).

The Red Guard art movement not only conducted extensive experiments with new modes of making art but also succeeded in producing a distinct visuality. By pushing to their logical extreme the fundamental tenets of a socialist visual culture, participants in the movement redefined art as well as the role of the artist and committed themselves to creating a far more comprehensive visual environment than mere art objects. They vowed to bring art back to life and rejected the notion of artistic autonomy, which was what had turned art into a superfluous and mystifying form of decoration. To return art to life meant to overcome the privileged institution of art and to make art a meaningful and accessible experience for the people. In the process, the artist was also to be transformed into an art worker whose task, analogous to that of an industrial or agricultural worker, was to contribute to the new socialist imagination.

On these core issues, the Red Guard art movement shared aspirations similar to those that had driven avant-garde movements in other parts of the world, especially in early twentieth-century Europe.[27] Some art historians have proposed to describe and understand it as a "red modernism," but it certainly was far from the variety of high-modernist revolution in the realm of fine art celebrated by Clement Greenberg, for example.[28] Others, especially some artists, prefer to see the Red Guard art movement, or Cultural Revolution art in general, as inseparable from or even foreshadowing contemporary art. Xu Bing 徐冰 (1955–), for instance, a leading conceptual artist, found it impossible to deny the legacy of Cultural Revolution art. While in New York, he was asked how, as an artist trained in a conservative country such as China, he ended up making conceptually challenging art. Xu Bing explained that his artistic sensibility had everything to do with his experience during the Mao era. "I know that my creative work reflects the genes of an artist with a socialist background," he wrote in 2008. "That is something which cannot be concealed and will always reveal itself in the end."[29] On another occasion, Zheng Shengtian 郑胜天 (1938–), who participated in the Cultural Revolution as a young artist and had his share of hardship and suffering, refused to disavow his youthful passion and experience. He felt puzzled when an American artist expressed sadness over what reportedly had happened in China. "I appreciated his sympathy," Zheng Shengtian wrote when reviewing his own career as an artist. "But I think the efforts of members of my generation have not been in vain. Many of us sought to create a new art for a new world, as artists in other countries and other times had tried to do. Their importance to the Chinese visual culture of the twentieth century cannot be denied and their influence can still be seen in contemporary Chinese art today."[30]

From the outset of the Cultural Revolution, its nature as a grassroots protest movement was expressed in a blasting visual environment consisting of aggressive posters, demeaning caricatures, and uncompromisingly bombastic graphics and language.[31] In 1967, Red Guard groups and factions in fine arts academies published scores of journals and pamphlets through which they conducted "great criticism" of the existing institution of art and issued their fiery manifestos, visual as well as textual. In June of that year, *Fine Arts Storm*, a journal published by a Red

Guard coalition at the Central Academy of Fine Arts, proclaimed the goal of the current movement: "Seize the power! Seize the power!! Seize the power!!!" "We will make the sky over the art field glowing with Mao Zedong Thought, and the ground underneath a warm and nurturing territory for workers, peasants, and soldiers."[32]

Red Guard art groups from art academies also organized massive and innovative art exhibitions in 1967, often in association with rebel groups from other work units, even from the army. The series of large-scale art shows in Beijing culminated in a spectacular national exhibition titled *Long Live the Triumph of Chairman Mao's Revolutionary Line.* It opened on National Day of October 1 and displayed over 1,600 objects ranging from ink-and-brush paintings to oil paintings, woodcuts, posters, and clay sculptures. Participating artists came from all over the country, and a large number of them were amateurs from all walks of life. After its run at the China Art Gallery, exhibition teams took some of the works and slides to remote rural areas in order to extend its impact far and wide. In November, the *People's Daily*, the party organ still firmly controlled by Mao and his fellow radicals, endorsed the exhibition and identified its three laudable features: The event was revolutionary in its theme, combative in its effect, and mass-based in its production. "The art exhibition constituted a popularization as well as an elevation of revolutionary artistic practices among the vast masses of workers, peasants, and soldiers."[33]

While the most iconic work of art from the Cultural Revolution era is probably the oil painting *Chairman Mao Goes to Anyuan* by Liu Chunhua (1967), the art form most favored by the Red Guard art movement was the black-and-white woodcut.[34] The cultural as well as political symbolism that the woodcut acquired in the twentieth century, in particular its position as a public, expedient, anti-elitist, and socially committed art form, made it a logical choice through which to express the ethos of a grassroots revolution. From the classics of modern Chinese woodcuts, some of which were directly influenced by German expressionist works, Red Guard artists drew inspiration and developed an energetic, assertive, and versatile graphic language. They also incorporated elements from satirical cartoons as well as folk art, such as paper cutouts. Yet given their impatience for action in a rapidly unfolding revolution, young artists were seldom willing to spend time actually working on wood blocks and then manually printing images. Instead,

FIGURE 4.2. Cover of the *Worker-Peasant-Soldier Pictorial* 工农兵画报, September 1968. Courtesy of the China Academy of Art Library, Hangzhou.

they would use a brush or marker to approximate the look and effect of a woodcut. In the process, a highly recognizable visual style and idiom specific to the Cultural Revolution was developed and codified (fig. 4.2).

As the Cultural Revolution moved on, the Red Guard art movement gradually lost momentum and was phased out as the Red Guard movement itself was fractured and eventually suppressed. By the early 1970s, "art by workers, peasants, and soldiers," or amateur art created with the assistance of professionally trained artists, would be promoted as the new socialist art. A prominent example of such art was the brilliantly colored peasant painting from Huxian (Hu County) in Shaanxi Province.[35] Nonetheless, the visual idiom of the woodcut would still have a broad appeal and find itself translated or adapted in other mediums, such as oil painting, ink-brush painting, and poster art.

One of the most common visual statements popularized by the Red Guard art movement in the late 1960s was that of a worker, peasant, and soldier conducting criticism. The critical agents could also be Red Guards in paramilitary uniforms and other groups. The visual impact of the image stemmed as much from the socialist subjects, depicted in stark black outlines as if printed from a wood block, against a background of a vibrant red, as it did from the striking transformation of earlier renditions of the same subjects from the socialist age before the Cultural Revolution. No longer optimistic socialist builders, the figures now appeared much more militant and more resolute as they focused their denunciatory force on a given enemy force, which could range from American imperialism to Soviet revisionism to capitalist values and practices. They were, in other words, a modification of an already prevalent visual paradigm. When they reappeared in Wang Guangyi's oil paintings of the 1990s, they had undergone yet another change, or what the artist would call, following E. H. J. Gombrich, a revision of schemata (plate 11).[36]

Wang Guangyi's resurrection of widely circulated but ephemeral and disposable print-based images in oils on canvas is an act therefore fraught with art-historical significance and self-consciousness. By amplifying those print images without leaving any gestural traces suggestive of an individual artist's presence, he gave them an afterlife as contemporary Pop art. He blew them up in a streamlined form for more intense visual impact. Also, by juxtaposing them with globally recognizable commercial logos, Wang Guangyi accorded the images created by anonymous Red Guard artists an unexpected status. They are brought back as a competing, if also equally significant, universal visual language.

Plural Histories

Apart from its art-historical references, the *Great Criticism* series had momentous conceptual consequences as well. Through its fractured double vision, it affirmed the inevitability of dissensus, which Jacques Rancière simply defines as the "manifestation of a gap in the sensible itself."[37] As a critical intervention, Wang Guangyi would come to identify and embrace a "socialist visual experience" in an effort to puncture the current visual order. He would become ever more invested in what had become a disavowed way of making art. This disavowal had taken place in the early 1980s when a reform consensus was reached in Chinese society after the Communist Party unequivocally denounced the Cultural Revolution as a grave error committed by Mao, who had died in 1976.

In a substantive interview with curator and art critic Charles Merewether in 2002, Wang Guangyi placed his creation of the *Great Criticism* series in the context of profound changes in the Chinese economy, politics, and culture that had occurred by the early 1990s. He clarified that when he proposed an analytical approach to art in the late 1980s, he was arguing against a tendency for an artist to be absorbed in metaphysical reveries. He wanted to find a way to reestablish the connection between art and social experiences. "In my view," Wang stated, "the real issue exposed in *Great Criticism* is the conflict between Western culture and socialist ideology. The meaning of this conflict may be better grasped through a study of different cultures than simply as an art problem."[38] This view of his most famous work has a different tenor from the artist's own initial exposition in 1990. He had suggested that by placing two cultural systems "in a relationship of irony and deconstruction," he was able to reveal or comment on "an absurd but total emptiness." By 2002, Wang Guangyi would underline the conflict that *Great Criticism* visualizes. Furthermore, he would argue that it was not a face-off to be dissolved through irony or sarcasm into nothingness, but an enduring conflict with global ramifications.

In the same interview with Merewether, Wang observed that it was in the 1990s that he came to see his double role as an artist and a social critic: "As an artist, I also exist as a critic of society." Yet he was clear about what kind of social criticism he was committed to. In response to the interviewer's follow-up question on the artist's relationship to history, Wang replied: "I don't think one's role should be simply that of a critic in this regard. To me at least, the most important task is to excavate, from a contemporary perspective, possible meanings of past history." From the perspective of a contemporary artist, he went on to elaborate, the Cultural Revolution was a meaningful event because "it provided a visual modality developed from the socialist experience of a given period of time." This "visual modality" was a complex one; it remained relevant because it was based on a systematic perception of the world and exerted a lasting impact. His recent work, Wang remarked, was an effort to recapture this complex visuality and to "remind the audience of the likelihood that a way of seeing and thinking may be forgotten or disappearing."[39]

Excavating the socialist visual experience therefore became a concerted project for Wang Guangyi around the turn of the new century.

He continued his *Great Criticism* series and expanded its scope to include more and more brand names and institutions. The piece *Great Criticism: WTO* (2001) was a timely response to the arrival of a new stage of globalization with China's accession to the World Trade Organization (plate 12). Yet in a series of installation and sculptural pieces, he sought to exert a greater impact, as he acknowledged in the Merewether interview. More than ever, he was interested in presenting a historical view of the contemporary, post–Cold War world. In a 2001 installation work titled *Elementary Education* and first exhibited in Hamburg, Germany, Wang extended the method of juxtaposition to include a miscellany of objects. He collected Chinese antiwar posters and graphics on safety measures in case of a nuclear bombing, all of which were published in 1967–68 at the height of the Cultural Revolution, and put them in picture frames next to a construction scaffold, spades, and boots for military personnel. (The military-grade spades provided by his German host were a welcome addition.) He wanted to recreate a work site where "everything is just about to begin." What would happen next was left to the viewers' imagination, but Wang was clear that his intention was to "show the education that our generation received and how, in the wake of the Cold War, we may continue to look at the current configuration of the world."[40] This installation work indeed retrieved a way of seeing that cannot be simply reduced to Cold War geopolitics or expunged as ideological indoctrination.

This desire to foreground the specific educational and cultural legacy defining a contemporary Chinese outlook underlay a set of seventy-two sculptural pieces that Wang Guangyi made between 2001 and 2002. The set is collectively called *Materialists*, as the philosophical opposite to idealists, rather than in the sense of individuals obsessed with material possessions. Wang regarded the concept of "a materialist" (more accurately, "a historical materialist," in contradistinction to an idealist) as particularly significant in the Chinese context because it has a revolutionary connotation and points to "an oppositional power of critique" against myopic thinking and self-deception. He also observed that even though the sculptural figures may have the gestures or facial features of the characters in his *Great Criticism* series, they form a simpler and purer presence because they are no longer caught in a confrontation with their opposites. They now stand on their own. "I want to restore a socialist spirit. . . . Without placing them in a dichotomous relationship,

FIGURE 4.3. Wang Guangyi, *Materialists* 唯物主义者, 2001–2, fiberglass-reinforced plastic and millet, 180 × 120 × 60 cm, 72 pieces. Courtesy of the artist.

I want these sculptures to reveal in and of themselves all the possible purity as well as the complexity of the socialist visual experience."[41] On another occasion, he stated, "I want to reconstruct the power and meaning of visual components drawn from the experience of socialism" (fig. 4.3).[42]

Making seventy-two fiberglass statues in honor of idealized and nameless socialist heroes was a monumental statement. It puts into visual terms Wang Guangyi's considered choice when faced with the conflict that *Great Criticism* spells out. After exposing the tension between two disparate systems and cultural choices, as it were, the artist now invites us to identify with the "great critics," assume their position, adopt their vision, and direct a critical gaze at the world around us. He no longer needs to include a reference to a "dichotomous relationship" because his artwork itself now stands in opposition to a prevailing order and seemingly entrenched reality. Instead of splitting our vision, as he does through *Great Criticism*, he urges us to look closely and focus on recognizing a vanished history and subjectivity against the clamorous surroundings of triumphant consumerism and the market economy.

In this sculptural work, the socialist subjects, some of them Red Guards, are restored as robust three-dimensional, larger-than-life monuments. They retain their self-confident gestures and exude a youthful optimism and defiance. They seem exaggerated in their expressions, and they are silent. A socialist spirit, according to Wang Guangyi, is observable in their torsos, gestures, expressions, and in the millet glued all over them. The fine, bright yellow grains of millet that cover the fiberglass sculptures are an important element because, as he told Merewether, "millet is full of revolutionary significance in China." As a staple food that sustained the Communist-led Eighth Route Army during the War of Resistance against Japanese Aggression in the 1930s, millet is a legendary object in the lore of the Chinese Revolution. To understand its meaning, Wang remarked, one has to study Chinese culture, just as one needs to delve into European culture to understand the significance and the Europeanness of the coarse felt fabric that Joseph Beuys repeatedly used in his work.[43]

Equally monumental as the group of sculptures from 2001–2 are two series of oil paintings that Wang Guangyi finished in 2003. The fifteen paintings under the general title *Forever Shining* present a striking visual counterpart to *Great Criticism*, in that the new work evokes a film negative that reverses black and white and reduces colors unnaturally. All are images based on familiar socialist posters, some of them having already appeared in *Great Criticism*. By bringing to our view their negatives, Wang Guangyi inserts a photographic dimension and possibility. They suggest not only an indexical relation to a photographed moment or experience but also the possibility of generating many fresh positive prints for our own present time (fig. 4.4).

As if to help us see from the negative a brilliant image, Wang Guangyi also created a mini series titled *Faces of Belief*. The five works in this series present the most archetypal and fantastic images retrieved from the socialist past. Three of these works can be viewed as a triptych that reenvisions the revolutionary trinity of the socialist imagination. Here the digits that once intrigued viewers of *Great Criticism* return, but even they seem to constitute orderly sequences. These inspired and inspiring faces are further enlarged in *The Face of Belief A* and *B*, in which the graphic property of a woodcut is also demonstrated as indispensable for a socialist iconography. Their radiating positivity, without ambivalence, as well as the sheer size of these canvases, bespeaks nostalgia for a longing that opened up a visionary world and left behind a distinct way of seeing and being seen (plate 13).

FIGURE 4.4. Wang Guangyi, *Forever Shining* 永放光芒 No. 3, 2003, oil on canvas, 300 × 200 cm. Courtesy of the artist.

What Wang Guangyi vows to retrieve from the socialist visual experience is more cultural identity and historical legacy than political ideology or doctrine. "The visual components drawn from the experience of socialism," an idiosyncratic phrase that the artist would also use to describe the object of his investigation, put the emphasis on concrete practices and experiences of socialism in China rather than on abstractions. For the same reason, he is very careful to distinguish the complex meanings of the Cultural Revolution, insisting that it had a very different impact on politics than on art. He also believes that the socialist visual experience is an inescapable cultural tradition for Chinese contemporary artists. "Before we judge its merits, we need to acknowledge it as a fact of our life. It shapes our perception, and determines the difference between our approach to depicting an object and anyone else's."[44] In actively claiming rather than disavowing or regretting this "fact of life," Wang

Guangyi puts himself at odds with the contemporary mainstream negation of the Cultural Revolution and thereby establishes a critical distance from many strands within the field of contemporary art.

As art historian Wang Mingxian 王明贤 has observed, Wang Guangyi is the most prominent contemporary artist who has consistently turned to visual images from the Cultural Revolution as sources for his artwork. With his theorization of a socialist visual experience around the turn of the new century, Wang Guangyi broadened his scope and became increasingly confident of his role as a cultural critic who refuses to accept the contemporary world as it is. On several levels, we see how this refusal leads to a productive insistence on history as meaningful difference. In terms of visual strategies, he shifts his attention from a deconstructive "double vision" to an excavating project that aims at "reconstructing a way of seeing." Monumentality is his preferred style and method by which to challenge the current visual regime and to force a conceptual breakthrough. (An installation he finished in 2001 is called *Monument to the Worker*.) Such a breakthrough reintroduces a past vision, or what Wang calls "the socialist spirit," which, once breaking into our view, haunts us like a specter and demands that we review and recount our relationship to the present.

Yet this critical review, which may express itself as a critique of consumer society, also reveals that there are contests over the present on another, more global level. This is where a divergence among different historical narratives and different cultural identities becomes observable. Thus, in *Materialists*, Wang Guangyi goes beyond the period of the Cultural Revolution and covers his sculptures with millet. When he asserts that one cannot understand the significance of millet in his work until one delves into Chinese culture, Wang explicitly turns revolutionary history into a source of cultural identity, and expands Chinese culture, in turn, beyond its usual association, especially for Western observers, with a remote and tranquil aesthetic tradition.

Only with the backing of this expanded cultural identity does Wang Guangyi feel confident enough to engage in a "cultural contest" with the hegemonic power of Euro-America.[45] It is a hegemonic power not only in having shaped the contemporary art discourse and market, but also for its capacity to reshape historical memories and narratives in its own image and interest. Wang foresees a protracted cultural contest because he remains skeptical of the triumphalist narratives that, in order

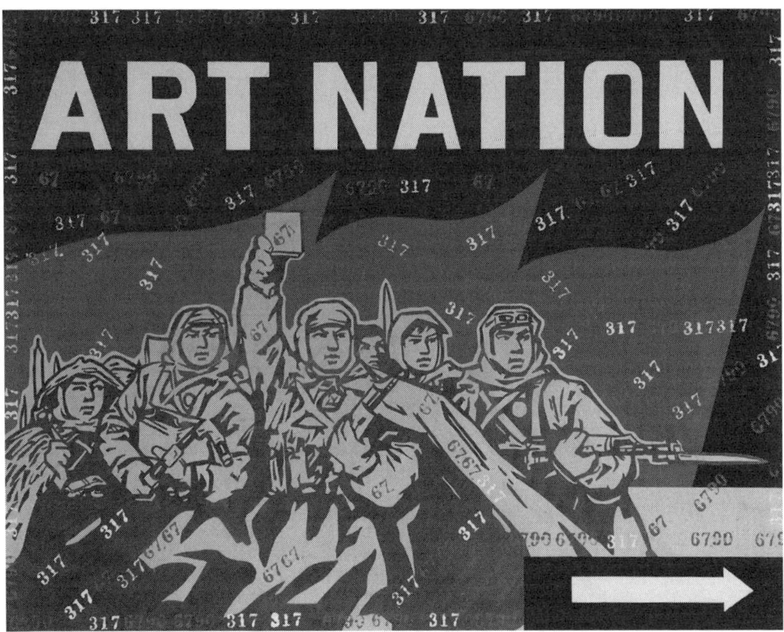

FIGURE 4.5. Wang Guangyi, *Great Criticism: Art Nation* 大批判—艺术 民族, 2005, oil on canvas, 140 × 180 cm. Courtesy of the artist.

to celebrate the outcome of the Cold War and the alleged "end of history," systematically reduce and rewrite twentieth-century world history. He, for one, believes the socialist history in China has left behind an enormous shadow. Regardless of its effect, "this shadow will have a long-lasting impact on China as well as on the world. . . . When you face it, you will feel its pressure," asserted Wang in 2004 (fig. 4.5).[46]

Coda: Global Resonances

Wang Guangyi remains the most prominent contemporary artist to have embraced the socialist visual experience and to have persisted in exploring its relevance. His efforts at reactivating a socialist way of seeing are provocative and often cause bewilderment and unease because he refuses to let the socialist subjects disappear, even when socialism is often taken to mean hardly anything more than a failed experiment or a misleading pretense. He brings those once widely disseminated images back in altered, monumental forms, and insists that we recognize them as our contemporaries, as embodying passionate human lives that still demand to be seen and to be heard. By inserting these disquieting forms into our field of vision, he hopes to make us see in a new light the way we see the world and ourselves.

For Wang Guangyi, socialist visuality is the powerful expression of a revolutionary culture that is based on the fundamentally political practice of differentiation and confrontation. This revolutionary culture is a complex living legacy not only because it has left an indelible mark on the identity of his generation of Chinese, but also because it was an inextricable product of the Cold War, which, in his view, continues to shape the geopolitics of the world today. A series of large-scale installation projects that Wang undertook in 2007–8 is directly called *Cold War Aesthetics*. Using a wide range of objects and resources (old public posters, fiberglass sculptures, cement blocks, and video displays) at different exhibition venues, he created scenes of Chinese citizens and militia preparing for nuclear, chemical, and biochemical attacks that were presumed to be an imminent danger in the mid-twentieth century. "My art is about searching for an opposition," the artist stated in an interview about the installations. "This is where the charm of the world lies, in this oppositional beauty, in the existence of opposites."[47] By restaging tensions that he regards as both historical and unresolved, Wang voices his skepticism of celebrations of globalization and insists on seeing the world as uneven, unequal, and haunted by past memories and promises. For him, dated political expressions turn into cultural legacies that in turn allow him to raise unsettling questions about the new world order, on both global and local levels.

Yet, as a major contemporary artist who openly declared his desire to "restore a socialist spirit" in his art, Wang Guangyi bears hardly any resemblance to artists working in the socialist era. On the contrary, he is a superstar in the bustling field of contemporary art, known for his acquired and expensive taste for a good cigar. An oil painting by Wang Guangyi may carry a price tag of hundreds of thousands if not millions of dollars, and his works are internationally sought after, collected, and forecast to continue to rise in value. In his splendid success in the marketplace, we see a vivid illustration of the ascendancy of the contemporary-art system and the simultaneous withdrawal of the socialist production system that was formally established in the early 1950s. We cannot lose sight of this side of the picture when we look at and examine Wang Guangyi's work. A double vision on our part is in order.

Wang Guangyi himself is no less aware of the price of his success. Shortly before *Great Criticism* began to be marketed and was sold briskly as Political Pop in the international art market, he had advocated the need to establish an art market in China, arguing that art and money would bring both good things and contentment.[48] Now, with a domestic art market in China that functions no differently than a stock market and with art fully globalized as an investment option, the success of the current art system appears to be nothing but a Pyrrhic victory. "Our entire society is in the business of humiliating art," Wang Guangyi complained bitterly in a 2008 interview, and he vowed to "restore the dignity of art and the artist" through his work.[49] The dignity that he wished to restore is not some sort of distinction or prestige on the part of the artist. On the contrary, it is respect for the artist as a committed cultural critic, and for works of art as purposeful interventions in the social and spiritual life of the nation. As such, art should not be reduced to commodities or invidious possessions. In deploring contemporary society's loss of respect for art, Wang turned against the domineering art market and also expressed his desire for an organic public art resonant with collective passions. Obviously related to his earlier program of restoring a socialist spirit, the new restorative project will have to start with a critique of the institution of art, which Wang has played an instrumental role in establishing, and of which he has been a notable beneficiary (plate 14).

And he knows that he is not powerful enough to alter the "powerful reality" that is the current art market. Nonetheless, starting with the *Cold War Aesthetics* installations, Wang Guangyi has articulated a new strategy regarding his work. His goal in this expansive project was to "make it not look like art" and to present the finished work as a textbook rather than an art exhibition. He has come to have little regard for "artsy art," because "such art is too easily aestheticized, too easily monetized." For this reason, he thinks his *Cold War Aesthetics* is better and more provocative than the *Great Criticism* series, because the latter still falls into the conventional category of collectible art objects.[50] What he seeks to bring about now is "antiart," or historical experience and imagination that cannot and should not be contained within the current system of art.

"I do not want art to be some rarified sphere," Wang Guangyi stated in 2008, and he went on to underscore the popular as well as public origins of his own work. It was "the power of the people," he claimed, that had enabled him to complete the *Great Criticism* series, because the familiar images of workers, peasants, and soldiers had come from nonprofessional artists and reflected the political imaginings of the ordinary people. "I try my hardest to use the people's hands to express my ideas; that is my ideal."[51] In the artist's new emphasis on the public nature of his art, we may hear a distant echo of the aspirations that once animated the Red Guard art movement half a century ago. It is also an emphasis with far-reaching global resonances as we continue to confront, in various locations and with different legacies, questions about art and its relationship to our contemporary life, collective as well as imaginary.

Notes

1. The epigraph is from Wang Guangyi, "Guanyu 'Qingli renwen reqing'" (On "Sorting out Humanistic Passions"), first published in *Jiangsu huakan* (Jiangsu art magazine), no. 10 (1990). An English translation of the text is available in *Wang Guangyi: Works and Thoughts 1985–2012*, ed. Demetrio Paparoni (Milan: Skira, 2013), pp. 317–18. Beautifully illustrated, this volume is an excellent resource, as it contains the artist's entire oeuvre until 2012, as well as critical assessments and key documents in English translation.

2. See Linda Sandler and Katya Kazakina, "Collector Farber Makes 63 Times Cost on Chinese Art," October 13, 2007, at http://www.bloomberg.com/apps/news?pid=newsarchive&sid=aIZq1q1ZrS3Q&refer=home (accessed October 5, 2015).

3. Quoted in Karen Smith, *Nine Lives: The Birth of Avant-Garde Art in New China* (Zurich: Scalo Verlag, 2006).

4. See Li Xianting, "Jiedu Wang Guangyi de sange jiaodu" 解读王广义的三个角度 (Three approaches to interpreting Wang Guangyi), in *Wang Guangyi* (Hong Kong: Timezone 8 Ltd., 2002), p. 60.

5. Huang Zhuan 黄专 and Pi Li 皮力, "Tuxiang jiushi liliang" 图像就是力量 (Image is power), in *Muji tuxiang de liliang: He Xiangning meishuguan zai 2002 nian* 目击图像的力量: 何香凝美术馆在 2002 年 (Witnessing the power of images: The He Xiangning Art Museum in 2002), ed. He Xiangning Art Museum (Nanning: Guangxi shifan daxue, 2003), p. 205.

6. See Huang Zhuan 黄专, introduction to *Shijue zhengzhi xue: Ling yige Wang Guangyi* 视觉政治学: 另一个王广义 (Visual politics: Another Wang Guangyi), ed. Huang Zhuan et al. (Guangzhou: Lingnan meishu, 2008), pp. 13–28. Regarding Wang Guangyi as "the most challenging contemporary artist in China," Huang

Zhuan asserts that at every turn in recent art history, the artist has come through with unexpected and stimulating questions. Through constant interrogation, Wang has formulated a unique visual politics in which historical and political resources are mobilized to enable a visual strategy and discursive intervention, rather than resorting to as an expression of political beliefs or agenda. An English translation of Huang's essay is available in Paparoni, *Wang Guangyi: Works and Thoughts*, pp. 343–55.

7. "Wang Guangyi: Wo meiyou chuangzao guo renhe dongxi" 王广义: 我没有创造过任何东西 (Wang Guangyi: I have not created anything by myself), *Nanfang zhoumo* 南方周末 (Southern weekly), November 5, 2008.

8. See Lü Peng 吕澎, "Tushi xiuzheng yu wenhua pipan" 图式修正与文化批判 (Schemata revisions and cultural critique), in Yan Shanchun 严善錞 and Lü Peng, eds., *Dangdai yishu chaoliu zhong de Wang Guangyi* 当代艺术潮流中的王广义 (Wang Guangyi in the currents of contemporary art) (Chengdu: Sichuan meishu, 1992), pp. 25–51.

9. See "Xinchao meishujia (er) Wang Guangyi" 新潮美术家 [二] 王广义 (New wave artists [2]: Wang Guangyi), *Zhongguo meishubao* 中国美术报 (Fine arts in China) 39 (September 28, 1987): 1. This issue of *Fine Arts in China* introduces Wang Guangyi as a cutting-edge artist.

10. See Yu Feng, "Wo kan 'wantong' zuopin" 我看"顽童"作品 (My view of the "daredevil's" work), *Zhongguo meishubao* 22 (December 21, 1985): 1. This issue of *Fine Arts in China* devoted most of its four pages to discussions of Rauschenberg's art and Pop art in general. One contributor cheered the Rauschenberg show as a refreshing "big joke" for the all-too-serious Chinese audience.

11. Jérôme Sans, "Wang Guangyi: A Pop Agitprop Aesthetic," in *China Talks: Interviews with 32 Contemporary Artists* by Jérôme Sans (Beijing: Timezone 8, 2009), p. 99.

12. Quotations are from "Li Xianting yu Wang Guangyi fangtan lu" (Li Xianting interviewing Wang Guangyi [2004]), in *Visual Politics: Another Wang Guangyi* pp. 78–94, esp. p. 84.

13. See Wang Guangyi, "On 'Sorting Out Humanist Passions'," pp. 317–18.

14. In a letter to a friend in 1988, Wang Guangyi made the following statement: "The existence of all cultural schemata does not mean absolute authority. We may regard them with a critical eye and then subject them to revisions. It is such acts of revision that prove the value of my existence." See Wang Guangyi, "Dui san'ge wenti de huida" 对三个问题的回答 (My answer to three questions), *Meishu* 美术 (Fine arts) 3 (1988): 57.

15. See Chang Tsong-zung, "A Politics of Engagement and Ideology of Strife," in *Wang Guangyi: The Legacy of Heroism*, ed. Susan Acret (Hong Kong: Hanart T. Z. Gallery, 2004), pp. 7–8.

16. See Huang Liaoyuan 黄燎原, "Shehui zhuyi de shijue jingyan" 社会主义的视觉经验 (The socialist visual experience), *Huasheng shidian* 华声视点 (Huasheng viewpoint) 11 (2002): 79–80.

17. See Wang Guangyi, "On 'Sorting out Humanistic Passions,'" p. 318.

18. Li Xianting, "Major Trends in the Development of Contemporary Chinese Art," *China's New Art, Post-1989* (Hong Kong: Hanart T. Z. Gallery, 1993), p. xxi. Wang Guangyi is the first artist to be introduced in the section on Political Pop, and the text in the catalogue offers a fuller description of his *Great Criticism* series: "In these works, the artist applies a deconstructionist approach to a clear language of symbols. . . . This seemingly arbitrary combination of political and commercial symbols creates a humorous and absurd effect that carries with it a biting satire of both the ideology of the Mao era and the blind craze for Western consumer products prevalent in China today, coupled with a frank delight in the silly glamour of Cultural Revolution and pop marketing images" (p. 3).

19. See Lü Peng, "Tushi xiuzheng yu wenhua pipan," pp. 50–51.

20. Gao Minglu, "Toward a Transnational Modernity: An Overview of *Inside Out: New Chinese Art*," in *Inside Out: New Chinese Art*, ed. Gao Minglu (Berkeley: University of California Press, 1998), pp. 29–30.

21. Gao Minglu, "From Elite to Small Man: The Many Faces of a Transitional Avant-Garde in Mainland China," in *Inside Out: New Chinese Art*, ed. Gao Minglu (Berkeley: University of California Press, 1998), p. 153. Here Gao offers a closer reading of *Great Criticism*: "The paintings are meant to show that though the two systems (political and commercial) are not united, the principal goal of each is to convince the population of the authenticity and singularity of its products. . . . Wang Guangyi's painting became a kitsch advertisement of an advertisement, and he himself became a producer of commodities instead of a preacher" (pp. 152–53).

22. Norman Bryson, "The Post Ideological Avant-Garde," in *Inside Out: New Chinese Art*, ed. Gao Minglu (Berkeley: University of California Press, 1998), pp. 52–53.

23. See "Zouxiang zhenshi de shenghuo" 走向真实的生活 (Toward a true life), *Beijing qingnian bao* 北京青年报 (Beijing youth daily), March 22, 1991, p. 6.

24. Known as the "May 16 Circular," the document, adopted by the Central Committee of the Chinese Communist Party under Mao's leadership in 1966, was not published in the *People's Daily* until May 16, 1967, by which time the Cultural Revolution had entered its most violent stage. The principal arguments and decisions contained in the circular were made public on June 1, 1966, in a *People's Daily* editorial titled "Sweep Away All Monsters and Enemies," which is widely regarded as the opening call for the Cultural Revolution across the nation. For the text of the "May 16 Circular" (in Chinese), see www.baike.baidu.com/view/136043.htm (accessed October 5, 2015). For an English translation of this historic document, see Harold C. Hinton, ed., *The People's Republic of China, 1949-1979: A Documentary Survey* (Wilmington, DE: Scholarly Resources, 1980), vol. 3, pp. 1508–11.

25. Arif Dirlik, "Socialism without Revolution: The Case of Contemporary China," *Pacific Affairs* 54, no. 4 (1981–82): 632–61, reprinted in Dirlik, "Back to the Future: Contemporary China in the Perspective of Its Past, circa 1980," in *China and New Left Visions: Political and Cultural Interventions*, ed. Ban Wang and Jie Lu (Lanham, MD: Lexington Books, 2012), pp. 3–42. The quote here is from p. 5.

26. See Julia F. Andrews, *Painters and Politics in the People's Republic of China, 1949–1979* (Berkeley: University of California Press, 1994), pp. 314–42, for a useful account of the Red Guard movement and Red Guard art in Beijing.

27. In his classic study, Peter Bürger argues that the central imperative of the avant-garde movements in early twentieth-century Europe was to deinstitutionalize artistic autonomy and return art to the praxis of life. See Bürger, *Theory of the Avant-Garde*, trans. Michael Shaw (Minneapolis: University of Minnesota Press, 1984).

28. See Wang Mingxian, "The Red Guards' Fine Arts Campaign," in *Art and China's Revolution,* ed. Melissa Chiu and Zheng Shengtian, pp. 187–98 (New York: Asia Society, New Haven, CT: Yale University Press, 2008). For a much more detailed and extended version of the essay in Chinese, see Wang Mingxian, "Hongweibing meishu yundong ji dui dangdai yishu de yingxiang" 红卫兵美术运动及对当代艺术的影响 (The Red Guard art movement and its impact on contemporary art), *Yishu tansuo* 艺术探索 (Art exploration: Journal of Guangxi Arts College) 19, no. 2 (2005): 32–40.

29. See Xu Bing 徐冰, "Ignorance as a Kind of Nourishment," in *Xu Bing Prints,* ed. An Su (Beijing: Wenhua yishu, 2010), pp. 220–37, quotation on p. 237. For the original Chinese text, see "Yumei zuowei yizhong yangliao" (愚昧作为一种养料) in the same volume, pp. 206–18.

30. Zheng Shengtian, "Art and Revolution: Looking Back at Thirty Years of History," in *Art and China's Revolution,* p. 39.

31. See Richard King and Jan Walls, "Introduction: Vibrant Images of a Turbulent Decade," in *Art in Turmoil: The Chinese Cultural Revolution, 1966–1976*, ed. Richard King, with Ralph Croizier, Shengtian Zheng, and Scott Watson (Vancouver: University of British Columbia Press, 2010), pp. 3–24, for a succinct narrative of art and art making during the Cultural Revolution.

32. Quoted in Wang Mingxian, "Hongweibing meishu yundong," p. 37.

33. Quoted in Wang Mingxian and Yan Shanchun, *Xin Zhongguo meishu tushi 1966–1976* 新中国美术图史 1966–1976 (An illustrated art history of New China 1966–1976) (Beijing: Zhongguo qingnian, 2000), p. 13.

34. For an introduction to this painting and an interview with its creator, see Melissa Chiu and Zheng Shengtian, *Art and China's Revolution* pp. 119–32.

35. For a recent account of Huxian peasant painting and its contemporary development, see Ralph Croizier, "Hu Xian Peasant Painting: From Revolutionary Icon to Market Commodity," in *Art in Turmoil: The Chinese Cultural Revolution, 1966–1976*, ed. Richard King, with Ralph Croizier, Shengtian Zheng, and Scott Watson (Vancouver: University of British Columbia Press, 2010), pp. 136–63.

36. An excellent resource for the study of visual culture in contemporary China is the website Chineseposters.net, supported by the International Institute of Social History, in Amsterdam.

37. Jacques Rancière, "Ten Theses on Politics," in his *Dissensus: On Politics and Aesthetics*, ed. and trans. Steven Corcoran (New York: Continuum, 2010), p. 39.

38. Charles Merewether, "An Interview with Wang Guangyi on the Socialist Visual Experience," in *Wang Guangyi* (Hong Kong: Timezone 8 Ltd., 2002), p. 28. Both the English and Chinese versions of the interview are included in this volume (pp. 26–35 and 50–57, respectively), with the English translation provided by Robert Bernell, but there are some discrepancies between them. I have opted to translate

Wang Guangyi's comments from the Chinese version. The English text is also included in Paparoni, *Wang Guangyi: Works and Thoughts,* pp. 319–25.

39. Merewether, "An Interview with Wang Guangyi," pp. 29–33.

40. Ibid., p. 31. For photos of this installation, see Paparoni, *Wang Guangyi: Works and Thoughts,* pp. 206–9.

41. Merewether, "An Interview with Wang Guangyi," p. 35.

42. See "Chongxin jiedu: Zhongguo shiyan yishu shinian" 重新解读: 中国实验艺术十年 (Rereading: Ten years of experimental art in China), *Beijing qingnian bao,* November 28, 2002.

43. Merewether, "An Interview with Wang Guangyi," p. 35. For a useful reading of Wang Guangyi's millet-covered sculptures, see Shu Kewen 舒可文, "Wang Guangyi de xiaomi weiwu zhuyi" 王广义的小米唯物主义 (The millet materialism of Wang Guangyi), in *Shijue zhengzhi xue: Ling yige Wang Guangyi* (Visual politics: Another Wang Guangyi), ed. Huang Zhuan et al. (Guangzhou: Lingnan meishu, 2008), pp. 286–88.

44. See Huang Liaoyuan, "Shehui zhuyi de shijue jingyan."

45. See "Li Xianting yu Wang Guangyi fangtan lu," p. 94.

46. Ibid.

47. "Faxian 'Lengzhan' zhi mei" 发现"冷战"之美 (Discovering the beauty of the "Cold War"), *Guangzhou ribao* 广州日报 (Guangzhou daily), December 29, 2007.

48. See "Yishu yu jinqian" 艺术与金钱 (Art and money), in *Yishu yu shichang* 艺术与市场 (Art and the market) 1 (Changsha: Hunan meishu, 1991): 3–4.

49. See "Wang Guangyi: Wo meiyou chuangzao guo renhe dongxi."

50. Sans, "Wang Guangyi: A Pop Agitprop Aesthetic," p. 103. For an introduction (by Sara Boggio) to this installation work and photographs, see Paparoni, *Wang Guangyi: Works and Thoughts,* pp. 262–77.

51. Sans, "Wang Guangyi: A Pop Agitprop Aesthetic," pp. 100–101.

PART 3
Red Classics

FIVE

PERFORMING THE "RED CLASSICS"

From *The East Is Red* to *The Road to Revival*

Xiaomei Chen

This chapter examines three "grand revolutionary music and dance epics" (*daxing geming yinyue wudao shishi* 大型革命音乐舞蹈史诗) created and performed from 1964 to 2009. Placing the first, *The East Is Red* (*Dongfang hong* 东方红), in the broader context of the international socialist movement, one can see it as dramatizing Mao Zedong's concern with the possibility that China might undergo a peaceful evolution from socialism to capitalism, an idea that emerged as a result of Khrushchev's denunciation of Stalin in 1956. Mao's rebuttal to Khrushchev's revisionist theories—which foresaw, for example, "peaceful coexistence and peaceful competition with the Western capitalist world, and a peaceful transition to a new world order without war" (*heping gongchu*, *heping jingsai*, *heping guodu* 和平共处, 和平竞赛, 和平过渡)—took shape as a call to "never forget class struggle." This summons inspired the creation, in the mid-1960s, of numerous "red classics" in fiction, poetry, music, drama, and film. Concerned about John Foster Dulles's prediction that a peaceful evolution to capitalism would occur in socialist countries and among the third and fourth generations of Communists in the socialist bloc (a prediction that would be manifested, astonishingly, in the fall of the Berlin Wall in 1989), Mao became increasingly worried about "capitalist tendencies" in some areas of socialist China, so much so that he resorted to the chaotic Cultural Revolution as the ultimate means of establishing a proletarian dictatorship.[1] Mao conceived of the Cultural Revolution as a perpetual insurrection aimed at countering "the many representatives of the bourgeoisie and counterrevolutionary revisionists" who had "sneaked into the party, the government, the army, and cultural circles."[2] In this way, he believed he would prevent China from regressing to a capitalist society in which poor people would have to suffer "bitterness" once again, for the second time (*shou er bian ku, zao er cha zui* 受二遍苦, 遭二碴罪), as they had "before liberation." The theme of *The East Is Red*, therefore, became that of the earliest "model theater," emphasizing the need for a continuing revolution to ensure that the socialist revolution would never "change its color from red to black." Subsequent model Peking operas, such as *The Song of the Longjiang River* and *The Seaport*, took up this same theme.[3]

Although claiming to be a "sister epic" to *The East Is Red*, *The Song of the Chinese Revolution* (*Zhongguo geming zhi ge* 中国革命之歌), which premiered in 1984, challenged the earlier one-sided narrative of CCP history, as it incorporated new research on the party's history in early post-Mao China. While presenting familiar revolutionary events, *The Song* contextualized Mao's "red legend" in light of Deng Xiaoping's "gray legend." Whereas the red legend refers to Mao's socialist revolution, which saw the capitalist free world as the archenemy in Cold War terms, the gray legend refers to Deng's semisocialist or even pseudosocialist ideology that was neither black nor white, as defined by Deng's own famous saying in the 1960s: "Black cat or white cat? It is only a good cat if it catches a mouse." Deng's practical approach subsequently led to his definition of China as "a socialist country with Chinese characteristics," or a "gray" socialist China with a capitalist market economy in many key sectors. *The Song* premiered in the 1980s, when Mao's legend had become both heritage and liability for the Deng regime, paving the way for Deng's revisionist approach to socialist China. This political shift—in the real-life experience of contemporary China in the 1980s and in its theatrical representation in *The Song*—created what Mao would have called "reactionary ideological groundwork" (*fan geming yulun zhunbei* 反革命舆论准备) for Deng Xiaoping's capitalist restoration, which in fact Mao had accused Deng and Liu Shaoqi of attempting during the Cultural Revolution.

The 2009 performance of *The Road to Revival* (*Fuxing zhi lu* 复兴之路) departed even further from the earlier two by congratulating the magnificent success of the Dengist regime and its capitalist approach, designed to rescue China from a disastrous past and set it on the road to modernity and prosperity. Justifying Deng's drive toward capitalism with "Chinese socialist characteristics," *The Road* demonstrates the power of the revolutionary epic performance to rewrite the red legend for the purpose of hailing a capitalist China. It accomplished this by using and manipulating the historical narrative, political orientations, popular stars and cultures, and nationalistic sentiment. These shifting, complex, and contradictory elements formed a new red legend for contemporary China, which remained "red" merely in name. Indeed, the legend now featured a "gray" approach, as seen in *The Song*, that could be situated between the red (socialist) and black (capitalist) approaches. (The black approach can be seen in *The Road*.) The crucial difference between the gray and black approaches in the last two epics, however, resides in *The Song*'s praise of the early success of a China amid reform and the signs of a promising future, in contrast to *The Road*'s lavish celebration of a grand capitalist reality in the twenty-first century as the sole alternative for China if it wanted to remain prosperous. Although both approaches maintained that they functioned effectively in the name of the red legend, the original meaning of the phrase suggests that only *The East Is Red* could truly lay claim to that label.

The East Is Red

Since its premiere in Beijing on October 2, 1964, under the close supervision of the state premiere, Zhou Enlai, the grand revolutionary music and dance epic *The East Is Red* has enjoyed unwavering popularity throughout the past half century. This became all the more evident in 2004, when it was revived to honor the PRC'S fifty-fifth anniversary. Its integral connection to political theater in general, however, was clear from its beginning in 1964. I have examined elsewhere the popular reception and numerous imitations of the epic from the 1960s on, and the intercultural connections between this first PRC music-and-dance epic and the North Korean socialist cult of Kim Il Sung and its performance tradition, which inspired the conception of *The East Is Red* in the first place. I have also examined the political and social environments of socialist China in the 1960s that necessitated this new performance genre.[4] Transformed from a local concert known as *The Spring of Shanghai: A Singing Event by the Masses* (*Shanghai zhichun qunzhong geyong dahui* 上海之春群众歌咏大会) to a variety show entitled *Performing Revolutionary History Songs* (*Geming lishi gequ biaoyan chang* 革命历史歌曲表演唱), *The East Is Red* finally evolved into a grand spectacle used to celebrate the fifteenth anniversary of the PRC's rise to power, and this last incarnation played a significant role in constructing a Mao cult during the Cultural Revolution. In post-Mao China, its signature songs continued to be featured in the programs of annual concerts celebrating the birth of the party, the army, and the nation, and even in the amateur performances of retirees and ordinary citizens in parks, on which occasions the songs gave voice to a nostalgia for a bygone Maoist society they remembered as characterized by equality, fairness, and idealism. The 2003 documentary about the Cultural Revolution, *Morning Sun*, introduced *The East Is Red* in university classrooms throughout the United States and Europe, depicting it as a central piece of socialist performance art that had an impact on Maoist youth and fueled their idealist pursuits even beyond the Maoist era.

For the historical and ideological context of the two later works, *The Song* and *The Road*, it is useful to reflect on the creative process that *The East Is Red* availed itself of, especially Premier Zhou Enlai's role in organizing top artists and performers to collaborate in staging this grand performance. Zhou was concerned above all with how to present the three episodes in *The East Is Red* that best memorialize Mao's irreplaceable role—that is, the founding of the CCP in 1921, the Autumn Harvest Uprising in 1927, and the Zunyi meeting during the Long March in 1935, which secured Mao's leadership of the CCP.[5] Recent scholarship reveals that Zhou Enlai himself had suggested using, in the "Dawn in the East" scene, the two flags that juxtaposed the image of Mao with those of Marx and Lenin, thereby implanting Mao as the founding father of the CCP, which is actually a distortion of the founding history.[6] To emphasize Mao's peerless leadership, Zhou further instructed the writers to add to the scene of several CCP martyrs walking toward the Nationalist Party, or Kuomintang (KMT), execution ground, a narrative partially blaming Chen Duxiu's appeasement of the KMT reactionaries for the failure of the 1927 revolution. Even though Chiang Kai-shek was "the external factor" responsible for the KMT massacre of CCP members on April 12, 1927, Chen would be depicted as "the internal factor," meaning he could have put together an effective response from the CCP had he not been so hamstrung by his appeasement policy and by his blind trust in the KMT reactionaries. Zhou believed that this "historical lesson stained with the blood of the CCP martyrs" that targeted Chen as a responsible party would help the Chinese people appreciate the way Mao's "correct line" had steered the revolution to victory and at the same time would teach "international socialist and Communist movements" that they must never make any concessions to their class enemies.[7]

Ironically, in the process of reinforcing Mao's authority, Zhou erased his own role in early party history. An earlier script of *The East Is Red*, for instance, displayed a flag of the "Nanchang Uprising Troops" in the scene depicting the first CCP military base in the Jinggang Mountains; to the producers, it would have been only natural to present the Nanchang Uprising, the CCP's first military action against the KMT, as having been led by Zhou Enlai, He Long, and others. Yet Zhou had suggested replacing this flag with that of the "Chinese Workers and Peasant Red Army" in order to emphasize the importance of the Autumn Harvest Uprising, led by Mao in September 1927, over that of the Nanchang Uprising more than a month earlier.[8] Accordingly, *The East Is Red* added a scene entitled "The Spark That Sets a Prairie Afire" ("Xinghuo liaoyuan" 星火燎原), in which a solo dancer introduces several groups of dancers as fire torches and red flags appear gradually on stage to signify Zhou's idea that "armed struggles in sync with Mao's correct military thoughts . . . survived and flourished; . . . those that were not, inevitably failed."[9]

The same impulse no doubt led Zhou to insist on creating a separate scene for the Zunyi meeting, which showed Mao taking over as CCP chief and about to lead the Long March to victory.[10] The writers and producers at first hesitated to stage such a meeting and circumvented the suggestion by presenting a dance and song they called "Ten Verses of Farewell to the Red Army" ("Shi song hongjun" 十送红军), a deeply moving scene of local peasants of the Jiangxi Soviet area sadly seeing off the Red Army soldiers about to depart on the Long March. Although touched by the scene, Zhou thought it was unrealistic because the Red Army retreated in a great hurry after being encircled and outnumbered by KMT troops; the Long March had evidently neither been planned nor announced to the Red Army commanders and soldiers. Zhou continued to believe that the epic would do well to focus on the Zunyi meeting, the significance of which lay in establishing Mao's "correct leadership" in party history.[11] Eventually the writers and producers came up with a dance and song called "The Red Army Soldiers Miss Mao Zedong"

("Hongjun zhanshi xiangnian Mao Zedong" 红军战士想念毛泽东), which conveyed the soldiers' and local people's longing for Mao in a moment of crisis. When the image of the two-story building where the Zunyi meeting was held was projected onto the background screen and then turned into a huge red flag with Mao's image in the center, audiences in the 1960s would often burst into loud applause, even though Zhou himself thought it was indeed "unrealistic" (p. 6). While it was unlikely that the soldiers and local people would have heard of the meeting at the time, or have understood its significance, "Mao's correct line had wide and deep roots among the people" and represented the "best interests of the people," Zhou explained, and he therefore accepted the scene as a combination of "revolutionary realism [*geming de xianshi zhuyi* 革命的现实主义] with revolutionary romanticism [*geming de langman zhuyi* 革命的浪漫主义]." Moreover, here was an instance in which a state leader, frequently eulogized for his love of theater and for protecting theater artists in PRC literary and cultural histories, managed to manipulate the "principles of proletarian art" in order to create a party history textbook, precisely because he appreciated and understood the dynamics of performance art.

Taking the dramatic plots of this epic performance seriously as records of the real historical past, Zhou laid out the framework to portray five wars, each illustrating the "victory of Mao Zedong Thought" during "different stages of the Chinese Revolution": the Northern Expedition, the "land reform revolution" (*tudi geming* 土地革命), the War of Resistance against Japanese Aggression, the War of Liberation, and the War to Resist U.S. Aggression and Aid Korea. Singling out Chen Duxiu again as the one who had failed to understand the significance of armed struggle during the Northern Expedition, Zhou Enlai praised Mao for his military strategy manifested during his lectures at the Guangzhou Peasant Training School (Nongmin yundong jiangxi suo 农民运动讲习所) and for his organization of worker and peasant troops while leading the Anyuan Workers' Strike (Anyuan gongren yundong 安源工人运动) with Liu Shaoqi; part of the Anyuan workers' group later joined forces with Mao's Autumn Harvest Uprising troops in the Jinggang Mountains (p. 7). During a rehearsal, Zhou was especially stirred when hearing the popular songs from the Northern Expedition section and could not help but sing along. To make sure that the epic cast Mao and the party in the best possible light, Zhou suggested revising the episode in which a couple of rich landlords were being denounced and paraded on stage as enemies of the people; we should not, he explained, give the impression that they would subsequently be executed, because very few landlords were killed when Mao led the Hunan peasant movement.[12] Thus Zhou saw to it that every detail and every episode "faithfully" and "undeviatingly reflected history"; in doing this, Zhou misrepresented history to cast Mao in a favorable light.

When Zhou Enlai was unsure about how to make a particular episode accord with the "historical truth," he sought Mao's and Liu Shaoqi's advice. The writers and producers wondered, for example, if they should mention the Fourth Division of the Red Army (*Hong di si fangmian jun* 红第四方面军) headed by Zhang Guotao 张国涛 under very difficult circumstances. Known in the official history as a "leftist separatist" who plotted to break away from Mao's main forces and establish his own CCP Central Committee, Zhang finally defected to the KMT side in 1938, after years of positions of leadership in the CCP cause.[13]

Zhou Enlai received Mao's clear instructions: in spite of Zhang Guotao's betrayal, the majority of the Fourth Division's commanders and soldiers had followed the "correct lines" of the CCP and made their own contributions and sacrifices. *The East Is Red* was to honor all the Red Army troops by staging the scenes "Capturing Luding River Bridge with Flying Colors," to portray the First Division; "Marching through the Yi Minority Area," to show off the Second Division; and "Crossing the Marshland," to give the Fourth Division its due. The epic also displayed the Fourth Division's flag, along with those of the First and Second Divisions, to symbolize their joining of forces at the end of the Long March, and to further ensure equal treatment of all forces involved, the same numbers of soldiers appeared for each division. As Mao's personal representative, Zhou had welcomed the Second and Fourth Divisions on their arrival in northern Shaanxi and thus felt confident editing and approving "The Song of Joining Forces [*huishi ge* 会师歌]," which "accurately reflected the historic event."[14] So here we have a survivor validating historical "truth," thanks to Zhou's privileged position as state head and his passion for the theatrical arts.

Zhou Enlai also had a role in alleviating some of the difficulties surrounding controversial events in the PRC's early history. Addressing the epic's directing group on the subject of its film adaptation, for example, Zhou spoke about eliminating the last two acts portraying events after

1949, namely, the "War to Resist U.S. Aggression and Aid Korea" and "The Call to Unite the Oppressed Peoples of the World to Resist Imperialism, Revisionism, and Reactionaries."[15] After seeing *The East Is Red*, Mao had suggested limiting the history to 1949.[16] He instructed that the film adaptation be part one of *The East Is Red*; part two could cover post-1949 events and be premiered in 1969 to coincide with the commemoration of the twentieth anniversary of the PRC's founding, a plan that would never be realized because the Cultural Revolution began in 1966 (p. 10). Mao's words brought Zhou a sense of relief, since "it was now easier to portray the problematic issues of reconciling the 'United Front' [*tongyi zhanxian* 统一战线] with the other democratic parties" when the epic ended with the "period of democratic revolution" (*minzhu geming jieduan* 民主革命阶段) before 1949. Prior to the PRC's founding, the CCP had allied with the leaders of other political parties. Zhou was perhaps aware of the rapidly diminishing role of the "democratic parties" (*minzhu dangpai* 民主党派) in the early 1950s, especially after the unpopular political campaign of 1957 targeting "antiparty Rightists"; some of those Rightists were "democratic [party] VIPs" (*minzhu renshi* 民主人士) who were silenced for criticizing the one-party system and its inevitable corruption. Now Zhou Enlai could sidestep the thorny issue of depicting a consistent United Front policy.[17] However, the once promising vision of—and fruitful political consultations with—the non-CCP leaders dedicated to "establishing a free, democratic, New China" (*zhengzhi xieshang, minzhu jianguo* 政治协商, 民主建国) surfaced in the 1984 revolutionary epic *The Song of the Chinese Revolution*.

All these developments imbued *The East Is Red* with the status of a red classic. Presented in a massive, effective theatrical form, it became the standard narrative of the party's revolutionary history, reflecting as it did the most recent dramatic twists and turns taken to revise the revolutionary past so that audiences would be schooled in the political correctness of the red legend. Bringing together all the major performers of the 1960s in song, music, dance, poetry recitations, and dramatic skits, and at the same time melding traditions of socialist realism, revolutionary romanticism, Western orchestral music, and Chinese folk and mass cultures, the epic, now in video and DVD form, has helped preserve a host of Maoist memories in contemporary China. Finally, the enterprise offers us a quintessential example of the passionate, sublime Maoist culture in terms of both its intimate relationship to everyday life and its mega-theatrical scale, rarely seen in other cultures except, to some extent, North Korea.[18] The film adaption of *The East Is Red*, released one year later, on October 1, 1965, to commemorate the sixteenth anniversary of the PRC's founding, opened on the eve of the Cultural Revolution, which would reject almost all prior literary and artistic creations, including post-1949 works, as a feudalist, capitalist, and revisionist black line (*feng, zi, xiu wenyi heixian* 封,资,修文艺黑线). *The East Is Red* can therefore be seen as a "lustrous, perfect coda to the seventeen years of PRC art before the Cultural Revolution," a period whose spirit and achievements are acclaimed in the twenty-first century as part of the red legacy of socialist art.[19]

Song of the Chinese Revolution

In 1984 a "sister show" of *The East Is Red*, entitled *The Song of the Chinese Revolution*, premiered to celebrate the thirty-fifth anniversary of the PRC's founding. Employing a similar organizational structure and similar direction by prominent art leaders, such as Zhou Weichi, a veteran of *The East Is Red*, *The Song* claimed to have followed the red-classic model in representing the Chinese Revolution with a music-and-dance epic, employing a cast of 1,500 artists from sixty performance groups, but it also strove to surpass its precursor, aided by a new angle on the material and an updated perspective on the past and recent developments.[20] *The Song* was praised for its dedicated cast, having produced a second revolutionary epic during the reform era when many actors and actresses had already abandoned the stage for more lucrative careers. The cast's challenge had been to make do with a much smaller production crew. Nonetheless, a sufficient number of artists and logistics staff had come on board from *The East Is Red* production some twenty years earlier. Many felt lucky to have survived the traumatic Cultural Revolution, when theater personnel in particular were persecuted for acting out "revisionist" and "counterrevolutionary" roles, and they were intent on weathering the current demanding times by creating a new red legend that would appeal to the younger audiences in contemporary China.[21]

Like its predecessor, *The Song* was inspired by a North Korean epic, in this case *The Song of Glory* (*Guangrong zhi ge* 光荣之歌), which, with its cast of five thousand, caught the attention of Deng Xiaoping and Hu

Yaobang 胡耀帮 during their 1982 state visit to North Korea.[22] Dedicated to Kim Il Sung on the occasion of his seventieth birthday, and produced under the personal supervision of his son, Kim Jong Il, who had considerable interest and expertise in the performing arts, *The Song of Glory* inherited the tradition of its own predecessor, *Three Thousand Miles of Motherland*, which had been the original inspiration for *The East Is Red*. Deng Xiaoping praised the Korean epic as "a vivid, visual textbook of the party's history." During his stay in North Korea, Deng declared, "We also have *The East Is Red*, which should be revised to commemorate Mao's ninetieth birthday."[23] Thus the North Korean and Chinese epics of the 1980s both celebrated the birthdays of their singular leaders, which marked a departure from their predecessors, *Three Thousand Miles of Motherland* and *The East Is Red*, which had commemorated the birth of their respective nations.

Following the example of Zhou Enlai's role in scripting *The East Is Red*, the second generation of party leaders also initiated and controlled the state production of this second epic. The secretariat of the Central Committee (*zhongyang shujichu* 中央书记处), for example, released an official directive in October 1982 to entrust the Department of Propaganda with the task of producing *The Song* as an updated version of *The East Is Red*. The new epic should borrow from its predecessor, the directive pointed out, but might want to expand the party's history from the May Fourth Movement to the new era of reform, to the successful conclusion of the Twelfth Party Congress.[24] The scriptwriters went through five different outlines and four draft scripts, all with the approval of the secretariat of the Central Committee.[25] Hu Yaobang, the general secretary of the Central Committee, passionately supported the new epic, even trying his hand at outlining its basic structure of eight episodes. The scriptwriters took this outline into account but did not end up using it, since they did not want to repeat the chronological order of *The East Is Red*.

In confronting the fundamental issues of how to select historical episodes, however, *The Song* followed its predecessor in skipping over problematic periods and policies since the late 1950s. After painstaking efforts and lengthy debates on how best to present a long and complex party history in two and one-half hours onstage, the scriptwriters finally came up with a much more condensed structure of five acts, with a prologue and an epilogue. Act 1 dramatizes more than one hundred years of Western imperialist history, especially the burning down of the Yuanming Yuan, the old summer palace, in 1900 by the Eight-Power Allied Forces, and the May Fourth Movement in 1919, and ending with the founding of the CCP in 1921 (see Chapter 1 in this volume, on the museumification of the First Party Congress). Act 2 covers the Northern Expedition, the tragic KMT/CCP split in 1927, the Nanchang Uprising, and the Autumn Harvest Uprising that led to the establishment of the Soviet government in the Jinggang Mountains. Act 3 combines the Long March, the War of Resistance against Japanese Aggression, and the War of Liberation into one coherent dramatic piece. Act 4 moves quickly from the PRC's founding in 1949 to the "smashing of the Gang of Four" in 1976.

These condensed acts left ample time to stage the lavish celebration of four short years in act 5: from 1978, when the Third Plenary Session of the Eleventh Party Congress passed its historic document to sort out Mao's achievements and mistakes and to shift the party's central task from class struggle to economic development, to 1982, when the Twelfth Party Congress convened. This crowning event received a second blessing in the epilogue, in which a grand chorus eulogizes "our motherland" marching toward "a new era," while documentary film clips projected on the background screen display images of party leaders attending the Twelfth Party Congress. *The Song* finally closes with the smiling face of Deng Xiaoping as the rising sun emerges from the ocean's horizon, an amazing imitation of the familiar image of Mao at the end of *The East Is Red*. *The Song* therefore promotes Deng as Mao's best successor, who began to realize Mao's dreams by correcting his errors, thus becoming a greater leader than the "greatest leader" of the past era.

Hu Qiaomu 胡乔木, known as the "number one cultural leader" (*touhao wenhua shouzhang* 头号文化首长) and an authority on CCP documents and history, carefully went over the entire script of *The Song* to make sure it "accurately" reflected past revolutionary events, in the same spirit as Zhou Enlai.[26] In doing so, however, Hu Qiaomu restored Zhou's historic role in *The Song*, which Zhou himself had denied in *The East Is Red*. Hu pointed out, for example, that in the scene depicting the Nanchang Uprising of 1927, the correct order of appearances onstage should be Zhou Enlai, Ye Jianying, He Long, and Zhu De, a directive that subsequent scripts and productions faithfully followed.[27] Nevertheless, the final production of *The Song* did not follow Hu's suggestion to have Qu Qiubai's character appear onstage before the scene of the Nanchang Uprising, in order to honor Qu's critical role in presiding over the August 7 Meeting (*ba qi huiyi* 八七会议), which had called for CCP uprisings against the KMT in 1927. It might have been too sensitive for the early post-Mao audiences to see the dramatic character of Qu, when his image as a traitor was still well known.

Nevertheless, Hu Qiaomu's intervention did shape the epic's narrative to some extent: the mere reference to the meeting as background information in the script indicated that Mao's leadership of the Autumn Harvest Uprising was the result of following Qu's directives to wage "armed struggles" as the new direction for the Chinese Revolution, a point impossible to make at the time *The East Is Red* was scripted, when Qu was still labeled as "a leftist opportunist."[28] When Mao appeared in person as a dramatic character in *The Song*—which did not happen in *The East Is Red*—he was anxious to look for the troops of Zhu De and Chen Yi, who had led their own uprisings and were on their way to join forces with Mao in the Jinggang Mountains, an image quite different from his dominant status in *The East Is Red*, which depicts him as the only leader. The stage directions in *The Song* point out several rural Soviet areas established in various parts of southern China that collectively achieved the goal of "the rural areas encircling the urban areas," which previous party histories—as well as *The East Is Red*—had attributed solely to Mao's so-called correct policies.

Even though Hu Qiaomu acted in a capacity comparable to that of Zhou Enlai in deciding how to represent the correct revolutionary past, in early post-Mao China Hu used his political capital to restore the neglected and misrepresented episodes and leaders. In his new capacity as Deng Xiaoping's secretary, Hu played a key role in revising party history to facilitate the legitimacy of Deng's regime and to build a theoretical basis for the otherwise difficult transition from the Maoist to the reform era. He successfully presided over the drafting of historic documents such as the party's "Resolution on Certain Questions in the History of Our Party since the Founding of the PRC," passed at the Sixth Plenum of the Eleventh Party Congress in 1981, which criticized Mao's Anti-Rightist Movement of 1957 and the Great Leap Forward of 1958. It also criticized Mao as "the person most responsible for launching the Cultural Revolution," which "had brought about tremendous disasters for the party, the country, and people of all ethnic groups" with his "over-emphasis on class struggle" and the unfounded theory of "continuing revolution under the dictatorship of the proletariat."[29]

In an interesting paradox, *The Song* essentially advocated a peaceful evolution from Mao's socialist revolution to Deng's "capitalist restoration," the very ideological mission *The East Is Red* battled against. How did *The Song* present a coherent history from socialism to the beginning of capitalism while still claiming to uphold the spirit of the red classic? The answer lies, first, in the paradoxical and complex role of the Dengist regime, which adhered to Mao's red legend of having established a socialist system after hard-won revolutionary wars, as portrayed in all three epics; the revolutionary past legitimized the CCP's absolute power in continuing a one-party system against any ideological deviations from the socialist norms, while pushing for semicapitalist economic reforms to build up China's economic and military power. The two epics therefore selectively celebrated "a better life and a stronger China" to boost national pride while dismissing the sensitive issues such as political reform, human rights, dissidents, environmental damage, and other thorny problems resulting from modernization. Second, cultural leaders in the Dengist regime, as well as in the Jiang Zemin regime after Deng's retirement in 1990, tapped into the rich resources of performance art to intervene, reshape, juxtapose, and complicate contradictory narratives, which were seamlessly merged and transformed into spectacles, body movements, and musical and theatrical elements that helped present "common ground" while whitewashing contradictions in political or public discourses.

Unlike *The East Is Red*, which confined the dramatic events to "the glorious twenty-seven years of party history" from 1921 to 1949, *The Song* expanded its historical scope to cover events from 1840 to 1984. It starts with a prologue, entitled "The Morning Melody of the Motherland" (*zuguo chen qu* 祖国晨曲), a spectacular scene designed to celebrate the magnificent reform era after the death of Mao, in sharp contrast to *The East Is Red*, which begins with sunflower dancers eulogizing the brilliant sun of Mao Zedong Thought (plate 15). The morning sun now allegorizes not Mao but the beginning of a new era in which hope for prosperity would not be possible without rejecting Mao's mistakes. As the solemn, graceful music is played by an ancient bell instrument, the 200-member chorus, accompanied by an orchestra of 130 musicians, lauds "a new generation that has created a new heaven and earth," "singing the morning song as brilliant as our nation," where "the great earth smiles" and "the universe blooms with life and vitality."[30] The ancient music from the bell instrument testifies to an emerging post-Mao intellectual discourse, which explores the ancient glories to appreciate them in light of today's successes (plate 16). At the end of this prologue, the curtains are drawn closed from both sides of the stage to form the background for a projected image of sculptures of revolutionary martyrs, analogous to those displayed in revolutionary museums. At one corner of the stage, a group of young people walk up to present flowers to those past martyrs who sacrificed their lives for the nation's present happiness.[31] From the vantage point of China in 1984, the epic travels back in time to illustrate how the reform era had indeed surpassed all previous historical periods. The nation-state in its modern glory has replaced the first epic's cult of Mao, but the grand leaders and their devoted martyrs still loom large on the stage as the inspirational source for a flourishing, contemporary China and, most important, to validate its legitimacy as the worthy successor of the Maoist legacy.

Unlike *The East Is Red*, which portrayed the KMT regime as "the old society cast in darkness" in order to praise the CCP cause, *The Song* pays equal tribute to all those who sacrificed their lives in the Opium Wars, the Taiping Rebellion, the Boxer Rebellion, and the 1911 Revolution.[32] *The Song*'s deviations from its predecessor, however, can be easily supported by Mao's own inscriptions on the Monument to the People's Heroes in Tiananmen Square, which commemorates those martyrs who had died for freedom and national sovereignty since 1884. The CCP movement thus became a part of a larger modern revolutionary history rather than constituting the only revolutionary history in China. When the dramatizations of the CCP/ KMT wars do appear (and these follow the parallel depictions in its predecessor), *The Song* reduces them to two acts, in contrast to the six acts in *The East Is Red*, thus leaving sufficient theatrical time to stage the post-1949 events with a focus on the "real" achievements of socialist China, made possible only after Mao's death.

Within its abbreviated representation of CCP history before 1949, *The Song* nevertheless pays equal attention to the significant contributions of other seminal leaders not affiliated with the CCP cause, such as Sun Yat-sen, the pioneering and visionary leader of the 1911 Revolution and the founding father of the KMT (p. 138). For example, act 1, entitled "From the May Fourth Movement to the Founding of the CCP" ("Wusi yundong dao jiandang" 五四运动到建党) stages the May Fourth Movement, in which young students from Peking University demanded "democracy" and "science" in an effort to "smash the old world" and herald "a new era of China's rise as a strong and modern nation," a dream that came true only belatedly in post-Mao China, as *The Song* implicitly suggests (p. 139). Ironically, however, the energetic, modern-style dance of the university students marching forward against police violence can be seen as foreshadowing the brutal suppression of student demonstrations in Tiananmen Square in 1989, when students expressed a similar demand for democracy against the corrupt government.

Unlike the first epic, which eulogized Mao as the only supreme leader, the second half of act 1 of *The Song* features various groups of early Communists, with a rotating stage presenting Zhou Enlai with his overseas student group in Paris; Li Dazhao with his disciples in Beijing; Mao Zedong with his friends reading his journal, the *Xiang River Review,* in Hunan; and Dong Biwu with his socialist activists in Wuhan. Most strikingly, act 1 ends with the dashing image of Liu Shaoqi, standing bravely in front of a moving locomotive surrounded by railway workers, in a close-up shot that moves rapidly toward the audience on the background screen (p. 35). The appearance of Liu Shaoqi highlights his early contributions to CCP history in organizing workers' strikes as well as his tragic death during the Cultural Revolution after having been accused, together with Deng Xiaoping, of being one of the biggest "capitalist roaders" attempting to restore capitalism in socialist China. The staging of the early history of the CCP thus points to the party's promises in its early years as well as to its blunders in the subsequent period. Nevertheless, *The Song*'s depiction of the birth of the CCP corrects *The East Is Red*'s historical error in portraying Mao as the sole founder, instead restoring him to his original status as a student and a colleague of other early leaders. The reception history of *The Song* recorded this "achievement" in emphasizing the changing course of post-Mao historiography and the dynamic nature of performance art that was best suited to publicize this transformation.

Not all errors were corrected, however. *The Song* repeated the accusation in *The East Is Red* that Chen Duxiu's rightist, defeatist policies were partially responsible for the 1927 KMT massacre of CCP members in the original script, even though the stage production did not go so far (p. 146). The writers and producers of *The Song* hotly debated how to best represent this important event—the birth of the party—from various angles. An expert musician, for example, insisted on using solos and a chorus to set the mood of that dark yet hopeful period of the early 1920s; a literary critic and theoretician supported this view in principle, but also believed that dancing should play a role in the scene. Wu Xue 吴雪, the former president of the China Youth Art Theater and an expert theater director, challenged the early use of a young fishing girl longingly gazing at the boat on Nanhu Lake in the suburbs of Shanghai, where the First Party Congress was held in 1921. As Wu argued, using this "eulogistic mode of representation" to express ordinary people's longing for the CCP was unrealistic, because the First Party Congress was held in extreme secrecy and was under constant threat of police surveillance. That was why the attendees of the First Party Congress had to move their meetings from an apartment in Shanghai's French Concession to the suburbs. "We were so used to eulogy as the main mode of representation," said Wu, "that we tended to neglect the historical background and environment of the historical past" (pp. 37–38). To illustrate his point, Wu acted out a movie scene showing Mao walking on a snow-covered road for a long time in a bitter storm, finally reaching a small room with a flickering light. As it turns out, Mao had walked all that time to locate one book—that was how difficult it was for the original party organizers. Seen in this light, the creative, collaborative energy that went into the numerous drafts of the second epic equaled, if not surpassed, that which was involved in the first epic; indeed, for artists and cultural officials such as Wu Xue, surviving the Cultural Revolution provided them with different insights into the party's history, as well as a more realistic and historically grounded view of how to represent it.

By the same token, *The Song* staged the 1927 massacre from a different, personal angle, as seen in act 2, "From the Northern Expedition to the Jinggang Mountains" ("Beifa dao Jinggangshan huishi" 北伐到井冈山会师). Departing from *The East Is Red*, in which mostly male martyrs marched fearlessly toward the execution ground, *The Song* presented a mezzo-soprano in the dramatic persona of a loving mother confronted with a terrible choice: having to entrust her infant child to the care of her comrades in a prison cell in the hours before dawn, when she will be executed. In a soothing voice, the mother speaks gently to her newborn:

> Mother is about to leave you
> In this dark night.
> I have so much to tell you.
> Oh, my child,
> How can you understand
> Life and death in this world?
> How can you understand
> The enemy has raised its knife?
> How can you understand
> The blood of Communists has stained the earth?

Surrounded by eight female prisoners dancing around her in white silk dresses, the mother tells her infant that as her legacy she is leaving "a sense of justice," "a red flag fluttering in the storm," and "the footprints of the revolutionaries marching forward." "Without regret," the mother promises her child "a brand-new world" that will belong to the younger generation "forever and forever!" (pp. 146–47). This gendered transformation neutralizes the otherwise male-dominated scene of the martyrs in *The East Is Red*; more importantly, it stages the catastrophic human casualties of the revolution, among which mothers, wives, and children paid a fearsome price. The charm of star singers, such as Guan Mucun 关牧村, softened the otherwise blatant call for collective sacrifice common to works in the Maoist era, meanwhile also sustaining a similar message on the importance of remembering the revolutionary past.

Act 3, "From the Long March to the War of Liberation" ("Changzheng dao jiefang zhanzheng" 长征到解放战争) quickly glides through three major wars: the KMT-CCP civil wars, the War of Resistance against Japanese Aggression, and the War of Liberation. In no uncertain terms, *The Song* repeats the core mission of *The East Is Red* in its chronological representations of these epic events in party history. At the same time, reflecting the difficult task of adapting to the new taste of contemporary audiences, *The Song* also dramatizes the tragic fate of a teenage Red Army soldier (*hong xiaogui* 红小鬼) in the Long March scene. The soldier freezes to death while standing on a cliff, still in his position of blowing the bugle to encourage others to persevere in the difficult march—in sharp contrast to the Zunyi meeting scene eulogizing Mao's leadership in *The East Is Red*. On seeing the young soldier's tragic figure, a female soldier performs a solo song and dance that lovingly and longingly eulogizes him as "a bright red star on the snow-capped mountains colored by a Red Army soldier's blood," whose "light will shine warmly upon generations to come" (pp. 152–53). The romantic sentiments of the young female soldier—reflecting a personal attachment or a utopian pursuit of Communist ideals, or a combination of both—adds another point of interest to the scene. Could the young soldier be seen as the symbolic son left behind by the mother in the previous act? Memoirs written about the Long March have described an International Youth Division (Shaogong guoji shi 少共国际师) of around ten thousand soldiers in the Jiangxi Soviet area, many of them the orphans of martyrs. These young soldiers—eighteen years old, on average, with the youngest being fourteen—learned to play the bugle, and many did not survive the Long March.[33] Seen in this context, *The Song* inherited both the realist and the romantic traditions perfected in *The East Is Red*. At the same time, it carved out a new space for narrating the fate of individuals in a national war. Concluding this episode with the three fluttering flags of the Red Army's First, Second, and Fourth Divisions to symbolize their final reunion—and the victory of the CCP—at the end of the Long March, *The Song* presents a faithful, panoramic representation of this key event with a group dance entitled "The Red Army Is Not Afraid of the Difficult Long March" ("Hongjun bupa yuanzheng nan" 红军不怕远征难). The dance features three dramatic characters—a cook, a flag bearer, and a teenage soldier—in order to project an imagined family bound together by a difficult and noble cause (p. 152).

In addition to the portrayals of these individuals, act 3 of *The Song* emphasizes the collective leadership during the Yan'an period, with appearances by dramatic actors portraying the characters of Mao, Zhu De, Liu Shaoqi, Zhou Enlai, and Ren Bishi, the "five great secretaries in the Central Secretariat" (*zhongyang shujichu wu da shuji* 中央书记处五大书记), elected by the party's Central Committee at the Seventh Party Congress in 1945 (plate 17). They join the cheering crowds on the stage—peasants, soldiers, intellectuals, students, and especially the artists and performers of the Yangge folk dance group of Lu Xun Art Academy—to celebrate the successful convening of the Seventh Party Congress under their collective leadership. Unlike the scene in *The East Is Red* that honors the Zunyi meeting as a way of celebrating Mao, the appearance here of other leaders with Mao becomes even more significant when one bears in mind that the Seventh Party Congress is known for putting into the party's constitution (*dangzhang* 党章) an acknowledgment that Mao Zedong Thought is the guiding thought for the Chinese Revolution.[34] *The Song*, however, opts not to present the beginning of the Mao cult but to give credit to the collective leadership. In a lively scene designed to reflect the historical past as closely as possible, as the producers claimed, *The Song* presents the five leaders joining the Yan'an masses in their Yangge folk dance, with Zhu De pulling up his sleeves to beat the drums, Mao holding a little peasant girl in his arms, and Liu Shaoqi chatting with Mao about the local ritual of a lion dance. According to the reception history of *The Song*, veteran leaders such as Xi Zhongxun and Yu Qiuli were so touched by the verisimilitude of this scene that they felt as if they had indeed returned to the memorable days of Yan'an more than forty years earlier (p. 58).

The Song's story highlights the challenges of realistic representation and the difficulties producers encountered in seeking actors who closely resembled those historical figures (*texing yanyuan* 特性演员). They invited Gu Yue 古月 to play the role of Mao after his successful performance in the award-winning film *Crossing the Chishui River Four Times* (*Si du chishui* 四渡赤水, 1983), premiered by the August First Film Studio (on Mao impersonators, see also Chapter 8 in this volume). Marshal Ye Jianying had personally chosen Gu for that film because he resembled Mao more closely than the other contenders. However, unlike in his other portrayals of Mao, including in another film, *Xi'an Incident* (*Xi'an shibian* 西安事变, 1981), Gu was expected to play a silent Mao in *The Song*, without any spoken words to express "Mao's mood and spirit." And Gu faced an additional challenge here, for he was also required to move through various stages of Mao's life in one performance: Mao is supposed to be thirty-four in the Jinggang Mountains scene, fifty-two in the Seventh Party Congress scene, and fifty-eight in the founding-the-nation scene, with invariably different temperaments, dispositions, and body language from scene to scene (p. 61). The reception narrative attributes Gu Yue's stunning success in *The Song* to his profound gratitude to Mao and his sense of personal debt to Feng Mu 冯牧, a veteran cultural leader who had "adopted" Gu from an orphanage after the liberation of Nanning 南宁 and trained him, sometimes on horseback while Feng marched with other soldiers, to become a teenage member of an army theater troupe.[35] It goes on to recount how, after having lost contact for forty years, Gu visited Feng and thanked him for writing a rave review of his performance as Mao in *Crossing the Chishui River Four Times*, which Feng wrote without knowing that Gu was the little boy he had initiated into a performance career for the revolution. Here and elsewhere, the historical past and personal journeys blended everyday life experience with performance practice.

In contrast to Gu Yue, who attained stardom because of his resemblance to a party leader, the actor Zhang Hanjun 张汉钧 had suffered a beating in the streets by Red Guards during the Cultural Revolution because he looked exactly like Liu Shaoqi, the so-called Chinese Khrushchev who had attempted to restore capitalism in socialist China. Zhang's misfortune turned to glory in 1980, however, when he was invited to play the dramatic character of Liu Shaoqi in the film *Conquering Nanjing in a Storm*, and then again in *The Song*. Even though Liu had only seven stage lines in the production, Zhang spent two months reading through historical documents about Liu, as well as Liu's own works, in order to best capture "his spirit and soul." At the age of sixty-two, Zhang was the oldest actor in *The Song*, but he poured his heart into the performance; he wanted his children and grandchildren to remember him as the lucky one who had played the dramatic role of former president Liu Shaoqi, who had not had Zhang's good fortune to survive the Cultural Revolution (pp. 66–70).

Because of his unique appearance, it was particularly challenging to find an appropriate actor to play the role of Ren Bishi. Finally the producers convinced Ren Yuanyuan, Ren Bishi's only surviving son, to play the role of his father, owing to their close resemblance. During the war, Ren Bishi's wife had given birth to nine children, but they lost four boys and one girl; some of the children were given to local peasants to raise during the war and were never found again, in spite of repeated searches after liberation. On October 27, 1983, the thirty-third anniversary of Ren Bishi's death, his widow brought her entire family, consisting of three generations, to attend the dress rehearsal of the Yan'an scene in *The Song*. She was moved to tears when she saw her "husband" looking exactly as he had three decades earlier and being played by her engineer son, who had never before performed on stage. The fact that Ren Yuanyuan, her youngest child, had survived because he was born in Yan'an gave further support to the CCP legend that credits Yan'an as the cradle of the revolution and a beacon for a new, hopeful China.

The most intriguing part of *The Song*, however, comes in act 4, "From the Founding of the Nation to the Smashing of the Gang of Four" ("Jianguo dao fensui siren bang" 建国到粉碎四人帮). Unlike *The East Is Red*, which avoided the complicated post-1949 history, *The Song* quickly covers the twenty-seven years from 1949 to 1976, from the founding fathers' establishment of a socialist China to their subsequent exit from the political stage in 1976, when Zhou Enlai, Zhu De, and Mao passed away in the same year. *The Song* takes the easy way out by sidestepping the mistakes of the Mao era and presenting three scenes that best represent Mao's triumphs: "The Founding Ceremony of the PRC," "Praise for the Socialist Motherland," and "The Smashing of the Gang of Four," which, according to the producers, best dramatized the essence of PRC history before the reform era.

"The Founding Ceremony of the PRC" focuses on a memorable moment in national history that has been depicted in paintings, photographs, movies, and television dramas, and has been recounted in diaries and memoirs. To the best of my knowledge, however, this was the first and only stage representation of the entire scene of the founding ceremony on the Tiananmen Rostrum on October 1, 1949. *The Song* presents not only the characters of Mao Zedong, Zhou Enlai, Liu Shaoqi, Zhu De, Song Qingling, and Dong Biwu but also Li Jishen 李济深, the chairman of the Revolutionary Committee of the KMT (Zhongguo Guomindang geming weiyuanhui 中国国民党革命委员会); Zhang Lan 张澜, president of the China Democratic League (Zhongguo minzhu tongmeng 中国民主同盟); and Shen Junru 沈钧儒, another prominent leader of the China Democratic League. Standing next to the CCP leaders are Li and Zhang, who were elected by the Chinese People's Political Consultative Conference (Zhongguo renmin zhengzhi xieshang huiyi 中国人民政治协商会议) as two of six vice chairpersons of the young republic's central government to join the newly formed Central People's Government. Their dream of building a new, democratic China, free from one-party autocracy under the leadership of the CCP and in consultation with other democratic parties, evaporated soon thereafter. During the Anti-Rightist Movement in 1957, 5,173 members of the Chinese Democratic Alliance were labeled "Rightists," representing 15.6 percent of the alliance's total membership.[36] Four out of the "five cardinal Rightists" whom the CCP has never rehabilitated were leaders or active members of the Chinese Democratic Alliance: Zhang Bojun 章伯钧, Luo Longji 罗隆基, Peng Wenying 彭文应, and Chen Bingren 陈炳仁. The staging of the PRC's founding ceremony could therefore be ironically perceived as a farewell ceremony for the past dream of a democratic China, initially envisioned before and right after 1949, when the CCP needed the independent parties' endorsement to establish its legitimacy. This was perhaps one of the reasons Zhou Enlai felt relieved by Mao's directive not to represent post-1949 events, which meant not having to deal with the thorny issue of the United Front in *The East Is Red*.

The next scene in act 4, "Praise for the Motherland" ("Zuguo song" 祖国颂), takes only seven minutes to represent the first seventeen years of the PRC's history, from 1949 to 1966.[37] Standing on an elevated platform that emerges from beneath the stage, a huge chorus merges with the chorus already standing on both sides of the stage to sing a popular song from the 1950s, "Praise for the Motherland," which begins thus:

The Sun jumped out of the Eastern Sea
Brilliant light shone upon the great earth
The rivers ceased their roaring sound
The mountains opened their arms
Oh, birds fly afar in the sky
Flowers blossomed everywhere
The land is magnificent
The people are proud
Our great motherland
Has entered the socialist era.

Behind the chorus, the background screen shows image after image of harvests, steel factories, oilfields, the Nanjing Bridge across the Yangzi River, and the first state road that connected Sichuan to Tibet (pp. 161–63). These selected images skip over traumatic events, such as the famine that followed the Great Leap Forward. Most significantly, *The Song* omits the entire history of the Cultural Revolution, a routine practice in history books and museum exhibitions in the PRC. In the scene entitled "The Smashing of the Gang of Four," the White Flower Dance evokes the April 5 Incident of 1976, when Beijing citizens took to Tiananmen Square to mourn Zhou Enlai's death. The white flowers worn by the crowds of mourners—who were suppressed by local police and the mobilized workers' militia—are employed thematically in *The Song* to express the Chinese people's mourning not only for Zhou Enlai, but for Mao Zedong and Zhu De as well, who had passed away in the same year. All in all, the White Flower Dance rejects the Cultural Revolution—and by extension Mao's socialist philosophy, which initiated it—as a disaster that necessitated a new era of reform. It also celebrates Deng Xiaoping, who was stripped of all his leadership positions and denounced as the behind-the-scenes architect of the April 5 Incident, with his attempt to reverse the "fruits of the Cultural Revolution" in order to "restore capitalism," as the official press at that time declared.

The White Flower Dance features a solo dancer appearing as Zhang Zhixin 张志新, a member of the CCP who was executed in 1975 as a "counterrevolutionary." The early post-Mao regime celebrated her as a heroic rebel against radical leaders of the Cultural Revolution, such as Lin Biao and Jiang Qing, even though her "real crime," as revealed in an article published in 2000, was daring to challenge Mao.[38] In 1968, at the peak of the Cultural Revolution when millions of people worshipped Mao and strove to carry out his great proletariat revolution, the young Zhang expressed her firm belief that Mao had made serious "leftist mistakes" in the Anti-Rightist Movement, in the Great Leap Forward, and especially during the Cultural Revolution. Mao increasingly became less modest, and he suppressed democracy, destroyed the unity within the party, and negatively affected the course of the Chinese Revolution and socialist construction with his erroneous theory of "continuous revolution." The cult of Mao placed Mao above the party, Zhang said, and could bring only disaster to the country. Her prophetic words anticipated the main points of the CCP's "Resolution on the History of Our Party after the Founding of the PRC," which was adopted in 1981, six years after Zhang's execution in 1975. Unable even to hint at these complicated historical events, *The Song* instead uses this one symbolic dance to redefine the Maoist years as either "red," "black," or "gray," leaving it to the audience to judge according to their individual standpoints, backgrounds, and experiences.

All these scenes lead to the climatic act 5, "From the Third Plenary Session of the Eleventh Party Congress to the Twelfth Party Congress" ("Shiyi jie san zhong quanhui dao shi'er da" 十一届三中全会到十二大). Numerous singers dressed to represent various ethnic minority groups gather on the stage to "welcome the rise of a New China" after "ten years of chaos and bitter winters" during the Cultural Revolution (p. 165). This display of cheerful ethnic groups echoes a scene in *The East Is Red* that celebrates the founding of the PRC; this formalistic similarity helps to conceal the ideological differences between the Mao and Deng regimes for some audiences, but it also supports divergent views for others who took to heart the CCP's resolution to condemn Mao's mistakes after 1949; it may appear to be neutral to still others, who simply enjoy the show without having to come to terms with any political interpretations, one way or the other.

The remainder of the seven episodes on the new achievements of workers, scientists, and soldiers in early post-Mao China blend together an otherwise complicated, at times contradictory, view of China under reform: on the one hand, happy peasants enthusiastically till their allocated plots of land and receive rewards, for the first time, according to their own labor—a radical break from the socialist collective farming system, a staple policy of Mao's rule. On the other hand, passionate children vow to become "the successors of the Communist cause" in "the spirit of Lei Feng" 雷锋, pledging to form a collective community to serve the people at the expense of personal interests. The stage direction explains that, "bathed in the party's sunshine, a young generation is growing up healthily, in the spring breeze of 'socialist spiritual civilization'" (*shehui zhuyi jingshen wenming* 社会主义精神文明) (p. 173), a catchphrase of the Dengist regime, which wanted to ensure that the importation of Western modernization and ideology, such as freedom and democracy, did not either threaten or replace the Maoist one-party system and the state's control over all aspects of people's lives. As the large, resounding chorus sings, the epilogue ends with images of Deng Xiaoping and other second-generation leaders projected on the screen, against the red sun shining on the magnificent motherland. When the cult of Deng finally replaces that of Mao, *The Song* completes its call for a peaceful evolution from socialism to semicapitalism in a grand performance that is consistent with its predecessor in tropes and imagery but rejects some of its most fundamental values in the socialist experience.

Critical reviews of *The Song* could not point out these thematic and ideological discrepancies, however, for the obvious reason of state censorship, although some critics and audience members did express disappointment with the show. The scene of rejoicing in the Jinggang

Mountains, for instance, was "too luxurious, without even a reference to the extraordinary hardships Mao and Zhu De's troops had experienced."[39] Likewise, the Yan'an scene celebrating the Seventh Party Congress painted too "lighthearted and happy" a picture of northern Shaanxi, where the local peasants had whole-heartedly supported the CCP revolution in spite of their own hardships during the war period, but who still lived in poverty even in contemporary China. By the same token, the important "smashing" of the Gang of Four that ended the Cultural Revolution appeared to be too "idealistic," with its depiction of a group of exultant people cheering the end of the Gang of the Four.[40] *The Song* could have dealt "more directly with the hardships and mistakes of our history in order to educate the audiences in this new era," one audience member argued.[41]

Critical success or not, *The Song* never seemed to enjoy the popularity of *The East Is Red*, in spite of similar efforts to have a film version made, which came mostly out of its very different historical times. Nevertheless, its performance history and the features it shared with its predecessor granted this second epic a place in the state performance culture—a culture that defined and defended the writing of history along the trajectory of the changing dynamics of official politics.

The Road to Revival: Post-epic Theatricality

Twenty-five years later, in 2009, when the scriptwriters and producers brainstormed about plans for *The Road to Revival* (*Fuxing zhi lu* 复兴之路), intended to commemorate the sixtieth anniversary of the PRC, they sketched out the "most earthshaking and colorful" thirty years of history in the reform era. Unlike the earlier productions, which were concerned mostly with how China had caught up with the rest of the world—through either a socialist or a capitalist approach—*The Road to Revival* benefited from the vantage point of a proud and prosperous China in the twenty-first century. Surveying the world in which China was now a leading nation, *The Road* could cheerfully reflect on 164 years of "Chinese" history from 1845 to 2009. Where was China then, in the 1960s, and how did it arrive at its present glory? This was what they intended to present to audiences in 2009.

Acknowledging *The East Is Red* as "a monumental epic" that they said they "still admire as a model" fifty years later, the scriptwriters and producers wanted to bypass the red classic to create their own classic, one that, in twenty years, the next generation would also look up to. They therefore focused on what I term "post-epic theatricality." To this end, Zhang Jigang 张继钢, the general director of *The Road*, conceived three performance spaces that combined "performance art in the square" (*guangchang yishu* 广场艺术) with "performance art on a stage" (*wutai yishu* 舞台艺术). Zhang designed a grand, arching structure that spanned the stage with a stairway of seventy-two steps and was as tall as a multistory building; on the stairway stood a chorus of a thousand people "singing brilliant songs" all night long to commemorate "our motherland's sixtieth birthday," similar to the ancient Greek's chorus rituals and the Mormon church's practice of singing congregational hymns all night during the holiday seasons. Looking on from above the performance throughout the entire show from "a global perspective," chorus members functioned as contemporary commentators, observing the historical events as they unfolded on the main stage. They presented a sense of contemporary time that was still ticking away during the show, and they invited reflection and critique from the audience.

Contained within the arched stairway, the conventional flat stage was transformed into a "raked stage" that sloped down toward the audience to improve visibility. Based on stage designs from the European Middle Ages and early modern theater, this raked stage created a more gradual platform for imagining walking into the depths of time, on "the road into history," according to Zhang (see plate 18). To add to the dynamics on the main stage, a huge LED screen displayed images from photographs, paintings, and clips from documentaries, providing reflecting historical backdrops, such as the image of foreigners burning down the imperial palace in 1900, the worker and peasant movements of the 1920s, the Long March, the launching of the atomic and hydrogen bombs and satellites, and the return to China of Hong Kong and Macao.[42]

Within this three-dimensional space, *The Road* presents five "poetic chapters," or acts: "A Memorial to the Anguished Land" ("Shanhe ji" 山河祭, 1840–1921), "An Epic of Heroic Martyrs" ("Rexue fu" 热血赋, 1921–49), "A Portrait of Socialist Pioneers" ("Chuangye tu" 创业图, 1949–78), "A Melody of the Great Waves" ("Dachao qu" 大潮曲, 1978–2008), and "Praise for a Magnificent China" ("Zhonghua song" 中华颂, 2009). No longer interested in interpreting history, which was assumed to be known to all, the producers of this epic focused on "opening one aesthetic door after another" to present a shining detail, an unforgettable image, a memorable plot, all under the most unusual and particular circumstances, so that they could "enlarge," "exaggerate," and "enrich" these images to create a sense of "freshness" that would win over contemporary audiences. For the prologue entitled "My Homeland," for example, they created a stage covered with huge pieces of sturdy brown paper that symbolized the hilly landscape of an ancient agricultural civilization; a peasant plows his land with his young, delicate wife following behind him. A group of 350 soldiers hiding beneath the stage create a waving motion that symbolizes the breathing of the yellow earth, its stress, tempo, and gestures. On this vast stretch of yellow earth, protected and watched over by the peasant couple, 470 emperors and empresses emerged, as well as countless thinkers, scientists, and poets, year after year, generation after generation.[43] From the minds of this couple, the epic of the homeland unfolds.

Chapter 1 of *The Road to Revival* begins with one plot that lasts only six minutes: in 1850, in front of the aristocratic members of the imperial family, the marvelous players of the Kunqu opera are in the midst of performing "Awakening from a Dream" ("Jingmeng" 惊梦) from *Peony Pavilion* (*Mudan ting* 牡丹亭) by Tang Xianzu 汤显祖. The song tells of Du Shiniang tearfully awakening from a beautiful dream about meeting her lover. Suddenly, gunshots from the Opium War interrupt the show, the bullets smashing to pieces a large painting entitled *The Magnificent Landscape of Ten Thousand Miles*. *The Road*'s audience can enjoy the elaborate Kunqu show as well as traditional poetry and painting, and meanwhile blame Western imperialists for their destruction.

Another shocking moment occurs in the next episode, entitled "Children's Ballads of the 1911 Revolution" ("Xinhai tongyao" 辛亥童谣), which presents a stunning group of 120 male performers dressed in traditional gentlemen's garments. They dance for four minutes, mostly with their knees on the ground, jumping up from their knees-folded position and then banging their bodies on the ground to express their total frustration, extreme pain, and desperate protest against the Qing court's persecution and execution of reformists. Having gone through two dozen revisions of the choreography, the dancers had in fact rehearsed twenty different dances in their effort to achieve a perfect moment that would best showcase the tumultuous spirit of the times.[44]

The following scene, entitled "Morning Light" ("Shuse" 曙色), stages another large image of "calling to arms" (*nahan* 呐喊) to express the patriots' fury against the status quo and their willingness to sacrifice themselves for a better life. For this sequence the producers created a brand-new theatrical form: 621 soldiers with angry faces appear onstage to form "a human wall of protest," with their 1,242 arms crossing over one another and reaching out toward the audience. This five-minute scene symbolizes, as the producers explained, eighty years of "calling to arms," and condenses the spirit of rebellion from the Opium Wars to the May Fourth Movement. The references to historical events, however, are not spelled out by poetic narrators, as in *The East Is Red* and *The Song*; rather, they are represented through stage props, such as the numerous flags with slogans from the May Fourth Movement printed on them, and through the titles of many of the "unequal treaties" imposed by foreign countries, projected on the LED screen.

To avoid repeating the earlier epics' familiar narratives of the birth of the CCP in 1921, in Chapter 2 a diary entry by Xie Juezai 谢觉哉, an early socialist, instead appears on the screen: "In the afternoon at six o'clock, Shuheng (He Shuheng 何叔衡) traveled to Shanghai, with Runzhi (Mao Runzhi 毛润之, Mao Zedong's style name) accompanying him, in response to the call from the Communists." Because of the secrecy of the event, the word "Communists" was signified by "xxxxx" in Xie's diary, the narrator explains. According to the producers, they chose to highlight this newly discovered, simple but valuable detail because it featured lesser-known early leaders, Xie and He. The image of the diary followed other references on the LED screen about Chen Duxiu's editorship of *The New Youth*, Li Dazhao's essays on the victory of the Bolshevik revolution, and the founding of the CCP by "Chen Duxiu in the south and Li Dazhao in the north (*nan Chen bei Li, xiangyue jiandang* 南陈北李, 相约建党)." Those few words finally restored Chen Duxiu's original status as one of the founding fathers, a claim previously dismissed in both *The East Is Red* and *The Song*.

Other key episodes also focused on shocking images from a new angle. The Nanchang Uprising of August 1927 was portrayed in a tense moment when numerous soldiers are passing guns to each other in secrecy to get ready for the uprising, with their commanders tying red scarves around their necks to identify them as members of the rebel troops. The Long March scene highlighted a small group of Red Army soldiers "flying over the snow-capped mountains" in a romantic spirit (plate 19). Through slow motion, achieved by having one leg of each dancer secured on a raised platform, with a wire connecting all of them, this modern dance presents "the magnificent beauty" of the red legend, instead of descriptions of death, starvation, and human tragedy, as in the other two epics. In contrast to the familiar images of soldiers in rags in other performance pieces, the stage designers here use silk costumes in a bright color scheme of white and light blue to suggest flowing motion and a free spirit.[45] Likewise, the scene portraying the memorable story of the soldiers sailing across the Yangzi River to wipe out the KMT troops and liberate the rest of China focuses on one dazzling spectacle: the stunning beauty of the shining helmets worn by numerous soldiers; together, they form "an ocean of waves" symbolizing the inevitable advance of one million soldiers. Similar to the two earlier epics, *The Road to Revival* also ends with elaborate scenes celebrating the founding of the PRC in 1949 with the songs and dances of ethnic minorities, to validate the solidarity and harmony of diverse ethnicities (plate 20).

Whereas *The Road to Revival* minimized the cult of Mao by honoring the ordinary people, this third epic created a cult of the artists, especially in the name of Director Zhang Jigang. According to his coworkers, all the most marvelous visual details in *The Road* came from the brilliant mind of Director Zhang, who processed "talent, courage, will power, and efficiency," who combined an army commander's style (because he came from an army performance troupe) with that of a passionate artist. Originally from a small town in Shanxi, Zhang achieved the enviable status of deputy director-in-chief in producing the Opening Ceremony for the Beijing Olympics, only to beat his own record by producing *The Road*, one of the most difficult revolutionary epics staged in a nonrevolutionary time. According to the reception history of *The Road*, when the cult of Director Zhang actually displaced the cult of Mao, *The Road* realized on stage a complete restoration of China to capitalism through its unique artistic form, with a cast of 3,200 performers and a team of 150 scriptwriters, composers, writers, stage designers, and staff members. One cannot help but reflect on Mao's early ideas, when he perceived Chinese artists and writers as deadly enemies of the proletariat dictatorship, and his force of will in initiating the Cultural

Revolution, which first targeted the cultural front to preempt the West's dream of a peaceful evolution from socialism to capitalism in China, even at the expense of destroying his own People's Republic. The power and danger of the performing arts, along with their potential to collaborate with and challenge the status quo, found their best manifestations in the evolutionary stories of these three red classics and the creative energies of the best performers in the past half-century.

Notes

1. Qiang Zhai, "Mao Zedong and Dulles's 'Peaceful Evolution' Strategy: Revelations from Bo Yibo's Memoirs," *Cold War International History Project Bulletin,* Issues 6–7 (Winter 1995–1996): 228–31.

2. CCP Central Committee, "The Cultural Revolution—Excerpts from 'Resolution on Certain Questions in the History of Our Party since the Founding of the People's Republic of China,'" in *China's Cultural Revolution, 1966–1969: Not a Dinner Party,* ed. Michael Schoenhals (Armonk, NY: M. E. Sharpe, 1996), pp. 296–303, see p. 296.

3. For studies in English of Maoist model theater, see Barbara Mittler, *A Continuous Revolution: Making Sense of Cultural Revolution Culture* (Cambridge, MA: Harvard University Asia Center, 2013), pp. 39–127: Xiaomei Chen, *Acting the Right Part: Political Theater and Popular Drama in Contemporary China* (Honolulu: University of Hawai'i Press, 2002); Rosemary A. Roberts, *Maoist Model Theatre: The Semiotics of Gender and Sexuality in the Chinese Cultural Revolution (1966–1976)* (Leiden: Brill, 2010).

4. Xiaomei Chen, "Fifty Years of Staging a Founding Father: Political Theater, Dramatic History and the Question of Representation," in *Representing the Past: Essays on the Historiography of Performance,* ed. Thomas E. Postlewait and Charlotte Canning (Iowa City: University of Iowa Press, 2010), pp. 303–30. The discussion of the production history of *The East Is Red* in this chapter does not overlap with my earlier essay.

5. Zhou Weichi 周巍峙, "Gaowu jianling, xizhe ruwei: Zhou Zongli lingdao women chuangzuo yanchu *Dongfang Hong*" 高屋建瓴，细致入微:周总理领导我们创作演出《东方红》 (Insightful guidance and caring support: Premier Zhou led us in creating *The East Is Red*), *Xin wenhua shiliao* 新文化史料 (Historical materials on the new culture) 1 (January 1998): 4–11, see p. 5.

6. Ibid., p. 5.

7. Ibid., pp. 5–6.

8. Zhou Enlai 周恩来, "Dui xiugai pailian hou de *Dongfang Hong* de yijian" 对修改排练后的《东方红》的意见 (My opinions on the revised version of *The East Is Red*), published in *Dang de wenxian* 党的文献 (Historical documents of the CCP) 6 (1995): 17–18, see p. 17. Zhou's document is dated March 5, 1965.

9. Zhou Weichi, "Gaowu jianling," p. 6.

10. Zhou Enlai, "Zai *Dongfang Hong* daoyantuan zuotanhui shang de jianghua" 在《东方红》导演团座谈会上的讲话 (A talk at the seminar attended by the directing group of *The East Is Red*), *Dang de wenxian* 6 (1995): 14–17, see p.16. Document dated January 8, 1965.

11. Zhou Weichi, "Gaowu jianling," p. 6.

12. Zhou Enlai, "Dui xiugai pailian hou," p. 18.

13. For Zhang Guotao's role, see Yao Jinguo 姚金果 and Su Hang 苏杭, *Zhang Guotao zhuan* 张国涛传 (A biography of Zhang Guotao) (Xi'an: Shaanxi renmin chubanshe, 2007), pp. 64–69. With regard to the problematic leadership of Zhang Guotao in the Soviet area and with the Fourth Division, Zhang's biographers present a complex assessment: "He carried out Wang Ming's erroneous leftist policies and initiated the 'grand-scale persecution' [*da sufan* 大肃反] that executed countless high- and middle-ranking officials and innocent soldiers, but he also led the Soviet area to its peak development. He was nevertheless responsible for the failure of the Fourth Division's anti-KMT elimination campaigns, which forced the Fourth Division to abandon its Soviet base area." See ibid., pp. 213–36.

14. Zhou Weichi, "Gaowu jianling," pp. 7–8.

15. Zhou Enlai, "Zai *Dongfang Hong*."

16. Wang Jianzhu 王建柱, "Yinyue wudao shishi *Dongfang Hong* shi zenyang dansheng de?" 音乐舞蹈史诗《东方红》是怎样诞生的? (How did the music-and-dance epic *The East Is Red* come into being?), *Dangshi wenhui* 党史文汇 (Materials on CCP history) 2 (2006): 34–36, see p. 36.

17. Zhou Enlai, "Dui xiugai pailian hou," p. 18.

18. For an insightful study of the sublime Maoist culture, see Ban Wang, *The Sublime Figure of History: Aesthetics and Politics in Twentieth-Century China* (Stanford, CA: Stanford University Press, 1997).

19. Mo Weiming 莫伟鸣 and He Qiong 何琼, "Daxing yinyue wudao shishi *Dongfang Hong* de chuangzuo youlai" 大型音乐舞蹈史诗《东方红》的创作由来 (The creation story of the grand music-and-dance epic *The East Is Red*), *Renmin yinyue* 人民音乐 (People's music) 12 (2006): 37–40, see p. 40.

20. Zhou Weichi 周巍峙, "Zhuangli de Zhongguo lishi geming huajuan" 壮丽的中国历史革命画卷 (A magnificent scroll on the history of the Chinese Revolution), *Xin wenhua shiliao* 新文化史料 (Historical materials on the new culture) 3 (1996): 28–31, see p. 3.

21. Wang Ying 王颖 and Shi Xiang 石祥, *Muhou zhenwen* 幕后珍闻 (Rare records between the stage curtains) (Beijing: Wenhua yishu chubanshe, 1986), p. 2. Chen Feng 晨枫, "Jiyi zhong de suiyue zai gesheng zhong yongheng" 记忆中的岁月在歌声中永恒 (Memorable years live forever in songs), *Gequ* 歌曲 9 (September 2007): 78–79.

22. "Mi yiyang de meili: Chaoxian zhuxi Jin Zhengri" 谜一样的魅力: 朝鲜主席金正日 (Mysterious charm: Kim Jong Il, the chairman of North Korea), at http://jishi.xooob.com/zz/20089/338549_896338.html (accessed June 14, 2014).

23. Wang Ying and Shi Xiang, *Mu hou zhenwen*, p. 2.

24. Chen Feng, "Jiyi zhong de suiyue," pp. 72–73.

25. Zhou Weichi, "Zhuangli de Zhongguo," p. 29.

26. Ye Yonglie 叶永烈, *Hu Qiaomu: Zhonggong zhongyang yi zhi bi* 胡乔木: 中共中央一支笔 (Hu Qiaomu A pen of the CCP Central Committee) (Nanning: Guangxi renmin chubanshe, 2007), p. 252.

27. Wang Ying and Shi Xiang, *Muhou zhenwen*, p. 18.

28. Ibid.

29. Ye Yonglie, *Hu Qiaomu*, pp. 218–19.

30. "Zhongguo geming zhi ge" 中国革命之歌 (The Song of the Chinese Revolution), in Wang Ying and Shi Xiang, *Muhou zhenwen*, pp. 134–35.

31. Ibid., pp. 134–35.

32. Ibid., p. 136. Hereafter, page numbers for "Zhongguo geming zhi ge" are cited directly in the text.

33. "Shaonian yingxiong: Zhongyang hongjun 'Shaogong guoji shi'" 少年英雄: 中央红军"少共国际师 (Teenage heroes: The Young Communist International Division in the Central Red Amy), in *Hong gushi* (红故事) (Red stories), December 29, 2010, p. 1, at http://www.honggushi.com/news/jindai/hgs9095.html (accessed August 15, 2015).

34. Lyman Van Slyke, "The Chinese Communist Movement during the Sino-Japanese War, 1937–1945," in *The Cambridge History of China*, ed. John K. Fairbank and Albert Feuerwerker, vol. 13, part 2 (Cambridge: Cambridge University Press, 1986), pp. 609–722, see p. 717.

35. Wang Ying and Shi Xiang, *Muhou zhenwen*, pp. 58–59.

36. Zhang Yihe 章诒和, "Shun Changjiang shuiliu canyue: Leiji Luo Longji" 顺长江水流残月: 泪祭罗隆基 (Floating on the Yangzi River with a crescent moon: A tearful obituary of Luo Longji), at http://www.edubridge.com/letter/zhangyihe_108.htm (accessed May 15, 2014).

37. Zhou Weichi, "Zhuangli de Zhongguo," p. 30.

38. Chen Shaojing 陈少京, "Zhang Zhixin yuan'an hai you xin de mimi" 张志新冤案还有新的秘密 (The new secrets in the wrongful case of Zhang Zhixin), *Nanfang zhoumo* 南方周末 (Southern weekend), June 16, 2000, at http://news.163.com/06/1115/14/2VVNJ92O00011244.html (accessed December 31, 2014).

39. Chen Yingbao 陈兴保, "Quzhe bu zu, huanle youyu: *Zhongguo geming zhi ge* shizhe yijian" 曲折不足, 欢乐有余: 中国革命之歌失着一见 (Not enough setbacks, and too much joy: Pros and cons of *The Song of the Chinese Revolution*), *Dianying pingjie* 电影评介 (Movies in review) 12 (1985): 16.

40. Ibid.

41. Ibid.

42. Liu Xing 刘星, "Zhe shi women Zhongguoren ziji chuangzao de shishi" 这是我们中国人自己创造的史诗 (This is an epic created by our Chinese people), in Mao Shi'an et al., *Fuxing zhi lu* 复兴之路 (The road to prosperity) (Shanghai: Shanghai wenyi chubanshe, 2009), pp. 101–2.

43. Wang Xiaoling 王晓岭, "*Fuxing zhi lu* cehua guocheng pianyi" 《复兴之路》策划过程片忆 (My recollection of the brain-storming sessions for creating *The Road to Prosperity*), in Mao Shi'an et al., *Fuxing zhi lu*, (Shanghai: Shanghai wenyi chubanshe, 2009), pp. 96–97.

44. Tan Guangpeng 潭广鹏, "Hanshui saman paiyan chang" 汗水洒满排演场 (Perspiration on the rehearsal site), in Mao Shi'an et al., *Fuxing zhi lu* (Shanghai: Shanghai wenyi chubanshe, 2009), p. 107.

45. Xing Shimiao 邢时苗, "Ling yi shan men de fengjing" 另一扇门的风景 (Scenery through another door), in Mao Shi'an et al., *Fuxing zhi lu* (Shanghai: Shanghai wenyi chubanshe, 2009), p. 111.

SIX

RED LEGACIES IN FICTION

David Der-wei Wang

Where historical orthodoxy falls apart, fiction thrives.
—Feng Menglong 冯梦龙 (1574–1645)

Amid a mixture of euphoria and controversy, the Chinese writer Mo Yan 莫言 (1955–) was awarded the 2012 Nobel Prize in Literature. Readers and critics in Chinese and Sinophone communities welcomed the news because since the mid-1980s, Mo Yan has proven to be a most eloquent and poignant storyteller of modern Chinese history, a writer, in the words of the Nobel Prize Committee, "who with hallucinatory realism merges folk tales, history and the contemporary."[1] The Chinese government took Mo Yan's honor most favorably, treating it as a belated recognition of Chinese socialist literature at its finest. For the Chinese public, however, the award may have mostly helped to appease the "Nobel complex" that has beset the nation since the 1930s.[2]

But Mo Yan's winning the award has also ignited heated debates, over issues from his political affinity with the party to his literary style, which verges on redundancy and repetition. Mo Yan is currently the deputy chair of the Chinese Writers' Association, a privileged position awarded only to select writers who follow the party line most closely. Just recently, in May 2012, Mo Yan joined another ninety-nine writers to hand-copy Mao Zedong's 1942 "Yan'an Talks on Literature and Art," in a manner reminiscent of the medieval Buddhist scripture transcribers, in commemoration of the talks' seventieth anniversary. The talks, it will be recalled, have served as the mandate for Chinese Communist literary and cultural policy for decades. Although they may have given rise to a unique type of literature on behalf of the regime, they have caused the purges, incarcerations, exiles, and executions of numerous writers and intellectuals.

However much one praises Mo Yan's earthy style and fantastic and rhetorical strategy from the repertoire originating with Yan'an literature. As I have discussed elsewhere, on the one hand, Mo Yan's fiction demonstrates three distinctive features of Chinese socialist fiction—nativism, realism, and national form.[3] He is particularly indebted to such writers as Zhao Shuli 赵树理 (1906–70) and Sun Li 孙犁 (1913–2002). On the other hand, one can easily recognize the ways in which Mo Yan has engaged in a radical dialogue with this tradition to the extent of parody and mockery. Not only did he draw inspiration from foreign writers such as William Faulkner and Gabriel García Márquez, he also managed to renew traditional narrative sources, which range from the storytelling tale to late Qing exposé fiction. The result is an extravaganza of styles and voices that both celebrates and deflates the red legacies he has allegedly been nurtured on. Thus, one cannot help wondering if any government leaders would still have endorsed Mo Yan had they read his works such as *The Republic of Wine* (*Jiuguo* 酒国, 1993), a carnivalesque prophecy of the capitalist degeneracy of socialist China; *Big Breasts and Wide Hips* (*Fengru feitun* 丰乳肥臀, 1999), an uncanny rewrite of the "revolutionary history" doctrine; and particularly *Life and Death Are Wearing Me Out* (*Shengsi pilao* 生死疲劳, 2007), a Buddhist layman's reflection on the gratuitous land reform system of the past six decades.

In their debates, many of Mo Yan's detractors, just like his governmental defenders, have focused on whether Mo Yan and his fiction can "represent" China and Chinese literature. They tend to discuss issues ranging from a revolutionary mandate to individual sovereignty, and from socialist justice to human rights.[4] One thing that seems to have been overlooked in their discursive engagement is, however, literature. Of course, as a discipline, literature has to be historicized and its definition and practice are always subject to revision.[5] But when a literary discussion takes up a rhetorical stance not unlike that of a historian or a political analyst, it risks the pitfalls of realist fallacy, the most rudimentary lesson for a literature student.

Above all, the power of literature and literary studies lies in invoking fictionality.[6] By fictionality, I mean not so much the intrinsic "play of text" as the intricate double bind between hermeneutics and politics embedded in the game of belle letters. I also have in mind Hannah Arendt's claim that the capacity to engage in storytelling and to communicate in fictional terms constitutes the foundation of a civil society.[7] Through linguistic and imagistic constructs, literature points to an intermedial sphere in which thoughts and actions, histories and desires are thrown into continuous interplay. Precisely because of its fictitious premise, literature enables one to traverse multiple contact zones where political scientists, historians, sociologists, among others, are denied access. Seen in this light, the "fiction" of Mo Yan demands a careful reading precisely because of its ties to the red legacies it inherits. As Mo Yan claims, his fiction is as murky as the reality it depicts; he writes not to indict any historical specificity but to incite multiple interpretations.[8]

This chapter argues that one cannot fully probe the significance of red legacies generally without first considering red legacies in fiction. By stressing the fictional dimension of red legacies, I am not only playing with its paradoxical implication—that is, treating red legacies either as facts reflected by fiction or as a simulacrum evaporating like fiction. Rather, I am more concerned with the tangled relationships among ideological imperatives, empirical contingencies, and narrative representations in the memory machine of Communist China. I contend that red legacies could not have exerted their impact on us had they been lacking in the evocative, metahistorical potential of fiction, something that helps both to dramatize the "moral occult" underneath political agendas and to cast utopian or dystopian visions onto the past and future of history.[9] Meanwhile, the power of red legacies is manifested by the treacherous terms in which history can be denounced as fiction, while fiction can be sublimated into history.

Above all, I call attention to the phantasmal nature of fiction, seeing it as a force propelling the dialectic of time and memory in red legacies. Insofar as "legacy" refers to a palpable or imaginary entity—a gift, artifact, or property, among others—handed down from the past, as from an ancestor or predecessor, red legacy entertains a twofold meaning. On the one hand, it points to a revolutionary tradition that is memorable and transmittable, as the past is believed to be enlivened and carried on by the generations to come. On the other hand, it points to a revolutionary tradition that is unmemorable and nontransmittable, as the past is believed to be long gone and what is left behind amounts to no more than its traces in dissemination. Either involves a politics of posterity.

Jacques Derrida has famously argued that, for all the fact that Marxism seems to have dissipated after the falling apart of the Soviet bloc, the "specters of Marx" continue to haunt the world. It is through the conjuration rather than the denunciation of the phantom of Marx that one comes to terms with the socialist legacy in a postsocialist era.[10] Following Derrida's insight, one can make a similar observation about the continued return of red legacies at a time when the history of the Chinese Communist Revolution seems to be fading into oblivion. Instead of ontology, it is the "hauntology" of the legacy that has to be taken seriously.[11]

With the above arguments in mind, I focus in the following pages on three dimensions of the red legacy in fiction: the dialogics of history after posthistory, enlightenment and enchantment, and utopia and dystopia. I argue that, compared with scholars of China studies, contemporary Chinese writers are more sensitive in teasing out the complex traces beneath historical dynamics, and more daring in describing the unnamable "Real" embedded in sociopolitical reality.[12] For instance, for those critical of the liberal marketization of contemporary China, *Brothers* (*Xiongdi* 兄弟, 2006) by Yu Hua 余华 (1960–) comes across as one of the darkest exposés of the postsocialist "vanity fair"; for those who question leftist communal solidarity, the same novel reads like a chilling indictment of revolutionary "bad faith." In view of the emergent New Leftist trend to justify the causes and effects of the Cultural Revolution, novels such as *Hard as Water* (*Jianying rushui* 坚硬如水, 2000), by Yan Lianke 阎连科 (1956–), teach us why one should think twice before hurrying to rehabilitate Maoist "politics." At a time when the rural economy demands more and more attention, Mo Yan's *Life And Death Are Wearing Me Out* provides a poignant observation that can hardly be emulated by scholars' lip service.

But fiction is more than a replica of reality; it encourages imagination and helps open up multiple representational strategies. Thus, where euphonic tunes are being played by the state, cacophony resounds in the world of *Qin Tune* (*Qin qiang* 秦腔, 2005) by Jia Pingwa 贾平凹 (1952–), and *Women's Idle Talk* (*Funü xianliaolu* 妇女闲聊录, 2008) by Lin Bai 林白 (1958–). Beyond the tiring calls for nationalism and sovereignty, scientific fantasies such as the *Earth Chronicles* trilogy (*Diqiu wangshi* 地球往事, 2008, 2010) by Liu Cixin 刘慈欣 (1963–) bring us to ponder social dynamics in outer space and their scientific and ethical implications. And speaking of "the future of New China," can any scholarly projections sound more compelling or controversial than those of Chen Guanzhong 陈冠中 (1952–) in *The Fat Years* (*Shengshi* 盛世, 2010), or Han Song 韩松 (1965–) in *2066: Red Star over America* (*2066: Xixing manji* 西行漫记, 2000)?

History after Posthistory

Enlightened Chinese intellectuals took up fiction as a vehicle for reforming politics and remaking history as early as the turn of the twentieth century. It became all the more polemical in the late 1920s when leftist writers and critics invested in it purposes ranging from critiquing the status quo to promoting a progressive agenda.[13] Mao Dun 茅盾 and Jiang Guangci 蒋光慈 both turned to fiction writing after the fiasco of the first Chinese Communist Revolution in 1927. Whereas the former's *Eclipse* (*Shi* 蚀) looks into the vacillation of the disillusioned young urban leftists, the latter's *Des Sans-culottes* (*Duanku dang* 短裤党) commemorates those who dedicated themselves unconditionally to the noble cause.[14] The early 1930s saw the boom of the "revolution plus romance" formula, which captured the sentimental appeal of the revolutionary campaign; meanwhile, critical realism emerged to become the dominant discourse on behalf of the "insulted and the wounded."[15]

How to compose fiction the "right way" in relation to revolutionary history was already a contentious issue during the Yan'an period. Fiction was expected to not only reflect reality but also rectify it; more, it was even expected to project Reality—the socialist state of plenitude as promised by the success of revolution. A new narratology was developed along with the institutionalization of a new politics and ethics of writing. One prominent case was Ding Ling 丁玲. In 1941 Ding Ling wrote "When I Was in Xia Village" ("Wozai xiacun de shihou" 我在霞村的时候), describing a female revolutionary's painful negotiation between the terms of gender and revolution. For this and several other writings, Ding Ling was "rectified" for spreading decadent thought and sentimentalism. When she remerged in 1948, with *The Sun Shines over the Sanggan River* (*Taiyang zhaozai sanggan heshang* 太阳照在桑干河上), she had become a cadre writer, and even her style—impassioned yet restrained—reflected the shakeup of her political bearings.

By the end of the Yan'an era, one can already discern at least three themes arising from revolutionary literature: the dialectic of revolution and history; the fashioning of an enlightened, progressive subjectivity; and the projection of a utopian vision. The first theme has to do with authenticating nationhood and the party line; the second highlights the epistemological and affective transformation of individuals as well as communities; the third helps substantiate the imaginary as prescribed by the ideological mandate. These three themes became the directives of literary creation after the founding of the People's Republic of China, their impact culminating in the heyday of the Great Proletarian Cultural Revolution.

The dialectic of revolution and history resulted in two trends in fictional writing from the 1950s to the 1970s, "revolutionary history romance," or *geming lishi xiaoshuo* 革命历史小说, which chronicles the "prehistory" of the founding of the republic, and the peasant novel that narrates the radical changes in Chinese rural communities resulting from land reform and other agricultural policies.[16] Neither trend should be taken merely at face value. They point instead to a well-orchestrated temporal scheme that advocates the inevitable triumph of the future over the past and the eternal return of lost justice, and an intricate spatial symbolism evoked by the loss, recovery, and redistribution of the homeland on both national and personal levels.[17] Millions of readers were moved by depictions of the ordeals the revolutionaries undertook in *Song of Youth* (*Qingchun zhi ge* 青春之歌) and *Red Crag* (*Hongyan* 红岩); heroic narratives such as *Defend Yan'an* (*Baowei Yan'an* 保卫延安) and *Red Sun* (*Hongri* 红日) helped crystallize the national yearning of one entire generation of Chinese. Meanwhile, novels about land reform and the rural cooperative movement, such as *A Chronicle of Creation* (*Chuangye shi* 创业史) and *Three Mile Bay* (*Sanli wan* 三里湾) observe peasants' desires and dilemmas vis-à-vis the national rural reform campaign.

It is against this background that we come to the contemporary scene. Much has been discussed about the 1980s, the New Era (*xinshiqi* 新时期) when fiction commanded enormous attention in terms of both formal experimentation and conceptual interrogation.[18] But more than twenty years after the "root-seeking" (*xungen* 寻根) and avant-garde (*xianfeng* 先锋) movements that shook "Maoist discourse" and unleashed waves of creative energy, one wants to ask: How have the writers of the New Era fared in the aftermath of the market economy and media explosions through the end of the past century? What are their concerns now with regard to their creative capacity and social agency? More important, how do they come to terms with the legacies of a literary system that once dominated the conception, production, and consumption of fiction?

Writing at a time when history has collapsed and revolution has lost its mandate, writers cannot take up the two subjects without pondering their inherent intelligibility. Thus Ge Fei 格非 (1964–), in "Misty Boat" ("Mizhou" 迷舟, 1987), envisions revolution as a labyrinthine game of desires, whims, and mishaps that ends up nowhere; Mo Yan's *Red Sorghum* (*Honggaoliang jiazu* 红高粱家族, 1986) depicts revolutionary history as a regressive rather than progressive sequence of national and family memories; Yu Hua's story "1986" simply likens the consequence of revolution to a gory theater of corporal mutilation and insanity. Whereas peasants were once hailed as the foundation of the new republic, Gao Xiaosheng 高晓声 (1928–1999) tells us in his "Chen Huansheng" 陈奂生 series that the peasants are as sly and self-interested as they are persevering and vulnerable. Su Tong 苏童 (1962–) further depicts, in "The Exile of 1934" ("Yijiusansi nian de taowang" 一九三四年的逃亡, 1986), peasants eternally condemned to the fate of decay and diaspora.

This is an era of posthistory, an era in which history—be it an ideology, an episteme, an institution, or a narrative form—is thrown into question. My definition of posthistory is derived from, but not confined to, the following threads. Aesthetically, it refers to A. C. Danto's observation of modern arts since the 1960s in terms of the decomposition of realist formulas and the dissipation of "aura."[19] Ideologically, it has to do with Francis Fukuyama's announcement of the end of (the Hegelian brand of) History in the aftermath of the meltdown of the Eastern European Communist bloc in the late 1980s, followed by leftist critics' rebuttal that, instead of demise, History is in effect about to be born again.[20] And intellectually it concerns Jacques Derrida's proposal that hauntology arises where the ontological versions of history are coming to an end. In the context of Chinese literary criticism, posthistory finds its subtle manifestation in campaigns such as the "farewell to revolution" (*gaobie geming* 告别革命) of Liu Zaifu 刘再复 and Li Zehou 李泽厚 and the call to "rewrite literary history" (*chongxie wenxueshi* 重写文学史) mounted by Chen Sihe 陈思和 and Wang Xiaoming 王晓明 in the late 1980s.[21] Although what is at stake here is nothing but "literary" history, these campaigns prompt one to consider whether, at a time when revolution has lost its legitimacy, revolutionary history cannot but betray its metaphorical nature. If that is true, to bid farewell to revolution and to rewrite literary history must point to a subversive interplay with Maoist ontology.

Fiction, rather than theory, serves as a more persuasive testimony to the arrival of posthistory in China. Yu Hua's short story "Life Is Like Smoke" ("Shishi ruyan" 世事如烟, 1987) is a case in point. By comparing things in life to smoke, the story captures the "structure of feeling" of the post–Cultural Revolution era. Gone is both the sublime figure that had once permeated China as well as all sensuous data that inform the intelligibility of everyday life. Trauma is invoked no sooner than it had been dissolved by irony.[22] Amid the ruins of memory roam the phantoms of nihilism. With the smoke-like infiltration of memories into everyday life, haunting becomes the affective and ideological trope of the Maoist legacy. The trope takes on even more menacing dimensions in historical hindsight, as an ominous anticipation of the Tiananmen incident and its aftermath.

Nevertheless, one discerns in most recent Chinese fiction a new sense of history and historicity "after" the era of posthistory. For instance, as if punning on the Chinese phrase *ruyan* (like smoke) of Yu Hua's "Life Is Like Smoke," Hu Fayun 胡发云 (1950–) titles his Internet novel *Ruyan@sars.come* (如焉@sars.come, Such is this world@sars.come). *Ruyan* has multiple implications in Hu's novel. Of concern here is that with the replacement of *yan* 烟 with the homonymic Chinese character *yan* 焉, a semantic twist takes place. It suggests that where Yu Hua envisages a reality "like smoke," Hu sees reality "the way it is" and concludes, "So be it." History makes the theme of Hu's novel, but this is a history that impresses not as a mere smoky (and spooky) haunting but as a palpable, lived experience.

Or, to take a broader perspective to assess the significance of *Ruyan@sars.come*, one can say that PRC fiction about revolutionary history up to the fin-de-siècle era, regardless of its political stances, has demonstrated a pendulum effect in aestheticizing politics—swinging from the sublime to the ironic; from a surplus of meaning to a hollowing out of meaning; from sanctioning the Real to disavowing the Real. The advent of a novel like *Ruyan@sars.come* indicates that on top of the dialectic between aesthetics and politics, writers are now paying more attention to the *ethics* of viewing and writing history. This ethics does not refer to moral schemata in the traditional sense any more than it represents an archaeological inquiry into the terms in which human relationships in the Communist regime are lived out and therefore become meaningful.

As *Ruyan@sars.come* develops, a lonely widow and mother comes across a group of political dissidents, governmental bureaucrats, and social activists, in either actual or virtual reality forming an intricate network of political and erotic relations that coincides with the severe acute respiratory syndrome (SARS) virus outbreak in 2003. Behind all these goings-on is the burgeoning Internet culture at the turn of the millennium. Hu seems to insinuate that if the past is still being remembered, it is already integrated into a world in which lived experience and virtual adventure, epidemic outbreak and ideological dissemination all happen at the same time and make sense, or nonsense, of each other in digital terms.

Equally provocative is *Breeze and Sunshine* (*Fenghe rili* 风和日丽, 2010) by Ai Wei 艾伟 (1966–), a novel about a young woman's quest for her father, a retired People's Liberation Army general. As the general is celebrated for embodying revolutionary history, his personal history is in eclipse—his failed pursuits of love, his being purged, and his unbearable sense of emptiness after the revolution. The return of his long lost daughter, therefore, is a reminder not only of the (un)desired part of the general's revolutionary history but also of a task of atonement long overdue.

The veteran writer Zhang Jie 张洁 (1935–), in *Without a Word* (*Wuzi* 无字, 2000), also reflects on the consequences of revolution in a postsocialist time, by relating the treacherous marital relationship between a senior cadre couple. History and revolution could not appear murkier when nostalgia about the heroic past is mixed with everyday bedroom warfare; in the end, nobody comes out with clean hands. In telling this revolution-plus-romance story turned sour, Zhang Jie poses a question: How would the heroines of fiction of the 1950s, such as Sister Jiang 江姐 of *Red Crag* or Lin Daojing 林道静 of *Song of Youth*, have turned out had they lived until today?

I will move on to two more radical cases, Mo Yan and Yan Lianke. They both come from a northern rural background, and each spent an extensive period of his life in military service.[23] To that effect, it is little surprise that they have written fiction that intertwines the two Communist fictional traditions mentioned above, the revolutionary-history novel and the peasant novel. In their hands, however, both traditions have undergone an unlikely transformation. Whereas Mo Yan has developed a fantastic, socialist brand of magical realism, Yan Lianke's writing is a mixture of macabre exposé and dark farce.

For example, in *Sandalwood Death* (*Tanxiangxing* 檀香刑, 2000) Mo Yan tries to revisit the violence and chaos of the Boxer Rebellion—presumably the origin of modern Chinese trauma and revolutionary momentum—in his hometown region. Instead of epic narrative, he adopts the local theatrical form known as "cat tune" (*maoqiang* 猫腔) to relate his story; politics and theater thus literally reciprocate each other. Mo Yan's *Life and Death Are Wearing Me Out* chronicles the changes in a village from the land reform era to the present, paralleling its protagonist's incarnations from human form into various animal forms: ox, mule, pig, and monkey. Change constitutes the leitmotif of Mo Yan's socialist version of *Metamorphosis*. The causes and effects of Maoist rural reform are recounted meticulously, only to bring forth a vertiginous sequence of associations from the Buddhist myth of transmigration to the Nietzschean myth of the "eternal return." By parading the reader through the protagonist's hilarious metamorphoses, Mo Yan reflects on how the numerous campaigns and movements have changed the Chinese rural landscape and mindscape and also on how the campaigns and movements have been changed when filtered through the layered textures of the folk imagination. It is through the frictions and fissures *between* these changes that Mo Yan comes to inscribe "his" history of the Communist regime.

Yan Lianke's *Hard as Water* scandalized his audience with its obscure look at human relationships during the Cultural Revolution. He makes two villains the protagonists of his novel; they are condemnable for their fanaticism and evil doings, but they are equally pitiable for their true love for each other, however illicit. More strikingly, the novel is narrated in the propaganda rhetoric that had once taken over every aspect of Chinese life. Yan obviously hints that what is supposed to be an ideological crusade is no more than a linguistic circus and sentimental spree—but one that nevertheless kills. Yan's *Lenin's Kisses* (*Shouhuo* 受活, 2002) relates the story of a "rural township enterprise" (*xiangzhen qiye* 乡镇企业) that seeks to develop a tourist site by exhibiting the corpse of Lenin.[24] To raise funds, an acrobatic troupe featuring an all-handicapped cast is sent on a tour of the nation and it wins wild popularity. As the novel becomes increasingly outrageous, Yan hits home the monstrous implications of the marriage between liberal marketization and socialist memorabilia, corporal grotesquery, and ghostly spectacle.

Even more noticeable are two banned novels by Yan: *Serve the People* (*Weirenmin fuwu* 为人民服务, 2005), in which the most memorable Maoist slogan is used as a password for the tryst between a young soldier and a general's wife; and *Dream of Ding Village* (*Dingzhuang meng* 丁庄梦, 2006), in which an AIDS epidemic resulting from blood-selling in a northern village spells not so much loss of life as a welcome gain of family income. Yan's stories are unfailingly bizarre and outlandish, but they are deeply rooted in the writer's sociopolitical concerns. Both *Serve the People* and *Dream of Ding Village* touch on body politics and fiction writing. Whereas the Maoist call to "serve the people" is interpreted in such a way as to betray its erotic appeal, the AIDS epidemic invites an allegorical reading about the "immune" system of the party/state being in disarray. Walking the tightrope of pornography and pathology, Yan Lianke's fictional diagnosis of contemporary China has made certain scholars' theoretical defenses of the status quo feeble, if not hypocritical.

Enlightenment or Enchantment

Fiction *as* enlightenment has occupied Chinese progressive writers since the May Fourth days. Mao Dun's *Rainbow* (*Hong* 虹) and Ba Jin's 巴金 *Family* (*Jia* 家), for instance, chronicle the ideological conversion of youth from blindness to insight, each with an ending that marks the beginning of further pursuit of knowledge and action. To that effect, they are said to have best demonstrated enlightenment in the vein of Marxism and anarchism, respectively.

Such a project of fictional enlightenment was reinforced by the party machine during the Yan'an era. As Tony Saich and David Apter suggest in their study, through "exegetical bonding" and the "phenomenology of confession," the party was able to install a discursive mechanism of thinking, reading, writing, and speaking that links individual life with collective solidarity, political exercise with ideological vision.[25] Mao's 1942 talks, to be sure, underline the curriculum for how enlightenment can be carried out through literature.

Apter and Saich also call attention to the mirage-like effect in the making of the Communist imaginary, such as the "myth" of Yan'an, and describe it in terms of Jean Baudrillard's notion of "simulacrum." Their polemical analysis notwithstanding, the two critics may have too readily couched their argument in postmodernist discourse. Above all, they cannot exempt themselves from the tautological circle by calling something a simulacrum while granting themselves a super-vision by default.

I would suggest an alternative approach. Instead of calling it "simulacrum," one should take seriously the sacrosanct charm inherent in revolutionary enlightenment, and understand it as a different kind of truth claim. To that end, the old Weberian model of enchantment versus disenchantment may shed more light than the Baudrillardean notion of simulacrum. For Max Weber, modernity registers its intellectual thrust through a disenchantment from premodern episteme.[26] If this is the case, one can argue that the Maoist brand of modernity takes on an additional dimension. It enacts enlightenment not merely through disenchanting Chinese people from preestablished values; rather, it at the same time enchants them by calling on the unrepresentable power of the Real.[27] This involves the "fusion of horizons" between iconoclasm and idolatry, modernist mythologies and "primitive passions," rationality and volition.[28] When enlightenment engenders enchantment, and enchantment substantiates enlightenment, Maoist discourse exudes its superpower.

Scholars have argued that if Western modernity is based on values such as rationality, individualism, and scientism, Maoist revolution indicates an endeavor to achieve "a modernity of anti-(Western) modernity."[29] But such criticism cannot fully explain Maoist modernity until it comes to terms with the element of the fantastic that lies beneath it. Fiction writers, nevertheless, have provided more viable examples for our reference. Take a look at *Long Live Youth* (*Qingchun wansui* 青春万岁, 1953; first published in 1979) by Wang Meng 王蒙 (1939–). This novel describes the life of a group of high school girls, their dreams and misgivings, visions and hesitations, on the eve of graduation. The girls' education culminates in a nocturnal visit to Tiananmen Square, where they run into a giant figure who turns out to be none other than Chairman Mao. A chance encounter becomes a miraculous moment of apotheosis, without which the girls' initiation into Communist knowledge would be incomplete.[30]

Wang Meng was twenty-three when he finished *Long Live Youth*. In a way, the novel is something he wrote for and about himself, in pursuit of an ideal bildungsroman. However, the novel ended up being censored, followed by Wang Meng's exile to Xinjiang for sixteen years. When it finally came into print after the Cultural Revolution, *Long Live Youth* was thus already inscribed with a subtext, about enlightenment turned into forbidden knowledge and enchantment into precarious enthrallment.

More than thirty years after Wang Meng wrote *Long Live Youth*, Yu Hua's "On the Road at Eighteen" ("Shibasui chumen yuanxing" 十八岁出门远行, 1986) relates a different kind of enlightenment story. At the age of eighteen, its protagonist is sent by his father to take a trip on his own. Unlike those aspiring girls of Wang Meng's novel, this young man has no destination to pursue, and he is on the road all by himself. The young man does have a dramatic encounter in the end, not with the Great Man but with a group of peasants turned robbers. In sharp contrast with the innocent ambiance and exuberant tone of *Long Live Youth*, "On the Road at Eighteen" impresses as a work of socialist absurd theater. One can read the story as an allegory that does away with all values of Maoism. Beyond such an approach, however, one may discern a more poignant message: the protagonist experiences only belatedly, on behalf of those girls of *Long Live Youth*, the dark side of Maoist enlightenment. Yu Hua's story is hauntingly illuminating not because it discovers anything new but because it represents "the return of the repressed."

The dialogue between enlightenment and enchantment continues to occupy Chinese novelists in the new millennium, and its tension can be neatly expressed by the titles of two works: *An Age of Enlightenment* (*Qimeng shidai* 启蒙时代, 2007), by Wang Anyi 王安忆 (1954–), versus *Wolf Totem* (*Langtuteng* 狼图腾, 2005), by Jiang Rong 姜戎 (1946–). Both novels deal with the coming of age of one generation of Chinese youth during the Cultural Revolution, and both are allegedly based on their writers' personal experiences. Nevertheless, the Cultural Revolution is cast in very different lights in the two novels. Wang's teenage characters participate in campaigns, strategize about revolutionary tactics, recite and debate Marx's and Mao's writings, and fall in and out of love. Meanwhile, the revolution has gone out of control, ultimately engulfing the young men's and women's ideals and yearnings. By contrast, the youth in *Wolf Totem* can no longer afford the kind of intellectual curiosity and ideological fervor of Wang's characters. They are "educated youth" sent down to the Mongolian prairie to be reeducated. In their effort to survive their harsh circumstances, they come to learn the virtue of being the wolf—sly, independent, lonely, and cruel. With the wolf totem, they believe they can replace the dragon symbolism of old China as well as the "sheep culture" of modern China.

This discovery brings home the ambivalent mentality of Chinese society, then as now. Whereas the invocation of the wolf totem both critiques and relishes a time consummated by the wolflike instinct, the same totem logic appears to apply just as well to the contemporary era, in which a new but equally ruthless law of the jungle thrives. That *Wolf Totem* was a best seller on the eve of the fortieth anniversary of the Cultural Revolution leads one to ask whether its appeal stems from memory of the revolutionary ordeal or from nostalgia about the primordial "collective unconsciousness" that made revolution possible in the first place.

Such ambivalence also becomes the subject of Su Tong's 苏童 *Boat to Redemption* (*He'an* 河岸, 2009). In this novel, a legendary martyr is enshrined in a town in the form of a stone tablet, a "totem pole," so to speak, that sanctions not only revolutionary history but also the martyr's family lineage. But the Cultural Revolution turns everything upside down. When the authenticity of that martyrdom is being questioned (as it should have been), the memorial quickly becomes a sign of stigma. As the truth of history becomes increasingly indiscernible, the teenage protagonist and last descendent of the martyr's family, already ostracized by the town, acquires his first lesson in socialist knowledge in the harshest way.

But it is Yu Hua's *Brothers* that truly brings into relief the tension inherent in enlightenment and enchantment. The novel depicts in two parts the fate of two brothers who have no blood kinship, from the time of the Cultural Revolution to the present. Part one is a sentimental exposé of the Cultural Revolution reminiscent of "scar literature" (*shanghen wenxue* 伤痕文学); part two is a farcical parade of contemporary absurdities, as if a rerun of the "strange events" (*guaixianxiang* 怪现象) of late Qing exposé fiction. The two parts generate a drastic emotional and thematic swing that could be disturbing to many a reader. But insofar as "excess" registers as the rhetorical and thematic mode of his novel, Yu

Hua can be excused for his hyperbole and cynicism. Indeed, his novel posits a series of questions: are the Cultural Revolution and the post-socialist market discrete phenomena, reflecting two political agendas of leftism and liberalism in conflict? Or are they indicators of a causal linkage, or even a historical isomorphism, of two apparently antagonistic ideologies? What if Mao and Mammon prove to be exchangeable icons in service of the new hybrid party line? Finally, in view of the fact that *Brothers* won huge market success thanks to its unabashedly bad taste and a well-manipulated publicity stunt, has not Yu Hua himself become what he sets out to ridicule, both an indicter and an instigator of socialist-capitalist degeneracy?

The examples discussed so far pertain mostly to the enlightenment of the urban or intellectual class of Chinese society. But there has been a PRC narrative tradition that deals with the underprivileged class's initiation into new social and historical consciousness. Zhao Shuli's *Changes of Li Village* (*Lijiazhuang de bianqian* 李家庄的变迁, 1946) and *Great Changes of a Mountain Village* (*Shanxiang jubian* 山乡巨变, 1958), by Zhou Libo 周立波, are examples from the 1940s and 1950s. In these works, peasants and proletarians at large are described as going through the trials of the old or the new society. Because the undesirable parts of their upbringings, such as superstition, illiteracy, cowardice, and parochialism, may keep them from recognizing either their limitations or their potential, their eventual conversion to socialist citizenship is all the more significant. This subaltern version of the enlightenment narrative reaches its peak during the Cultural Revolution, as illustrated by Hao Ran 浩然 in *The Golden Road* (*Jinguang dadao* 金光大道, 1977).

Enlightenment in the socialist rural vein regained attention in the new century, ironically coinciding with the mounting problems besetting the contemporary Chinese village. However, from the pen of conscientious writers the subject does not merely beget its antithesis, showing how illusory the erstwhile Chinese rural vision is. Rather, these writers take note of the fact that enlightenment has indeed taken place in Chinese rural communities, but that it manifests itself in ways other than expected. While they still tend to fall prey to social changes, Chinese peasants, after all, have learned their lessons from years of interacting with "history" and "revolution." They make use of their newly acquired (sociopolitical and economic) wisdom and their "local knowledge," and bring about laudable or lamentable consequences.

In comparison to Mo Yan's *Life and Death Are Wearing Me Out* and Yan Lianke's *Dream of Ding Village*, here we focus on a different type of writing, one that reads as less provocative than Mo Yan's or Yan Lianke's works but conveys no less significant messages. Jia Pingwa's *Qin Tune*, for instance, describes the rapid decline of *Qin qiang*, the most ancient form of Chinese theater, in the face of a rampant consumer culture. Such a subject may sound like a cliché of nativist literature. But instead of following any extant formula, Jia adopts a slow, sprawling "thick narrative" to relate his story, detailing the mysterious origin of the theater and its multiple modern-day adaptations. As Jia implies, *Qin qiang* may become extinct someday, but its "tune," its sound, has long penetrated the deep layers of Chinese social consciousness.

Lin Bai's *Women's Idle Talk* is allegedly a firsthand account of the ramblings of a country woman who makes a living in Beijing as a handywoman in the author's household. The "novel" is fragmentary in structure and has almost no plot to speak of. Through this poorly educated woman's seemingly endless gossip, daydreams, chatting, and stories about her life, however, Lin Bai the narrator comes to learn about the profound economic and moral crisis of rural China. In a way, the woman is a twentieth-first-century version of Xianglin's Wife 祥林嫂, the archetypal suffering peasant woman of modern Chinese literature. Lin Bai's heroine still has the naive impulse to tell her stories, but unlike her early modern counterpart, she knows only too well that she will have to make do with her life by herself instead of relying on either feudalist or socialist superstitions. As a result, it is Lin Bai the narrator/listener who is fascinated, indeed enchanted, by the proliferating stories, while revealing her own ineptitude.

Where Lin Bai's protagonist fascinates her readers with seemingly endless talk, the characters in *One Sentence for 10,000 Sentences* (*Yiju ding yiwanju* 一句顶一万句, 2009) by Liu Zhenyun 刘震云 (1958–) come across as people unable to articulate. This is a novel about the futile search for love and companionship among a group of lower-class people, over two generations. Despite their boisterous life on the surface, Liu's characters are consumed by unfathomable loneliness. Underlying the novel is the phrase "One sentence for ten thousand sentences," a quote from Marshal Lin Biao 林彪 on the eve of the Cultural Revolution, praising Chairman Mao for his mastery of revolutionary truth.[31] While Lin Biao's praise of Mao eventually proved to be a sham, his statement has since taken on a life of its own. Throughout the novel, Liu Zhenyun's characters seek to express themselves to no avail; the magical "sentence" that supposedly summarizes the truth of trust and love remains a mystery. But if a popular saying about Mao's prescient wisdom should have come from someone who ended up being Mao's primary traitor, one wonders if there is any word uttered by anyone that can be taken seriously. Given such a paradox, Liu insinuates that truth and its disavowal may well be two sides of the same coin, and that the longing for sociality and intimacy among his characters evaporates after all, like a failed incantation.

"The Best of All Best Possible Worlds"

Utopia constitutes one of the most important themes at the budding of modern Chinese literature. Works such as *The Future of New China* (*Xin Zhongguo weilaiji* 新中国未来记), by Liang Qichao 梁启超; Wu Jianren 吴趼人, *The New Story of the Stone* (*Xin shitouji* 新石头记); and Biheguan zhuren 碧荷馆主人, *New Era* (*Xinjiyuan* 新纪元) imagine either a futuristic time in which China regains its superpower, or a fantastic space in which China has transformed into an ideal state.[32] By writing the incredible and the impractical, late Qing writers set the terms of China's modernization project, both as a new political agenda and as a new national myth.

This utopian impulse, however, dissipated in the May Fourth era, when writers appeared to be so preoccupied by the canon of realism that they could not even entertain any fantastic thought. Among the few nonrealistic works produced around this time, it was dystopia, not utopia, that became the norm, as evinced by Shen Congwen 沈从文 in *Alice in China* (*Alisi Zhongguo youji* 阿丽思中国游记); Zhang Tianyi 张天翼, *A Diary of Hell* (*Guitu riji* 鬼土日记); and Lao She 老舍, *City of Cats* (*Maochengji* 猫城记).

But utopia had found a new venue—Communist discourse—to demonstrate its power. I have indicated elsewhere that the Communist Revolution is predicated on the vision that the socialist Promised Land is accessible through a radical shakeup of the status quo.[33] To that end, literature is only part of a grand narrative projecting what China should become. One could even argue that the utopian trope always occupied a space in the mainstream literature from 1942 to 1976, be it called socialist realism, revolutionary realism, or revolutionary romanticism. Whatever happens to the past and present, the party/state is supposed to lead the Chinese people to "the best of all best possible worlds."

Operating in conjunction with utopia is science fantasy, a genre that features fantastic marvels and technological novelties in service of a utopian (or dystopian) agenda. Rudolf Wagner has indicated that the genre enjoyed a short-lived boom in China from the mid-1950s to the end of the 1960s, as part of the "marching toward science" campaign.[34] The genre then staged a brief comeback in the late 1970s, following the fall of the Gang of Four; it assumes, as Wagner argues, a new role as "lobby literature," "presenting scientists' group aspirations in the form of the fantasy future, and portraying how scientists would operate in the larger framework of society if their demands were met."[35] Of course, all scientific aspirations were supposed to be sublimated into the Marxist-Maoist brand of science.

Utopia and science fantasy underwent an ambiguous transformation in the fin-de-siècle era. Writers sent mixed signals when looking forward and backward. Despite the ongoing murk of politics, they were able to create more personal visions, and in that sense they remind us of their late Qing predecessors. For instance, Bao Mi 保密 (1953–), in *Yellow Peril* (*Huanghuo* 黃禍, 1991), presents an apocalyptic vision of a China engulfed by civil wars and nuclear holocaust, which result in an exodus and a new "yellow peril" worldwide; Liang Xiaosheng's *Floating City* (*Fucheng* 浮城, 1993) describes a southeastern Chinese metropolis mysteriously disconnected from the mainland. By envisioning China on the verge of either a miraculous rejuvenation or eternal destruction, or by foreseeing China as either a postnuclear wasteland or an instigator of a new "yellow peril," these writers create different temporal and spatial zones through which to ponder the fate of their nation.

The new century witnessed the resurgence of writing and reading utopian and science-fiction fantasy, especially among the younger generation of readers. The recent wave may have something to do with the increasingly open public sphere, which grants writers more leeway to imagine China's past and future.[36] It may also serve as a fictional counterpart to the visionary government campaigns, such as "a great country is rising" (*daguo jueqi* 大国崛起) and "harmonious society" (*hexie shehui* 和谐社会). One hundred years after the appearance of *The Future of New China* and *New Era*, contemporary writers are again negotiating the future of New China and bearing witness to a new era. They have more reasons to think big because China is indeed stronger and more prosperous than at any moment in the preceding century. Sober voices reverberate as well, however. Particularly for our concern, select writers have proposed that any futuristic projection of China presupposes a deep reflection on the meanings of red legacies that have proven both utopian and dystopian.

In Han Song's *2066: Red Star over America*, the year 2066 marks a turning point in Sino-American relations. America has suffered a series economic and political disasters while China has become a "gardenlike" superpower. A prodigy of the Chinese game of Go is sent to a competition in the United States, only to be caught in the Second Civil War there. He undergoes numerous adventures, including surviving a deluge on a ship named *Noah*, and he returns to China in the end. Han Song seems to be relating a revanchist fantasy that has obsessed many writers since the late Qing. But he has more to tell us. China is said to have achieved its superpower status by succumbing to "Amando" 阿曼多, an intelligence that preprograms everyone's life and oversees their happiness in every possible way. But Amando proves to have collapsed when mysterious Martians descend on Earth, turning China into the Land of Promise (*fudi* 福地). Incidentally, the Chinese expression *fudi* is also a euphemism for cemetery—a land for the dead. Thus on top of the conflict of nationalism versus globalism, Han Song entertains a much darker view of the human condition as a whole.

For Han Song, Go is not so much a game of China's intellectual culture as it is a game-like undertaking that incites belligerent desires and political schemes. As a corollary, Amando is but a futuristic version of a "game" that outwits human wisdom and brings about destruction. This leads to Han Song's critique of the intelligibility of history. It will be recalled that part of his novel's title is inspired by *Red Star over China* (1937), a work of reportage by Edgar Snow (1905–72) and arguably the first account in the English-speaking world to unveil life in Yan'an, the wartime Chinese Communist Mecca. By playing off of Snow's title, Han Song prompts one to rethink the geopolitics of utopia in terms of socialist (China), capitalist (America), and extraterrestrial space. His conclusion could not be more ambiguous. Above all, the novel is a flashback set in 2126, the future of the future, when Earth's civilization, be it socialist or capitalist, has been terminated. Over the Land of Promise shines Mars, or Fire Star (Huoxing 火星), in place of Red Star.

Arguably one of the most ambitious works of contemporary Chinese fiction, Liu Cixin's *Earth Chronicles* trilogy—*Three Body* (*Santi* 三体, 2007), *Dark Jungle* (*Heian senlin* 黑暗森林 2008), and *God of Death Lives Forever* (*Sishen yongsheng* 死神永生, 2010)—assumes an epic scope that spans millions of years.[37] Mixing the Cultural Revolution with *Star Wars*, historical pathos with outer-space marvels, Liu has created a chronotope his peers can hardly emulate. But Liu's works are not only a fantastic spectacle; they are also an inquiry into the ethical terms of such a spectacle. *Three Body* relates how a woman scientist exacts revenge for the purging and death of her father in the Cultural Revolution by inviting the extraterrestrial creatures called Three Body to invade Earth. A group of Chinese citizens are drafted to help prevent the impending global holocaust. These heroes travel through the tunnel of time, engage in ingenious tactics, and fight cosmic battles. Meanwhile, it turns out that Chairman Mao had long foreseen these futuristic "star wars" and has implemented a preemptive plan.

Because of its grand scope and majestic style, critics have called Liu's trilogy a sublime work.[38] True, Liu's works are awe-striking in their introduction of an apocalyptic view of the world's civilization in crisis. He asks if human rationality can generate a (political) science that is anything but rational; if history presented in the "future perfect" mood can redeem bygone or ongoing mishaps; if a filial daughter's vengeful wrath can override her professional commitment to social well-being; if a national leader can be both a rescuer and a destroyer of humanity. Liu refuses to give easy answers to his questions; instead he plays them out against the gigantic cosmic backdrop, thereby soliciting an effect that sustains as much as it subverts the "Maoist sublime" that his fictional vision originates with.

In contrast to Han Song's and Liu Cixin's utopian fantasies, the renowned avant-garde writer Ge Fei's *Southlands Trilogy* (*Wutuobang sanbuqu* 乌托邦三部曲)—part 1, *Bygone Beauty* (*Renmian taohua* 人面桃花, 2005); part 2, *Land in Dreamland* (*Shanhe rumeng* 山河入梦, 2007); part 3, *Spring Ends in Southlands* (*Chunjin jiangnan* 春尽江南, 2012)—relates in a more classical style how a utopian project turns into a dystopian nightmare. Ge Fei packages his trilogy in circuitous symbolism, such that it sounds less provocative when compared with the works of two exiled writers, Cao Guanlong 曹冠龙 (1945–) in the United States and Ma Jian 马建 (1952–) in the United Kingdom. Both engage in a revisionist account of the past. In *Sinking* (*Chen* 沉, 2009), Cao Guanlong focuses on a most atrocious incident during the Cultural Revolution: the cannibalism that reportedly took place in Guangxi Province. The incident has been recounted in detail by Zheng Yi 郑义 (1947–) in his report, *Red Memorial* (*Hongse jinian bei* 红色纪念碑, 1993). Cao, however, gives it a twist by writing in a farcical mode. He describes how "eating man" becomes a gastronomic and political necessity in a society immersed in fanaticism, and how, at its most outrageous, cannibalism becomes a culinary art and is transformed into a ghoulish carnival. Lu Xun's "A Madman's Diary" ("Kuangren riji" 狂人日记) thus has an extravagant twenty-first-century edition.

Whereas Cao Guanlong invests his dystopian critique in the cannibalized body, Ma Jian finds in the paralyzed body a site for corporal politics at its most poignant. In *Beijing Coma* (*Rouzhitu* 肉之土, 2010), a young Tiananmen protestor who was gunned down on the night of the June Fourth massacre has been in a coma ever since. Although his body is withering away, the young man's subconscious remains vibrant. This is where Ma Jian's story takes off. In dreams, his protagonist wanders into the world of the classic text *Classic of the Mountains and Seas* (*Shanhai jing* 山海经), where immortals and monstrous creatures, bizarre vegetation and astonishing landscapes interact and form a robust, ever-changing world. By calling on ancient mythology, Ma Jian may be trying to rescue the post-Tiananmen society from the stupor of amnesia. But his narrative is punctuated with moments of uncertainty. Insofar as the world of the *Classic of the Mountains and Seas* is also a grotesque world, crowded with unruly forces and vicious beings, Ma Jian seems to insinuate that he cannot recapitulate the creative energy of the mythical world of ancient times without calling forth its destructive potential at the same time.

Finally, we come to *The Fat Years* by Chen Guanzhong, a Hong Kong writer currently residing in Beijing. The novel starts with a global economic crash in 2011 that paralyzes all the leading countries except China. Thanks to shrewd national leadership, China is able to take advantage of the crisis to further its economic development and sociopolitical solidarity. As a result, as early as 2013 China can already boast of the arrival of *shengshi*, a historical epoch of peace and prosperity. While the majority of Chinese citizens welcome the golden time, there are signs—such as a prevailing mood of jubilation called "high lite lite" and a mass case of amnesia—that arouse a few nonconformists' suspicions. To find out the truth they kidnap a "national leader," only to be persuaded by the latter's self-justification, and they end up quitting their dissident activities.

Compared with the other utopian/dystopian works discussed in this chapter, *The Fat Years* may fall short in presenting either an epic vision or a sinister prophecy. It nevertheless creates a style of its own by linking futuristic fantasy with contemporary issues of journalistic relevance. Contrary to fiction in the vein of *Brave New World* or *1984*, *The Fat Years* does not aim merely to expose the evil scheme of a seemingly benign regime; it seeks instead to tell the other side of the story, thus making the "national leader" in captivity its hero. According to this leader, the primary goal of his government is to make people happy; to that end, market liberalization is only one of the measures China adopts to enhance the quality of life. Our leader may sound like a pragmatist, but he could not be a more firm believer that the Communist Party should be the only and the best ruler of China. When Chairman Mao meets Machiavelli, a new breed of ideologue-cum-technocrat is born. Suave, cool, and a little jaded, this national leader is familiar with the rhetoric of both liberals and New Leftists and does not mind playing with their terms. His nightlong, tell-all confession, which constitutes almost half of the novel, must be the longest lecture ever in contemporary Chinese fiction. In the end, he manages to persuade his kidnappers to release him so that he can better serve the people.

But we are also told that the people are served MDMA, the "ecstasy" drug, in their drinking water, which helps them forget anything that would hamper a healthy "revolutionary memory." This biopolitical episode is a predictable device of science fiction. What Chen Guanzhong really achieves is a story in which the national leader turns out to be not only a competent administrator but also the most mesmerizing storyteller. His story about the golden time turns out to be an even more potent prescription for national ecstasy. According to him, China is securing her sovereignty, and her people believe they are enjoying a wholesome and harmonious life.

We thus see that red legacies in fiction have run full circle. A sublime state has been achieved, not in the sense of the "Maoist sublime" but of the "phantom sublime" as defined by Slavoj Žižek.[39] Still, Chen Guanzhong arranges for his dissident characters to turn their backs on the golden time at the end of the novel, a conclusion that brings to mind Lu Xun's words:

> There is something I dislike in heaven; I do not want to go there. There is something I dislike in hell; I do not want to go there. There is something I dislike in your future golden world; I do not want to go there.[40]

Coda

In his essay "China's Rise: Experiences and Challenges" ("Zhongguo jueqi de jingyan jiqi mianlin de tiaozhan" 中国崛起的经验及其面临的挑战, 2010), the prominent PRC scholar Wang Hui 汪晖 (1959–) argues that although China has been ruled by one political party since 1949 and therefore has been deemed undemocratic, the fact is that "during the 1950s, 1960s, and 1970s, there existed within the party a self-correction mechanism. Theoretical debate, particularly open theoretical debate, has played an important role in the course of the party's and the state's self-adjustment and self-reform."[41] This mechanism of self-correction within the party, according to Wang Hui, was supplemented by the platform of open debate among intellectuals during the 1990s. Either way, it indicates that China watchers are not justified in criticizing China as completely lacking in democratic experience. Wang Hui is also known to have suggested that the Cultural Revolution should not be unconditionally condemned, for it may have paved the way for the rise of the New Era; and that Mao should be credited for his endeavors, at least at select moments in his rule, to promote an authentic "politics" of revolutionary utopia, in contrast to the "depoliticized politics" that has plagued China and the world in recent decades.[42]

Wang Hui's observations have drawn vehement responses. As a matter of fact, the controversy can be regarded as a most recent example of the "open debates" among Chinese intellectuals regarding how to reassess red legacies. His controversial stance aside, Wang Hui deserves merit for trying to rethink revolutionary history and defend the Chinese political system against models prescribed by the West. But Wang may only barely keep a delicate balance when he expresses his yearning for Maoist politics, on the one hand, and conducts a Foucauldian archaeology of history, on the other. And he has yet to account for the tension between the reported polyphony among contemporary intellectuals, which he believes is a welcome addition to the party's "self-correction" system, and the muted dissonant voice of someone like the dissident literary critic and Nobel Peace Prize winner Liu Xiaobo 刘晓波 (1955–).

My intent here, however, is not to critique either Wang Hui or his opponents. Rather, I contend that neither side has gone far enough if they truly aim to discuss the dynamics of red legacies at their most intricate. For Wang Hui, his reassessment of the Cultural Revolution and Maoism could have been more subtly addressed had he taken into account the atrocious human costs involved in the party's "self-correction" system, and the grave ethical and affective consequences Mao's utopian projects have brought about in the lives of millions of Chinese. For Wang's critics, their charges could have been more (de)constructive had they recognized the multiple threads that gave rise to red legacies as well as the nuanced overtones of Wang Hui's argument.

This is where fiction—literature—can contribute more to a critical understanding of red legacies. As I have suggested elsewhere, precisely because fiction, or *xiaoshuo* 小说, can take advantage of its being "small talk," it serves as a remedy for a society inundated with "big talk," or *dashuo* 大说, from theories to criticisms, doctrines, and manifestos.[43] Fiction plays with intellectual exegesis or ideological critique, but it need not assume any highbrow mannerisms or pompous agenda. Moreover, it enjoys a license—even in the heyday of ideological strictures—to imagine what reality is and is not, and what reality should be and should not be. In Mikhail Bakhtin's terminology, fiction *is* heteroglossia by nature; it accommodates as many truth claims as abjurations.[44]

Accordingly, where Wang Hui and his critics are trapped in antagonistic views of red legacies, fiction writers have told us that Mao was both the charismatic leader who inspired Chinese youths to pursue pure "politics" (*Song of Youth*) and the mastermind who directed Chinese youths to depoliticize politics (*Hard as Water*); the Cultural Revolution was both an "age of Enlightenment" and an age that saw human dignity and rationality degenerate into a performance of totems versus taboos

(*Wolf Totem*; *Boat to Redemption*); the postsocialist era both bids farewell to socialist cannibalism (*Women's Idle Talk*) and welcomes capitalist cannibalism (*Brothers*).

Most importantly, fiction is more than a replica of reality; it encourages imagination, projects plural discursive trajectories, and maps allegorical horizons. Thus, from the fictional perspective, one can take another look at Wang Hui's endorsement of the "self-correction" mechanism of the Communist Party and contemplate its implications. It brings to mind the allegory of "immunity" that revolutionary forerunners such as Lu Xun and Chen Duxiu once conceived.[45] For Lu Xun, as for Chen Duxiu, just as white cells help immunize the body against the attack virus, so literature bears the agency that helps a society forestall and "self-correct" its wrongs.

Wang Hui would have liked to follow Lu Xun's provocation. But writing in the new century, can he make his "self-correction" theory as critical *and* allegorical as someone like Yan Lianke does in *Dream of Ding Village*, which treats the spread of the AIDS—a disease caused by the immune system's being "autoimmunized"—a sign of both bodily malfunction and sociopolitical degeneration?[46] One recalls that Yan's fiction was banned, a fact that may indicate either that the "self-correction" mechanism of the party-state was well at work, or more likely, that the mechanism works so well as to nullify from within any elements meant to help immunize the national body against malaise and corruption.

Or, one wonders if the "self-correction" mechanism may have had its moment of oversight in approving a novel such as Mo Yan's *Life and Death Are Wearing Me Out*. In that novel, the ups and downs of land reform throughout the PRC's history proceed like a cycle of self-corrections. Instead of directly assessing the outcome of the Maoist machine of self-correction, Mo Yan attributes the pains, absurdities, and inconsistencies arising therefrom to a different kind of machine of self-correction, the layman-Buddhist belief in retribution and transmigration. As his protagonist undergoes a series of metamorphoses, from a human into different species of animals, throughout the history of socialist China, Mo Yan casts a most dubious light on red legacies.

To conclude this review of fiction's red legacies, I turn to Voltaire's *Candide*, arguably the most powerful fictional testimony to the age of Enlightenment. Candide grows up in a sheltered life, indoctrinated in

Leibnizian optimism by his mentor, Dr. Pangloss. As a young man, he is nevertheless thrown into a sequence of most horrible trials, to the point that he realizes that the utopia he is seeking is actually unlivable; his sweetheart has become a shrew, and rationality is forever haunted by contingencies.

In the end, Candide and Pangloss seem to have found a way to live a peaceful life. Looking back, Pangloss concludes that the sufferings they have undergone make sense after all, and that "all is for the best in the best of all possible worlds." All wrongs are corrected by the universal Divine Design. Candide, while not rejecting his mentor's optimism outright, simply responds, "We must cultivate our garden."

With the ending of *Candide* in mind, I suggest that, whereas theoreticians and literary critics explain by explaining away the twists and turns of China's red legacies, fiction writers and readers restore, nay, cultivate them. In their imaginary gardens, realities and fantasies graft onto each other, politics take root in necessity and desire, and legacies, whatever color, are nurtured on fiction.

Notes

1. "The Nobel Prize in Literature 2012 Mo Yan," *Nobelprize.org*, October 11, 2012, at http://www.nobelprize.org/nobel_prizes/literature/laureates/2012/ (accessed June 30, 2014).

2. David Der-wei Wang 王德威, "Kuangyan liuyan, wuyan moyan" 狂言流言, 巫言莫言 (Crazy talk, fluid talk, bewitched talk, no talk), in *Yijiu sijiu yihou* 一九四九以后 (After 1949), ed. David Wang, Chen Sihe 陈思和, and Xu Zidong 许子东 (Hong Kong: Oxford University Press, 2010), pp. 1–21.

3. David Der-wei Wang and Michael Berry, "The Literary World of Mo Yan," *World Literature Today* 74, no. 3 (Summer 2000): 487–94.

4. The scholars siding with New Leftism are particularly vociferous when they critique globalism versus indigenous autonomy and capitalist imperialism versus postcolonial resistance. See, e.g., Wang Hui, *The End of Revolution: China and the Limits of Modernity* (New York: Verso, 2009); *China's New Order: Society, Politics, and Economy in Transition*, trans. Ted Huters and Rebecca Karl (Cambridge, MA: Harvard University Press, 2003); Xudong Zhang, *Postsocialism and Cultural Politics: China in the Last Decade of the Twentieth Century* (Durham, NC: Duke University Press, 2008); Lydia Liu, *The Clash of Empires: The Invention of China in Modern World Making* (Cambridge, MA: Harvard University Press, 2004).

5. See, e.g., the meticulous analysis by Leonard Chan (Kwak-kau Chan) on the formation of "literature" as a discipline at the turn of the twentieth century:

Wenxue ruhe chengwei zhishi? Wenxue piping, wenxue yanjiu, yu wenxue jiaoyu 文学如何成为知识? 文学批评, 文学研究与文学教育 (How did literature become knowledge? Literary criticism, literary studies, literary education) (Hong Kong: Hong Kong Institute of Education, 2010).

6. I am referring to the long genealogy of theoretical endeavor that highlights the creative and evocative dimensions of literary engagement, ranging from Aristotelian and Confucian presuppositions to romantic and deconstructive provocations. As far as this chapter is concerned, I would call attention to the fact that the mutual implication of historicity and (fictional) narrativity has always been the case in Chinese historiographical and literary studies. But never have we seen such a moment as we have in modern times, when official history has been so dictated by the ideological and institutional imaginary as to verge on the discourse of make-believe, a discourse often associated with traditional fiction, and fiction so arrested by a desire to reflect the past *and* future as to appropriate the functions of traditional history with respect to completed fact. Hence the genesis of the peculiar double bind of Chinese literary modernity.

7. Hannah Arendt, *The Human Condition* (Chicago: University of Chicago Press, 1968), p. 105: "Storytelling reveals meaning without committing the error of defining it."

8. Mo Yan, afterword to the Chinese edition of *Shengsi pilao* 生死疲劳 (Life and death are wearing me out) (Taipei: Rye Field, 2007), p. 611.

9. Hayden White, *Metahistory: The Historical Imagination in Nineteenth-Century Europe* (Baltimore: Johns Hopkins University Press, 1973). For a definition of the "moral occult," see Peter Brooks, *The Melodramatic Imagination: Balzac, Henry James, Melodrama, and the Mode of Excess* (New Haven, CT: Yale University Press, 1976), chap. 1; also see Brooks, *Reading for the Plot: Design and Intention in Narrative* (Cambridge, MA: Harvard University Press, 1992).

10. Jacques Derrida, *Specters of Marx: The State of the Debt, the Work of Mourning and the New International*, trans. Peggy Kamuf (New York: Routledge, 1994). For discussions of Derrida's theory, see Peggy Kamuf, "Violence, Identity, Self-Determination and the Question of Justice: On *Specters of Marx*," in *Violence, Identity, and Self-Determination*, ed. Hent deVries and Samuel Weber (Stanford, CA: Stanford University Press, 1997), pp. 271–83; Nigel Mapp, "Specter and Impurity: History and the Transcendental in Derrida and Adorno," in *Ghosts: Deconstruction, Psychoanalysis, History*, ed. Peter Buse and Andrew Stott (New York: St. Martin's Press, 1999), pp. 92–124. For a critique of Derrida's theory, see Michael Sprinker, ed., *Ghostly Demarcations: A Symposium on Jacques Derrida's Specters of Marx* (London: Verso, 1999).

11. For Derrida's theory in the Chinese context, see Chen Xiaoming's *Delida de dixian: Jiegou de yaoyi yu xinren wenzhue de daolai* 德里达的底线: 解构的要义与新人文主义学的到来 (The bottom line of Derrida: The meaning of deconstruction and the arrival of new humanism) (Beijing: Beijing daxue chubanshe, 2009); see chap. 10 for the "specters of Marx" and the Chinese socialist legacy.

12. I consider the "real" in terms of Slavoj Žižek's definition in *The Sublime Object of Ideology* (London: Verso, 1989).

13. See my discussions on Mao Dun, Lao She, and Shen Congwen, in *Fictional Realism in Twentieth-Century China* (New York: Columbia University Press, 1992), chap. 3; David Der-wei Wang, *The Monster That Is History: History, Violence, and Fictional Writing in Twentieth-Century China* (Berkeley: University of California Press, 2004), chap. 3.

14. Wang, *The Monster That Is History*, chap. 3.

15. See Jianmei Liu, *Revolution Plus Love: Literary History, Women's Bodies, and Thematic Repetition in Twentieth-Century Chinese Fiction* (Honolulu: University of Hawai'i Press, 2003).

16. See my discussion in Wang, *The Monster That Is History*, pp. 161–69.

17. Ibid., p. 262.

18. See, e.g., Xiaobin Yang, *The Chinese Postmodern: Trauma and Irony in Chinese Avant-Garde Fiction.* (Ann Arbor: University of Michigan Press, 2002); Xudong Zhang, *Chinese Modernism in the Era of Reforms: Cultural Fever, Avant-Garde Fiction, and New Chinese Cinema* (Durham, NC: Duke University Press, 1997); Jing Wang, *High Culture Fever: Politics, Aesthetics, and Ideology in Deng's China* (Berkeley: University of California Press, 1996).

19. Arthur C. Danto, *Beyond the Brillo Box: The Visual Arts in Post-Historical Perspective* (Berkeley: University of California Press, 1998).

20. Francis Fukuyama, *The End of History and the Last Man* (New York: Free Press, 1992).

21. Li Zehou and Liu Zaifu, *Gaobie geming: Ershi shiji Zhongguo duitanlu* 告别革命: 二十世纪中国对谈录 (Farewell to revolution: A dialogue on twentieth-century China) (Taipei: Rye Field, 1999). "Rewrite literary history" refers first to a column hosted by Chen Sihe and Wang Xiaoming in the journal *Shanghai wenlun* 上海文论 (Shanghai literary criticism) in 1988; the column sought to reevaluate the canon of modern Chinese literature as instituted by the party line, and it quickly ignited debates among intellectuals as to the "rewritability" of literary history and even history as such.

22. See Yang, *The Chinese Postmodern.*

23. Mo Yan was born in the rural town of Gaomi in Shandong Province; he joined the PLA in 1976 and took an early retirement in 1997. Yan Lianke is a native of Song Prefecture in Henan Province; he joined the PLA in 1978 and was discharged in 2004.

24. On *Lenin's Kisses*, see Chapter 10 in this volume.

25. David Apter and Tony Saich, *Revolutionary Discourse in Mao's Republic* (Cambridge, MA: Harvard University Press, 1994).

26. Max Weber, *The Protestant Ethic and The "Spirit" of Capitalism and Other Writings*, trans. Peter Baehr and Gordon C. Wells (New York: Penguin Books, 2002); for a detailed discussion, see, e.g., Malcolm H. Mackinnon, "Max Weber's Disenchantment Lineages of Kant and Channing," *Journal of Classical Sociology* 1, no. 3 (2001): 329–51.

27. Here I am referring to the "Real" in Slavoj Žižek's definition; see Žižek, *The Sublime Object of Ideology.*

28. Rey Chow, *Primitive Passions: Visuality, Sexuality, Ethnography, and Contemporary Chinese Cinema* (New York: Columbia University Press, 1995), chap. 1.

29. Wang Hui, "Dangdai Zhongguo de sixiang zhuangkuang yu xiandaixing wenti" 当代中国的思想状况与现代性问题 (The intellectual dynamics of contemporary China and the question of modernity), in *Qu zhengzhihua de zhengzhi: Duan ershi shiji de zhongjie yu jiushi niandai* 去政治化的政治: 短二十世纪的终结与九十年代 (Depoliticized politics: The end of the short twentieth century and the 1990s) (Beijing: Sanlian shudian, 2008), pp. 58–97.

30. This scene appears only in the 2003 edition of *Long Live Youth*, which partly restores Wang Meng's 1953 manuscript; in all the earlier versions of this novel, this scene of more than six pages is deleted. See Wang Meng, *Qingchun wansui* 青春万岁 (Beijing: Renmin wenxue chubanshe, 2003), pp. 315–20. See Mingwei Song's succinct discussion in "The Taming of the Youth: Discourse, Politics, and Fictional Representation in the Early PRC," *Journal of Modern Literature in Chinese* 9, no. 2 (July 2009): 108–38.

31. Lin Biao: "The thought of Mao Zedong represents the apex of contemporary Marxism and Leninism and is the highest directive of our military forces. The books by Chairman Mao are the highest directive of our military forces. The words of Chairman Mao are of the highest standard, authority, and power. Every sentence of his is truth; every single sentence is as useful as ten thousand sentences" (毛泽东思想是当代马克思列宁主义的顶峰, 是我们全军各项工作的最高指示.毛主席的书, 是我们全军各项工作的最高指示. 毛主席的话, 水平最高, 威信最高, 威力最大. 句句是真理, 一句顶一万句.) *Renmin ribao* 人民日報 (People's daily), January 24, 1966.

32. See my discussion in David Der-wei Wang, *Fin-de-siècle Splendor: Repressed Modernities of Late Qing Fiction, 1849–1911* (Stanford, CA: Stanford University Press, 1997), chap. 5.

33. Ibid.

34. Rudolf Wagner, "Lobby Literature: The Archaeology and Present Functions of Science Fiction in China," in *After Mao: Chinese Literature and Society, 1978-1981*, ed. Jeffrey C. Kinkley (Cambridge, MA: Council on East Asian Studies, Harvard University, 1985), p. 334.

35. Ibid., p. 335.

36. For recent studies on utopia, see, e.g., Fredric Jameson, *Archaeologies of the Future: The Desire Called Utopia and Other Science Fictions* (London: Verso, 2005).

37. *Santi*, or "Three-body," refers to a specific mathematical term, a theoretical problem that scientists have been trying to solve for the past two centuries. Basic information about it can be found at http://en.wikipedia.org/wiki/Three-body_problem (accessed June 30, 2014).

38. Jia Liyuan 贾立元, "Zhujiu women de weilai: Jiushi niandai zhijin Zhongguo kehuan xiaoshuo zhong de Zhongguo xingxiang yanjiu" 筑就我們的未來: 九十年代至今中国科幻小说中的中国形象研究 (Achieving our future: Study of China's image in Chinese science fiction since the 1990s), masters thesis, Beijing Normal University, 2010, pp. 30–46.

39. See Žižek, *The Sublime Object of Ideology*.

40. Lu Xun, "The Shadow's Leaving-Taking," in *Wild Grass*, trans. Feng Yu-sheng (Peking: Foreign Languages Press, 1974), p. 8.

41. Wang Hui, "Zhongguo jueqi de jingyan jiqi mianlin de tiaozhan" 中国崛起的经验及其面临的挑战 (China's rise: Experiences and challenges), *Wenhua zongheng* 文化纵横 2 (2010), at http://www.aisixiang.com/data/33011.html (accessed June 30, 2014).

42. Wang Hui, "Qu zhengzhihua de zhengzhi, baquan de duochong goucheng yu 60 niandai de xiaoshi" 去政治化的政治, 霸权的多重构成与 60 年代的消逝 (The politics of depoliticization, the multiple constructs of hegemony, and the fading of the 1960s), in Wang, *Qu zhengzhihua de zhengzhi*, pp. 1–57.

43. David Der-wei Wang, preface to *Narrating China* (*Xiaoshuo Zhongguo*, 小说中国) (Taibei: Rye Field, 1993), pp. 1–5.

44. Mikhail Bakhtin, *Dialogic Imagination, Four Essays*, ed. Michael Holquist, trans. Vadim Liapunov and Kenneth Brostrom (Austin: University of Texas Press, 1982), chap. 1.

45. See Carlos Rojas, "Cannibalism and the Chinese Body Politic: Hermeneutics and Violence in Cross-cultural Perception," *Postmodern Culture* 12, no. 3 (May 2002), at http://www.pomoculture.org/2013/09/19/cannibalism-and-the-chinese-body-politic-hermeneutics-and-violence-in-cross-cultural-perception/ (accessed October 5, 2015).

46. Jacques Derrida, "Autoimmunity: Real and Symbolic Suicides," in Giovanna Borradori, *Philosophy in a Time of Terror: Dialogues with Jürgen Habermas and Jacques Derrida* (Chicago: University of Chicago Press, 2003); for an extensive analysis, see J. Hillis Miller, "Derrida Enisled," *Critical Inquiry* 33, no. 2 (2007): 248–76.

SEVEN

POST-SOCIALIST REALISM IN CHINESE CINEMA

Jason McGrath

In the climactic moment of the 1955 film *Dong Cunrui* 董存瑞, a classic war film from Mao-era China, the eponymous hero commits a suicide bombing to destroy an enemy machine gun nest that threatens a wave of attacking Communist troops. The scene brings to the fore two notable aspects of Chinese socialist realist cinema: its melodramatic romanticism and its propensity to indulge in formalist techniques during moments of maximum emotional and ideological impact.[1] In this scene, editing is particularly foregrounded; the seven shots preceding the explosion take approximately sixteen seconds in all, for a quick editing rate of just over two seconds per shot. Especially striking are the cuts before the explosion that bring the audience suddenly much closer to the character in his life's final moments. These edits, which in three quick shots cut from an extreme long shot to a medium close-up of the hero holding the dynamite (fig. 7.1), resemble jump cuts because the camera distance changes dramatically while the frontal position changes hardly at all (thus violating the "30-degree rule" of classical continuity editing).[2] The technique recalls the radical use of similar editing in films like *Arsenal* (1929) by the Russian and Soviet director Vsevelod Pudovkin (whose theories of montage were influential in China), thus pointing to the continued Soviet influence on Chinese cinema of the time.[3] Such films combined elements of what David Bordwell has called the "historical materialist" (that is, early Soviet) narrative mode with the more predominant, Hollywood-based "classical" narrative mode, as moments of

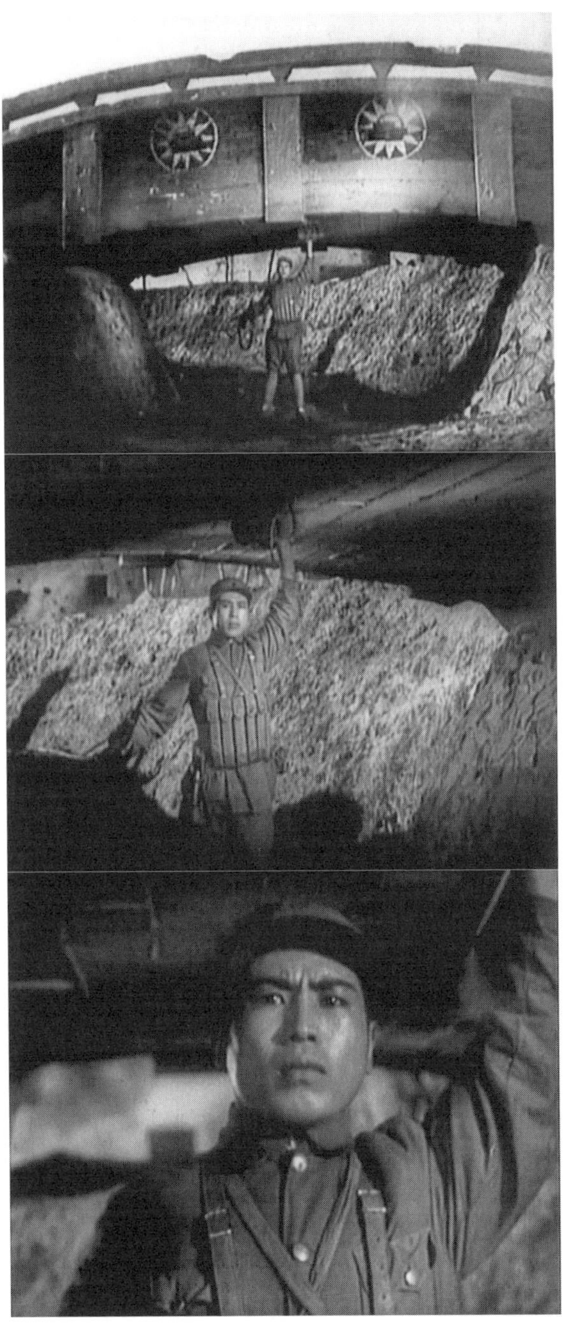

FIGURE 7.1 Final three shots of the hero in the 1955 film *Dong Cunrui* 董存瑞, directed by Guo Wei.

"socialist formalism" are interspersed with mostly classical socialist realism.[4]

In the context of red legacies in the films of postsocialist China, one other moment in *Dong Cunrui* is significant. It takes place earlier in the film, when a band of Communist soldiers are hunkered down along a grassy hillside, waiting to do battle with a larger group of Japanese soldiers. When the latter come charging up the hill, one of the Communist soldiers announces, "The devils have come!" (*guizi laile*! 鬼子来了!), using the standard derogatory term for the Japanese enemy. Forty-five years later, the actor and director Jiang Wen 姜文 would use this exact phrase as the title of his own film about the anti-Japanese resistance—a darkly funny, irreverent, and occasionally shocking dismantling of the foundational myth of the People's Republic of China, the master narrative of how the Communist army saved the Chinese people, in part through resistance against the Japanese occupation.

That film, rendered in English as *Devils on the Doorstep* (2000), is one good example of the phenomenon I call "post–socialist realism," a term I define against the precedent of socialist realism. Beginning with critical discourse in 1979 and the early 1980s, which we will consider here in detail, post–socialist realism in Chinese cinema developed over the course of three decades, revealing continuities among the so-called Fourth, Fifth, and Sixth (and beyond) "generations" of filmmakers.[5] Post-socialist realist cinema conforms aesthetically in many ways to the neorealist model theorized by André Bazin—a set of stylistic preferences that implicitly oppose both Mao-era socialist realism and post-Mao entertainment cinema, while also deliberately cueing and then subverting genre and narrative conventions from Mao-era films such as *Dong Cunrui*. *Devils on the Doorstep*, for example, cites that tradition in its very title but then proceeds to undermine it in both style and story. Post–socialist realism thus invokes the legacy of Maoism not simply through nostalgic or parodic citation, but by developing as its dialectical other in form even as it subverts the narrative content of socialist realism and its mainstream successors in post-Mao China—including both state-sponsored "leitmotif" or "main–melody" cinema (*zhuxuanlü dianying* 主旋律电影) and commercial entertainment cinema (and the increasingly common blends of the two).[6]

In his brief but indispensable 1921 essay "On Realism and Art," Roman Jakobson highlights the inherent historicity of any claim to realism, showing how any dominant code or set of conventions that is widely claimed to be the most realist eventually will generate two opposing tendencies: the conservative tendency to follow the tradition and view it as the way to be faithful to reality, and the progressive tendency to deform the given code, viewing it as in fact a distortion of reality, and its deformation, therefore, as more faithful to reality than its maintenance.[7] At the time of his writing, for example, the conservative hegemonic code in literature was that of late nineteenth-century realism, while the emerging modernist avant-garde attempted to undermine its tired conventions and thus bring art closer to life. Jakobson's broader insight is that every form of realism implicitly constitutes itself by reference to some previous mode that is thought to have become stale and formulaic, even if that previous mode also had called itself "realism." By the same token, the newer, more authentic realism inevitably establishes a set of conventions—conventions, no doubt, that initially are "unconventional" and said to give access to the real—which, once they become habitual, may themselves appear equally ossified and cut off from reality. Thus, my assay of post–socialist realism must address not just its development against the precedent of socialist realism but also its own eventual consolidation in some cases into cliché.

Socialist and Post-Socialist Realism

Chinese socialist or "proletarian" realism arose in part as an intended dialectical improvement on the critical or social realism inspired by nineteenth-century Western literature, and evident also in Shanghai's left-wing cinema of the 1930s and 1940s. Such "old" realism was said to stop at merely reflecting the current ills of society, without inspiring action and showing the way forward.[8] Socialist realism, in contrast, does not merely seek to hold a mirror up to a corrupt world or society, "objectively" reflecting or recording its appearance; instead, it tries to demonstrate society's inner structure and history's direction. Thus, for example, it highlights the class nature of society through the representation of social types in Marxist moral melodramas. One way in which "revolutionary romanticism" is added to supplement socialist or "revolutionary realism" is in the depiction of socialist heroes, who propel history forward and thereby reveal its direction (often through gallant self-sacrifice, as in the case of Dong Cunrui), while also modeling the ideal Communist citizen of the future.[9] In terms of style and narrative structure, socialist realist cinema generally includes such "classical" Hollywood elements as continuity editing, clear goal-driven protagonists, obvious chains of cause and effect that develop through scenes highlighting the most significant story events, and some sense of resolution at the end. Formal ostentation—in the form of montage sequences, superimposed shots, and so on—is occasionally seen in moments of great dramatic impact and is clearly motivated by the narrative.

In contrast, post–socialist realism manifests a loss of historical certainty in terms of narrative content, while in its style it emerges as a reaction against both Hollywood-style classicism and the intermittent Soviet-style formal artifice of socialist realism. The term "post-socialism," though rarely used in China itself, has been employed frequently by scholars in the West to describe the conditions in China after Mao, during the so-called era of reform and opening that Deng Xiaoping launched in late 1978. Arif Dirlik first proposed the term in 1989 to refer not to a capitalist China that had completely discarded socialism, but rather to a still ostensibly socialist China that nonetheless sought to redefine the relation between Chinese socialism and capitalist modernity.[10] Within a few years, it became increasingly difficult to conceive of the emerging "socialism with Chinese characteristics" as anything other than Chinese capitalism, owing to the ongoing economic boom and the accompanying marketization, if not outright privatization, of more and more sectors of the economy—including the film industry and other cultural institutions. A number of recent scholarly books on China have featured the term "post-socialism," just as many works on Eastern Europe and the former Soviet Union have used either "post-socialist" or "post-communist" to describe those societies since 1989.[11]

Specifically in the realm of Chinese cinema studies, the term "post-socialism" has been used by Chris Berry, first as part of the phrase "post-socialist strategies" in an essay (with Mary Ann Farquhar) on the early Fifth-Generation films *Yellow Earth* (*Huang tudi* 黄土地, dir. Chen Kaige 陈凯歌, 1984) and *Black Cannon Incident* (*Hei pao shijian* 黑炮事件, dir. Huang Jianxin 黄建新, 1985), and then in his book *Postsocialist Cinema in Post-Mao China*, which covers a slightly earlier group of Chinese films, those made in the years immediately following the Cultural

Revolution.[12] However, so far as I know, among scholars of contemporary China the specific phrase "post–socialist realism" has been used only by myself in a discussion of the early films of Jia Zhangke 贾樟柯, in which I argue that those films are post-socialist realist in two senses: first, they are a realism of the post-socialist social and economic condition; and second, they self-consciously supplant and oppose the cinematic aesthetics of socialist realism and its successor, state-studio "leitmotif" cinema. I hyphenate "post-socialist" partly in order to highlight this second sense, more clearly retaining the implied "socialist realism" against which post–socialist realism began to differentiate itself soon after the Cultural Revolution.

Although my previous use of the term referred in particular to Jia Zhangke's student works and his first feature film, *Xiao Wu* 小武 (1997), post–socialist realism goes back to the dawn of the so-called New Era (*xin shiqi* 新时期). In 1979 a dramatically new discourse on cinema became evident in China's film periodicals. The dominant trend in those critical essays was to argue for the autonomy of film from other arts such as literature and—especially—drama, and to promote, in the words of the most well-known of the essays, the "modernization of film language" as a set of techniques that would reconnect film to real life by overcoming the conventions that Chinese cinema was said to have drawn, in far too great a measure, from dramatic traditions.[13] Those techniques included on-location shooting, natural lighting and sound, naturalistic performances that might involve nonprofessional actors, long shots and long takes, deep-focus photography, handheld camerawork, episodic narratives, attention to seemingly irrelevant details, an openness to contingency in the profilmic event, and lack of unambiguous plot resolution.

In fact, the new conventions—which constituted the means of breaking the old conventions of socialist realism—fall largely into two broad sets of stylistic options, which often are found mixed together even within the same post-socialist realist films. First, there is what can broadly be defined as elements of a pseudo-documentary style, including handheld camerawork, a relatively fast pace of cutting, nonprofessional actors, on-location shooting, natural lighting and sound, and openness to contingency in the event filmed. Second, there is a more aestheticized long-shot/long-take style and an episodic/elliptical narrative structure that show the overarching influence of French film theorist André Bazin—

as do some of the "documentary" techniques—but possibly also the influences of modernist art cinema and even "traditional" expressionist Chinese aesthetics.

Genre Subversion

Before examining the stylistic conventions of post–socialist realism in more detail, it will be useful to look briefly at those aspects of the phenomenon that have to do more with subverting the genre conventions—and thereby the historical claims and political ideology—of Mao-era socialist realism. A variety of Mao-era genres—war epics, spy thrillers, even musicals and comedies—served to reinforce the master narrative of the liberation of the Chinese people by the Chinese Communist Party and the ongoing vigilance against reactionary forces that seek to compromise the people's victory. Communist and Communist-sympathizing protagonists thus face a whole host of villains, including feudal authorities such as landlords, Nationalist Party (KMT) officials and soldiers, and imperialist Japanese occupiers or American aggressors. Even in the reform era, officially sponsored "leitmotif" films selectively repeat these narratives and reinforce the idea of CCP-led prosperity and progress.

In *Devils on the Doorstep*, the setup immediately cues the viewers' expectations of the historical master narrative of resistance against imperialism: a Communist guerrilla fighter enlists the local peasantry to assist the underground resistance in an area occupied by the Japanese army. The conventions of socialist realism would dictate that the Communist cadre be handsome, courageous, and in solidarity with the peasants on whose behalf he fights to liberate the country, and the peasants whose help is enlisted would in turn be inspired to revolutionary consciousness by the brave cadre. In the film, however, the lone Communist character is never seen except as a handgun and then a sword extended into the frame from off screen. The weapons are used to threaten the hapless peasant Ma Dasan 马大三, who is ordered to watch over a kidnapped Japanese soldier and his translator. The film is in fact devoid of heroism, and the Chinese people under occupation are depicted hardly more favorably than either their brutal Japanese occupiers or the dimwitted American soldiers who appear at the end of the film.

Even the casting of the film plays on its Mao-era generic precedents.

PLATE 1. *Paying Respects at the First Party Congress Site*, 1974, Shanghai People's Art Publishing House. Image courtesy of the Shanghai Propaganda Poster Art Center.

PLATE 2. Pan Jiajun 潘家峻, *Wo shi haiyan* 我是海燕 (I am a petrel), 1972. Courtesy of the artist.

PLATE 3. Chen Yanning 陈衍宁, *Yugang xinyi* 渔港新医 (New doctor at the fishing port), 1975. Courtesy of the artist.

PLATE 4. Zhang Shaocheng 张绍城, *Guangkuo tiandi xin miaozhuang* 广阔天地新苗壮 (New saplings of the vast universe), 1973. Courtesy of the artist.

PLATE 5. Anonymous artist, *Shenye bu mian* 深夜不眠 (Awake late into the night), 1975. China Poster Collection, University of Westminster.

PLATE 6. *Zhaodaole hongqi* 找到了红旗 (I've found the red flag), 1971. Photograph of Wu Qinghua, heroine of the revolutionary modern ballet *Red Detachment of Women*. Paul Crook Collection, on loan to the China Poster Collection, University of Westminster.

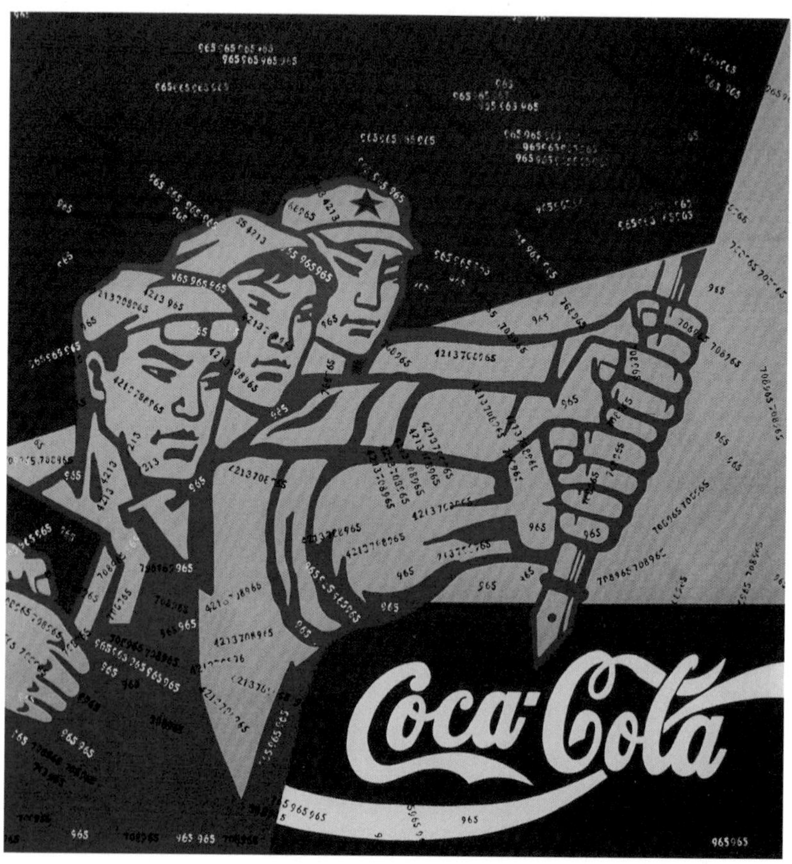

PLATE 7. Wang Guangyi 王广义, *Great Criticism: Coca-Cola* 大批判—可口可乐, 1990–1993, oil on canvas, 200 × 200 cm. Courtesy of the artist.

PLATE 8. *(left)* Wang Guangyi, *Mao Zedong: Red Grid No. 1* 毛泽东—红格1号, 1988, oil on canvas, 150 × 130 cm. Courtesy of the artist.

PLATE 9. *(below)* Wang Guangyi, *Great Criticism: Pepsi* 大批判—百事可乐, 1998, oil on canvas, 200 × 180 cm. Courtesy of the artist.

PLATE 10. Red Guard artists at work, 1967, photographer unknown. Collection of Wang Mingxian.

PLATE 11. *Down with American Imperialism! Down with Soviet Revisionism!* 打倒美帝！打倒苏修！(Wuhan: Hubei renmin chubanshe, 1969), poster, 77 × 35 cm. Image courtesy of the International Institute of Social History, Amsterdam.

PLATE 12. Wang Guangyi, *Great Criticism: WTO* 大批判—*WTO*, 2001, oil on canvas, 200 × 200 cm. Courtesy of the artist.

PLATE 13. Wang Guangyi, *The Face of Belief B* 信仰的面孔 B, 2002, oil on canvas, 200 × 200 cm. Courtesy of the artist.

PLATE 14. Wang Guangyi, *Great Criticism: Warhol* 大批判－沃霍尔, 2005, oil on canvas, 200 × 160 cm. Courtesy of the artist.

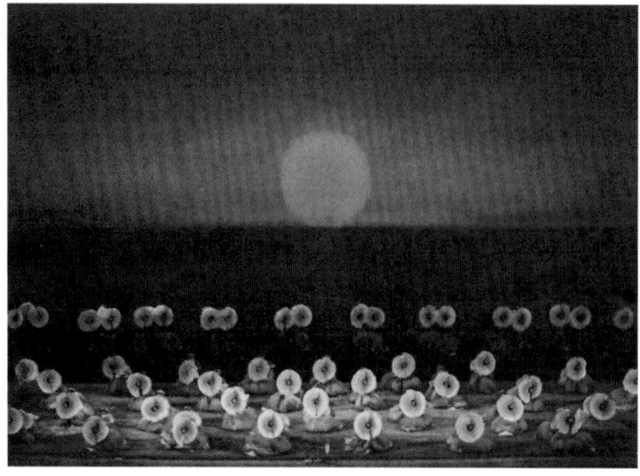

PLATE 15. The Sunflower Dance, from the prologue to *The East Is Red* (1964).

PLATE 16. "A Morning Melody of the Motherland," from the prologue to *The Song of the Chinese Revolution* (1984).

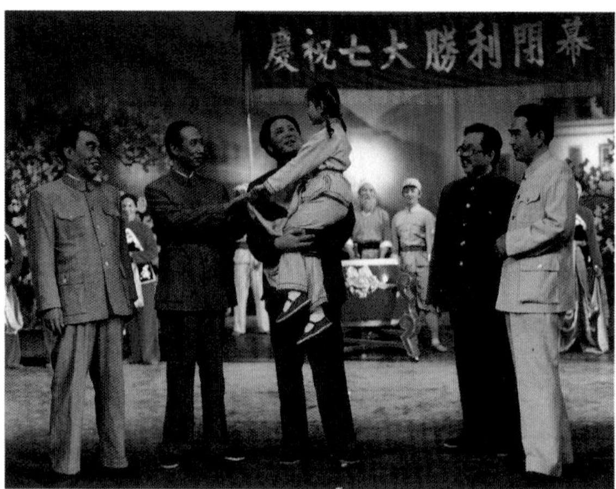

PLATE 17. "From the Long March to the War of Liberation," act 3 of *The Song of the Chinese Revolution* (1984).

PLATE 18. The dance "Fighting across the Yangzi River," from act 2 of "An Epic of Heroic Martyrs," in *The Road to Revival* (2009). This image also shows an arched stairway over the "raked stage," which created a gradually sloped platform for imagining "the road back into history."

PLATE 19. The song and dance "On the Long March," from act 2 of "An Epic of Heroic Martyrs," in *The Road to Revival* (2009).

PLATE 20. Act 5, "The Song of China," in *The Road to Revival* (2009) celebrates the founding of the PRC in 1949 with the songs and dances of ethnic minorities, such as the Chinese Muslims shown in this scene.

PLATE 21. Farmers in the 1984 film *Life* 人 生, directed by Wu Tianming.

PLATE 22. Farmers in the 1984 film *Yellow Earth* 黄土地, directed by Chen Kaige.

PLATE 23. *(above)* Peng Tian as Mao, Hunan, ca. 2007, in *Ready Made* (2008), directed by Zhang Bingjian.

PLATE 24. *(left)* Chen Yan as Mao, Sichuan, ca. 2007, in *Ready Made* (2008), directed by Zhang Bingjian.

PLATE 25. The countdown segment of the Opening Ceremony for the 2008 Olympic Games featured 2,008 drummers.

PLATE 26. Prince Jai (Jay Chou) leads a digital multitude into battle in *Curse of the Golden Flower* (2006).

PLATE 27. Slow-motion footage of the 1984 National Day parade closes the film *The Big Parade* (1986).

PLATE 28. In *Red Sorghum* (1987), the Japanese army assembles an audience and forces them to witness an execution.

PLATE 29. Displays in the Jianchuan Museum's Red Era series. Photo by Denise Y. Ho.

PLATE 30. Views of the Red Guard Graveyard in Chongqing. Photo by Jie Li.

Attentive viewers would have recognized the actor playing the would-be executioner "One-stroke Liu," a legendary swordsman who turns out to be merely a crazy old man, as the eighty-plus-year-old Chen Qiang 陈强, who portrayed the evil landlords Huang Shiren 黄世仁 and Nan Batian 南霸天 in the Mao-era classics *White-Haired Girl* (*Bai mao nü* 白毛女, dir. Shui Hua 水华 and Wang Bin 王滨, 1950) and *Red Detachment of Women* (*Hongse niangzi jun* 红色娘子军, dir. Xie Jin 谢晋, 1961), respectively—his menacing performances in those films now being reduced to ridiculous parody.

Stylistically, much of *Devils on the Doorstep* employs aspects of neorealism, with mostly handheld cameras, shooting often in claustrophobic interior spaces lit by a single light source, plunging much of the frame into darkness. Many minor characters are played by nonprofessional actors, some of whom also served as crew members. With the exception of the final two shots, the entire film is in black and white, which adds to the low-budget documentary aesthetic but simultaneously recalls the film's generic precedents in Chinese black-and-white war movies from the 1950s, including the film from which it takes its title.[14]

Devils on the Doorstep, in its deconstruction of the socialist realist war movie, shares continuities with many other post-socialist realist films, including those of both preceding and subsequent "generations." Its director, Jiang Wen, is sometimes considered a Sixth-Generation filmmaker, but the basic strategy of undermining the mythology of heroic resistance to the Japanese occupation can be found in films as early as *The One and the Eight* (*Yige he bage* 一个和八个, dir. Zhang Junzhao 张军钊, 1983)—generally considered to be the first film of the Fifth Generation—and it is still evident in the recent *City of Life and Death* (*Nanjing! Nanjing!* 南京! 南京!, 2009), directed by one of China's most promising post–Sixth Generation directors, Lu Chuan 陆川. All of these films undermine, with more or less subtlety, the genre conventions of Mao-era war films. Other classics of the postsocialist period perform similar generic subversions of the party-promoted master narrative of China's delivery from poverty and feudal oppression. In the landmark early Fifth-Generation film *Yellow Earth*, for example, a handsome Communist cadre is idolized by a young woman oppressed by the unenlightened patriarchal traditions of her poverty-stricken region. For the mainland Chinese spectator, this immediately brings to mind the structure of apprenticeship found in such red classics as *Song of Youth* (*Qingchun zhi ge*

青春之歌, dir. Cui Wei 崔嵬 and Chen Huai'ai 陈怀皑, 1959) and *Red Detachment of Women*, in which a spunky young woman with instinctive revolutionary tendencies is mentored by an attractive young Communist man. In those cases, a romantic bond between heroine and cadre is suggested through the visual conventions of Hollywood romance, even if it is absent in explicit form in the script.[15] In *Yellow Earth*, however, the young woman is a girl of fourteen, complicating the audience's perception of any implicit romance, and to make matters worse the cadre utterly fails to save her from her awful fate according to the local feudal customs—the girl is married off against her will to a much older man, and she eventually dies trying to flee across the Yellow River to search for the Communist base.

Stephanie Donald has conducted a brilliant close reading of one moment in the film, when what she calls the "socialist realist gaze"—an authoritative look toward an offscreen horizon that indicates the sure ideological vision of the Communist hero—is subtly but devastatingly subverted through a combination of performance and editing.[16] Here I will add one more example of the genre references in the film. I have noted elsewhere that one of the central messages of Mao-era cinema can be summed up as "Communists have more fun!"[17] In revolutionary films of the 1950s and 1960s, regions controlled by the Nationalists are usually depicted as literally darkened areas in which the common people weep, their oppressors frown or sneer, and nobody seems truly happy. In contrast, the Communist base areas are always depicted as bathed in bright light and filled with lighthearted, unalienated laborers at work—people laughing and splashing each other as they wash clothes in *Red Detachment of Women*, for example. Often the people and soldiers in the Communist-held territories break into joyful and energetic song or dance. This message, that Communists have more fun—a staple of socialist realism in China—is severely problematized (possibly even lampooned) by the famous drum-dance sequence in *Yellow Earth*. The film cuts temporarily to the Communist base in Yan'an, from which the Communist cadre had come to the girl's village and to which he had returned after falsely promising that he would return for her before the date of her forced marriage. True to generic precedent, the flower-drum sequence depicts vigorous Communist soldiers performing an energetic, joyous dance in the bright sunlight, enjoying the blessings of living in a liberated area. However, the entire sequence is undermined by the shot that immediately precedes it—a subtly horrifying shot of the girl's bridal veil being raised by the dark, grizzled old hand of the man who essentially is about to rape her. The joy of the liberated area is put directly in the context of the fate of the helpless girl for whom communism held only a false promise.

Initial viewers of *Yellow Earth* reacted with disapproval or even incomprehension, in part because of such twists on its socialist realist precedents. The leading critic Li Tuo compared watching it to answering the door at a party expecting to welcome an old friend, only to be confronted by a complete stranger, resulting in an awkward silence and even possible hostility.[18] One of the film's most controversial aspects was its "depiction of the poverty of the land and its people."[19] This would not have been as awkward for viewers—the film being set in the 1930s, depicting people who are *supposed* to have been suffering from the deprivation of preliberation feudalism—except that the filmmakers used mostly local farmers to play roles other than the four main characters. This neorealist technique provoked the unsettling realization that local farmers *of the early 1980s*, more than three decades after liberation, continued to live under great hardship, thus subverting the narrative of progress under communism. That is, the documentary technique of using local nonprofessionals as extras in the film severely disrupts the historical master narrative of socialist realism insofar as it places the poverty of peasants in the Communist present in direct comparison with the feudalist past, thus questioning the entire master narrative of the Mao era as bringing liberation from oppression and hardship.

Of course, the critiques of the Mao era found in Fourth- and Fifth-Generation films of the 1980s arguably helped to legitimate the policies of the new reform-minded Communist leadership. However, later waves of post–socialist realism would extend the critique of the myth of progress to the reform era itself. While the generation that emerged in the 1980s could be seen as subtly undermining the legitimacy of the previous party regime while implicitly endorsing the new one, by the 1990s a successive generation of post-socialist realist filmmakers would challenge the myth of progress during the post-Mao era as well. The early films of the pioneering independent directors Zhang Yuan 张元 and Wu Wenguang 吴文光, for example, often focused on disillusioned youth who had lost the idealism of the 1980s, while many slightly later independent films—particularly those following in the footsteps of Jia

Zhangke's early films, such as *Xiao Wu*—reinforced the critique of the reform-era economy by featuring its losers—pickpockets, prostitutes, migrant laborers, small-time hustlers—again, often played by nonprofessional actors. The latter trend continues well into the new millennium, including in the form of low-budget, "underground" fictional films and documentaries shot on digital video (DV).

Stylistic and Narrative Techniques of Post–Socialist Realism

The examples discussed thus far show how post–socialist realist films set about undermining the generic touchstones of socialist realism. It is equally important, however, to address in more detail the neorealist style and narrational mode of post–socialist realism—meaning the particular formal techniques, beyond generic conventions of character and story—that position post-socialist realist films as a dialectical response both to socialist realism and to the Hollywood-based classical style on which socialist realist and reform-era mainstream Chinese filmmaking drew.

In their landmark 1979 essay "On the Modernization of Film Language" ("Tan dianying yuyan de xiandaihua" 谈电影语言的现代化), filmmaker Zhang Nuanxin and critic Li Tuo in many ways anticipated the course of development of post–socialist realism in Chinese cinema over multiple decades and "generations." As Yingjin Zhang has recently written, though the essay was first known as a manifesto for the Fourth-Generation filmmakers, who emerged immediately following the Cultural Revolution, many of the ideas in the essay did not come fully to fruition—or result in films that gained widespread recognition, particularly internationally—until the Fifth- and Sixth-Generation Chinese filmmakers (many of whom had studied with instructors from the Fourth Generation at the Beijing Film Academy) began to produce their work.[20] Indeed, it is remarkable how well the essay both obliquely encapsulates the significance of its historical moment—just months after Deng Xiaoping had consolidated power and launched the reform era—and portends developments in Chinese cinema that would play out over the decades to come. The authors not only addressed and deepened points that recently had been made by others—most notably a critique of Chinese film as having become overly dramaturgical—but also began what would be a decades-long engagement with inter- and postwar Western film theory and practice, in particular the methods championed by André Bazin.

The polemic against the overdramatization of Chinese film had been launched earlier the same year, when Bai Jingcheng 白景晟 had argued for "throwing away the walking stick of drama" (*diudiao xiju de guaizhang* 丢掉戏剧的拐杖).[21] The essence of drama, according to Bai, was conflict (*chongtu* 冲突), and Chinese filmmakers were all too apt to use dramaturgical methods of plot construction. Film, he argued, does not have to focus so exclusively on characters and their conflicts, but can express things through natural landscapes or objects as well as through techniques distinctive to film.

In their essay, Zhang Nuanxin and Li Tuo reiterate the same principal criticisms as Bai Jingcheng, but they place them in the context of a teleological narrative of the history of world cinema, the urgent overall message of which is that Chinese cinema has "fallen behind" and must "catch up with the development of world film art."[22] However, even in this larger frame, drama becomes cinema's foil, with the progress of film art measured by how much it distances itself from drama. Early film is said to have been dependent on drama but to have gradually established its own cinematic aesthetic. The coming of sound prompted a temporary retrogression in which dramatic principles again came to dominate film, but movements such as Italian neorealism and the French New Wave helped to steer film back to its own path and made significant advances in film aesthetics. The overarching history told by Zhang and Li is summed up by their claim that "a trend in the modern development of world film art is that the narrative mode of film language (or one could say film's structural method) has increasingly shed its theatrical influence and instead in every respect advanced toward becoming more cinematic."[23]

Like Bai Jingcheng, Zhang and Li associate theatrical influences with an excess of "dramatic conflict."[24] However, one has to consider the extent to which "drama" may be a convenient whipping boy for a somewhat different but more sensitive set of issues. The cinema of the Cultural Revolution had been determined in part by the theories put forth by Mao as early as his "Talks at the Yan'an Forum on Literature and Art" and then refined into the formulas of Cultural Revolution art—theories that rely on the idea that class struggle should be at the center of both art's function and its content. In lamenting the excessive influence of drama, with its overreliance on "conflict," this handful of critics of the late 1970s undoubtedly were obliquely critiquing not just dramaturgical film aesthetics but, more broadly, the overinstrumentalization of film by the agenda of revolutionary class struggle. Zhang and Li repeatedly make the obligatory gesture of blaming the Gang of Four for the stalled development of cinema in China, but at one point, shortly after their very first mention of the Gang of Four, they somewhat daringly go further: "What needs to be pointed out is that the trend that, in artistic creation, one can speak only of politics rather than of art, only of content rather than of form, only of the artist's worldview rather than of artistic skill, did not completely begin with the rampage of the Gang of Four."[25] They go on not to reject Marxism but to urge a more sophisticated view of the Marxist theory of the relation of form to content and, implicitly, the relation of art to political economy, or superstructure to base.

Therefore, insofar as "drama" stands in for the aesthetics of socialist realism (or the Chinese variant of "revolutionary romanticism") in general, the call for film to evolve from the dramatic to the properly cinematic is not simply about the intermedial relationship of film to theater, but more fundamentally about a new ideology of depoliticization, calling here for an increased autonomy of art from politics in the reform era. Nevertheless, we must take seriously the essay's particular prescriptions for "modernizing" Chinese film language and thus catching up with world cinema. Aside from a general endorsement of "cinematic" over "dramatic" methods, in particular the essay launched what would become a decades-long fascination with Bazinian aesthetics among many Chinese critics and filmmakers—in terms of both the promulgation of Bazin's film theory and the championing of Italian neorealism as a model. Zhang and Li credit Bazin with leading a group of critics and filmmakers in challenging montage theory and proposing the "long-take theory."

The introduction of Bazin in general, and long-take aesthetics in particular, to Chinese cinematic discourse in the reform era may have been gradual at first, but it would have a lasting influence. As Cecile Lagesse puts it in an essay on the topic, Bazin's "approach to cinematic realism would allow filmmakers and critics to rethink cinema's relationship to reality after the Cultural Revolution and to free cinema from its former role as an ideological conduit."[26] Less than a year after the landmark essay on the modernization of film language, Li Tuo followed with a more specific essay titled "An Attention-worthy School of Cinematic Aesthetics—On the Long-Take Theory," coauthored with Zhou Chuanji 周传基.[27] Lagesse documents a number of other significant articles that would follow over the years, and even those only scratch the surface of Bazin's penetration into the Chinese discourse on cinema and the remarkably consistent importance of his ideas for various filmmakers from the Fourth Generation through the Sixth Generation. Bazin's preferences for long shots, long takes, on-location shooting, natural lighting and sound, episodic narratives, and so on are manifested to varying degrees in key Fourth-Generation films such as *Evening Rain* (*Ba Shan yeyu* 巴山夜雨, dir. Wu Yigong 吴贻弓, 1980), *Narrow Street* (*Xiao jie* 小街, dir. Yang Yanjin 杨延晋, 1981), *Life* (*Rensheng* 人生, dir. Wu Tianming 吴天明, 1984), and *Wild Mountains* (*Ye shan* 野山, dir. Yan Xueshu 颜学恕, 1985), as well as early Fifth-Generation films like *The One and the Eight*, *Yellow Earth*, and, by director Tian Zhuangzhuang 田壮壮, *On the Hunting Ground* (*Liechang zhasa* 猎场札撒, 1985) and *Horse Thief* (*Dao ma zei* 盗马贼, 1987).

Bazin and his ideas continued to be discussed in Chinese cinematic discourse throughout the 1980s and 1990s.[28] Jia Zhangke, a film theory concentrator in the BFA literature department during the mid-1990s who would go on to eventually become the most world-renowned Sixth-Generation filmmaker, virtually paraphrases Bazin in many of his interviews, though he rarely mentions him by name. Bazin's influence continued into the new century; the leading film journal *Contemporary Cinema* (*Dangdai dianying* 当代电影), for example, published a special section on Bazin in 2008. A full-text search for Bazin in the Chinese Academic Journals Database turns up references to him in 601 articles published from 1979 to 1989, 799 articles published from 1990 to 2000, and an astounding 2,407 articles published between 2001 and 2011.[29]

The Long Take

What exactly was the appeal of Bazin's ideas in the context of the transition from socialist realism to post–socialist realism? Let us begin with his so-called long-take theory. Zhang and Li's 1979 "Modernization" essay introduced the long-take theory of the Bazinian school as having raised a challenge to "montage theory" in the West decades earlier, and it suggested that, at the least, long-take techniques should be combined with montage to allow for more artistic possibilities.[30] Bazin had advocated long takes (along with long shot distances and deep-focus photography) as intrinsic to a realist style, owing to their preservation of objects and events in their actual duration. Whereas montage *constructs* an event rather than simply *showing* it, thus leading the spectator to a particular meaning, long-take cinema preserves the continuity of space and time, the freedom of the spectator, and the ambiguity of the image.[31] For post-socialist realist critics and filmmakers, the long-take aesthetic goes hand in hand with the desire to wrest more autonomy for art from politics, and the fact that montage was tied to Soviet film theory only reinforced its association with conflict-based revolutionary cinema.

While post-Mao Chinese theoretical interest in long-take aesthetics clearly began to take hold in 1979, the actual practice thereof was a more gradual process. Taking the Fourth-Generation films already mentioned as examples, the average shot length (ASL) of *Evening Rain* (1980) was 7.1 seconds, which is actually slightly shorter than those of the Mao-era narrative films mentioned previously, such as *Dong Cunrui* (8.3 seconds) and *Red Detachment of Women* (8.7 seconds).[32] With *Narrow Street* (1981), however, shot length was clearly expanding, up to 9.5 seconds, and by *Life* (1984) it had increased further, to 12.1 seconds.

Life is thus one example of how the Bazinian long-take method championed by early reform-era critics clearly found its way into the films of the Fourth Generation; its average shot length was significantly higher than the norm for Mao-era cinema, many other films of the early 1980s, and Hollywood cinema, for that matter.[33] Like the last of the Fourth-Generation films mentioned above, *Wild Mountains* (1985)—which had an even longer ASL of 12.7 seconds—*Life* incorporated other elements of Bazinian neorealist conventions, including natural lighting, on-location shooting, and naturalistic performances.

Indeed, *Life* illustrates the extent to which the Fifth Generation—much ballyhooed as representing a major rupture in Chinese film history—was in fact dependent on the previous generation for both its freedom to experiment and many details of its stylistic decisions. Wu Tianming, the Fourth-Generation director of *Life*, in 1984 became the head of the Xi'an Film Studio and would go on to produce such Fifth-Generation landmarks as *The Black Cannon Incident*, *The Horse Thief*, and *Red Sorghum* (*Hong gaoliang* 红高粱, dir. Zhang Yimou 张艺谋, 1987). With *Life*, Wu shot in the same area and among the same sorts of peasants as Chen Kaige in the Fifth-Generation classic *Yellow Earth*, even including similar local folk singing, similarly daring compositions—juxtaposing farmers or beasts of burden precariously on a slanted horizon, for example (plates 21 and 22)—and a wedding scene very much like that in *Yellow Earth*, in terms of both its false joviality and its visual appearance and musical accompaniment.

The early Fifth-Generation films, like these selected Fourth-Generation counterparts, did significantly lengthen the average shot length compared with Mao-era feature films, and thus helped to put the critics' promotion of Bazinian aesthetics into practice. The first Fifth-Generation film to be distributed, *The One and the Eight*, had an ASL of 11.6 seconds, while *The Horse Thief* had an ASL of 11.8 seconds; on the other hand, *The Hunting Ground* and *Yellow Earth* both averaged less than 10 seconds per shot, so there is no apparent trend toward longer shot lengths from the Fourth to the Fifth Generation; rather, there was a common preference in the mid-1980s for a significantly longer-take style than in either Mao-era or contemporary Hollywood cinema.

Despite the increase in shot length in Fourth- and Fifth-Generation post–socialist realism in the 1980s, it really was not until the Sixth Generation, in the 1990s and early 2000s, that the long-take aesthetic was taken to an extreme, no doubt owing not just to the continuing relevance of Bazin in Chinese cinematic discourse but also to the influence of such globally recognized long-take auteurs as Taiwan's Hou Hsiao-hsien 侯孝贤 and Tsai Ming-liang 蔡明亮, as well as others such as the Iranian filmmaker Abbas Kiarostami and the Hungarian Béla Tarr. Sixth-Generation director Jia Zhangke, in particular, used ASLs of well over one minute in films such as *Platform* (*Zhantai* 站台, 2000) and *Unknown Pleasures* (*Ren xiaoyao* 任逍遥, 2002).

The importance of the long-take aesthetic to Chinese art cinema of the reform era certainly has been long recognized. It must itself be understood, however, as a "red legacy," if only in the form of a dialectical negation, since post–socialist realism must be seen as a reaction to the socialist realism that preceded it as well as to the mainstream cinema to which it offered an alternative during the reform era. The long-take preference emerged first in critical discourse as an alternative to a style of montage that was associated with dramatic conflict, and thence with the political instrumentalization of cinema. Beginning in 1979, Bazinian long-take realism was framed in part as an assertion of an autonomous cinematic aesthetic.

The Detail

Another key feature of post–socialist realism, mentioned in the earliest critical writings of the reform era, was the importance of incidental detail. In their seminal essay on the modernization of film language, Zhang Nuanxin and Li Tuo approvingly noted that "in Italian neorealist cinema, life is generally depicted through ordinary details," in contrast to films that follow "theatrical rules," with their "complicated twists, outlandish plots, and exaggerated, violent conflicts."[34]

In a later essay published in 1984, Yang Ni 杨妮 continues and deepens the critique of overly dramatic film.[35] Like Zhang and Li, Yang points to Italian neorealism as the model for making films nondramatic. For her, this does not mean that a film should lack a plot or conflict, but that the plot should be relatively loose and possibly have multiple strands, and that any conflicts should be realistic rather than overly dramatized. Film narratives, Yang argues, should not necessarily have "dramatic plots in which closely related events, cause-and-effect relationships, and step-by-step developments lead to a climax," but rather should have "parallel plots," "few or no dramatic climaxes created out of intensified contradictions," and—most important—narrative lines that are frequently interrupted by minor details.[36]

Also like Zhang and Li, Yang invokes Bazin as she argues for film as a fundamentally documentary medium that depends most crucially on the indexicality of photography: "Between the recorded image on film and the object there should be a relationship like that of fingerprint to finger."[37] In keeping with the idea of film as what Kracauer called "the redemption of physical reality"—a phrase quoted in Yang's essay—the natural development of the art, according to Yang, involves "discarding theatricality and absorbing documentary devices."[38]

Zhang and Li had explicitly praised what they called French and Italian "political films" that "do not rely on the concept of dramatic conflicts to develop the plot" but instead "employ a 'realist' method from beginning to end, imbuing the films with a very strong documentary style, making it seem as if what we see is not a fabricated story but rather like an actual record of a real political incident."[39] The methods of cinematic realism are explicitly tied to a realistic representation of history, in implicit contrast to the highly formalized revolutionary myths that came to dominate filmmaking in the PRC by the time of the Cultural Revolution. The word used here that I have translated as "realist," *jishi* 纪实, has the connotation of "reportage," or the on-the-spot recording of events as they happen.[40] The implication is that such a realist or reportage style will capture all the messy details of historical events rather than just presenting them according to a simplistic and predetermined master narrative.

In these essays, while filmmakers are urged to deemphasize methodical progress toward a dramatic climax, film as an art must, on the contrary, get on with things. As is stated many times and in various ways, China "lags behind the circumstances" (*luohou yu xingshi* 落后于形势) and needs to catch up with the rest of the world after being cut off from the main current of film art for decades.[41] Zhang and Li's teleological narrative of film history suggests that cinema has a universal history from which China has quite simply been absent. Of course, the idea that China must catch up with the world was not at all subversive for the essay's historical moment, but rather played into the overall ideology of the Four Modernizations during the early Deng era.

Such appeals to the teleology of progress, however, do not necessarily need to be accepted at face value, particularly when looking back from the vantage point of decades later. Arguments for particular cinematic forms that are couched in a rhetoric of progress, of China's lagging behind and needing to make up for lost time, may themselves be indicative of rhetorical strategies more than core concerns. If filmmakers and film critics wanted to see more attention paid to form and less to political content—if they hoped to carve out some autonomy for film art in the early reform era—it would only make sense for them to frame their arguments within the master narrative of the Four Modernizations, whether or not that was the real motivating issue.

What is perhaps more interesting in retrospect is the idea of *detail*, to which Yang repeatedly returns. She clearly wants to draw attention to, and to cause to proliferate in the art of film, a plethora of minor details from real life that are not directly motivated by the plot of the film as a whole. This, for her, is the essence of the new realist style that Chinese filmmakers should adopt. In the context of dismantling the founding myths of Mao-era socialist realist cinema, the minor detail functions not just as a marker of realism in the Bazinian or Italian neorealist sense; it also participates directly in the process of generic subversion. Films of the Mao era exhibited what I have called a formalist drift—progressing from moments of socialist formalism, such as the occasional deployment of Pudovkin-style editing patterns in the 1950s, to the extreme stylization that dominated the whole of the Cultural Revolution's model-opera films.[42] This drift toward formalism in film style goes hand in hand with an increasingly rigid conventionalization of ideological rhetoric, with important consequences. In historical films on the fights against feudalism and Japanese occupation, the illusion of bearing witness to history is lessened as the depictions become more obviously stylized and codified. More broadly, as Alexei Yurchak has argued occurred in the Soviet Union after the death of Stalin, ideological discourse itself becomes more obviously performative rather than constative, which ultimately destabilizes it and leaves it open to subversion through techniques such as parody.[43]

The focus on detail in post–socialist realism plays into this process in a very specific way. Mao-era cinema, as noted, was not above indulging in formalist technique, despite its claims to realism. However, such indulgences always served a clear narrative and ideological goal—emphasizing the drama of the moment of heroic self-sacrifice in the *Dong Cunrui* scene described at the beginning of this chapter, for example. As Xia Yan, the most influential Chinese Communist script writer from the 1930s to the 1980s, put it in a key guide published in 1958, every film technique must have *purpose* (*mudixing* 目的性).[44] In this sense, while moments of "socialist formalism" were implicitly allowed, the deliberate cultivation of pure cinematic excess was clearly forbidden.[45]

This emphasis, by arguably the leading film theorist of the Mao era, on every technique having a purpose in the narrative indirectly betrays the somewhat scandalous extent of the relationship between Maoist revolutionary film style and classical Hollywood style, in which, as David Bordwell has shown, film technique as a rule is subordinated to narrative motivation.[46] Beginning in the post-Mao era, therefore, the deliberate focus on incidental detail itself contributed to the subversion of socialist-realist convention and also represented a departure from the conventions of Hollywood-based entertainment cinema, in that the incidental detail was by its very nature resistant to *purpose* in Xia Yan's sense or to *motivation* in Bordwell's sense. Here again the priorities of post-socialist realist filmmakers overlap with and draw upon Bazin's ideas of a "cinema of time" or a "cinema of duration," which organize time not dramaturgically but according to "life time"—the experience of ordinary life replete with quotidian moments and relative inactivity.[47]

I have described elsewhere how this emphasis on quotidian moments in the duration of everyday life plays out in such classics of post-socialist realism as Jia Zhangke's *Platform*.[48] Here I will note a very different instance of the irruption of detail in a moment from the climax of *Devils on the Doorstep*. The antihero protagonist Ma Dasan has gone on a vengeful rampage in which he tried to hack to death Japanese prisoners of war after their surrender to Chinese troops. He is sentenced to death, and the Chinese commander assigns the task of execution to none other than the Japanese soldier whom Ma Dasan previously had been hiding at the behest of the anonymous Communist guerrilla. At the moment when the soldier is poised with his samurai sword to behead the kneeling Ma Dasan, an ant suddenly appears on the neck of the prisoner just where the sword is to cleave his flesh (fig. 7.2). Distracted, in a moment of bizarre dark humor, the executioner stops what he is doing to flick the ant off the condemned man's skin. Given the conventions of heroic execution and other forms of martyrdom that can be found in countless Chinese revolutionary films, the interruption of this crucial dramatic moment by a meaningless ant crystallizes the intervention of post–socialist realism as a whole, serving simultaneously as the sort of true-to-life detail celebrated in Bazin's writings on Italian neorealism and also as a disruption of the codes of socialist realism, in which executions follow a very specific form of cinematic representation that Chinese viewers of the Mao era would have internalized and expected.[49]

The detail of this moment in *Devils on the Doorstep* shares something in common with the ambiguity Chris Berry has identified as characteristic of Fourth-Generation films of the late 1970s and early 1980s, the aimless chatting of soldiers in the early Fifth-Generation classic *The Big Parade* (*Da yuebing* 大阅兵, dir. Chen Kaige, 1986), the long stretches of silence and boredom in Jia Zhangke's Sixth-Generation films, and even the random moments of life captured by the younger generation of DV-camera-wielding independent filmmakers shooting on the streets of China today.[50] Throughout the post-Mao era, post–socialist realism

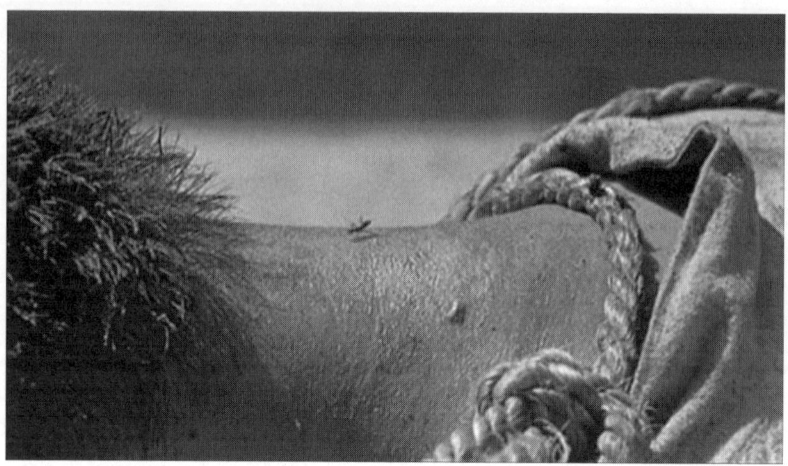

FIGURE 7.2. Irruption of detail in *Devils on the Doorstep* 鬼子来了 (2000), directed by Jiang Wen.

has drawn on the cinematic and theoretical resources of one realism in order to undermine another that held sway for the three preceding decades. That is, bearing in mind the historical dialectics of realism as described by Jakobson, the broad trend of post–socialist realism, insofar as it developed as a self-conscious reaction against the aesthetics of socialist realism, must itself be understood as part of the red legacy of the Mao era—as one of the myriad ways in which post-Mao culture draws on and defines itself in terms of the preceding revolutionary period.

Late Post–Socialist Realism

What happens to post–socialist realism as reform-era China progresses from the shadow of the Cultural Revolution to the center of the twenty-first-century capitalist world economy—while the dynamics of realism, as described by Jakobson, inevitably transform the post-socialist realist aesthetic from a progressive tendency seeking to counter and replace Mao-era socialist realism into a conservative tendency that sustains post–socialist realism as a potentially hegemonic realism of its own age?

As Jakobson's theory would suggest, one inevitable result is that post–socialist realism itself becomes formalized. This tendency became particularly clear with post–Sixth Generation cinema, which seemed to repeat the "realist" conventions of filmmakers like Jia Zhangke in a way that began to appear formulaic. As Shelly Kraicer observed in 2009, "Jia-ist cinema, through its profound effect on most younger independent Chinese directors, seems lately more restrictive than liberating in its influence. Film language in 'mainstream' indie Chinese films (both docs and features) seems to have temporarily congealed into something like formulaic liturgies: fetishization of the long take, the distant camera, the objective tone, the unedited minutiae of daily life."[51] The primary features that had seemed to counter socialist realist cinema with the bracing realism of Bazinian aesthetics themselves begin to appear as mere formulaic conventions reproduced for the global art-cinema market to which the Chinese independent and art-film scenes had long since adjusted themselves; the "progressive" tendency became the "conservative" tendency, at least insofar as it conformed to the expectations of its limited global film-festival audience.

Meanwhile, Jia Zhangke himself, for example, had moved on to new things, manifesting broader trends that in part challenged the earlier post-socialist realist aesthetic that his work had exemplified. His films—including *The World* (*Shijie* 世界, 2004) and *Still Life* (*Sanxia haoren* 三峡好人, 2006)—began to make use of blatantly nonrealist features such as animation and computer-generated imagery, placed sometimes jarringly alongside his usual Bazinian long-take realism. Films such as *Dong* (东, 2006) and *Still Life* blurred documentary with fiction in a way that called into question the truth claims of both.[52] His latest feature film at the time of this writing, *A Touch of Sin* (*Tian zhuding* 天注定, 2013), experiments with the conventions of popular genre cinema and uses a style of continuity editing that departs greatly from his early "slow cinema" aesthetic.

Other filmmakers who had contributed to the post-socialist realist trend went mainstream in various ways. The most prominent Fifth-Generation directors, Chen Kaige and Zhang Yimou, despite the latter's experiments in realism in the 1990s with *The Story of Qiu Ju* (*Qiuju da guansi* 秋菊打官司, 1992) and *Not One Less* (*Yi ge dou bu neng shao* 一个都不能少, 1999), were both working in the decidedly nonrealist genre of the martial-arts-themed historical epic in the early years of this century, with films such as Chen's *The Promise* (*Wuji* 无极, 2005) and *The Sacrifice* (*Zhaoshi gu'er* 赵氏孤儿, 2010) and Zhang's *Hero* (*Yingxiong* 英雄,

2002) and *House of Flying Daggers* (*Shi mian maifu* 十面埋伏, 2004), to name just a few.

Still other filmmakers, including Jiang Wen and Lu Chuan, gravitated not toward the sort of contemplative long-take realism of international art cinema in the Bazinian tradition, but to the mainstream contemporary global style that David Bordwell has identified as "intensified continuity"—a style that does not so much depart from classical Hollywood narration as accentuate some of its options, including a quicker rate of cutting, more use of both long (telephoto) and short (wide-angle) lenses, closer framings, and a constantly prowling camera that makes use of contemporary handheld camera technologies.[53] In terms of shot length, for example, Jiang Wen's *Devils on the Doorstep* and Lu Chuan's *Mountain Patrol* (*Kekexili* 可可西里, 2004) and *City of Life and Death* all fall within the ASL range of 3 to 7 seconds that Bordwell finds characteristic of Hollywood films from the 1980s to the first decade of this century.[54]

A number of films from mainland China, beginning around the turn of the twenty-first century, arguably went further than "intensified continuity" all the way to what some have argued is a "postclassical" style of narration, including such features as multiple or "spliced" plot lines, a highly episodic structure with loose causality, hypermediated or subjective realism, genre hybridity, unmotivated technical play, and a high degree of self-consciousness.[55] Elsewhere I have called such an aesthetic the "new formalism" in Chinese cinema, a style that is too ostentatious to be mainstream, yet also far from the aesthetic of post–socialist realism.[56]

The nonmainstream *realist* alternative in China (to belabor a perhaps overly fine semantic distinction) seems to have moved increasingly from "post–*socialist realism*"—a realist style that consciously seeks to supplant socialist (or proletarian or revolutionary) realism—to "postsocialist *realism*"—or simply a realism of the postsocialist condition that continues to employ stylistic elements of Bazinian and documentary realism. Such a style continues and even extends aspects of the preceding post–socialist realism, such as long takes, on-location shooting, "amateur" methods such as nonprofessional actors, and a faith in reality that includes an "on-location" (*xianchang* 现场) aesthetic and openness to contingency. This style often blurs the boundary between documentary and fiction in film, and it has if anything become even more widespread in the independent Chinese film scene with the arrival of DV technology in the late 1990s.

One example of the ongoing vitality of this aesthetic, Liu Jiayin's *Oxhide II* (*Niupi II* 牛皮II, 2009), is a masterpiece of extreme long-take minimalism, featuring just nine shots in 132 minutes and including only three characters: a mother, father, and daughter played by the filmmaker herself and her two actual parents. The action, such as it is, takes place mostly in real time and merely covers a family making and eating a meal of dumplings together while having intermittent conversations about the task at hand as well as about the family shop run by the father. Stylistically, the film exemplifies a long-take realism that lingers exclusively on details rather than moments of high drama or conflict (though there is subtle drama in the family dynamics). However, we arguably no longer have reason to label this style post–socialist realism because the genre-deconstruction characteristic of that trend seems to have disappeared entirely; what lingers as a backdrop for the film's style or story is no longer the red legacy of the Mao era so much as the legacy of post–socialism itself.

Notes

1. See my more lengthy discussion of these features in Jason McGrath, "Cultural Revolution Model Opera Films and the Realist Tradition in Chinese Cinema," *The Opera Quarterly: Performance + Theory + History* 26, no. 2–3 (Spring–Summer 2010): 343–76.

2. The 30-degree rule, violated often in early cinema but rarely in "classical" Hollywood movies, states that a cut between two shots of the same subject from different distances should involve a change in the camera position of at least 30 degrees; otherwise, the cut will resemble a jump cut and will strike the viewer as a "mistake."

3. Viewers may also be reminded of the very similar cuts in Alfred Hitchcock's *The Birds* (1963), released eight years after *Dong Cunrui*.

4. See the relevant chapters in David Bordwell, *Narration in the Fiction Film* (Madison: University of Wisconsin Press, 1985), pp. 156–204, 234–73; on "socialist formalism," see p. 271.

5. The categorization of Chinese filmmakers by generations started in the mid-1980s, when a new post–Cultural Revolution class graduated from the Beijing Film Academy (BFA) and was called China's "fifth generation" of directors. In this schema, the First-Generation directors were the cinematic pioneers of the 1910s and 1920s; the Second were the filmmakers during the golden age of Shanghai cinema in the 1930s and 1940s; the Third-Generation directors were those who began making films in the "Seventeen Years" before the Cultural Revolution, or 1949–66; the

Fourth were trained before the Cultural Revolution but only began making films afterward; and the Sixth-Generation directors completed their BFA education after members of the Fifth Generation already had made their mark.

6. For an overview of this commercial-state hybrid cinema, see Yomi Braester, "Contemporary Mainstream PRC Cinema," in *The Chinese Cinema Book*, ed. Song Hwee Lim and Julian Ward (London: Palgrave Macmillan, 2011), pp. 176–84.

7. Roman Jakobson, "On Realism in Art," in Jakobson, *Language in Literature*, ed. Krystyna Pomorska and Stephen Rudy (Cambridge, MA: Belknap Press of Harvard University Press, 1987), pp. 19–27.

8. See, e.g., Zhou Yang, "Thoughts on Realism," in *Modern Chinese Literary Thought: Writings on Literature, 1893–1945*, ed. Kirk A. Denton (Stanford, CA: Stanford University Press, 1996), pp. 335–44.

9. Beginning in 1958 in China, "revolutionary realism plus revolutionary romanticism" replaced "socialist realism" as the official slogan in the arts.

10. Arif Dirlik, "Postsocialism? Reflections on Socialism with Chinese Characteristics," in *Marxism and the Chinese Experience: Issues in Contemporary Chinese Socialism*, ed. Arif Dirlik and Maurice Meisner (Armonk, NY: M. E. Sharpe, 1989), pp. 361–84.

11. Just a few examples in the China field include Jason McGrath, *Postsocialist Modernity: Chinese Cinema, Literature, and Criticism in the Market Age* (Stanford, CA: Stanford University Press, 2008); Xudong Zhang, *Postsocialism and Cultural Politics: China in the Last Decade of the Twentieth Century* (Durham, NC: Duke University Press, 2008); Robin Visser, *Cities Surround the Countryside: Urban Aesthetics in Postsocialist China* (Durham, NC: Duke University Press, 2010); Deborah S. Davis and Wang Feng, eds., *Creating Wealth and Poverty in Postsocialist China* (Stanford, CA: Stanford University Press, 2008); Judith Farquhar, *Appetites: Food and Sex in Post-Socialist China* (Durham, NC: Duke University Press, 2002); and Haomin Gong, *Uneven Modernity: Literature, Film, and Intellectual Discourse in Postsocialist China* (Honolulu: University of Hawaiʻi Press, 2012). Those covering Eastern Europe and the former Soviet Union are too numerous to mention, but one notable work that covers those areas as well as China is Aleš Erjavec, ed., *Postmodernism and the Postsocialist Condition: Politicized Art under Late Socialism* (Berkeley: University of California Press, 2003).

12. Chris Berry and Mary Ann Farquhar, "Post-Socialist Strategies: An Analysis of *Yellow Earth* and *Black Cannon Incident*," in *Cinematic Landscapes: Observations on the Visual Arts and Cinema of China and Japan*, ed. Linda Erlich and David Desser (Austin: University of Texas Press, 1994), pp. 81–116; Chris Berry, *Postsocialist Cinema in Post-Mao China* (New York: Routledge, 2004).

13. Zhang Nuanxin 张暖忻 and Li Tuo 李陀, "Tan dianying yuyan de xiandaihua" 谈电影语言的现代化 (On the modernization of film language), *Dianying yishu* 电影艺术 (Film art), no. 3 (1979): 40–52; published in English as Zhang Nuanxin and Li Tuo, "The Modernization of Film Language," trans. Hou Jianping, in *Chinese Film Theory: A Guide to the New Era*, ed. George S. Semsel, Xia Hong, and Hou Jianping (New York: Praeger, 1990), pp. 10–20. The following quotations

from Zhang and Li's essay will cite the page number in the original Chinese version first and the relevant page of the English translation second, though I have largely rendered my own translations for greater faithfulness to the original.

14. Jie Li argues that Jiang Wen's black-and-white cinematography is not intended to achieve an unmediated *realist* effect, but rather that he "is far more interested in reproducing and subverting the *mediated* collective memories of the period," particularly through "the cinema of the Cold War." Jie Li, "Discoloured Vestiges of History: Black and White in the Age of Colour Cinema," *Journal of Chinese Cinemas* 6, no. 3 (2012): 250, 252.

15. Jason McGrath, "Communists Have More Fun! The Dialectics of Fulfillment in Cinema of the People's Republic of China," *World Picture* 3 (Summer 2009), at http://www.worldpicturejournal.com/WP_3/McGrath.html (accessed October 5, 2015).

16. Stephanie Hemelryk Donald, *Public Secrets, Public Spaces: Cinema and Civility in China* (Lanham, MD: Rowman & Littlefield, 2000), pp. 59–62.

17. McGrath, "Communists Have More Fun!"

18. Geremie Barmé and John Minford, eds., *Seeds of Fire: Chinese Voices of Conscience* (New York: Hill and Wang, 1988), p. 253.

19. Bonnie McDougall, *The Yellow Earth* (Hong Kong: Chinese University Press, 1991), p. 6.

20. Yingjin Zhang, "Directors, Aesthetics, Genres: Chinese Postsocialist Cinema, 1979–2010," in *A Companion to Chinese Cinema*, ed. Yingjin Zhang (Oxford: Wiley-Blackwell, 2012), pp. 62–64.

21. Bai Jingcheng, "Throwing Away the Walking Stick of Drama," in *Chinese Film Theory: A Guide to the New Era*, ed. George S. Semsel, Xia Hong, and Hou Jianping (New York: Praeger, 1990), pp. 5–9.

22. Zhang and Li, "Tan dianying yuyan de xiandaihua," pp. 40, 10.

23. Ibid., pp. 44, 15.

24. Ibid.

25. Ibid., pp. 40–41, 11.

26. Cecile Lagesse, "Bazin and the Politics of Realism in Mainland China," in *Opening Bazin: Postwar Film Theory and Its Afterlife*, ed. Dudley Andrew (Oxford: Oxford University Press, 2011), p. 316.

27. Zhou Chuanji and Li Tuo, "Yi ge zhide zhongshi de dianying meixue xuepai: Guanyu chang jingtou lilun" (一个值得重视的电影美学学派: 关于长镜头理论) (An attention-worthy school of cinematic aesthetics: On the long-take theory), *Dianying wenhua congkan* 电影文化丛刊 (Film culture anthology), vol. 1 (Beijing: Zhongguo shehui kexue chubanshe, 1980), pp. 148–60.

28. An early 1990s graduate of the BFA recently told me that Bazin was more foundational in the curriculum than any other single film theorist.

29. These figures do not take into account the variable coverage of certain journals in the database over the decades, but the point remains that interest in Bazin certainly appears not to have diminished in the twenty-first century compared with earlier years.

30. Zhang and Li, "Tan dianying yuyan de xiandaihua," pp. 46, 16–17.

31. André Bazin, "The Evolution of the Language of Cinema," in Bazin, *What Is Cinema?* trans. Hugh Gray, vol. 1 (Berkeley: University of California Press, 1967), pp. 23–40.

32. In fact, some of the more experimental films of the early 1980s—including *Evening Rain*, *Narrow Street*, and *Life*—would have had longer ASLs had it not been for the directors' tendency to indulge in the occasional very rapid montage sequence, often tied to the psychological states of the protagonists, which itself came off as the kind of modernist (as opposed to socialist realist) technique recommended by critics such as Bai Jingcheng, Zhang Nuanxin, and Li Tuo.

33. For comparison's sake, the ASL of Hollywood films between 1930 and 1960 ranged from 8 to 11 seconds, but that had decreased to 5–8 seconds by the 1970s, and it became even shorter thereafter, to the point that many Hollywood films today have ASLs of as little as 2 seconds or less. See David Bordwell, "Intensified Continuity: Visual Style in Contemporary American Film," *Film Quarterly* 55, no. 3 (Spring 2002): 16; and Bordwell, *The Way Hollywood Tells It: Story and Style in Modern Movies* (Berkeley: University of California Press, 2006), p. 122.

34. Zhang and Li, "Tan dianying yuyan de xiandaihua," pp. 45, 15.

35. Yang Ni, "Lun jishixing gushi yingpian de xushi jiegou: Jian yu Tan Peisheng tongzhi shangque" 论纪事型故事影片的叙事结构: 兼与谭霈生同志商榷 (On the narrative structure of documentary-style fiction films: A response to Comrade Tan Peisheng), *Dianying yishu*, no. 7 (1984): 17–30. Published in English as Yang Ni, "Film Is Film: A Response to Tan Peisheng," trans. Hou Jianping, in *Chinese Film Theory: A Guide to the New Era*, ed. George S. Semsel, Xia Hong, and Hou Jianping (New York: Praeger, 1990), pp. 59–75. The following notes provide page numbers for the original and the translation, in that order.

36. Ibid., pp. 19–20, 63.

37. Ibid., pp. 26, 69.

38. Ibid., pp. 26, 72. Siegfried Kracauer, *Theory of Film: The Redemption of Physical Reality* (Princeton, NJ: Princeton University Press, 1960).

39. Zhang and Li, "Tan dianying yuyan de xiandaihua," pp. 16, 45.

40. Chris Berry has elaborated on the concept of "on-the-spot realism" (*jishizhuyi* 纪实主义) in "Facing Reality: Chinese Documentary, Chinese Postsocialism," in *The First Guangzhou Triennial: Reinterpretation: A Decade of Experimental Chinese Art (1990–2000)*, ed. Wu Hung et al. (Guangzhou: Guangzhou Museum of Art, 2002), pp. 121–31; and "Getting Real: Chinese Documentary, Chinese Postsocialism," in *The Urban Generation: Chinese Cinema and Society at the Turn of the Twenty-first Century*, ed. Zhang Zhen (Durham, NC: Duke University Press, 2007), pp. 115–34. During the reform era, the intentional rendering of "realism" as either *jishi* or *xieshi* 写实 rather than the officially favored *xianshi* 现实 is itself a marker of the transition from socialist realism to post–socialist realism.

41. Zhang and Li, "Tan dianying yuyan de xiandaihua," pp. 40, 10.

42. McGrath, "Cultural Revolution Model Opera Films and the Realist Tradition in Chinese Cinema."

43. Alexei Yurchak, *Everything Was Forever, Until It Was No More: The Last Soviet Generation* (Princeton, NJ: Princeton University Press, 2006).

44. Xia Yan 夏衍, "Xie dianying juben de jige wenti" 写电影剧本的几个问题 (A few questions on screenwriting), in *Bainian Zhongguo dianying lilun wenxuan* 百年中国电影理论文选 (Selected works from one hundred years of Chinese film theory), ed. Ding Yaping 丁亚平 (Beijing: Wenhua yishu, 2002), pp. 446–73. Originally a speech delivered at the Beijing Film Academy in 1958.

45. Cinematic excess refers to anything that lacks or exceeds narrative motivation in a film. Kristin Thompson, "The Concept of Cinematic Excess," in *Narrative, Apparatus, Ideology: A Film Theory Reader*, ed. Philip Rosen (New York: Columbia University Press, 1986), pp. 130–42.

46. See Bordwell, *Narration in the Fiction Film*, pp. 156–204.

47. André Bazin, "De Sica: Metteur en Scène," in Bazin, *What Is Cinema?* trans. Hugh Gray, vol. 2 (Berkeley: University of California Press, 1971), p. 76.

48. McGrath, *Postsocialist Modernity*, esp. pp. 150–51.

49. The conventional representation of a protagonist's martyrdom by execution would have included, for example, his or her dignified straightening of clothing during the last minute of life, the shouting of slogans such as "Long live the Communist Party!" at the moment of death, and the surging of the *Internationale*, the Communist anthem, on the film's soundtrack to indicate that the cause is only made stronger by the individual's death.

50. Berry, *Postsocialist Cinema in Post-Mao China.*

51. Shelly Kraicer, "Finding Ways to Fit: Mainland Chinese Films at Toronto and Vancouver," dGenerate Films, November 18, 2009, at http://dgeneratefilms.com/critical-essays/finding-ways-to-fit-mainland-chinese-films-at-toronto-and-vancouver (accessed October 5, 2015).

52. For a discussion of this, see Jason McGrath, "The Cinema of Displacement: The Three Gorges Dam in Feature Film and Video," in Wu Hung et al., *Displacement: The Three Gorges Dam and Contemporary Chinese Art* (Chicago: Smart Museum of Art, University of Chicago, 2008), pp. 33–46.

53. David Bordwell, "Intensified Continuity: Visual Style in Contemporary American Film," *Film Quarterly* 55, no. 3 (Spring 2002): 16–28.

54. Ibid., p. 17.

55. For a systematic argument for this style as an emerging option in world cinema in recent decades, see Eleftheria Thanouli, *Post-Classical Cinema: An International Poetics of Film Narration* (New York: Wallflower Press, 2009).

56. Jason McGrath, "The New Formalism: Mainland Chinese Cinema at the Turn of the Century," in *China's Literary and Cultural Scenes at the Turn of the 21st Century*, ed. Jie Lu (London: Routledge, 2008), pp. 207–21.

PART 4

Red Bodies

EIGHT

MAO'S TWO BODIES

On the Curious (Political) Art of Impersonating the Great Helmsman

Haiyan Lee

In the Chinese-American writer Yiyun Li's prizing-winning short story "Immortality" (2003), a carpenter's wife conceives a child on the day Mao Zedong declares the founding of the People's Republic of China.[1] During her pregnancy, she is inundated with Cultural Revolution–style cult-of-Mao propaganda, and as a result of her constant gazing at Mao's portrait, she gives birth to a son who is the spitting image of Mao. Years later, soon after Mao's death, the now grown-up son is whisked to the capital to be trained as Mao's impersonator. As such, he becomes his hometown's pride and joy. But when the reforms deepen, his utility diminishes and he is finally publicly disgraced in a prostitution-cum-extortion scandal. He returns home and castrates himself at his mother's grave, thus adding himself to the long line of barren males from the town, which was famous in imperial times for supplying the court in Beijing with eunuchs.[2]

Li's story belongs to a familiar corpus of sensationalized narratives about the horrific Mao years, of which certain segments of the Western readership never seem to tire. Told in a first-person plural voice that chillingly blends naivety and zeal, the story telescopes PRC history into a montage of clichéd images and sound bites that accentuate the madness and absurdity of the entire Mao era. Li lards the text with a smattering of Mao's most memorable and, in hindsight, reprehensible utterances in italics, much like the way Jung Chang uses Maoist stock phrases as chapter headings in her best-selling memoir *Wild Swans*, giving the impression that life under Mao was one frenzied and often botched implementation after another of a megalomaniac's warped utopian vision. The political mysticism that once imbued these utterances with the power to throw millions off their feet now merely sounds foolish. "[Mysticism's] baffling metaphors and highflown images," notes Ernst Kantorowicz, "when deprived of their iridescent wings, may easily resemble the pathetic and pitiful sight of Baudelaire's Albatross."[3]

Yet the story departs from the usual scenario of a blameless individual being arbitrarily persecuted on grounds of "difference," be it family background (landlord/capitalist parentage or overseas connections) or personality (too independent-minded). Instead, the rise and fall of the nameless young man in the story is propelled by a freakish magnetism that draws him to the white-hot center of political orthodoxy until he is symbolically burnt by the sun. Unlike the earlier castrated boys whose families carefully preserved their "male roots" so that their bodies could be made whole again at their burial, the Mao look-alike's severed member goes missing, causing considerable anxiety among the collective "we," who do not know how they shall bury him in his "incompleteness": "For the peace of our own minds, everyday we pray for his health. We pray for him to live forever as we prayed for the dictator. He is the man whose story we do not want to end, and, as far as we can see, there will be no end to his story."[4]

With these lines, the story draws to a close even as it disavows real closure, as if to enjoin the reader to go on looking, elsewhere, for a sequel. The observant reader need not look far to find contemporary replays of the young man's story, albeit in a different key and with a more motley cast. Since the late 1970s, the state-run film and television industry has been grooming "special actors" and casting them in historical epics that depict the nation's founding fathers and their rivals: most notably Mao Zedong (1893–1976), Zhou Enlai (1898–1976), Zhu De (1886–1976), and Chiang Kai-shek (1887–1975). By the time *The Founding of a Republic* (*Jianguo daye* 建国大业, dir. Han Sanping 韩三平 and Huang Jianxin 黄建新), a lavish tribute on the occasion of the nation's sixtieth birthday, came out in 2009, two generations of special actors had cycled through numerous paeans to the Chinese Communist Party and its pantheon of demigods. Most of these productions were made-to-order propaganda potboilers that have quickly receded from collective memory. Nonetheless, the posthumous cult of Mao, driven in part by expedient political pieties and in part by commodified mass nostalgia, has kept open a career option for those with a fortuitous resemblance to the great leaders, a taste for party history and lore, and a knack for mimicry. This chapter takes a closer look at the institutionalized practice of using special actors to portray Mao, and at the emerging phenomenon of freelance impersonators performing in entertainment and hospitality venues. My goal is to situate Mao impersonation on the spectrum of performative practices from spirit mediumship, at one end, to satirical art, at the other, not only to make sense of the fraught relationship between Mao's "image magic" and its aesthetic and commercial appropriations, but also to critique the problematic aspects of Li's story that seem to underlie much of the West's (mis-)understanding of China.

Mao's Image Magic

The narrator in Li's story claims there is a folk belief that "the more a pregnant woman studies a face, the greater the possibility of the baby owning that face."[5] If we leave aside the story's compression of PRC history—in asking us to imagine a totalitarian society blanketed by official propaganda and terrorized by an omnipresent state from the moment of the PRC's founding—we can take this folkloric creed as an apt comment on the voodooish dimensions of the cult of Mao. The way in which Mao's image was disseminated at the height of the Mao cult bore a strong affinity with religious or magical cults. *Pace* Walter Benjamin, Mao's image, though mechanically reproduced ad infinitum and ubiquitously visible, lost little of the aura accrued to him as the supreme leader of the CCP, the liberator of the downtrodden, and the sacred symbol of the consolidation of splintered Chinese sovereignty and the suturing of a dismembered Chinese body politic.[6] His pictures were treated not as mere representations but as something on the order of divine iconography possessing magical potency and commanding homage. In other words, they were imbued with "image magic," a powerful and abiding form of magic known in many premodern cultures that assumes the magical identity between an image (such as a portrait) and its object.[7] Political rituals, such as criticism and self-criticism meetings, struggle sessions, loyalty dances, morning instructions and evening reports, were typically conducted under Mao's gaze, usually emanating from the standard Tiananmen Gate portrait in which he looked straight at the camera lens and hence at all who stood before him. Image magic can also be a dark art. Defacing Mao's image, by accident or by design, was treated as an act of *lèse-majesté*, a political crime most commonly evoked in post-Mao writing to highlight the fanatic excesses of Maoism.

In Li's story, Mao essentially impregnates the carpenter's wife through image magic. Indeed, the birth of Mao's future impersonator is eerily evocative of the Christian myth of immaculate conception, especially considering that the carpenter is summarily dispatched early in the story for making an irreverent joke about Mao's population policy and the wife is widowed at the tender age of eighteen. If the mishandling of Mao's portrait can spell disaster for anyone anywhere, having a dead ringer for Mao walking in their midst, once the child is born, raises the stakes that much higher for the entire community: "With the boy living among us, we are constantly walking on a thin layer of ice above deep water. We worry about not paying enough respect to the face, an indication of our hidden hatred of the dictator. We worry about respecting that face too much, which could be interpreted as our inability to tell the false from the true, worshipping the wrong idol."[8] The value of his face, however, is only fully realized after the great leader's demise, when the young man is brought to the capital to take part in an audition. He triumphs for having allegedly captured the sassy spirit of Mao: While the other candidates all choose to quote Mao solemnly announcing the birth of the nation, he impulsively spurts out this jaunty dictum: "A man cannot conceal his reactionary nature forever, just as a widow cannot hide her desire to be fucked."[9]

The young man goes on to enjoy a glorious career enacting Mao in propaganda films and televised national celebrations. In his mimetic perfection, he becomes a political spirit medium, surrendering his body to possession by an apotheosized personage that still looms large in the collective psyche. Through him, the audience is reconnected with a spiritual father and the nation is made whole again—but at the cost of making the medium a sacrificial lamb. The young man is consigned to a state of exception in which he lives an ersatz life and cannot partake of the everyday—an exclusion from ordinary humanity that is encoded as his inability to secure a wife. In the early stage of his career, no girl is good enough for him; later he is spurned by young girls drawn to more modish faces. When the young man tries to satisfy his sexual urges with a prostitute, he is framed by her and her pimp and extorted for an exorbitant sum when they recognize his face. He is unceremoniously turned out by his official handlers for sullying the great leader's image and sent back to his hometown. With his self-mutilation in the graveyard, the story loops back to the opening gambit about the town's lineage of "great papas" who, having had their male bodies "cleaned," were sent to the palace to serve the emperor and his women, and brought riches and glory to their families and hometown. But what precisely does the young man share in common with the eunuchs of yore? Why does Yiyun Li contrive to have him issue from the same town and be regarded by the townsfolk with the same abject deference and delusional pride?

The eunuch-impersonator genealogy suggests that the specter of Oriental despotism continues to haunt China long after the fall of the last imperial dynasty. The collective "we" that rhapsodizes about the "great papas" as well as the young man for getting so very close to the epicenter of power, whatever the cost to individual integrity and dignity, is subtly satirized for its masochistic self-delusion. To the extent that the people have come to love their despot, the story seems to suggest, they deserve tyranny and oppression, and are certainly in no position to recognize the truth of their subjection and to agitate for freedom—all except the young man, when his one-of-a-kind career draws to an ignominious close. His act of self-mutilation may be read as a belated attempt to be rid of the last vestige of the self that has caused him such grief. But unlike a certain legendary ten-year-old boy of yesteryear who "cleaned" himself and went on to become the greatest of all great papas, the young man's body has already been used and abused in the service of power. His postservice castration can thus be read as a protest against the state of exception to which he, along with those who adored him as the great leader's double and willingly subjected themselves to the charisma of absolute power, had been condemned. He therefore stands for the hope that the Chinese people are perhaps not inexorably afflicted with a slavish mentality or doomed to live in the shadow of imperial tyranny, however much Mao may have resembled or consciously aspired to be an emperor.

Mao Is Dead, Long Live Mao!

The idea of Mao as China's new emperor has considerable currency in both elite and popular circles. Though few historians take it seriously, it has acquired the stubborn staying power of myth, defying refutation, and is readily mobilized as a rhetorical weapon in ideological jousts. Commenting on Jung Chang and Jon Halliday's damning 2005 biography, *Mao: The Unknown Story*, Geremie Barmé notes the wanton use of imperial metaphors that are redolent of "the image of oriental obliquity" and that effectively place Mao "at some quaint, incomprehensible oriental remove, reducing a complex history to one of personal fiat and imperial hauteur."[10] While it is true that the Communist regime has appropriated elements of the Confucian tradition of statecraft, particularly the moralization of politics, or what Susan Shirk calls "virtuocracy," Mao is not a modern reprisal of the long lineup of absolutist emperors.[11] Barmé rightly warns against letting the appeal of imperial metaphors, glibly deployed by Mao himself and his admirers and detractors alike, blind us to the gulf between dynastic rule and modern political rationality.[12]

To begin with, Mao as ruler sat astride a vast and complex modern administrative machine that no Chinese emperor could have dreamed of devising or overseeing. Moreover, the idea of Mao as "the savior of the Chinese people" was less an expression of "disguised monarchism" than shorthand for a radically modern ideology that asserted the identity of the party, the state, and the people as the collective agent of history and the sovereign subject of the new political order.[13] Instead of mediating, as the emperor did, between heaven and humanity, Mao stood for the incorporation of the people into the body politic. He was their corporate self-image, and the cult of Mao was in essence communal self-worship *à la* Émile Durkheim. Whereas the emperor's forbidden countenance had to be enshrouded in mystery and shielded from the common eye, Mao's visage was all pervasive. He had to be seen in order to be truly powerful, and his charisma was the congealment of pious gazes and votive chants. In other words, the potency of his persona was a collective construct, buoyed by projected desire and misrecognized agency, as is the case with all deity worship. However, in the cult of Mao, the demiurge was a real human being in control of formidable state apparatuses and having multitudes at his beck and call. The damage he was capable of inflicting on the body politic, even without his having to pull any lever directly, is all too painfully evident to students of PRC history.

According to Kantorowicz, in medieval England a king was theorized by court jurists as having two bodies, the body natural, which was mortal, and the body politic, which makes the king a "corporation sole" that never dies: "King is a Name of Continuance, which shall always endure as the Head and Governor of the People (as the Law presumes) as long as the People continue . . . and in this Name the King never dies."[14] It is possible to see Mao as also possessing two bodies. The Mao body natural is rumored to have had down-to-earth taste, sloppy personal hygiene, cravings for the company of young women, and an irascible temperament. Throughout the first three decades of the socialist period, he clashed impetuously with the party establishment, just as the English king became a nuisance to the Parliament. The Mao body politic, however, was synonymous with political legitimacy and thus remained indispensible to the party's rule. As the official formulation has it, "Mao Zedong Thought" is the "crystallization of the collective wisdom of the CCP." Thus even as Mao cannibalized the party from within, the party relied on the Mao cult to prop up its fitful rule. Those who opposed Mao's rogue radicalism nonetheless had to act in the name of defending Mao's "revolutionary line," much like the Puritans "fighting the king to defend the King."[15] Repudiating Mao is tantamount to repudiating the regime's very legitimacy and the fundamental premise of the political order: that the party stands for the unity of the people and executes the dictatorship of the proletariat on behalf of the people. In this light, Mao is only the personification of the coterminousness of popular sovereignty and one-party autocracy.

Mao's two bodies bear out Eric Santner's thesis that in the transition from royal to popular sovereignty, the king's two bodies did not simply vanish, but rather became dispersed horizontally among the people. The challenge then becomes how to represent the people's "sacral soma" as the locus of sovereign power and authority.[16] Claude Lefort has famously argued that the center of power in a democracy is an empty place that politicians only provisionally inhabit on behalf of the electorate: "There is no power linked to a body."[17] Likewise, Victoria Kahn suggests that the king's two bodies have morphed into the distinction between person and office.[18] But PRC history shows that the "surplus of immanence," in the absence of a transcendent source of legitimacy, can be condensed and displaced onto a new, fleshly bearer of the principle of the popular sovereign: the charismatic populist hero.

Although Santner does not consider a figure like Mao, the bifurcation of Mao was the party's greatest ideological achievement, insofar as it managed to survive the mortal blows dealt by Mao. Mao the populist hero—the savior of the Chinese people and the red-hot sun in their breasts—supplied a solution to the predicament of representing an empty place by occupying it. On the one hand, the party shielded the coarser, more appetitive aspects of the Mao body natural from public knowledge; on the other hand, a simultaneously beatific and corporeal Mao was in constant public view: the sweaty body wielding a hoe, the vigorous body in a bathrobe, the avuncular body in the midst of smiling children, the ebullient body shaking hands with model workers. It was this body that formed the somatic basis of Mao's sacred iconography. The immortality of this body— Mao's *corpus mysticum*—was endlessly exalted in liturgical speech and practice, in tales of magical healing and breakthrough, and by taboos against blasphemy and desecration.[19] The horizontal dispersal of sovereignty of which Santner speaks was thus dramaturgically elaborated on in the recitations of quotations and loyalty dances and mass rallies, merging the sacral soma of the people into the Mao body politic while subjecting their flesh to the mortifications of the proletarian dictatorship.

Today, the political theology of Mao's two bodies is discernible in the two oddities in the post-Mao reckoning with the Maoist past. First, while the Mao body natural is good and dead, the corpse has not been buried or cremated but embalmed and put on permanent display in a memorial hall in the heart of Tiananmen Square, the most symbolically charged site in the nation's capital. In his extensive account of Mao's funeral and the disposition of his remains, Frederic Wakeman notes how, notwithstanding its flagrant contradiction of the Communist ethos of egalitarianism, the memorial hall allows the party to take permanent possession of "a body whose very corporeality continued to radiate the charisma of Mao Tse-tung's [Mao Zedong's] personal power."[20] Rudolf Wagner deftly unpacks the rich religious connotations of the structure and the pilgrimage it prescribes against the background of a shifting Communist sacred geography. Like a holy relic, the flag-draped mummy is there to commune with the bodies that file past its crystal sarcophagus in hushed reverence, and to affirm their corporate immortality as well as the perpetuity of the party's rule.[21] Second, Mao's life is commonly assessed as composed of 70 percent accomplishments and 30 percent errors, a schizophrenic formulation that seems to trouble few, resting as it does on the political theology of Mao's two bodies. Exposing Mao's failings can thus be safely confined to Mao the fallible human being without impugning Mao the anchor of regime legitimacy and articulator of the cumulative wisdom of the party's revolutionary experience.[22]

In the reform era, during which the party has given itself an overtly nationalist and covertly capitalist makeover, Mao's immortal body is retooled to sanction developmental goals rather than class struggles. Mao's persona acquires a new aura as the guardian angel of a newly awakened nation striving to accede to world-power status. Tellingly, the use of special actors to impersonate Mao and other revolutionary leaders got its start in this same period of collective refashioning. While it may have seemed a natural step to put Mao back on stage once the original was no longer available, the theatricalization of Mao was in fact the beginning of Mao's depoliticization, or de-Maoification. Writing on Shakespeare's revolutionary contribution to the "democratization of fame," Leo Braudy argues that in the Bard's historical plays, "kingship and rule are turned into a show in which one might play a good part or a bad one, but always a part, while the audience, usually the subordinates of the great, for a time become their judges."[23] Again, "acting took kings and turned them into possibilities that anyone could aspire to imitate. When the king begins to compete visually with other men, how long will it be until he must compete politically?"[24] It is no accident that there was no theatrical *representation* of Mao during the first three decades of PRC history, when Mao could *present* himself in highly orchestrated political rituals as a singular personage to be worshipped rather than judged. The post-Mao theatricalization of Mao sought to recapture that mystical presence, but it invariably also opened the door to the secularizing ramifications of representation.

In his attempt to make sense of Soviet cinema's "audacity" to portray Stalin while he was still living, André Bazin comes to the conclusion that the celluloid Stalin, almost always solitary and pensive, is for all intents and purposes "mummified," that is, reduced to pure allegory, as the end of history and as incarnated transcendence: "His biography is literally identical with History and shares the absoluteness of History."[25] As such, Stalin is treated as "a dead hero" whose "meaning of life has already and definitely been attained" and whose destiny is irreversible.[26] In other words, the cinematic representation of Stalin presupposes a terminated biography, hence the solemn rigidity of his image, which is practically indistinguishable from its documentary counterpart.[27] Had Mao been put on screen before his death, the treatment would have been equally mummifying in effect: every precaution would have been taken to deplete him of any ordinary character traits, psychology, or personality. Not surprisingly, early post-Mao representations of Mao were largely constrained by this documentary inertia, and as a result, the performances were redolent of a programmatic spirit possession, of a powerful deity taking possession of a passive vessel—the special actor.

The veteran special actor Gu Yue 古月 (1939–2005) is reported to have been selected to portray Mao by Marshal Ye Jianying in 1978, and he appeared in more than eighty films as Mao's double, winning both broad popular acceptance and official approbation.[28] (See Chapter 5 in this volume for a discussion of Gu Yue's performance in the music-and-dance epic *Song of the Chinese Revolution*.) He and other special actors of his generation, most notably Wang Tiecheng 王铁成 (as Zhou Enlai) and Lu Qi 卢奇 (as Deng Xiaoping [1904–97]), played no other roles during their entire careers than the one they were groomed to play, and sported no distinct personality aside from the larger-than-life personae of their avatars. Their personal lives were kept in low profile, and they had few opportunities to leverage their public image for personal gain. In an interview with a Hong Kong journalist, Gu Yue speaks resignedly of his low pay and his inability to cash in on his famous face, and consoles himself in a philosophic tone: "To play a leader you have to be prepared to make some sacrifices."[29] Barmé points out that the party expressly forbade Gu Yue from doing product endorsements and that the one rare appearance he made at a "charity concert" for which he was remunerated handsomely was harshly criticized in the media for damaging Mao's mystique.[30] In the same interview, Gu Yue ruefully dreams of playing "China's Gandhi" in a Hollywood blockbuster production that Oliver Stone was rumored to be contemplating.[31] Needless to say, this did not pan out for him, and he died in relative obscurity.

Since the 1990s, a new generation of actors has vied, with varying degrees of success, to portray the great leader on the stage and screen. Of note is Tang Guoqiang 唐国强, who plays Mao in the 2009 "main melody" blockbuster *The Founding of a Republic*.[32] Before this role, Tang had already played Mao on screen a good dozen times, though he is better known among mainland audiences as a matinee idol, from the romantic comedies he did in his youth and, later, for playing mature statesmen in period dramas. Pointing to his less-than-striking resemblance to Mao and his long and variegated acting career, some critics questioned the wisdom of choosing him for the all-important role in the all-important cinematic event of the decade. But the gamble paid off: the film became the highest grossing domestic production in China, thanks not only to the casting of Tang as Mao, but also to the dozens of celebrity actors (who offered their services gratis) who portrayed the entire constellation of power players during the fateful years between Japan's surrender in 1945 and the founding of the People's Republic in 1949. For a while, figuring out who was who became a national pastime, and the combined drawing power of the stars (together with many officially organized screenings) kept the film at the top of the box-office chart and online entertainment sites. The new generation of moonlighting special actors has thus subtly redefined the nature of political impersonation, from rigidly codified spirit possession to improvisational performances that place a higher premium on character acting and psychological verisimilitude (*shensi* 神似) than on superficial resemblance and mimicry (*xingsi* 形似). The younger actors, moreover, are usually celebrities in their own right and have played and will likely go on to play very different kinds of roles in both mainstream and entertainment media. They are no longer marionette-like state props dutifully acting out hackneyed historical scripts.[33]

Gu Yue and company had to undergo rigorous training to internalize their avatars' regional accents, speech patterns, gestures, and comportment while effacing their own personalities as much as possible. Less-than-perfect resemblances were remedied through plastic surgery. Their performances are highly scripted and formalized, as befitting the near-documentary nature and pedagogical function of the films in which they appear. Tang Guoqiang and others like him, however, are able to bring their own star power to bear on their roles. The figurative "possession trance" they enact is thus less structured and more open to improvisation in which, as Kathryn Wylie puts it, "the gods have human attributes closely allied with the personalities of the devotees."[34] Not surprisingly, the newer productions tend to give more screen time to portraying the leaders in mundane or casual circumstances in which comedy and a looser style are permissible. In *The Founding of a Republic*, for example, the top CCP leaders celebrate a major military victory against the KMT by drinking into the wee hours. At the end of the scene, a tipsy Mao, cheeks aglow, leans against a pillar while watching Zhou Enlai and Zhu De belt out *The Internationale* together. The scene is widely and fondly noted by commentators for highlighting the "human" (*renxing* 人性) and "everyday" (*shenghuo* 生活) side of the great leaders. Indeed, rather than merely acting out the standard mythology of the revolution, the actors are more intent in recent films on transmitting the human attributes of the demigods: "their likes and dislikes, activities, and personal quirks."[35] In other words, they have inched the practice of impersonation closer to the marketplace and its culture of celebrity, and further away from the elevated theater of political ritual.

Thus the Mao body politic lives on, but in a framework quite different from the one that once endowed him with mystical and lethal powers. Today, Mao's persona straddles the increasingly blurred boundary between political ritual and mass entertainment. In a sense, the party has been playing catch-up with the popular Mao craze of the 1990s, attempting to anchor the floating symbol that Mao has become while channeling the popular yearning for the sacred and the sublime. It is a struggle, trying to prevent the appropriation of Mao as either a blatant commercial brand or "a vehicle for nostalgic reinterpretation, unstated opposition to the status quo, and even satire."[36] However, even as the party works hard to slow the process of secularization and marketization, its own brand of state capitalism has few qualms about turning Mao into a bankable star capable of reaching both the hearts and pockets of audience members. This it does by bundling old-fashioned propaganda with slick productions and savvy publicity campaigns. As such, Mao's persona is more and more dissociated from the system that created and sustained it and more and more attached to Mao's person as the genius statesman and author of his public image.

The post-Mao Mao craze has largely taken leave of Durkheim's "conscience collective" and embraced John Locke's possessive individualism, whereby its natural habitat is the capitalist marketplace rather than the temple of secular religion. Anodyne biographies written in "a cloying and affected prose style" about Mao the private man have proliferated, converging with official boilerplate depictions of Mao as a flesh-and-blood hero: earthy, witty, feisty, and dazzling, all at once.[37] Quasi-academic works have sought to explain Mao the tragic hero by honing in on his private demons and idiosyncrasies, on the assumption that he is, in the last analysis, the author/owner of his own deeds and that his character flaws go a long way toward making sense of the high tragedy of both his personal life and that of the nation.

In recent years, freelance Mao impersonators, or what might be called "*shanzhai* Maos" 山寨毛, to adapt a term widely used in China to designate knockoffs, counterfeits, and unofficial versions of almost anything, have been cropping up at tourist sites and entertainment venues, giving rise to a veritable rent-a-Mao cottage industry.[38] For the first time ever, the question of Mao's "publicity rights" has been brought up by newly legal-minded opinion makers. In the age of the market, a person is assumed to be the sole legitimate owner of his or her publicly identifiable likeness, particularly in the case of a celebrity whose prominent profile is typically attributed to his or her unique personal qualities and hard striving.[39] The celebrity's distinct persona comes under the protection of publicity laws in many Western societies, because recognition value, even the posthumous variety, can be easily translated into exchange value in a media-saturated commercial economy. But the real question is not whether Mao owns his persona or whether he should be protected by publicity laws—if there were any in place in China. Rather, it is whether the party can maintain its monopoly over Mao's persona in the face of centrifugal market forces that threaten to decentralize the Mao industry into a freewheeling culture industry.[40] One wonders how long the party will regard unauthorized, playful, and potentially ironic impersonations of Mao as symbolic dismemberment of the Mao body politic, instead of disregarding them as harmless mass entertainment, which is the standard treatment of political satire in secular Western societies.

In 2005, a story in the newspaper *Xin jing bao* told of a "fake Mao," surnamed Sun, who hung out in a resort called Miniature Old Beijing on the outskirts of the capital city, plying a specious trade.[41] According to the report, Sun was in partnership with the resort's restaurant and made a pretty good living entertaining the diners by reciting Mao's famous speeches, giving autographs in imitation of Mao's calligraphic style, and posing for pictures at a price of 20 yuan per photo. Sun claimed to have played Mao in numerous film and television productions, though the story stresses that few of his claims had been substantiated. Still, the customers appeared to be little troubled by the flimsiness of his credentials and were quite willing to have him grace their tourist snapshots. The article cites the opinions of both state officials and legal experts with regard to the legality of Sun's enterprise, noting their hemming and hawing in the absence of any explicit prohibition.[42]

The first in-depth look at these enterprising, grassroots impression artists comes from the Beijing-based independent filmmaker and artist Zhang Bingjian 张秉坚.[43] In his documentary film *Readymade* (*Xianchengpin* 现成品, 2008), Zhang adopts the "direct cinema" style that is the signature of the new Chinese documentary movement, and quietly lets two freelance impersonators act out their triumphs and tribulations for their audiences on and off the screen.[44] The first individual is a farmer named Peng Tian 彭天 from Mao's native province of Hunan (plate 23). We are introduced to him as his disembodied voice, vividly raspy, proclaims the founding of the People's Republic, echoing Mao as the latter stood on the balcony of Tiananmen Gate in the iconic archival footage. At the time of the filming, Peng is enrolled in the Performance Art Program at the prestigious Beijing Film Academy (BFA), an incubator for China's most accomplished filmmakers and screen artists. Despite having to commute to campus by public transportation and dine in the school cafeteria with twenty-year-olds, Peng unfailingly remains in character and is never seen without his Mao suit and slicked-back hairdo. Soon we follow him to Changsha, the capital of Hunan, where he rehearses in someone's living room with local amateur actors, in preparation for an appearance in a public celebration. On the same trip, he returns to his native village in the mountainous western region of Hunan and is given a hero's welcome by the village folk and his extended family (who identify themselves as belonging to the Tujia ethnic minority group). Pooling their resources to pay his hefty tuition at the BFA, Peng's family members appear exceedingly proud and supportive of his career choice, though no one, including Peng himself, knows what is in store for him upon graduation. He entertains his fellow villagers by alternately reciting Mao's speeches and singing amorous folk ditties. The villagers join in the conviviality by shouting Communist slogans, belting out Mao-era revolutionary songs, and crooning sentimental ballads. The scene has the infectious mood of a rousing revivalist congregation.

The jovial cacophony recedes as the film transitions to the second story, and we hear the bombastic marching music cranked out by a band of garishly clad women escorting "Mao" to some ceremony in a smoggy provincial town. This Mao is played by Chen Yan 陈燕, a Sichuanese housewife who waited twenty years after her mother discovered her special endowment before she made herself up and posed at various events as a chain-smoking and perpetually waving Mao (plate 24). Unlike Peng Tian, Chen cannot mimic Mao's speeches with her female voice. Yet as a mute Mao, she approximates the iconicity of the Mao body politic with uncanny precision. In contrast to Peng Tian's self-sacrificing family, Chen Yan's husband and daughter are dead set against her new-found avocation and refuse to appear in the documentary. In an interview program at a local television station, Chen reveals, in between sobs, the hurt and abuse she endures from her husband. He reportedly resents the idea of "sleeping with" Mao in his marital bed. To him, Mao has taken possession of his wife's body and blotted out her submissive, housewifely self as she becomes more and more celebrated for her public guise, absorbed by the thrills of role playing and self-reinvention, and identified (by herself and by her fans and clients) with her theatrical self. He can be forgiven for not being too keen on bedding the Great Helmsman, but underlying his objections is the familiar sexist insistence that a woman should ideally be a private person with no significant public identity, or at least not one so colossal and obliterating as Mao's. In fact, he should be thankful that there is a radical break between the public and private in Chen's high-octane transvestitism, so that the Mao body politic is barred entrance into their private life where it might upset the gender hierarchy. The same cannot be vouchsafed for male impersonators.[45]

In the same television interview, Chen tells the host that the only thing that keeps her going is the "people's" (*laobaixing* 老百姓) recognition and demand. Near the end of her segment, we learn that the local government has more than once put a damper on her activities, though whenever she does appear in public in full Mao regalia (including a pair of custom-made boots that elevate her height by 25 centimeters), passersby are always eager to seek out her hand and pose for photos with her. Indeed, their excitement seems only augmented by the open secret of her gender. The public, after all, is consuming the Mao body politic and what matters is mimetic perfection. As Chen Yan makes it clear, public enthusiasm has greatly fortified her resolve to "serve the people," whatever it might cost her privately. In both her case and Peng Tian's, it is this sense of mission—sustained by the public recognition and media profile bestowed on these otherwise marginal, anonymous individuals (a farmer and a housewife)—that seems to guarantee the seriousness of their Mao impersonations even as they bring palpable pleasure, evidenced by moist eyes or hysterical giggles, to spectators. Ultimately, what generates the pleasure is the evocation of a bygone age of collective effervescence. Satire or irony would be quite beside the point.[46]

Taken in aggregate, the growing crop of *shanzhai* Maos seems to point to a lax attitude on the part of the state so long as it is assured that their amateur performances do not cross the line and degenerate into caricature or burlesque. That is, so long as Mao's image magic is not dissipated in free play. According to Ernst Kris and E. H. Gombrich, caricature "is a play with the magic power of the image, and for such a play to be licit or institutionalized the belief in the real efficacy of the spell must be firmly under control. Wherever it is not considered a joke but rather a dangerous practice to distort a man's features, even on paper, caricature as an art cannot develop."[47] It is in the party's interest to make sure that Mao impersonation does not slide into the domain of art and become the occasion for mirth, and so far the party has been largely successful in stanching the parodic impulse. Nonetheless, the freelancers have taken a bold step away from the institutionalized practice of Mao impersonation. They usually moonlight as Mao's double either to supplement their income or as a hobby. Their lives, therefore, are not entirely subsumed or circumscribed by their role. They are more like shamans who go on a quest to incorporate the spiritual into their own persona, whereas the professional special actors more closely resemble mediums who are involuntarily possessed by spirits. Even more so than the second-generation special actors, the freelancers are assertive authors who poach from the orthodox repertoire to craft a more or less licit and resonant cultural commodity for the marketplace. They are generally cognizant of the prohibition against parody and emphatic about the high moral purpose of their art. However, how their performances are interpreted and appreciated by viewers cannot always be dictated by the party or even themselves. Irony may well be in the eyes of the beholder, especially if the beholder is sensitized to a different regime of political art in the age of global mass entertainment.

Chairman Mao Would Not Be Amused

The compliance in refraining from parody, at least on the surface, among Mao doppelgangers and their audiences proves quite baffling to foreigners for whom the entire point of mimicking politicians is to mock them and knock them down a few pegs. Viewed from the Western tradition of political satire, the Chinese ritual theater of impersonation is oddly straight-laced and dour. Absent any Rabelaisian laughter, its mass appeal is a poser to those who believe in the universality of art. David Moser, a program consultant and host for China Central Television in the first decade of the 2000s, wrote about the phenomenon with a candid confession of befuddlement:

> I'm at a popular Peking duck restaurant in Beijing, chatting with Chairman Mao. He sits a few feet from me, drinking Coca-Cola and chain-smoking Marlboros. His jet-black hair is immaculate, his gray revolutionary suit perfectly pressed, his smooth skin marred only by the familiar mole on his chin. I am mesmerized, awed to be in the presence of this historical icon. He asks me for my email address. I have trouble understanding his thick Hunan accent. He hands me his business card.
>
> The name on the card breaks the spell. He is Du Tianqing, a Mao impersonator who has played the Chairman in many movies and television programs. . . . In addition to his movie and TV work, Du also travels around China gracing various meetings, variety shows, and factory openings with a once-in-a-lifetime visit from the Great Helmsman himself. He typically greets the crowd in the hortatory style of the revolutionary days ("Comrades! Under no conditions forget class struggle!"), and then delivers one of Mao's famous speeches, mimicking every aspect of the leader's body language and vocal intonation. Like many Mao portrayers, he has even put some effort into learning to imitate Mao's unmistakable calligraphy, and he concludes his performances by producing, on the spot, a large character scroll in Mao's hand.[48]

To Moser, impersonating Mao at meetings, celebrations, and variety shows is both like and unlike what Elvis impersonators do. Both pay "complex homage" to a great personage: "Whether the slogan is 'imperialist running dogs' or 'You Ain't Nothin' but a Hound Dog,' both . . . seem to evoke powerful resonances of a turbulent past that now seems mythic, larger than life." But only the Elvis impersonation is imbued with an aesthetic of kitsch, of condescending to a cultural hero and exploiting his human foibles for humorous or satirical effect. The Chinese, it seems to Moser, have not developed a taste for the pleasure of kitsch.[49] Another reporter also finds it paradoxical that "the Mao ersatz [can] work a lively circuit of banquets, holiday celebrations and weddings" in a land where political satire is strictly off limits.[50]

In a recent blog for *Foreign Policy*'s "In Other Words" political humor edition, Eric Abrahamsen ponders the sad fate of irony in Mao's China: "'Socialism is great!' Was there ever a statement riper for ironic mockery than this erstwhile catchphrase of the infant Chinese republic? How could a thinking people accept this and a host of other bald statements at face value, without so much as a raised eyebrow or a silently murmured *really*?"[51] If there *were* any such murmurs, they were not for us to hear—not until the coming of the Internet. In the late 1990s when the Internet was still uncensored, a site called Black Humor Wire Service set out to mock the Xinhua News Service in the manner of *The Onion*.[52] Once the "net nannies" were mobilized to patrol cyberspace in the middle of the next decade and, as a consequence, most official targets were placed out of bounds, political humor morphed into a decidedly kitschy form of Internet humor called *egao* (naughty play 恶搞).

Moser's piece was written just before *egao* took off. It began in 2006, when an obscure techie named Hu Ge 胡戈 made a spoof of the ponderous, megabudget film *The Promise* (2005), directed by Chen Kaige 陈凯歌.[53] Lately Hu has taken on CCTV's anchor program *News Simulcast* (*Xinwen lianbo* 新闻联播), notorious for its soporific chronicles of official meetings and its hunky-dory brand of journalism. Hu and others like him enjoy enormous followings online and have so far eluded threats of lawsuits and official sanctions. This is evidence enough that the Chinese are not completely indifferent to the pleasures of kitsch. The absence of Mao spoofs, in contrast, has complex political and cultural determinations, not the least of which is the essentially theological nature of Chinese politics. Chen Kaige and CCTV are fair game because one operates in a nonpolitical orbit and the other has refashioned itself as a modern communications organ dedicated to professional journalism. Both can have their *craft* judged and critiqued (and ridiculed) on an aesthetic register, just as a Shakespearean actor is subject to audience evaluation even when he is playing the king.

Western societies have largely jettisoned the mystical idea of the king's two bodies and inserted an institutional wedge between a politician and the office she or he temporarily occupies, hence the democratic fiction of an empty place at the center of power. In theory, therefore, lampooning politicians should not undermine the sacrality of the polity or its constitutional principles. In modern times, political parody in the West is constitutionally protected under the principle of freedom of speech and is often valorized by scholars as a weapon for the weak. From great statesmen and pompous politicians to charismatic artists and glamorous stars, no one is exempt from the barbs of satire, even if some media darlings fight hard to seek the protection of publicity laws when their reputation or commercial interest is on the line. On the whole, it is considered poor taste to lose one's composure over a cartoon rendition of one's image or a riff on one's pronouncements. After all, in societies predicated on the separation of church and state, impersonation has decidedly moved out of the ritual domain and consequently lost its magical, incantatory power. At historic tourist sites in the United States, the founding fathers are brought back to life in a somewhat reverential manner owing to their stature in the nation's founding mythology, but such pockets of pious performance lie at the outer peripheries of a shrinking core of political rituals that include presidential inaugurations, Memorial Day at Arlington National Cemetery, singing of the national anthem at sporting events, and reciting the Pledge of Allegiance in schools. In general, instead of representing a miraculous reincarnation, impersonation has become an art form that is discontinuous with political life. Kathryn Wylie writes: "As faith declines . . . the elements of comedy and parody increase. The lived theatre of possession becomes the theatre performed, 'the serious part diminishes in rapport to that of the frivolous. . . . ' The diminishing seriousness of ritual is especially prevalent where rites are held as a part of carnivals or festivals," or staged for thrill-seeking tourists.[54] In a similar fashion, Robert Elliott traces the trajectory of dance from primitive hunting ritual to modern spectatorial art form: "In the beginning the dancers were 'making' magic: they were 'making' the death of the animal or of their foes; but when belief in the magical efficacy has gone, the makers, like the dance, become something else. They may become performers and the dance, detached from its immediate practical purpose and from the practically directed emotion which impelled it, a thing to be witnessed. The dance, in fact, may become art."[55]

Art is thus a sublimation of magic, replacing concerns about ritualistic efficacy with those about aesthetic value. Moser notes how Westerners carry their aesthetic taste for the irreverent and frivolous over to their imaginings of and dealings with China, from Andy Warhol to the enthusiasm for schlocky Mao artifacts and Mao-themed Pop art. In their eyes, the Mao industry is indistinguishable from the culture industry, and anything that can be bought and sold on the market is fair game for the stage, real or metaphorical. Mao's image or name has been deployed as a sort of eye-catcher or rhetorical device on the covers of countless academic and journalistic books about post-Mao China. An anthology of contemporary short stories, for example, is entitled *Chairman Mao Would Not Be Amused: Fiction from Today's China*, calling attention to the compiler's facetious effort to imagine Mao's displeasure if he were to read the subversive or frivolous stories collected therein.[56] The promise of (political) mischief, of Chinese authors thumbing their noses at political orthodoxy, serves to flag contemporary Chinese literature's welcome distance from Communist propaganda for the benefit of the mistrustful foreign reader.

* * *

In this investigation of how the political-theological idea of Mao's two bodies lives on in the performative art of Mao impersonation in contemporary China, we have examined both the institutionalized practice of using "special actors" to portray Mao (and other political leaders) in PRC main-melody film and television and the emerging "rent-a-Mao" phenomenon of freelance impersonators reenacting Mao's speeches and calligraphy at tourist sites and entertainment venues. Framing this discussion is a close reading of Yiyun Li's short story "Immortality," about the fate of a man born with Mao's face and groomed to be his official impersonator. Although Mao impersonation tilts toward the spirit mediumship end of the spectrum of performative practices (with satire on the other end), it is still a fluid and volatile practice alive to the exuberant "unruliness of the persona" and the naughty polysemy of culture, which neither censorship nor publicity laws can permanently rein in.[57] The practice has had the paradoxical effect of both prolonging the lifespan of the Mao body politic and killing it off, softly but surely. Indeed, it was the party itself that inaugurated the process of transforming Mao from a "cosmic savior" and the "subject and master" of history to the object of collective nostalgia.[58] Nonetheless, the wheel of de-Maoification, of turning Mao from godhead to celebrity, has been slowly but steadily slipping out of the party's grip.

China's cyber generation seems quite prepared to savor the delicious irony of party-sponsored and market-enabled Mao mimesis that renders him a quotidian god jostling for elbow room in the higgledy-piggledy of everyday life, a fate shared by countless historical worthies.[59] Yu Hua 余华, a contemporary writer noted for his satirical take on post-Mao Chinese society, relates an Internet joke in his *China in Ten Words*: Suppose Mao were to wake up from his thirty-odd years of "repose" and amble to the front steps of the memorial hall. As he scans sunlit Tiananmen Square, at once familiar and strange, a gaggle of tourists discovers him and rushes over, hollering: "Gu Yue, may we have your autograph please?"[60] While living, Gu Yue was not allowed to cultivate any personal cachet; posthumously, however, the special actor has apparently come to stand for the extent to which Mao's image magic has been vitiated by those who are carrying on his art, with or without official blessing.

In keeping with the hypothetical drift of the foregoing anecdote, we might say that the young man in Yiyun Li's story does not have to sink to such depths of despair after all. He could very well embark on a second career, making the rounds at weddings, birthday parties, and television programs, finding satisfaction and fulfillment as a shamanic hero and celebrity in his own right. And if someday Mao finally falls victim to the logic of the market and is crowded out by edgier pop icons, the young Mao impersonator will have made his contribution to killing off the Mao body politic without any collateral damage to his own body and manhood. Sometimes fiction has to play catch-up with life.

Notes

I would like to thank Alexander Cook, Prasenjit Duara, Paul Festa, Daphne Lei, Jie Li, Zhanara Nauruzbayeva, Xiaobing Tang, Jeffrey Wasserstrom, and Yu Zhang for their help with this chapter.

1. Yiyun Li, "Immortality," *Paris Review*, no. 167 (Fall 2003): 24–43. Winner of the *Paris Review*'s Plimpton Prize, the story is reprinted in Yiyun Li, *A Thousand Years of Good Prayers: Stories* (New York: Random House, 2006), pp. 44–67. Subsequent citations refer to the *Paris Review* edition.

2. Historically, several towns in Hebei in proximity to Beijing, most notably Nanpi, Cangzhou, Hejian, and Qingxian, supplied practically all of the castrated males who served the imperial court. I thank Weijie Song for this detail.

3. Ernst Hartwig Kantorowicz, *The King's Two Bodies: A Study in Mediaeval Political Theology* (Princeton, NJ: Princeton University Press, 1957), p. 3.

4. Li, "Immortality," p. 43.

5. Ibid., p. 28.

6. According to statistics compiled by the National Printing Management Office, more than 4.3 billion posters of Mao were printed between 1949 and 1976, the bulk of these cranked out during the Cultural Revolution. Daniel Leese, "Mao the Man and Mao the Icon," in *A Critical Introduction to Mao*, ed. Timothy Cheek (Cambridge: Cambridge University Press, 2010), pp. 219–39, see p. 220. Geremie Barmé points out that in the first decade after Mao's death, his "votary image" quickly disappeared, only to be brought back with a vengeance in the 1990s: the number of Mao portraits printed rose from 370,000 in 1989 to 50 million in 1991. Geremie Barmé, *Shades of Mao: The Posthumous Cult of the Great Leader* (Armonk, NY: M. E. Sharpe, 1996), p. 9.

7. Robert C. Elliott, *The Power of Satire: Magic, Ritual, Art* (Princeton, NJ: Princeton University Press, 1960), p. 87.

8. Li, "Immortality," p. 32.

9. Ibid., p. 35.

10. Geremie Barmé, "'I'm So Ronree,'" in *Was Mao Really a Monster? The Academic Response to Chang and Halliday's Mao: The Unknown Story*, ed. Gregor Benton and Lin Chun (London: Routledge, 2010), pp. 73–83, see p. 82.

11. Susan Shirk, "The Decline of Virtuocracy in China," in *Class and Social Stratification in Post-Revolution China*, ed. James L. Watson (Cambridge: Cambridge University Press, 1984), pp. 56–83.

12. Geremie Barmé, "For Truly Great Men, Look to This Age Alone: Was Mao Zedong a New Emperor?" in *A Critical Introduction to Mao*, ed. Timothy Cheek (Cambridge: Cambridge University Press, 2010), pp. 243–72, see pp. 246–47.

13. Ibid., p. 269.

14. Kantorowicz, *The King's Two Bodies*, p. 23.

15. Ibid.

16. Eric Santner, *The Royal Remains: The People's Two Bodies and the Endgames of Sovereignty* (Chicago: University of Chicago Press, 2011), p. xxi. Santner is centrally concerned with the ways in which the sovereign exception, as theorized by Giorgio Agamben and Roberto Esposito, is transmuted into the bifurcated body of the people as citizens (bearers of rights) and as creaturely life (flesh). I engage this general topic in my book *The Stranger and the Chinese Moral Imagination* (Stanford, CA: Stanford University Press, 2014).

17. Claude Lefort, *The Political Forms of Modern Society: Bureaucracy, Democracy, Totalitarianism* (Cambridge, MA: MIT Press, 1986), p. 303.

18. Victoria Kahn, "Political Theology and Fiction in *The King's Two Bodies*," *Representations* 106 (Spring 2009): 79.

19. On the Mao cult, see Daniel Leese, *Mao Cult: Rhetoric and Ritual in China's Cultural Revolution* (Cambridge: Cambridge University Press, 2011); Ban Wang, "In

the Beginning Is the Word: Popular Democracy and Mao's Little Red Book," in *Mao's Little Red Book: A Global History*, ed. Alexander Cook (Cambridge: Cambridge University Press, 2014), pp. 266–77.

20. Frederic Wakeman, Jr., "Mao's Remains," in *Death Ritual in Late Imperial and Modern China*, ed. James L. Watson and Evelyn S. Rawski (Berkeley: University of California Press, 1988), pp. 254–88, see p. 274.

21. For this reason, the removal of Mao's remains from the square will have to await a time when his image no longer underpins the sacrality and immortality of the nation. Public calls for Mao's removal, however earnest and reasonable, can only fall on deaf ears and bring negative repercussions on the courageous advocates—see Richard McGregor's discussion of the petition entitled "An Appeal for the Removal of the Corpse of Mao Zedong from Beijing," in *The Party: The Secret World of China's Communist Rulers* (New York: Harper, 2010), p. 246.

22. When queried about his view on Mao's "errors" by an American journalist, the veteran Mao impersonator Gu Yue responded with a rhetorical question: "What do you think of the statue of Venus? Her arms may be broken but she's still beautiful. I see Mao Zedong in the same way. Flawed beauty is more alluring." Quoted in Barmé, *Shades of Mao*, p. 178.

23. Leo Braudy, *The Frenzy of Renown: Fame and Its History* (New York: Vintage Books, 1997), p. 319.

24. Ibid., p. 335.

25. André Bazin, "The Stalin Myth in Soviet Cinema," in *Movies and Methods: An Anthology*, ed. Bill Nichols (Berkeley: University of California Press, 1985), pp. 29–40, see p. 36.

26. Ibid., pp. 36–38.

27. On the Stalin cult, see Jan Plamper, *The Stalin Cult: A Study in the Alchemy of Power*, (Stanford, CA: Hoover Institution Press; New Haven, CT: Yale University Press, 2012).

28. Zhou Yong 周勇, "Cong Gu Yue qushi kan texing yanyuan shengcun xianzhuang" 从古月去世看特型演员生存现状 (The present state of special actors: Reflections occasioned by Gu Yue's passing), *Xin jing bao* 新京报, July 9, 2005, at http://ent.163.com/ent/editor/star/050709/050709_434673.html (accessed October 5, 2015). Sun Zhong 孙仲, "'Texing yanyuan' linian dao le gai dapo de shihou le" '特型演员'理念到了该打破的时候了 (It's time to do away with the idea of special actors), August 26, 2010, at http://big5.taiwan.cn/plzhx/wylz/201008/t20100826_1505205.htm (accessed October 5, 2015).

29. Quoted in Barmé, *Shades of Mao*, p.182.

30. Ibid., p. 177.

31. Ibid., p. 181.

32. See Yi Lijing 易立竞, "Tang Guoqiang: Wo shi changpao yundongyuan" 唐国强: 我是长跑运动员 (Tang Guoqiang: I am a long-distance runner), September 28, 2009, at http://www.infzm.com/content/35310 (accessed October 5, 2015). Tang Guoqiang also stars in the thirty-part television serial version of *The Founding of a Republic*.

33. Perhaps one of the most decisive breaks effected by the second-generation

actors is the double role played by Ma Xiaowei 马晓伟 in *Song Qingling, Mother of the Nation* (*Guomu Song Qingling* 国母宋庆龄, 2010) as both Mao Zedong and Chiang Kai-shek. See Sun Zhong, "'Texing yanyuan.'" Also jaw-dropping was the decision to cast the art-house favorite Liu Ye as Mao in *Beginning of the Great Revival* (*Jiandang weiye*, dir. Han Sanping and Huang Jianxin, 2011), a tribute to the CCP's ninetieth anniversary.

34. Kathryn Wylie, *Satyric and Heroic Mimes: Attitude as the Way of the Mime in Ritual and Beyond* (Jefferson, NC: McFarland, 1994), p. 31.

35. Ibid.

36. Barmé, *Shades of Mao*, pp. 13, 16.

37. Ibid., p. 29.

38. Yu Hua, *China in Ten Words*, trans. Allan H. Barr (New York: Pantheon Books, 2011), p. 183.

39. Sheryl N. Hamilton, *Impersonations: Troubling the Person in Law and Culture* (Toronto: University of Toronto Press, 2009), pp. 184–86.

40. Michael Dutton, "From Culture Industry to Mao Industry: A Greek Tragedy," *boundary 2* 32, no. 2 (Summer 2005): 151–67.

41. Gongye Xiangbo 公冶祥波 and Geng Xiaoyong 耿小勇, "'Texing yanyuan' jiaban Mao Zhuxi yu youke heying shoufei ershiyuan" "特型演员"假扮毛主席与游客合影收费20元 ("Special actor" impersonating Mao, charging 20 yuan for tourist pictures), April 25, 2005, at http://news.xinhuanet.com/fortune/2005-04/25/content_2874485.htm (accessed October 5, 2015).

42. The 1994 advertising law bans the exploitation of Mao's image in advertising, largely in response to rampant commercial development. Yet the practice of inviting special actors "to do a turn" at major celebrations began to take off in the early 1990s and apparently fell below the radar of policy makers. See Barmé, *Shades of Mao*, pp. 31–43.

43. Zhang Bingjian, *Xianchengpin* 现成品 (Readymade), B.X.N. Productions, 2008.

44. Chris Berry, Xinyu Lü, and Lisa Rofel, eds., *The New Chinese Documentary Film Movement: For the Public Record* (Hong Kong: Hong Kong University Press, 2010).

45. In one of Qiu Xiaolong's Inspector Chen thrillers, *The Mao Case*, a real-estate tycoon develops a secretive hobby of impersonating Mao the private man with kinky appetites and imperial privileges, apparently drawing inspiration from the aforementioned biographies. He gets his hands on the orphaned granddaughter of a former actress and a mistress of Mao's, modeled on Shangguan Yunzhu (1920–68), installs her in an apartment decorated like Mao's residence in Zhongnanhai, and acts out his Mao-as-emperor fantasy during their trysts: "He started talking like Mao, thinking like Mao, living like Mao, and fucking like Mao too." Xiaolong Qiu, *The Mao Case* (New York: Minotaur Books, 2009), p. 275. Although one does not have to "fuck" like Mao in order to "talk" like Mao, a man can plausibly shift between playing Mao in bed and Mao at Tiananmen Gate. The tycoon would have gotten away with it—after all, a "big buck" keeping "a little concubine" for himself is nothing unusual in

today's China, and the party is in no position to stop people from trying to spice up their erotic life by mimicking Mao's private vices—had he not begun recklessly to knock off those who got in his way. This secretive Mao wannabe forms an interesting contrast to the impersonators profiled in the media: the latter invariably strive to live a virtuous private life in order to live up to their public, theatrical persona. It seems that a fascination with the sordid tidbits of Mao's private life, shared by domestic and foreign readers alike but disapproved of by the party, is per force divorced from the part-official, part-popular enthusiasm for the Mao body politic.

46. According to director Zhang Bingjian (private communication), Peng Tian returned to his village after completing his studies at the BFA and failing to secure a steady acting job in Beijing. He is now a pig farmer, though he has not given up hope of portraying Mao on screen. Chen Yan, on the other hand, is faring much better. See Patrick Boehler, "Housewife Turns Mao Zedong Impersonator," *South China Morning Post*, November 21, 2013, at http://www.scmp.com/news/china-insider/article/1361934/housewife-turns-mao-zedong-impersonator (accessed October 5, 2015). Her story is also briefly recounted in Yu, *China in Ten Words*, p. 184.

47. Quoted in Elliott, *The Power of Satire*, p. 88.

48. David Moser, "Red Stars over China: The Mao Impersonators," *Danwei*, October 7, 2004, at http://www.danwei.org/tv/david_moser_on_mao_impersonato.php (accessed October 5, 2015).

49. Ibid.

50. Pete Brook, "Chinese Mao Impersonators Are Devoid of Irony, Satire," *Wired*, October 7, 2010, at http://www.wired.com/rawfile/2010/10/tommaso-bonaventura-mao-zedong/ (accessed October 5, 2015).

51. Eric Abrahamsen, "Irony Is Good! How Mao Killed Chinese Humor . . . and How the Internet Is Slowly Bringing It Back Again," *Foreign Policy*, January 12, 2011, at http://www.foreignpolicy.com/articles/2011/01/12/irony_is_good (accessed October 5, 2015).

52. Ibid.

53. Haomin Gong and Xin Yang. "Digitized Parody: The Politics of *Egao* in Contemporary China," *China Information* 24, no. 1 (2010): 3–26.

54. Wylie, *Satyric and Heroic Mimes*, pp. 32–33.

55. Elliott, *The Power of Satire*, p. 55.

56. Howard Goldblatt, ed., *Chairman Mao Would Not Be Amused: Fiction from Today's China* (New York: Grove Press, 1995).

57. Hamilton, *Impersonations*, pp. 198–99.

58. Wakeman, "Mao's Remains," pp. 269, 286.

59. Consider the evolution of Guan Yu from a fearsome warrior to the god of war and god of wealth (see Prasenjit Duara, "Superscribing Symbols: The Myth of Guandi, Chinese God of War," *Journal of Asian Studies* 47, no. 4 [1988]: 778–95), sharing space with the kitchen god and a host of other Buddhist and Daoist deities on the domestic or communal altar. The process of superscription is certainly also at work in Mao's transformation from a deified supreme leader to a quotidian god.

60. An earlier example in this genre is the Hong Kong author Yau Ma Tei's short

tale "Mausoleum," in which Mao wakes up to and is dismayed by a crassly commercialized China, and is literally knocked back into his coffin so that he cannot reverse (again) the course of history. See Geremie Barmé and John Minford, *Seeds of Fire: Chinese Voices of Conscience* (New York: Noonday Press, 1988), pp. 189–92.

NINE

"HUMAN WAVE TACTICS"

Zhang Yimou, Cinematic Ritual, and the Problems of Crowds

Andy Rodekohr

Crowds and Form

Under the creative direction of master filmmaker Zhang Yimou 张艺谋, the 2008 Beijing Olympic Games Opening Ceremony drew on China's rich cultural resources and seemingly unlimited assets in capital and manpower to exhibit an unprecedented visual and technological extravaganza. Though it won high praise and commendations for its spectacular achievement, the huge crowd formations that structured the narrative of the exhibition unsettled many observers. Zhang's use of such "human wave tactics" (*renhai zhanshu* 人海战术) not only partakes of the global imaginary of masses and multitudes made emblematic during the twentieth century's "era of crowds" but also evokes the powerful and haunting visual legacy of the Maoist era.[1] Zhang's Opening Ceremony expresses a red legacy both in how it re-engages with the questions of mass representation at the heart of China's revolutionary narrative, and how it informs the changing notion of the crowd's role in the post-revolutionary era beginning in the 1980s. Zhang's uncanny staging of the crowd in 2008 thus marked a haunting return of the spectacular revolutionary masses, resurrected for the very ritual celebrating China's ascendance to the global stage.

At the same time, Zhang's use of the crowd in the Opening Ceremony alerts us to his own filmic inquiry into the visual, narrative, and ideological dilemmas posed by the crowd image. A closer look at Zhang's work as a director and a cinematographer reveals his persistent interest in the power and continuing resonance of the crowd image, suggesting a keen awareness of the possibilities and contradictions of collective representation, the dynamic of visual desire between spectator and spectacle, and the particular entanglement of the crowd and historical authority. From his early work as a Fifth-Generation cinematographer on *The One and the Eight* (*Yige he bage* 一个和八个, dir. Zhang Junzhao 张军钊, 1983; with co-cinematographer Xiao Feng 肖风) and *The Big Parade* (*Dayue bing* 大阅兵, dir. Chen Kaige 陈凯歌, 1986), to his more recent historical epics *Hero* (*Yingxiong* 英雄, dir. Zhang, 2002) and *Curse of the Golden Flower* (*Mancheng jindai huangjin jia* 满城尽带黄金甲, dir. Zhang, 2006), examining the use of the crowd image in Zhang's work provides a certain measure of continuity within his highly variable film career, while also bringing into focus the visual legacy inherited from the Chinese revolutionary culture. On the one hand, his restaging of the crowd image takes part in the active forgetting of the revolutionary imperative by adopting the spectacular value of such images for service in the global marketplace, while on the other, Zhang Yimou's use of the crowd speaks to the revolution's unfinished business. Working in the age of the deterioration of revolutionary ideology, when the telos of its historical narrative is fading into the past, Zhang's films appropriate the crowd image in a way that deconstructs the ontology of the collective subject while rebuilding it for contemporary political and commercial purposes.

Zhang's repeated use of the crowd image is characterized especially by two interrelated notions that run through his work: ideological ritual and the technologies of mass reproduction. In the films examined in this chapter, the crowd serves as a ritualizing agent that gives form to the abstract, qualitative idea of the masses and marks the image it produces as a medium of expansion with the potential to produce a "perfect circuit," to borrow Haun Saussy's term, of spectacularity between image and the audience.[2] Ritual, according to the authors of *Ritual and Its Consequences*, enacts the crowd formation to imagine, reconstruct, and project a unified social body in the subjunctive tense, for "the creation of an order *as if* it were truly the case."[3] This approach to ritual also foregrounds the artifice of Zhang's crowd forms, drawing attention to the *impossibility* of achieving the wholeness they point toward.[4] The inherent ambiguity displayed in the ritualizing crowd also allows Zhang some room to maneuver around the overly didactic pitfalls of political filmmaking, as shown in his defense against the charges of using human wave tactics. In the Maoist period, as well, the constant refiguring of belonging and exclusion (of which Zhang and his family were victims) drove a continual restaging of revolutionary devotion in material practice (a target of absurdist critique in *To Live* [*Huozhe* 活着, 1994], for example).[5] The kind of contrived ritual that saturates his films, a point of both admiration and criticism, and his use of the crowd in these contexts is crucial to understanding the visual legacy of the crowd he inherits.[6]

While ritual suggests the crowd's role as a mediator between the symbolic and the real, Zhang's films also testify to the crowd's intimate relationship with technological media. The emergence of the crowd in modern consciousness is rooted not just in the conceptual notions of imagining it but also even more fundamentally in the technological means of showing it. In a footnote to his famous essay on the work of art, Walter Benjamin discusses how, through the developing technologies of photography, sound recording, and, most important, film, "the masses are brought face to face with themselves," and Benjamin states plainly, "Mass reproduction is aided especially by the reproduction of the masses."[7] The technological, and specifically visual, methods of propaganda employed on a vast scale during the Maoist era propagated not only the ideological call of revolution but also the medium of the crowd itself. Interpellation is carried out by replicating what Rey Chow calls the "projectional mechanism of filmic projection"—the technologized, reproducible, mass object the audience sees in posters and film.[8] Zhang Yimou's works demonstrate this mechanism at work diegetically (as in the Opening Ceremony's collective celebration of the "Four Great Inventions" [*si da faming* 四大发明]), but also in his extradiegetic commitment to spectacle as the ideal way of attracting a commercial audience. The crowd itself can be seen as a kind of peculiarly cinematic effect, neither purely ideological nor market-driven, but a modern invention that reshapes and multiplies bodies, onscreen and off.

Zhang Yimou's red legacy is therefore not limited to depictions of China's revolutionary history; it may also be recognized in his approaches to representing and mobilizing crowds. Throughout his career, he has deployed the crowd image in a variety of methods, evidence of a long-held engagement with questions fundamental to the structure and subject of Chinese history. The proliferation of crowd images in nearly all facets of social and visual life during the Cultural Revolution (surpassed in magnitude and sublimity only by the figure of Mao, himself a key figure in the crowd's constitution) represents for Zhang a framework for historical narration that he has repeatedly challenged, deconstructed, amplified, and exalted over the course of his career. The selection of films analyzed in this chapter (which passes over Zhang's directorial efforts in the 1990s) is not meant to imply a uniform approach to Zhang's dealings with the crowd; rather, by starting with the Olympic Games Opening Ceremony and his recent imperial epics *Hero* and *Curse of the Golden Flower* before jumping back to his earlier cinematographic work in the 1980s, I mean both to complicate the conventional reading of his later work (as an appeal to authoritarian, or even fascist, aesthetics) by juxtaposing it with his initial, deconstructive inquiries into the nature of the Chinese masses, and to suggest that these inquiries have persisted and continue to yield new figurations.

Human Wave Tactics: The Olympic Crowd in 2008

Reaction to the 2008 Beijing Olympics Opening Ceremony promptly focused on the event as spectacle, marked most prominently by its massive crowd formations (some 15,000 performers were used in the 50-minute presentation) and technical innovation (most notably the gigantic LED scroll unrolled on the stadium floor). Taken together, these aspects comprised a language of people and technology through which China would, in Geremie Barmé's words, "speak directly to the world of China's vision of itself."[9] This stylized narrative of cultural heritage, on the one hand, and technological modernization, on the other, moving from a mythic recitation of Confucian aphorisms and elaborate exhibitions of three of the Four Great Inventions, to shining, youthful visions of a high-tech future, nearly omits any depiction of China's revolutionary history.[10] It is instead in the medium of the crowd, constant almost throughout the production, that we discern a visual link to the revolutionary heritage of contemporary China (plate 25).

While the success of the Opening Ceremony garnered Zhang heaps of praise in the international and domestic media for his creatively "human-powered" use of technology and visually arresting style, his use of the crowd image remains the primary point of unsettled criticism and has provoked a range of commentary that never strays too far from the political.[11] Whether menacing or hospitable, the image of the Chinese crowd consistently evokes questions of nation and political representation; as one *New Yorker* correspondent, perhaps echoing twentieth-century German cultural critic Siegfried Kracauer, succinctly wondered, "What kind of society is it that can afford to make patterns out of its people?"[12] National pomp and lavish production are elements expected of any country hosting the Olympic Games, but the foregrounding of crowd images in the 2008 Opening Ceremony in Beijing not only set the bar in terms of extravagance and spectacle but also intensified a long-simmering apprehension over the significance of collective representation.

The crowd image was a particular focus of sarcastic criticism in the domestic Chinese netizen reaction to the Opening Ceremony. Even on the semiofficial discussion forum Strong Nation (*Qiangguo luntan* 强国论坛), part of the state-run *People's Daily* (*Renmin ribao* 人民日报) website, one commentator wondered during the show, "What does China have except people?" and a respondent noted acerbically, "This kind of opening ceremony is possible only in China, because nobody else has that many people."[13] Some of the most biting criticisms accused Zhang of employing so-called human wave tactics, a negative term leveled at Zhang's film work as well (especially *Hero* and *Curse of the Golden Flower*). Originally a militaristic phrase describing a massed, headlong attack on the frontlines that favors overwhelming scale over strategic maneuvering (a technique used extensively by the PLA in Korea and elsewhere), the Chinese term took on new meaning in the reform era.[14] Nowadays the phrase is used to disparage theatrical and cinematic productions that overcompensate for their lack of narrative substance with attempts to galvanize the audience with pointless crowd formations. The cynical turn behind its contemporary usage suggests that staged crowd formations are perceived not only as inherently and overtly political but also as symptomatic of an age in which revolution itself is an anachronism and human wave tactics are an outmoded relic.

Zhang defended his use of these human wave tactics in an interview with *Southern Weekend* (*Nanfang zhoumo* 南方周末) in the days following the Opening Ceremony. According to Zhang, human wave tactics are a precondition for this kind of "plaza art" (*guangchang yishu* 广场艺术) and offer a method for maximizing the sensations such a performance is intended to produce:

> If there is a plaza performance, you definitely need to use "human wave tactics" to a certain degree. You cannot assume that thirty people will be able to pull it off unless it is an avant-garde show; for one thing, they will not be visible, and for another, it's exceedingly desolate. This kind of performance must possess something impassioned; you definitely need tens of thousands to take the stage. Technological devices, artificial things, and ornaments are all lifeless. For this performance, the most soul-stirring is the human, and most meaningful are still the kinds of things humans can convey to others.
>
> What is a plaza? The plaza is what maximizes the power produced by people gathered together. Regardless if it is an assembly, a political parade, or a performance, when many people gather together, even if they do nothing they still produce a peculiar feeling that this is humanity, the physiological meaning of hearts beating ever faster, *aiya*, so many people.
>
> From the point of view of an individual, within his own physiology, seeing so many people gathered and doing something together will move him and produce a very distinct kind of aesthetic response and a vastly different psychological feeling. In a plaza performance, how can you not use people or make use of so many people? If you do, they mock you and say you're just using "human wave tactics." If I feared this kind of mockery, then I wouldn't use people in this way. But this kind of approach is absolutely incorrect. In fact, any director of such a large-scale plaza performance who does not use these tactics, leaving aside the question of exactly how many to use, will find it damn impossible to pull off the show.[15]

For Zhang, the spectacle of a unified crowd performance remains the only viable technique able to generate the distinct psychological effects of power (*liliang* 力量) and peculiarity (*yiyang* 异样) on the self, brought about through the immediate physiological (*shengli* 生理) connection between the crowd and the observer.[16] In his formulation of the affective power of the crowd image, however, Zhang interestingly stresses the public architecture of such an event, the plaza. The Chinese term *guangchang*, literally a public space or square, is indelibly associated with mass movements, and similarly conflates the contradictory associations that make up the crowd. As cultural critic Dai Jinhua 戴锦华 explains, the plaza connotes the revolutionary legacy of protests and campaigns in modern Chinese history, especially those at Tiananmen Square such as the May Fourth protests in 1919, the Red Guard rallies in the autumn of 1966, and the student protests in 1989: "The phrase *Tiananmen Guangchang* signifies a mighty authoritarian state power and *the people* [*renmin* 人民], that great homogenous mass [*qunti* 群体] without classes or individuality."[17] By calling the Opening Ceremony a kind of plaza art, Zhang Yimou is not just tapping into the legacy of a physical space but also attempting to recuperate a technique of plaza art that imagines the *guangchang* as the revolutionary stage inhabited by the crowd.

As Dai goes on to explain, however, since the mid-1990s the term *guangchang* has become ubiquitous in Chinese cities as, simply, a shopping center, thus displacing the sacred aura of revolution and instead partaking in "the spectacle of globalization" that transforms the revolutionary masses into a crowd of consumers.[18] Zhang Yimou's Opening Ceremony likewise simultaneously draws on a legacy of revolution in its appropriation of the crowd image while engaging the global market, advertising an image of China to the world that signals a break from its revolutionary past and announces that China is open for business. The homogeneity of the masses, no longer based on the elimination of class divisions, is presumed in the illusion of equality under the market economy. Having been purged of its ideological vitality, the crowd in China's Olympics therefore serves as a reminder of the loss of the utopian vision promised by revolution. The ritual of crowd formation, in this sense, is an empty gesture, a "ritualization of utopia" that suggests, as Maurice Meisner puts it, "not the simple failure of revolution but rather a process of degeneration which seems inherent in its very success."[19] From this perspective, the 2008 Olympic Games, referred to as the long-awaited opportunity for China to showcase its remarkable economic development and exhibit its openness to the world, is a finale of sorts.

Zhang's explanation of his use of human wave tactics in the Opening Ceremony suggests a recognition of the embodied power of such crowd forms, along with a measured ambivalence toward the function of the plaza. This equivocation, mindful of the passing of the once-immanent revolutionary utopia the crowd signals, is magnified by a repeated correlation Zhang locates between the fullness of the crowd and its absence. In the same *Southern Weekend* interview, Zhang discusses the number of performers used in the production and remarks that the logistics and uniformity required for such a performance involving so many will confound the Western viewer who cannot see the whole for the parts:

> I think when [Westerners] watch something like this, they do marvel at its technical proficiency, but I think they see it as a matter of 1 + 1. If they watch the North Korean Arirang . . . , they would also marvel at its perfection in this sense.[20] It is people, so many people moving together in unison, but the Westerner doesn't see this. This is something they should have, not us in our ancient Eastern countries. In the end, if the Westerner again watches this technique, he will see the human element; after he sees it as 1 + 1, the feeling of amplification will be produced, and this is truly the feeling of astonishment he should have.[21]

The figure of the crowd cannot be accounted for through the mere totaling of the sum of its participants; rather, it produces an expansive sense of wholeness and totality, embodied through the uniformity of movement (*dongzuo de zhengqi* 动作的整齐). The inability to understand that Zhang attributes to his imagined Western observer recalls a similar sentiment expressed by Chairman Mao in 1964 when, speaking to an American journalist, he asked rhetorically, "Is Communism only the piling of brick on brick? Is there no work to be done with man?"[22] Both Zhang and Mao perceive inadequacy in the simple arithmetical aggregation of individuals to represent the whole, and depend instead on the affective sensation of the sublime produced through spectacle, a fusion of political ritual and aesthetic possibility. The "feeling of amplification" (*fangdagan* 放大感) Zhang aims for is akin, in this way, to what Ban Wang calls the "overwhelming explosion of sensory stimulus" in his discussion of the Cultural Revolution's rhetorical creation of a "sea of red" (*hong haiyang* 红海洋).[23] Impossible to achieve through mere accounting, the sense of the humanity that underlies the ritual staging of the crowd is, for Zhang, a feeling conditioned in red culture and revolutionary history.

The mathematical quandary Zhang Yimou identifies underscores one of the fundamental paradoxes of crowd representation. According to Arjun Appadurai, the idea of the masses is represented numerically by the numeral zero "because it is the key to converting integers into numbers in the hundreds, the thousands, the millions."[24] Using "0" to break free of the limits of seeing the crowd as merely a matter of "1 + 1" manifests the metonymic potential of the crowd to point toward the totalized masses, but also produces a parallel vision of emptiness alongside it. Mao's famous assertion that one of the most revolutionary features of the Chinese masses is that they are "poor and blank" (*yiqiong erbai* 一穷二白) also realizes this special capacity for the simultaneous expression of exponential growth and a hollow void.[25] In this sense, the operation of the crowd image resembles that of a Derridean supplement, producing "the *fullest measure* of presence," which nonetheless "produces no relief, [as] its place is assigned in the structure by the mark of emptiness."[26] In Zhang's exhibition, the "mark of emptiness" is the very source of the crowd's ideological and imagistic authority, the figure of Mao. A couple of oblique references notwithstanding, Mao's invisibility in the 2008 Beijing Olympics Opening Ceremony is pronounced.[27] The revolutionary plentitude once promised by the crowd invokes the specter of the chairman, but in doing so it also reenacts his erasure from the narrative of China's Olympic dream.

Without Mao's ruddy visage to catalyze the crowd into being, what can be proffered as the organizing framework of the postrevolutionary masses? The program's celebration of the Four Great Inventions, together with the vision of the future of China's technological innovation, comprise a powerful and appealing narrative of Chinese culture that stresses invention, ingenuity, and modernity. The crowd image, no longer mobilized to wage ideological warfare, becomes instead a vehicle for technological progress in a globalized, international future.[28] Tech is the new telos. Though the discourse of "technological utopianism" has a long history in Chinese cultural production, the emphasis on its *collective* realization in the 2008 Opening Ceremony finds its most direct visual authority in the modernization propaganda of the Maoist era, when technological advancement and innovation were constantly juxtaposed with the themes of socialist revolution.[29] The visually fantastic link between industrialization and collectivity that began with the Great Leap Forward campaign of the late 1950s remained a prominent theme of posters and political films during the following two decades. The impossible excess that characterizes the crowdlike figure of multiplicity is summoned in exhibitions of successful production and reproduction; technological achievements, crop yields, manufacturing bounty, and other fantastic signifiers of utopian modernization are pictured necessarily as collective triumphs. The means of propaganda production take the explosive growth of the crowd as a model; the techniques (and messages) of mass reproduction during the Maoist era, marked by "detachability and infinite repeatability," in Rey Chow's words, are shared and propagated in the medium of the crowd.[30]

Crowd, Ritual, and History: *Hero* and *Curse of the Golden Flower*

Placing the connections among the crowd image, ritual, and technology that underpin the mythic narrative of the 2008 Opening Ceremony in context with Zhang's depictions of epic "histories" in the films *Hero* and *Curse of the Golden Flower* further complicates the picture of how the crowd is figured in his cinematic vision. In each of these examples, the crowd serves a highly ritualistic and militaristically technological function, existing, ostensibly, as a subordinate player in the more qualified drama among the main actors (roles unfailingly filled by the biggest stars in contemporary Chinese film). Though the role of the crowd in these examples can be described as merely ornamental, Zhang's maximalist techniques of depicting the crowd interrogates the problematic relationship between leaders and masses, a dilemma with immediate ramifications for how history is written and, perhaps more significantly, expunged. In this sense, history making is itself caught up in "human wave tactics," an aesthetic spectacle masking the violence and sacrifice that contribute to its formation.

Hero weaves together several narrative threads, told in flashback, that relate an elaborate endeavor to assassinate Ying Zheng 嬴政 (who would become the First Emperor, Qin Shihuang 秦始皇; played by Chen Daoming 陈道明). As layers of narrative, related in multiple and competing interpretations (and color schemes), propel the assassin, Nameless (Jet Li [Li Lianjie] 李连杰), gradually closer to his target, the characterization of the First Emperor grows more sympathetic, transforming the cruel tyrant of the Chinese popular imagination into a compassionate, strong, and solitary figure.[31] Much like the reciprocity between the revolutionary crowd and Chairman Mao, the crowd formations of soldiers and officials serving Ying Zheng are a near-constant accessory to his absolute authority and images of imperial ceremony. However, what becomes clear by the end of the film is how the ornament of the crowd image isolates the First Emperor, foreclosing other narrative possibilities (particularly the ritual execution of Nameless at the end of the film). Zhang not only demonstrates the emperor's own inability to break free of the ritual trappings he has created for himself but also highlights historical erasure as a consequence of the same resolute will to unify China that the film celebrates.

Although Zhang consistently denies that any of his films are intended to be political in nature, there is nonetheless a suggestive connection between his sympathetic depiction of the Qin emperor and Mao's own reappraisal of the First Emperor. While his historical significance was never in doubt, Qin Shihuang was for centuries reviled as a ruthless tyrant who slaughtered scholars and burned books in pursuit of his monomaniacal aims. In the first decades of the People's Republic, however, the emperor was gradually exonerated of his excesses, even gaining measured praise from Chairman Mao.[32] After it was discovered that Vice Chairman Lin Biao, in his outline for a failed coup d'état, had vilified Mao as "a contemporary Qin Shihuang," a major mass campaign was launched in 1972 to posthumously criticize Lin, along with Confucius. Mao's association with the First Emperor was embraced, and numerous articles, along with a best-selling biography, praised Qin Shihuang in historical materialist terms as a progressive ruler.[33] One such article exalts the First Emperor's decree to officially designate the common people as *qianshou* 黔首, literally "the black-headed," a nomenclatural shift that, according to the author, acknowledges their status as "the principal force of the war of unification."[34] Zhang's film *Hero,* nearly three decades after Mao's promotion of the First Emperor, continues the process of historical revision by paying special attention to the crowd image and the way it manifests the singular hegemon, while endowing the massed soldiers with his titanic will and unifying the disparate kingdoms into national wholeness. This kind of sublime spectacle of immanence suggests, therefore, a legacy of crowds that Zhang remythifies into the past while also querying the practice of ritual itself, and in particular the practice of ritual that serves as a proxy for writing history.

Curse of the Golden Flower similarly emphasizes the constructedness of the historical narrative and the violence and erasure underlying the accumulation of political power, a process that holds particular resonance in the catastrophic power struggles that engulfed China during the Cultural Revolution. Of particular interest in the film is Zhang's deft embrace of computer-generated imagery (CGI) in its production. At the climax of *Curse*, an attempted overthrow of the emperor (played by Chow Yun-fat [Zhou Runfa] 周润发), orchestrated by the empress (Gong Li 巩俐) and led by her son, Prince Jai (Jay Chou [Zhou Jielun] 周杰伦), unleashes tens of thousands of soldiers on the palace courtyard, where they battle an equally massive army whose advantage in ingenious weaponry ensures the insurgency's swift and brutal suppression. Zhang Yimou's proclivity for technological exhibition in the spectacular battle scenes works doubly, both through the extradiegetic CGI effects that multiply the expanse of the crowd, and through the imaginative military hardware the soldiers deploy (plate 26).

The way that Zhang connects crowds and the technology that mobilizes them underscores the original, militaristic sense of the phrase "human wave tactics," rendering the military crowd as a cinematic effect whose means of visibility condition its spectacular extermination at the film's resolution.[35] For Zhang, summoning these "digital multitudes" indulges his interest in plaza art while also revealing the violence and the mass death underscoring state ritual, as in the ceremonial spectacle of the Chrysanthemum Festival that ends the film. The massive casualties fail to impede the ceremony, as hundreds of palace workers methodically remove the corpses and replace them with arranged flowers in pots.

Film critic Sek Kei (Shi Qi 石琪) writes, in a brief review of *Curse of the Golden Flower*, that only someone who had experienced the Cultural Revolution could have made a film of such excessive proportions, and finds irony in the film's ending, in which all traces of the bloody, failed coup are whitewashed with an image of peace and prosperity.[36] Though both *Curse of the Golden Flower* and *Hero* are set in an ancient past, their concerns with historical erasure, as Sek suggests, are much more contemporary. The constant rewriting of revolutionary history in China during the Maoist years, through rectification, purges, and revisions, found legitimation in the name of the "mass line" (*qunzhong luxian* 群众路线), even while traces of the political machinations driving the historical narrative were distorted, forgotten, and excised. Much more than an expression of the ruler's might, the crowd image, oscillating between visual plentitude and historical erasure, highlights the violence, sacrifice, and ghostly void that accompanies these power struggles.

Deconstruction of the Red Crowd: *The One and the Eight* and *The Big Parade*

Zhang Yimou's historical epics of the first decade of the twenty-first century seem far removed from his initial forays into cinema as one of the Fifth-Generation filmmakers in the 1980s. In the films *The One and the Eight*, *Yellow Earth* (*Huang tudi* 黃土地, dir. Chen Kaige, 1984), and *The Big Parade*, Zhang's cinematographic work powerfully revisualizes the foundations of the historical narrative of revolution and confronts the mythic image of the cultural origins of collectivist ideology in China. While the plots of these films overlap significantly with the filmic narrative of national liberation present in most PRC cinema after 1949, Zhang's cinematography visually interrogates a sacred totem of party ideology, the constitution and sublimation of the crowd.[37]

For the Fifth-Generation filmmakers, forging a new aesthetics for Chinese film meant not only challenging the master narrative of revolutionary Maoist ideology but also dismantling the visual dynamic of the crowd image. In response to the radical profusion of crowds and crowd images of the Cultural Revolution, the Fifth-Generation films hailed both a vigorous renewal of the engagement with individuality and nature as well as a deconstruction of the revolutionary myth. A closer look at the visual and cinematographic style developed in these works, however, also exhibits a persistent fascination with the crowd image. Director Chen Kaige remarked of the drum dance scene in his 1984 film *Yellow Earth* that "the unified way people dress up and dance is a thing all in itself, too."[38] The way in which the Fifth Generation and their films picture this "thing all in itself" in the wake of the Cultural Revolution manifests the crowd as an uncanny, haunting compulsion, a hollow gesture toward the utopia it once promised.

The One and the Eight was granted limited public release on October 8, 1984, following an almost year-long process of re-editing to meet the requirements for certification from the Film Bureau.[39] Though the film has never gained the recognition of the international breakout *Yellow Earth*, released just a couple of months later, it prefigures that film and other Fifth-Generation works in both style and theme. Set in 1941 during the War of Resistance against Japan, in the desolate plains of central Hebei province, *The One and the Eight* focuses on a group of nine prisoners being held for various crimes by the Eighth Route Army. The titular "one" is Wang Jin (Chen Daoming), an army officer who, after being separated from his unit, is falsely accused of treason. Wang is differentiated from the motley "eight," a group of bandits, deserters, an informant, and a well-poisoner, from the beginning, both through the camera's reverential treatment of him and the other characters' recognition of his principled behavior. Zhang (with Xiao Feng) notes in the "Cinematographers' Statement" that "comparing [the '1' and the '8'] in either numerical terms or in terms of 'substance' [*zhi* 质], they are opposites; but when this individual's words and actions shock, influence, and resonate among the others, through a series of events we get a sense of the Communist's fearless spirit made manifest by his resolute faith, as well as the integrity that comes from his devotion to the cause."[40] By the end of the film, Wang's righteous comportment and unfailing devotion to Communist Party principles convinces the others to give up their selfish ways and fight on behalf of their nation against the Japanese. Communist principle serves as the interface through which the disparate integers can, at least temporarily, achieve common purpose.

The film's storyline of how a disparate group achieves a sense of belonging, camaraderie, and loyalty to the nation may sound familiar in the socialist realist tradition, and it certainly hews to the demands of ideological correctness. However, in contrast to the war films of the 1950s and 1960s, in which the shining flawlessness of the Eighth Route Army heroes strikes fear into sickly and evil foreigners or traitors, this ragtag bunch finds redemption in spite of their nefarious backgrounds. After coming across a massacre at a small village, the prisoners undergo a transformation; they give up their selfish pursuits and begin to understand the need for collective action as a response to such mass atrocities (this scene was suggested by Zhang and used around two hundred extras as corpses).[41] The film boldly bestows the possibility of "redness" on characters previously "unrepresentable" and precluded from such a distinction.[42] In terms of its formal aesthetics as well, *The One and the Eight* stands out compared with war films made in the Maoist era; Dai Jinhua notes how the variety of technical stylizations and the unorthodox camerawork complete "the defamiliarization of historical myth" of the founding of the nation.[43] Even the film's title poses a mathematical query without a definite sum; instead it uses discreet fragments that suggest the possibility of adding up to something but does not assume a latent unity of the parts in a cohesive whole.

The most striking thing about the film's depiction of the crowd and the process of its formation is found in the aesthetics of visualizing the collective. The opening sequence of the film shows a collection of historical photos of the war while an authoritative voiceover (reminiscent of the narrator of the 1964 propaganda film *The East Is Red* [*Dongfang hong* 东方红]) describes the national struggle against the Japanese imperialists, highlighting the contributions of the Communist Party. Unlike a conventional newsreel, however, the sequence of photos does not follow a regular pattern or timing sequence; when the montage connects the historical background to the film's plot, we see a slow pan across a still photo of the nine prisoners. Silhouetted against a blue background, each of the criminals faces a different direction, seemingly unconnected in any way to the other members of the group (save for the rope that ties them together). This panning shot is followed by the rapid juxtaposition of extreme close-ups of the prisoners faces, spliced together in a seemingly random fashion. The incongruity of the narration, told in the standard and familiar voice of the party with the modernist visual montage that accompanies it, sets up a remarkable contradiction between the master narrative of history and the visual sense of fragmentation and shock.

Modernist and avant-garde film techniques offer a different perspective on the crowd than the uniform image of the heroic masses that flourished during the Cultural Revolution. Close-ups of faces and torsos, glimpses of body parts in shafts of light surrounded by darkness, and an alternation between deep and shallow focus to contrast faces in the foreground and background all serve to fragment the typically homogenous and unified crowd image, demystifying the idea of totality. What Zhang Yimou's cinematographic style here suggests is that such unity is constructed, and that the idea of the masses is at best a cinematic projection. The film ends with a long shot of Wang Jin carrying the wounded section chief on his back across a flat, desolate landscape dominated in the frame by the bleak, washed-out sky (a technique Zhang would repeat to great effect in *Yellow Earth*). As the two make their way into the distance, their bodies merge to form a somewhat grotesque amalgamation of the human form whose fusion is no more than a visual trick, a mirage captured on film.[44]

The visual problem of the crowd is made even starker in the 1986 film *The Big Parade*. *The Big Parade* was the second collaboration between director Chen Kaige, cinematographer Zhang Yimou, and art director He Qun 何群, following the remarkable success of *Yellow Earth*. Shot over a sweltering summer in Hubei Province's heat, the film was commissioned to commemorate the 1984 National Day parade through Tiananmen Square that marked the thirty-fifth anniversary of the founding of the PRC. It follows a division of servicemen enduring the physically and mentally grueling training required to participate in the parade. On the training ground, collectivity and uniformity of action are instilled in the soldiers, systemizing every aspect of the group, from their posture to the height of each of their steps. Zhang's cinematography in *The Big Parade* deconstructs both the crowd as a mass unit and the ritual of its formation. Slow pans across assembled torsos, arms, and legs, as doctors take careful stock of each soldier's height, shoulder width, and relative knee position reveal some of the visual tricks involved in the party's use of crowd aesthetics. The intensity of the discipline drilled into the soldiers, which Zhang shoots in a manner that Eugene Wang refers to as "formalizing impulse toward bodiless geometry," produces the impression of a singular entity, emphasized by Zhang's repeated use of long shots and overexposed takes that merge bodies together in the shimmering heat waves rising from the pavement.[45]

Over the course of the film, the soldiers, originally chosen on the basis of their physical similarity and visual cohesiveness, are gradually differentiated through characterization. Each struggles with his own personal tribulations (and shares voiceover narration duties), and the strict training regimen taxes them physically and emotionally, as the visual tension implicit in their individuality and occasional isolation in the barracks contrasts with the highly regulated scenes of the training ground. Placing the characters' psyches at stake effectively breaks down the unified crowd into its individual components; as Yingjin Zhang puts it, "Performing in state-sponsored events inevitably fragments the unified subjectivity (people as 'pedagogic object'—the nation-people)."[46] Near the end of the film, the squad leader Li Weicheng (played by Wang Xueqi 王学圻, who also starred as the Communist soldier in *Yellow Earth*) gives a moving speech highlighting both the futility and the nobility of their task; after walking nearly ten thousand kilometers in preparation for just ninety-six steps before the rostrum in Tiananmen

Square, Li asks, "Is this not a Long March?" evoking the crucial event in Chinese Communist historical mythology; he concludes by reciting a line from the national anthem, "March of the Volunteers" ("Yiyong junjin xingqu" 义勇军进行曲): "Let our flesh and blood forge our new Great Wall!" Each of these statements not only evokes a revolutionary genealogy (another implicit allusion to the crowd) but also calls for an ideological resolution to the visual problem of how the collective whole can be pictured and realized.

The latter image from "March of the Volunteers" is particularly resonant in Chinese revolutionary film culture, as it recalls the leftist classic in which the song first appeared, the 1935 film by Xu Xingzhi 许幸之, *Children of Troubled Times* (*Fengyun er nü* 风云儿女). That film concludes with "March of the Volunteers," as its protagonists take up arms and join the masses in song as they march against the invading Japanese. The marching sequence dialectically constructs the masses through a modernist montage of close-ups on faces and marching feet, and suggests a sense of unity through unidirectional movement and rousing music. The film ends as the group marches forward to unknown ends, galvanized in spirit and ready to sacrifice their lives for the national cause. *The Big Parade*, like *Children of Troubled Times*, also concludes with "March of the Volunteers," this time matched with footage shot at the 1984 National Day parade. However, what seems at first to be standard, newsreel-like coverage of the marching units as they pass in front of the rostrum takes a more contemplative turn during the final minute or so of the film as the rousing march, accompanied by sounds of feet marching in lockstep, segues into a more somber, nostalgic melody while various military units pass in slow motion. These plaintive shots, filmed in a highly ritualistic manner and edited together through slow fades, are protracted in a way that emphasizes the overwrought ideological formality of their action as well as the ephemeral nature of such rituals (plate 27).

Like *The One and the Eight*, the release of *The Big Parade* was delayed by more than a year owing to disagreements with the Film Bureau. Director Chen Kaige's original intention was to end not with the parade but with a series of shots of a deserted Tiananmen Square. The bureau's objection to the ambivalent connotations of the image of an empty Tiananmen, and its insistence that the ending instead include footage from the parade demonstrates the bureau's apprehension about the crowd's erasure. Wu

Hung recalls how the pivotal 1949 decision to locate the government in Tiananmen Square found justification in Friedrich Engels's notion of "the zero point" as "the point on which they are all dependent, to which they are all related, and by which they are all determined."[47] Recalling Zhang Yimou's remarks on plaza art, one can see how, in *The Big Parade*, filmmakers were already exploring the ghostly dimensions of the crowd, either in its absence or as a cinematic effect of ritualization.

The 1984 National Day parade was the largest official mass demonstration in Tiananmen Square since the Red Guard rallies in the summer and autumn of 1966.[48] At the time, the issue of how China would reconcile its market-oriented reforms and its revolutionary history was an unresolved question. By the time of the next National Day parade, in 1999, the spectacle of nationalism would become so carefully circumscribed that Beijing's residents were told to stay home and watch it on television.[49] For the sixtieth anniversary celebration in 2009, much of the creative team that executed the Opening Ceremony for the Olympics the previous year reconvened to design the ritual spectacular that, Barmé notes, is now "primarily produced for a TV audience." The mediatization of the crowd image makes clear Haiyan Lee's observation that the subject of representation in the parades, "the people," are to recognize themselves as "the absent signified."[50] Juxtaposing the films *The Big Parade* with the 2008 Olympics and the 2009 National Day festivities, one can see indications of how Zhang's sense of the crowd image, even its post–Cultural Revolution cinematographic deconstruction, is mediated through the cinematic apparatus.

The ambivalent final shot in *The Big Parade*, an unidentifiable silhouette of a soldier's head facing the red sun, foreshadows the final shot of Zhang Yimou's directorial debut, *Red Sorghum (Hong gaoliang* 红高粱, 1987). The regeneration of the body politic in that film, in contrast to the deconstruction of the crowd through the excavation of its desolate ritualization in *The Big Parade*, is celebrated as a cultural myth predating the ruptures of modern history. The accessible, commercial appeal of *Red Sorghum*, the way it "announces to the people the continuation of history," also signaled a new era of filmmaking for the masses, based on the crowd not so much as an object of ideological interpellation (or aesthetic deconstruction, in the films of the Fifth Generation), but as a viewing and consuming audience.[51]

Conclusion: *Red Sorghum*

With *Red Sorghum*, Zhang regenerates the notion of a Chinese body politic, in the sense of visualizing a mythological "redness" that precedes political systemization, as well as reapprehending the film audience not merely as a collective, ideological subject, nor an analytical, critical viewer, but, in the end, as a popular one. *Red Sorghum* often serves as the exemplary transitional film between the art-house, modernist style of the Fifth Generation and the commercialized, entertainment-driven mode of filmmaking that emerged as part of the state studios' institutional restructuring in the late 1980s.[52] Released in the midst of an ongoing debate over the social value of the "entertainment film" (*yule pian* 娱乐片), the success of *Red Sorghum* was proved not just by its enthusiastic domestic reception but also by the critical praise and awards it earned internationally. As cinema's ability to address its audience as a cohesive, collective unit (in the manner of the political films of the Maoist era) diminished, the film industry's aims shifted from ideological edification to the release of individual desires, including those of a consumerist nature.[53] Zhang refers to his film as a "bastard" (*zazhong* 杂种) work, the product of both an artistic sensibility and popular instincts, noting in his "Director's Statement on *Red Sorghum*" that commercial and national interests are not opposed in his work:

> As the nation becomes strong and prosperous, the nature of its people is also inspired to develop. The people rely on this spirit just like trees depend on their bark; this is one layer of this film's most practical significance.
>
> The sense of legend [*chuanqi secai* 传奇色彩] makes this film attractive. While just one may seem feigned, many together make it real; the bizarre details in this film keep everyone firmly in their seats.[54]

Zhang reconciles his "red" use of the crowd with domestic profitability and his international acclaim through the very figure of the crowd, manifesting it onscreen through powerful motifs of earthy ritual and historical spectacle, as well as in the cinematic attraction of the offscreen audience. Prioritizing entertainment and box-office appeal over ideological didacticism (or art-house-style deconstruction of such ideology) allows Zhang's film, much like the Opening Ceremony more than two decades later, to operate as mass media in the dual sense: as a product both for and of the masses (plate 28).

In the end, Zhang's use of the spectacular image and his construction of a visual dynamic between the onscreen crowd and its audience is primarily not about ideological propagation but the mobilization of the visual medium of crowds to address collectivity. The way in which Zhang uses the crowd image to galvanize his work speaks to the ongoing appropriation of the revolutionary visual grammar of crowds in contemporary China. In Zhang's case, these human wave tactics become, perhaps ironically, a vehicle for audience expansion, a kind of currency that at once highlights the visual spectacularity of the crowd image and effectively renders its immediacy and revolutionary potential through absence. Borrowing the Maoist rhetoric of mass ritual and technological reproduction, Zhang's production of the visual spectacular at the Olympic Games in 2008 carries traces of the fascination with the crowd image from his early film career, and also reveals an understated relation to the revolutionary era.

Notes

1. In his 1896 treatise *La psychologie des foules,* Gustave Le Bon ominously predicted "the age we are about to enter will in truth be the ERA OF CROWDS." See Gustave Le Bon, *The Crowd: A Study of the Popular Mind* (New York: Macmillan, 1896), p. xv.

2. Haun Saussy, "Crowds, Number and Mass in China," in *Crowds,* ed. Jeffrey T. Schnapp and Matthew Tiews (Stanford, CA: Stanford University Press, 2006), p. 259.

3. Adam B. Seligman et al., *Ritual and Its Consequences: An Essay on the Limits of Sincerity* (New York: Oxford University Press, 2008), p. 20. Haiyan Lee deserves credit for first making the connection between *Ritual and Its Consequences* and the 2008 Olympic Games Opening Ceremony in a post for the China Beat blog "It's Right to Party, En Masse," since published in Kate Merkel-Hess, Kenneth Pomeranz, and Jeffrey N. Wasserstrom, eds., *China in 2008: A Year of Great Significance* (New York: Rowman & Littlefield, 2009), pp. 173–77.

4. The authors of *Ritual and Its Consequences* also note how the effectiveness of ritual "in part arises from the sense that one never creates a full unity, but one can, through ritual, develop more productive ways of connecting with other people and with the larger world." Seligman et al., *Ritual and Its Consequences,* p. 42.

5. Zhang's father was labeled "historically anti-revolutionary" for his service in the Nationalist Army prior to 1949. See Paul Clark, *Reinventing China: A Generation*

and Its Films (Hong Kong: Chinese University Press, 2005), pp. 15–16, and Ni Zhen, *Memoirs from the Beijing Film Academy: The Genesis of China's Fifth Generation*, trans. Chris Berry (Durham, NC: Duke University Press, 2002), pp. 44–50. The rhetorical query, "Who are our enemies? Who are our friends?" from the 1926 essay, "Analysis of the Classes in Chinese Society" ("Zhongguo shehui ge jieji de fenxi" 中国社会各阶级的分析) opens the collection of Mao's selected works. See Mao Zedong, *Mao Zedong xuanji* 毛泽东选集 (Selected works of Mao Zedong) (Beijing: Renmin chubanshe, 1961), p. 3.

6. See, e.g., Donald S. Sutton, "Ritual, History, and the Films of Zhang Yimou," *East-West Film Journal* 8, no. 2 (July 1994): 31–46.

7. Walter Benjamin, "The Work of Art in the Age of Mechanical Reproduction," in *Illuminations: Essays and Reflections*, trans. Harry Zohn (New York: Schocken Books, 1969), p. 251.

8. Rey Chow, *Primitive Passions: Visuality, Sexuality, Ethnography, and Contemporary Chinese Cinema* (New York: Columbia University Press, 1995), p. 33.

9. Geremie R. Barmé, "China's Flat Earth: History and 8 August 2008," *China Quarterly* 197 (March 2009): 64. Barmé's detailed analysis is an invaluable resource for understanding the Opening Ceremony in its cultural, political, and historical contexts.

10. The first act was titled "Brilliant Civilization" ("Canlan wenming" 灿烂文明), and the second was called "Glorious Age" ("Huihuang shidai" 辉煌时代). See Barmé, "China's Flat Earth," pp. 69–70.

11. *New York Times* columnist David Brooks, for example, perpetuated the hackneyed trope of a menacing "oriental horde," an artifact of the fears of a "Yellow Peril" from the turn of the twentieth century, in drawing a trembling distinction between "individualist" Western societies and "collectivist" Asians in his editorial a few days later, concluding forebodingly, in reference to Hu Jintao's signature propaganda campaign for a "harmonious society" (*hexie shehui* 和谐社会), that "the ideal of a harmonious collective may turn out to be as attractive as the ideal of the American Dream." Brooks's column, thoroughly excoriated online by commentators less ignorant of China's political and cultural history, betrays the deep and ongoing anxiety on the part of the mainstream American media toward images of Chinese crowds. See David Brooks, "Harmony and the Dream," *New York Times*, August 11, 2008, at http://www.nytimes.com/2008/08/12/opinion/12brooks.html (accessed July 3, 2014). For a roundup of reactions to Brooks's column from such frequent China commentators as James Fallows at the *Atlantic Monthly* and John Pomfret of *Newsweek*, see Elliott Ng, "The Online Evisceration of David Brooks," *CNReviews*, August 18, 2008, at http://cnreviews.com/china_cultural_differences/david-brooks-china_20080818.html (accessed July 3, 2014).

12. Anthony Lane, "The Only Games in Town: Week One at the Olympics," *New Yorker*, August 25, 2008, at http://www.newyorker.com/reporting/2008/08/25/080825fa_fact_lane (accessed July 3, 2014).

13. Comments quoted in a *China Times* (*Zhongguo shibao* 中国时报) article (no longer available online). English translation posted by Roland Soong in his blog,

EastSouthWestNorth; see Roland Soong, "Chinese Internet Reacts to Olympics Opening Ceremony," *EastSouthWestNorth*, August 8, 2008, at http://zonaeuropa.com/20080808_1.htm (accessed July 3, 2014).

14. Edward C. O'Dowd's examination of the paradox of the PLA's use of *renhai zhanshu*, or the human wave tactic, as it was deployed in the Sino-Vietnam War of 1979 is relevant here, especially his discussion of the importance of the soldiers' political devotion when using such a technique. See Edward C. O'Dowd, *Chinese Military Strategy in the Third Indochina War: The Last Maoist War* (New York: Routledge, 2007), pp. 143–55.

15. Zhang Ying 张英 and Xia Chen 夏辰, "Zhang Yimou jiemi kaimushi" 张艺谋解密开幕式 (Zhang Yimou reveals the secrets of the Opening Ceremony), *Nanfang zhoumo* 南方周末 (Southern weekly), August 14, 2008, p. A3.

16. Zhang's choice of words reflects long-standing aims in his film work as well. Although the exact terms differ, his 1983 "Cinematographers' Statement on the Film *The One and the Eight*" (cowritten with Xiao Feng) discusses how the aesthetic design of the film was intended to produce a "beauty of strength" (*li zhi mei* 力之美) through the contrast of colors, light, and so on. See Zhang Yimou and Xiao Feng, "Yingpian *Yige he bage* sheying chanshu" 影片《一个和八个》摄影阐述 (Cinematographers' statement on the film *The One and the Eight*), in *Lun Zhang Yimou* 论张艺谋 (On Zhang Yimou) (Beijing: Zhongguo dianying chubanshe, 1994), pp. 92–99.

17. Dai Jinhua, "Invisible Writing: The Politics of Mass Culture in the 1990s," trans. Jingyuan Zhang, in *Cinema and Desire: Feminist Marxism and Cultural Politics in the Work of Dai Jinhua*, ed. Jing Wang and Tani E. Barlow (New York: Verso, 2002), p. 215; Chinese terms cited are from the original published text, Dai Jinhua, *Yinxing shuxie: 90 niandai Zhongguo wenhua yanjiu* 隐形书写: 90年代中国文化研究 (Invisible writing: Research in Chinese cultural studies in the 1990s) (Nanjing: Jiangsu renmin chubanshe, 1999), p. 261.

18. Dai, "Invisible Writing," p. 217 (p. 263 in the Chinese version).

19. Maurice Meisner, *Marxism, Maoism, and Utopianism: Eight Essays* (Madison: University of Wisconsin Press, 1982), p. 214. The authors of *Ritual and Its Consequences* make a similar point, writing, "The subjunctive world created by ritual is always doomed ultimately to fail—the ordered world of flawless repetition can never fully replace the broken world of experience. . . . Ritual should be seen as operating in . . . 'the register of the tragic.'" Seligman et al., *Ritual and Its Consequences*, p. 30.

20. North Korea's Grand Mass Gymnastics and Artistic Performance Arirang Festival, held annually from August until October in Pyongyang, celebrates the birthday of Democratic People's Republic of Korea founder Kim Il-sung. The 2007 Arirang was recognized by Guinness World Records as the "Largest Gymnastics Display," with more than 100,000 performers.

21. Zhang and Xia, "Zhang Yimou jiemi kaimushi," p. A6.

22. From an interview with journalist Anna Louise Strong on January 17, 1964. See Tracy B. Strong and Helene Keyssar, "Anna Louise Strong: Three Interviews with Chairman Mao Zedong," *China Quarterly* 103 (September 1985): 502. The first part of this quote is also used as the epigraph to Meisner, *Marxism, Maoism, and Utopianism*.

23. Ban Wang, *The Sublime Figure of History: Aesthetics and Politics in Twentieth-Century China* (Stanford, CA: Stanford University Press, 1997), p. 198.

24. Arjun Appadurai, *Fear of Small Numbers: An Essay on the Geography of Anger* (Durham, NC: Duke University Press, 2006), pp. 59–60.

25. Mao Zedong, *Quotations from Chairman Mao Tse-tung* (Beijing: Foreign Languages Press, 1966), p. 36; Chinese term cited from *Mao zhuxi yulu* 毛主席语录 (Quotations from Chairman Mao) (Beijing: Zhongguo renmin jiefangjun zongzhengzhibu, 1966), p. 33. This idea is also discussed in Maurice Meisner, *Mao Zedong: A Political and Intellectual Portrait* (Malden, MA: Polity Press, 2007), pp. 148–49.

26. Jacques Derrida, *Of Grammatology*, trans. Gayatri Chakravorty Spivak (Baltimore: Johns Hopkins University Press, 1997), pp. 144–45.

27. Geremie Barmé identifies two such allusions to Mao, one of which is the similarity of the impressionistic landscape painting to one of the canonical paintings of the Maoist era, *How Splendid the Rivers and Mountains* (*Jiangshan ruci jiao* 江山如此多娇), based on one of Mao's poems, "Snow" (*Xue* 雪). See Barmé, "China's Flat Earth," pp. 74–76. Painters Fu Baoshi 傅抱石 and Guan Shanyue 关山月 were commissioned to paint the enormous work as part of the 1958 campaign that saw the development of Tiananmen Square, including the Great Hall of the People, where the work hangs. Landscape painters were a frequent target of criticism during the Maoist era, and they justified their work by claiming a correspondence between the vast landscape and the sublime idea of the masses. Mao's wife, Jiang Qing 江青, expressed disapproval of *How Splendid the Rivers and Mountains* because it contained no evidence of human activity. See Ellen Johnston Laing, *The Winking Owl: Art in the People's Republic of China* (Berkeley: University of California Press, 1988), p. 77.

28. Siegfried Kracauer's 1927 essay "The Mass Ornament" shows the intense visual association between modern industrial production techniques and the patterns and repeatability of the crowd image. See Siegfried Kracauer, "The Mass Ornament," in *The Mass Ornament: Weimar Essays*, trans. and ed. Thomas Y. Levin (Cambridge, MA: Harvard University Press, 1995), pp. 75–86.

29. For an examination of Soviet, Eastern European, and North Korean rhetoric of technology, see Paul R. Josephson, *Would Trotsky Wear a Bluetooth? Technological Utopianism under Socialism, 1917–1989* (Baltimore: Johns Hopkins University Press, 2010).

30. Chow, *Primitive Passions*, p. 34.

31. Zhang's fascination with Qin Shihuang is not limited to *Hero*. Zhang's collaboration with the composer Tan Dun 谭盾 (who wrote the score for *Hero*), the opera *The First Emperor*, premiered in New York in late 2006. Like the Opening Ceremony that Zhang would direct less than two years later, the opera's production was praised for its spectacular set design (including a near-constant chorus of hundreds), costuming, and choreography. For a critical reading of Zhang's multiple depictions of Qin Shihuang's quest for immortality from a different perspective, see Carlos Rojas, *The Great Wall: A Cultural History* (Cambridge. MA: Harvard University Press, 2010), pp. 60–66.

32. In Mao's 1958 "Speech at the Second Plenum of the Eighth Central Committee," he used the First Emperor as a positive example of "emphasizing the present while slighting the past" (*houjin bogu* 厚今薄古). After being reminded by Vice Chairman Lin Biao of the emperor's infamous crimes of "burning books and burying Confucians alive" (*fenshu kengru* 焚书坑儒), Mao queried, "What did he amount to? He only buried alive 460 scholars, while we buried 46,000. In our suppression of the counter-revolutionaries, did we not kill some counter-revolutionary intellectuals?" Quoted in Li Yu-ning, ed., *The First Emperor of China* (White Plains, NY: International Arts and Sciences Press, 1975), pp. xlix–l. Mao performs exactly the same arithmetical flourish with the integer "0"; see Appadurai, *Fear of Small Numbers*, pp. 59–60.

33. For a detailed account of the reinterpretation of Qin Shihuang during the "Criticize Lin, Criticize Confucius" campaign (*pi Lin pi Kong yundong* 批林批孔运动), see Wang Gungwu, "'Burning Books and Burying Scholars': Some Recent Interpretations Concerning Ch'in Shih-huang," *Papers on Far Eastern History* 9 (March 1974): 137–86.

34. Shih Lun, "On the 'Black-Headed People,'" in Li Yu-ning, ed., *The First Emperor*, pp. 250–51. According to the *Shiji* 史记, Qin Shihuang's decree was handed down in the twenty-sixth year of his reign (221 BCE). See Sima Qian, *Records of the Grand Historian: Qin Dynasty*, trans. Burton Watson (Hong Kong: Renditions; New York: Columbia University Press, 1993), p. 44.

35. One of the key promotional points for the film was the extravagant reality of these war crowds. In television spots and interviews before the film's 2006 release, Zhang and others repeatedly divulged the fact that more than 20,000 extras were used in the climactic battle scenes. As in the Opening Ceremony, these crowds were assembled in cooperation with the PLA. See Yu Deshu 喻得术, "Dianying dachangmian qianjunwanma 'shang bu qi'" 电影大场面千军万马'伤不起' ('Invincible' crowds in huge film scenes), *Fazhi wanbao* 法制晚报 (Legal evening news), November 18, 2011, at http://www.fawan.com/Article/yl/jd/2011/11/18/124530136862.html (accessed July 3, 2014).

36. Sek Kei, "'Mancheng jindai huangjinjia' guguai" 《满城尽带黄金甲》古怪 (The bizarre *Curse of the Golden Flower*), *Mingbao* 明报 (Ming Pao), December 27, 2006, at http://ol.mingpao.com/cfm/star5.cfm?File=20061227/saa02/mee1.txt (accessed July 3, 2014).

37. Director Zhang Junzhao stated in a 1984 interview that the main thrust of the film is "to grasp the strength of those in war—the strength of Communists, the strength of the masses across all social strata. It is precisely these disparate, isolated elements of power that the CCP brought together in strength that thus enabled it to triumph over Japanese imperialism and set the nation on a course of continuous development." See the interview with Zhang Junzhao in Luo Xueying 罗雪莹, *Huiwang chunzhen niandai: Zhongguo zhuming dianying daoyan fangtanlu* 回望纯真年代: 中国著名电影导演访谈录 (Looking back on a sincere age: Interviews with famous Chinese film directors) (Beijing: Xueyuan chubanshe, 2008), pp. 120–21.

38. George S. Semsel, "Interviews: Chen Kaige and Zhang Yimou, Fifth Generation Director and Cinematographer," in *Chinese Film: The State of Art in the People's*

Republic, ed. George S. Semsel (New York: Praeger, 1987), pp. 139–40. Chen also characterizes the drum dance scene as an expression of the peasants' "consciousness of power in taking control over their own destiny." See *Huashuo Huang tudi* 话说《黄土地》 (Telling the story of *Yellow Earth*) (Beijing: Zhongguo dianying chubanshe, 1986), p. 278. Zhang echoes this sentiment and notes how, in order to prevent the camera movements from becoming too disorienting and "subjective," he included a panning shot of the bystanders watching the spectacle, hands tucked into their sleeves: "If they could take control over their own destiny, they could erupt with a strength that could move mountains and fill the sea." Ibid., p. 287. Ni Zhen credits Zhang with the idea for the drum dance scene in *Yellow Earth*; see Ni, *Memoirs from the Beijing Film Academy*, pp. 180–81.

39. Clark, *Reinventing China*, p. 79. For a list of changes made to the film, see Luo Xueying, *Huiwang chunzhen niandai*, pp. 134–37.

40. Zhang and Xiao, "Yingpian *Yige he bage* sheying chanshu," p. 92.

41. Ni, *Memoirs from the Beijing Film Academy*, pp. 166–67.

42. "Unpresentable" is Ma Ning's term to describe these characters. See Ma Ning, "Notes on the New Filmmakers," in *Chinese Film: The State of the Art in the People's Republic*, ed. George S. Semsel (New York: Praeger, 1987), pp. 73–77.

43. Dai Jinhua, "Severed Bridge: The Art of the Sons' Generation," trans. Lisa Rofel and Hu Ying, in *Cinema and Desire: Feminist Marxism and Cultural Politics in the Work of Dai Jinhua*, ed. Jing Wang and Tani E. Barlow (New York: Verso, 2002), p. 36.

44. Ma Ning notes that the out-of-focus figures form the shape of a tripod, which he reads as *ren* 人, or "person." Though I appreciate how this visualization dovetails with his humanist interpretation of the film, the three-legged nature of a tripod implies much more heavily, I think, the character *zhong* 众, or "crowd." See Ma Ning, "Notes on the New Filmmakers," p. 77.

45. Eugene Wang, "Film and Contemporary Chinese Art: Mediums and Remediation," in Carlos Rojas and Eileen Chow, eds., *The Oxford Handbook of Chinese Cinemas* (Oxford: Oxford University Press, 2013), p. 576.

46. Yingjin Zhang, *Screening China: Critical Interventions, Cinematic Reconfigurations, and the Transnational Imaginary in Contemporary Chinese Cinema* (Ann Arbor: Center for Chinese Studies, University of Michigan, 2002), p. 173.

47. Friedrich Engels, quoted in Wu Hung, *Remaking Beijing: Tiananmen Square and the Creation of a Political Space* (Chicago: University of Chicago Press, 2005), p. 8.

48. Haiyan Lee, "The Charisma of Power and the Military Sublime in Tiananmen Square," *Journal of Asian Studies* 70 (May 2011): 411.

49. Ibid., p. 419.

50. Ibid. Lee also notes the shift since the brutal 1989 crackdown on student protestors that substituted the display of military hardware for the Maoist notion of a "people's war."

51. Dai, "Severed Bridge," p. 34.

52. See, e.g., Ying Zhu, *Chinese Cinema during the Era of Reform: The Ingenuity of the System* (Westport, CT: Praeger, 2003), pp. 111–23; and Yingjin Zhang, *Chinese National Cinema* (New York: Routledge, 2004), pp. 238–40.

53. For more on the debates over the entertainment film in the second half of the 1980s and early 1990s, see "The Entertainment Film," in *Film in Contemporary China: Critical Debates, 1979–1989*, ed. George S. Semsel, Chen Xihe, and Xia Hong (Westport, CT: Praeger, 1993), pp. 83–139; and the essay by director Wu Yigong, "We Must Become Artists Who Deeply Love the People," in *Perspectives on Chinese Cinema*, trans. and ed. Chris Berry (London: British Film Institute, 1991), pp. 133–40.

54. Zhang Yimou, "*Hong gaoliang*: daoyan chanshu" 《红高粱》导演阐述 (Director's statement on *Red Sorghum*), in Luo Xueying, *Hong gaoliang: Zhang Yimou xiezhen* 《红高粱》张艺谋写真 (*Red Sorghum*: Portrait of Zhang Yimou) (Beijing: Zhongguo dianying chubanshe, 1988), p. 72.

TEN

TIME OUT OF JOINT

Commemoration and Commodification of Socialism in Yan Lianke's *Lenin's Kisses*

Carlos Rojas

The time is out of joint: Oh cursed spite,
That ever I was born to set it right.
—William Shakespeare, *Hamlet*

In Alejandro Brugués's 2011 film *Juan of the Dead* (*Juan de los Muertos*), contemporary Havana suddenly finds itself confronted with a plague of flesh-eating zombies. As terror strikes the city, a band of intrepid locals led by the eponymous protagonist (played by Alexis Días de Villegas) decides to capitalize on the crisis by hiring themselves out as zombie exterminators, with the deliciously macabre slogan, "Juan of the dead, we kill your loved ones. How may I serve you?" (Juan de los muertos, matamos a sus seres queridos. ¿En qué puedo servirle?).

Marketed as Cuba's first zombie movie, this $3 million Spanish-Cuban coproduction was the most expensive privately financed movie in Cuba's history, and was also the first independent Cuban film to receive official state approval. Released in Cuba in December 2011, just eight months after an increasingly decrepit Fidel Castro officially stepped down as head of the Cuban Communist Party and four months after it had been announced that the government would, for the first time, legalize the purchase and sale of private real estate, the film may be seen as a product of—as well as a commentary on—Cuba's apparent impending transition from communism to capitalism. Just as Brugués's title plays on George Romero's classic zombie flick, *Dawn of the Dead* (1978) (in which zombies famously symbolize both a consumerist impulse as well as the structural contradictions within capitalism itself), the arrival in Cuba of this cinematic riff on Romero's iconic film may be seen as a symptom of the ineluctable entry of global capitalism into what had been an isolated Communist bulwark.

The zombies in *Juan of the Dead* are overdetermined, contradictory figures. On one hand, their maimed and wounded bodies mirror the dilapidated urban landscape of contemporary Havana, in a precarious state of disrepair after half a century of Communist rule. On the other hand, the invading zombies symbolize the inexorable force of global capitalism that is currently transforming the entire nation. Not only do these Cuban zombies mirror the consumer-driven undead figures in Romero's earlier film, Brugués adds another twist wherein his zombies are also linked to American imperialism. Soon after locals start reporting sightings of the zombies, for instance, Cuba's government-controlled television news service broadcasts a denial that there exist any zombies at all, insisting instead that the cadaverous figures are actually dissidents hired by the United States in an attempt to destabilize the Castro regime. The zombies, in other words, are imagined in the film as a symbolic manifestation of both a Communist legacy and the capitalist forces against which communism is theoretically opposed, while simultaneously articulating an ironic critique of U.S. attempts to foment dissent within Cuba as well as of Cuba's paranoia about U.S. intervention.

Some of the contradictory implications of the film's zombies are concisely captured in a sequence in which Juan and his companions are detained by a heavily armed Cuban soldier, who forces them to strip naked and then proceeds to handcuff them together and load them onto a military convoy truck. The soldier explains that the military is in the process of rounding up all the survivors of the epidemic, in order to arm them and have them fight the undead invaders. Shortly after he finishes his explanation, however, one of the other prisoners in the truck starts to display zombie-like symptoms and begins attacking everyone around him. Bedlam ensues, and when the proverbial smoke clears, Juan and the other prisoners have managed to escape from the truck, though Juan remains handcuffed to another member of his original group—an effeminate Asian-looking young man who goes by the name China. The next morning, it is revealed that China was inadvertently injured in the previous night's melee, leaving him infected with the zombie virus. When he, too, begins displaying zombie-like symptoms, Juan—to whom China remains shackled at the wrist—finds it necessary to sacrifice his half-human/half-zombie companion in order to save himself from a similar fate.

While the pairing of the Cuban Juan and the Asian-looking China in this sequence may be viewed as an allegorical commentary on the relationship between two of the world's last surviving Communist regimes (Cuba looking askance as post-Maoist China is transformed by a frenzy of capitalist excitement), perhaps more significant for our purposes here is the earlier intermixing, on the military convoy truck, of abject and undead bodies. Stripped naked and chained together like animals, the prisoners in this scene are reduced to a state of extreme degradation, and virtually the only thing they manage to retain is the very quality that distinguishes them from the zombies they are fleeing—life itself. In this way, the Cuban state transforms Juan and his companions into radically desocialized beings, precisely in order to defend itself from the destabilizing threat of an invasion of the living dead.

The detainees in this scene may be seen as examples of what the Italian political philosopher Giorgio Agamben calls *homo sacer*, or "bare life." Taking inspiration from a provision in ancient Roman law that stipulates that a citizen may be punitively removed from the social order, thereby rendering him or her a sacrificial figure on which the law's putative legitimacy is itself theoretically grounded, Agamben describes this figure of the *homo sacer* as "human life [that is] included in the juridical order solely in the form of its exclusion (that is, of its capacity to be killed)."[1] He argues that these subaltern figures mark the ideological limits of the polis, while at the same time symbolizing the pragmatic ground on which political regimes establish their authority. Working along similar lines, South African political philosopher Achille Mbembe extends Michel Foucault's argument that modern biopolitical governance is predicated on the institutional regularization of life, and instead emphasizes the importance of the state's "power and capacity to determine who will live and who will *die*."[2] In the resulting necropolitical system, Mbembe argues, it is from this power to apportion death and reduce individuals to the status of bare life that the modern state derives its power and political sovereignty. In Brugués's film, therefore, the Cuban military's act of stripping the protagonists down to their bare humanity directly mirrors the way in which it seeks to use the threat of what are literally living corpses to ground its authority.

Although neither Agamben nor Mbembe specifically applies the concept of bare life or necropolitics to China, their analyses have useful implications for our understanding of the political dynamics of modern China. Just as the Maoist era was characterized by a systematic process of political scapegoating to buttress the state's authority, the post-Mao era has witnessed a wide-scale process of sociopolitical disenfranchisement in the name of economic development. In particular, even as Beijing has encouraged rapid growth over the past three and a half decades, it has nevertheless done relatively little to loosen the residency permit (*hukou* 户口) system that makes it difficult for Chinese citizens to officially relocate to a different area of the country. As a result of the precipitous increase in the wealth gap between China's urban and rural areas, combined with the explosive growth in the cities' need for cheap labor, a vast "floating population" of more than a hundred million rural-to-urban migrants has congregated in and around the nation's urban centers. Even as these migrants are recognized as one of the key elements of the nation's continued growth, they nevertheless find themselves stripped of many of the basic social benefits that the state offers its citizens. The state's efforts to promote growth and stability, in other words, are predicated on its partially disenfranchising nearly 10 percent of its own population.

Taking my lead from *Juan of the Dead*'s depiction of the fictional character China's abrupt transformation from a state of *homo sacer* to nascent zombie, in this chapter I examine a similar pairing of disabled bodies and a figuratively reanimated corpse in the 2004 novel *Lenin's Kisses* (*Shouhuo* 受活) by Yan Lianke 阎连科. The novel explores a set of structural tensions inherent in contemporary China's transition from communism to capitalism by deploying a dialectic of bare life and living death, focusing in particular on the way in which the two intersect around the figure of the commodity.

The Livening of Lenin

Lenin's Kisses opens with a description of time out of joint—a freak midsummer blizzard that befalls a rural, mountainous region in central China:

> Look, in the middle of a sweltering summer, when people couldn't liven, it suddenly started snowing. This was hot snow.
>
> Winter returned overnight. Or, perhaps it was more that summer disappeared in the blink of an eye—and since autumn had not yet arrived, winter instead came hurrying back. During that year's sweltering summer, time fell out of joint. It became insane, even downright mad. Overnight, everything degenerated into disorder and lawlessness. And then it began to snow.
>
> Indeed, time itself fell ill. It went mad.[3]

The blizzard lasts for seven days, blanketing the region's wheat crop and raising fears of the possibility of a famine the following winter. The crisis prompts the local county chief to visit the village and proffer assistance, which in turn sets in motion a series of events with consequences that extend far beyond the village itself.

Broadly speaking, the untimely blizzard that afflicts this remote region may be seen as a symptom of the temporal disjunction in which contemporary China currently finds itself. The novel opens in the summer of 1998, precisely two decades after Deng Xiaoping's 1978 "Reform and Opening-Up" (*gaige kaifang* 改革开放) campaign, which helped catalyze China's strategic shift from high communism to hypercapitalism.[4] Thanks in part to Deng's initiatives, China's gross domestic product has increased more than a hundredfold over the past three and a half decades, though most of this growth has been concentrated in the country's urban regions, with its largely rural interior lagging behind. For instance, central China's landlocked Henan Province, in which Yan Lianke's novel is set, is one of the nation's poorest and most populous regions, and the story suggests that the 110,000 residents of the province's fictional Shuanghuai 双槐 County have similarly derived little benefit from the nation's overall economic growth. The main plot of *Lenin's Kisses* is set against the backdrop of this concern that Shuanghuai may be left behind in the nation's rapid development—and the novel's opening blizzard sets in motion a series of initiatives designed both to help the fictional county capitalize more effectively on the nation's growing wealth and, at the same time, to permit a remote village at the county's outer margins to sever its ties with the state and reassert its former independence.

In particular, it turns out that when the Shuanghuai County chief—

a local bureaucrat by the name of Liu Yingque 柳鹰雀—visits the blizzard-stricken village of Liven at the beginning of the novel, he is already pursuing an ambitious plan to jumpstart his county's economy. After hearing that Russia, in dire economic straits since the collapse of the Soviet Union in the early 1990s, might not be able to afford to continue maintaining Lenin's preserved corpse, kept on display in Moscow's Red Square, and was considering cremating it, Liu Yingque resolves to purchase the corpse and bring it back to China. Inspired by the popularity of Chairman Mao's embalmed corpse, on view in Beijing's Tiananmen Square, together with contemporary China's more general interest in red tourism (visiting sites with historical significance for Chinese communism), Liu has come up with a plan to install Lenin's corpse in a special Lenin Memorial Hall that he is building in Shuanghuai County. He is confident that the new mausoleum will draw so much tourist revenue that he will then be able to provide the residents of his county with everything they might desire. First, however, he must figure out a way to raise the vast sum of money he will need to purchase the corpse, and it is during his visit to Liven that he finally devises a solution.

Liu Yingque's fund-raising scheme is rooted in the unique nature of the village itself. Owing to a peculiar set of historical circumstances, the vast majority of the residents of Liven have a physical disability: they might be blind, deaf, or mute; lack an arm or a leg; or suffer from paralysis or stunted growth. As a result of their disabilities, many of the villagers have acquired "special skills"—an unusually acute sense of hearing, for example, to compensate for being blind, or an extremely strong left leg to compensate for having merely a stump for a right leg. While the villagers normally use these special skills only to help them carry out their day-to-day responsibilities, they have a tradition of demonstrating their skills for one another's entertainment during the village's annual festival. During his postblizzard visit, Chief Liu comes up with the idea of organizing the villagers into performance troupes that would tour the region—with some of the ticket revenue being returned to the villagers themselves but the majority being earmarked for the county's Lenin Fund.

Lenin's Kisses revolves around a twin focus on Lenin's embalmed corpse and the villagers' disabled bodies, each of which carries a set of contradictory associations. While in theory Liu is interested in Lenin's corpse because it symbolizes the political and philosophical ground on which China's Communist regime is based, in reality his interest in the corpse is primarily driven not by a theoretical or ideological commitment to Lenin's work, but by his conviction that he will be able to use the corpse to develop an immensely profitable regional tourist industry. Added to the irony that a quintessential socialist relic is desired for its ability to generate a vast profit is the suggestion that Chief Liu desires the tourism revenue not for its own sake, but so that he may provide more effectively for the needs and desires of his county's residents. He wants the corpse, in other words, because it will allow him to provide his county with a degree of social support that would exceed even that which they received under communism. As a commoditized icon of China's Communist heritage, therefore, the corpse is positioned at the hinge between communism and capitalism, underscoring the dialectical tensions implicit in each.

Liven's disabled villagers, meanwhile, may be regarded as paradigmatically subaltern figures whose debased position is strategically inverted once they begin performing for a wider public to help raise money for the county's Lenin Fund. This transformation of the villagers' disabled bodies into cultural commodities speaks to the pervasive spread of a capitalist logic into even the most remote regions of rural China, and in this respect the condition of the villagers symbolizes the socioeconomic contradictions that characterize contemporary China at this moment of transition from socialism to capitalism. Like contemporary China's vast floating population of internal migrants, Liven's disabled villagers constitute a key element in plans for economic growth, even as their own (economic) value is directly tied up with their marginal, subaltern status.

Driving the parallel between the figure of the corpse and that of the disabled villagers, meanwhile, is the specific history of Liven itself. It turns out that the reason why the village matriarch, Grandma Mao Zhi 茅枝婆, agrees to allow the villagers to go on tour in the first place is so that the village might then be able to return to the idyllic state it had enjoyed *before* becoming integrated into China's socialist regime. Just as the utopian community in the famous fifth-century CE fable "Peach Blossom Spring" (*Taohua yuan ji* 桃花源记) by Tao Yuanming 陶渊明 is so isolated that its residents do not even know which dynasty is in power, Liven is presented as having long been so removed from the surrounding region that the village remained blithely unaware of the historical developments transforming the rest of the country.[5] When Grandma Mao Zhi belatedly realized that the rest of the nation had already been divided into communes and cooperative societies, she became determined to have Liven do the same—resulting in a process that came to be known as "entering society" (*rushe* 入社). After discovering that none of the three nearest counties even recognized the village's existence, Grandma Mao Zhi proceeded to visit each of the three county seats, demanding that one of them acknowledge Liven as falling under its jurisdiction. She eventually found a county chief who was willing to do so, but when the village was then victimized during the ensuing famines and political persecutions associated with the Great Leap Forward and the Cultural Revolution, Grandma Mao Zhi came to regret her actions and vowed to do everything in her power to help the village regain its former autonomy. When Liu Yingque visits Liven immediately following the summer blizzard of 1998, Grandma Mao Zhi quickly seizes the opportunity to try to make good on her promise. She agrees to permit Liu Yingque to use the villagers to raise money for his Lenin Fund in order that the village might then be allowed to withdraw from the county altogether and regain its former independence.

Even as Liu Yingque's attempts to purchase Lenin's corpse gesture back to the philosophical and historical origins of Chinese communism while simultaneously looking forward to the capitalist wealth that the nation is striving to attain, for Liven itself, the purchase of the corpse is tightly bound up with an attempt to capitalize on the nation's economic growth in order to regain the idyllic, autonomous state that the village had previously enjoyed. As the agreed-upon date for the troupes' disbandment and the village's "withdrawal from society" approaches, however, many of the villagers become so seduced by the amount of money they find they are able to earn in the performance troupes that they begin to have second thoughts about the prospect of severing Liven's ties with the county, and by implication disbanding the troupes. Both the purchase of the corpse and the establishment of the performance troupes pivot on a fantasy of plentitude that had originally been the promise of Communist theory, but that in practice is presented as an alternative to the disasters suffered under China's actually existing Communist state.

Sandwiched between Liven's memory of a prerevolutionary era in which the villagers always had more than enough to meet their needs and Liu Yingque's plan to use Lenin's corpse to bring in enough tourism revenue to allow him to satisfy the county residents' every desire, there were more than three decades of Maoist rule, during which Liven suffered a devastating series of famines and political persecutions. One sequence in the novel, for instance, relates how, at the beginning of the Cultural Revolution, the local commune demanded that Liven divide its residents based on their sociopolitical status and periodically send a landlord or rich peasant to the commune to be publicly humiliated and beaten—or "struggled against," to use the political lingo of the time. The villagers initially resisted this demand, claiming that, historically, everyone in the village had been equal and that consequently the distinctions between rich and poor peasants simply did not apply to them. The commune responded by issuing *every* household in the village a black booklet with the household's name on the cover and a Mao quote and the phrase "Serve the People" printed inside, and demanded that every two weeks one household would assign someone to take its booklet and go to the commune and be struggled against. Unable to divide the village along economic and ideological lines, the commune thus adopted a solution wherein every household—and, indeed, every villager—embodied these same tensions. The irony, however, is that the Cultural Revolution struggle sessions that were being carried out in the name of promoting social equality were themselves being played out against the backdrop of a village in which class distinctions allegedly did not exist in the first place.

For the residents of Liven, therefore, the act of "serving the people" involved submitting to a ritual of public humiliation and corporeal desecration. One villager, for instance, was viciously beaten at one of these struggle sessions, and when his tormentors demanded that he hand over his family's grain, he replied that it had already been confiscated. The people from the commune then proceeded to "beat him even more severely than before, their fists raining down on his nose, mouth, and eyes, and their clubs striking his head and legs. When they punched his nose, it started bleeding, and when they hit his mouth, his teeth were knocked loose. They hit his face so hard that they left him with a huge black eye, and struck his legs so violently that he would have been left a cripple if he hadn't already been one."[6] Ironically, this beating figuratively recapitulates the conditions of the villager's original disability when the people from the commune strike his legs "so violently that he would have been left a cripple if he hadn't already been one." In the context of the overall novel, this scene serves as an important reminder of how the villagers' physical disabilities structurally mirror the abject status to which they are relegated after "entering society."

In particular, this Cultural Revolution scene rehearses a logic of corporeal desecration that lies at the heart of the collective identity of Liven itself. Legend has it that the village dates back to the Ming dynasty, when three disabled peasants were permitted to drop out of a mass relocation procession and establish a remote community deep in the mountains. This community ended up attracting disabled villagers from throughout the region, and even as the village became defined by its residents' disabilities, the collaborative arrangements that the villagers adopted to compensate for their respective physical limitations helped make possible an idyllic existence in which all of their basic needs were easily satisfied. The villagers' disabilities, therefore, contributed not only to their community's self-imposed isolation but also to the idyllic existence that they were subsequently able to enjoy.

Liven's position at the margins of the Chinese body politic is underscored by the relationship between the villagers' disabled bodies and those of their able-bodied neighbors. While the novel refers to able-bodied subjects as "wholers" (*quanren* 全人), the disabled are referred to as *canren* 残人—which is presumably a shortened form of *canji ren* 残疾人 ("disabled person"), but which could be literally translated as a "fractured or remnant person." The villagers' incomplete bodies function as potent reminders of the ideological fissures that underlie the sociopolitical ground of the nation itself. The nation's ideological coherence, in other words, is structurally predicated on its strategic exclusion of marginal peoples and dissonant ideologies.

A comparable supplemental logic, meanwhile, applies to the novel's thematization of Lenin's preserved corpse. The narrative consistently refers to Lenin's corporeal remains as *yiti* 遗体—wherein the character *yi* literally means "remnant" or "vestige." For instance, people who maintained loyalty to a fallen dynasty after it had been superseded by a new one were traditionally called *yimin* 遗民—"loyalists," or literally "vestigial people." In *Lenin's Kisses*, the embalmed corpse functions as a symbol of a comparable kind of loyalism, wherein an iconic symbol of communism (Lenin's remains) is used to promote a paradigmatically capitalist enterprise (tourism), though this is done precisely to enable a subsequent critical intervention in the nation's capitalist logic of uneven development (as seen in Liu Yingque's plans to redistribute the projected profits from his Lenin mausoleum to all the residents of his county). As an *yiti*, therefore, Lenin's corpse functions as a locus of loyalty to the ideological origins of Chinese communism, and as a reminder of the structural tensions that haunt communism itself.

In psychoanalytic terms, the supplementary status of the villagers' disabled bodies and of Lenin's embalmed corpse may be viewed as examples both of what Julia Kristeva calls the abject and what Jacques Lacan calls a partial object. For Kristeva, abjection refers to the process by which the coherence of the Self is grounded on the violent ejection of extraneous corporeal elements such as blood, feces, and vomit, which are perceived as posing a threat to the Self/Other binary on which the symbolic order is predicated.[7] For Lacan, meanwhile, the partial object, or *objet petit a*, is conceived as an "object-cause of desire," or "something from which the subject, in order to constitute itself, has separated itself off as organ."[8] Both the Kristevan abject and the Lacanian *objet a*, therefore, are conceived as fundamentally separable elements of the Self, on which the Self relies for its own process of self-constitution. The difference, however, is that whereas the abject is viewed as an object of revulsion and disgust, the *objet a* is regarded as an object of desire. If we combine these two concepts, we have a model wherein the imaginary coherence of the Self is a product of a dialectical engagement with corporeal or ideological fragments that function simultaneously as objects of disgust and desire.

For Kristeva, a sense of abjection is most apparent in elements associated with death: "The corpse, seen without God and outside of science, is the utmost of abjection. It is death infecting life. Abject." It is appropriate, therefore, that one of the most iconic of the villagers' "special skills" routines is Grandma Mao Zhi's own performance as an extraordinarily elderly woman who claims that her unusual longevity is the result of her insistence on preemptively wearing her burial clothing, day in and day out. In other words, it is by embracing the possibility of death that Grandma Mao Zhi's stage persona is able to forestall her own actual death—and it is this same simultaneous embracing and rejection of death, in turn, that becomes the focal point of the audience's enthusiastic fascination with, and strategic marginalization of, the disabled performance troupe itself. A similarly paradoxical logic also applies to the figure of Lenin's corpse. The corpse is a paradigmatic symbol not only of death but also of the ability of history and memory to transcend individual mortality, and consequently Lenin's embalmed remains symbolize not only the socialist theoretician's own mortality but also the enduring legacy of his works and accomplishments. It is, moreover, precisely the specter of the corpse's potential demise (because Russia may no longer be able to afford to maintain it) that inspires Liu Yingque's plan to grant it a new life (by proposing to purchase the corpse and bring it back to China).

In both Lenin's corpse and Grandma Mao Zhi's elderly woman performance (and, by extension, Liven's "special skills" performances in general), what mediates between these inverse qualities of the abject and the partial object is a logic of commodity fetishism. Not only are Lenin's embalmed corpse and the villagers' disabled bodies viewed as potential sources of immense profit, they also both illustrate a process wherein a material commodity comes to assume a mystical character that occludes the human labor and social relations responsible for the commodity's actual production. Whereas Marxian theory seeks to reaffirm the corporeal labor and social relations underlying a commodity's production, in *Lenin's Kisses* this critique is effectively turned on its head through an emphasis on the commodity status of *the body itself*—with both Lenin's corpse and the villagers' disabled bodies being reimagined as objects of fetishistic investment in their own right. Just as Yan Lianke repeatedly thematizes in several of his other novels processes of corporeal self-commodification, in *Lenin's Kisses* what is being commoditized is quite literally the very fragmentedness and incompleteness of the villagers' bodies themselves.[9] The abject subaltern, in other words, is transformed, through a process of self-commodification, into an *objet a* of the contemporary capitalist economy.

While Kristeva and Lacan argue, in psychoanalytic terms, that the imaginary constitution of the Self is predicated on a simultaneous rejection of and desire for bodily elements that have become symbolically separated from the Self, *Lenin's Kisses* illustrates a comparable logic wherein the constitution of the Chinese *nation* is grounded on the simultaneous rejection of and desire for embodied figures positioned at the symbolic margins of the body politic. Both Lenin's corpse and Liven's disabled villagers are positioned in a paradigmatically peripheral position with respect to contemporary China's self-conception, though in both cases their perceived alterity is reinvented as an object of desire through a process of commodity fetishism. In other words, even as the corporeal materiality of Lenin's embalmed corpse and the villagers' disabled bodies function as a critical reminder of the Marxian validation of the value of labor and the importance of an equitable social distribution of wealth, the emphatically marginal status of both the corpse and the disabled villagers emblematizes the degree to which contemporary China's sociopolitical self-conception is predicated on a strategic elision of these very same Marxian principles.

"Serve the People!"

A similar set of concerns is developed Yan Lianke's first major work after *Lenin's Kisses*: his 2005 novella *Serve the People!* (*Wei renmin fuwu* 为人民服务). Set in 1967, at the height of the Cultural Revolution, *Serve the People* focuses on a low-ranking PLA soldier and his relationship with his division commander's attractive young wife. The soldier, Wu Dawang 吴大旺, is assigned to work in the compound where the commander's wife, Liu Lian 刘莲, lives, and she convinces him that the Maoist injunction "Serve the People" may be interpreted transitively—such that by "serving" Liu Lian, Wu Dawang would therefore also indirectly be serving "the people." It turns out, however, that the kind of "service" Liu Lian desires is specifically of a sexual nature, given that her husband, an older military commander, was apparently rendered impotent by a groin injury suffered in combat. Wu initially declines Liu's overtures, but when he realizes that his reluctance may affect his career, he eventually accedes to Liu's demands. Liu and Wu develop a code: whenever she moves a placard inscribed with the Maoist motto "Serve the People" away from its usual place in her dining room, Wu Dawang understands that this is her signal that he should come up to her bedroom and "service" her. The placard's being "out of place" thus symbolizes a more general displacement of the highly politicized rhetoric and ideology that dominated China during this period.

This perverse reinterpretation of one of Mao's best-known mottoes takes another twist when, during one sexual encounter, Wu Dawang accidentally knocks down and tramples on a framed sign bearing another Maoist slogan. Wu and Liu Lian's horror at this sacrilegious act is quickly sublimated into erotic desire, as they immediately proceed to enjoy unusually passionate intercourse. Shortly afterward, Wu and Liu abandon themselves to three days of nonstop sexual activity, and at one point during this sexual marathon, they begin scouring the house for more Maoist icons to deface and destroy. With each act of political desecration, their passion grows, spurring them to engage in even more enthusiastic lovemaking.

This climactic sequence in the novella hinges on the double reversal of a conventional understanding of Maoist political culture. First, the scene takes place during one of the most destructive periods of the Cultural Revolution—though in a precise inversion of the familiar image of Red Guards systematically destroying artifacts associated with the "Four Olds" in the name of Maoism, here we instead find a systematic destruction of *Maoist* icons in the name of sexual passion. Second, the scene inverts the logic of sublimation that arguably underlies much of the political passion observed under Maoism. Rather than channeling libidinal energies into political ones, here we find politically driven impulses redirected into nakedly sexual ones. In this scene we see a convergence of the psychopolitical logics of the abject and the partial object, wherein the Maoist icons are transformed from paradigmatic objects of desire into abject objects of destruction—even as each new act of desecration serves to reinforce the libidinal bonds linking the two partners.

Serve the People concludes with another reversal of fortune. Liu Lian reveals to Wu Dawang that she is pregnant, and then arranges for him to return to his hometown for an extended leave of absence. When Wu eventually comes back to the military base where he had been stationed, he discovers that the entire base has been dismantled while he was away, and everyone with any knowledge of his relationship with Liu Lian has been transferred somewhere else. At this point, Wu realizes that his entire relationship with Liu had been merely a setup designed to enable Liu to become pregnant with a child whom she and her husband could treat as their own. It turns out, in other words, that Liu Lian's insistence on a transitive understanding of the phrase "Serve the People" was actually a screen for a scheme premised on a transitive understanding of paternity. By treating her son by Wu Dawang as though he were her husband's child, Liu Lian is effectively transferring the attribution of paternity from one figure to another and, in the process, underscoring the socially constructed nature of paternal-filial relationships.

A similarly transitive approach to paternity and filiation also drives *Lenin's Kisses*. In particular, Liu Yingque's determination to acquire the corpse of one of the forefathers of Chinese socialism is directly rooted in his own conflicted relationship with his foster father. In one of the work's many flashbacks, we are told that Liu was abandoned as an infant on the doorstep of a school for training local cadres and ended up being adopted and raised by the local schoolmaster. After his adoptive father's death, Liu discovers that the schoolmaster had bequeathed him a "Hall of Devotion" containing writings by twenty leading Chinese and foreign socialist theoreticians and military leaders, together with a set of biographical charts listing key milestones in their respective lives. The room also contains an extra chart that has been left largely blank, and which Liu Yingque concludes corresponds to his own life and career. Part of the room's attraction for Liu, therefore, lies in the bifurcated glimpse it offers of both the past and the future, and he memorizes the biographical charts of his figurative forefathers while filling out his own. The room's association with themes of surrogate paternity and filiation is reinforced by the fact that it was handed down to Liu by his foster father, whose postmortem portrait also occupies a prominent position in the room. Liu's attempts to map out his own future, moreover, are closely tied to his efforts to symbolically reaffirm his relationship with such political father figures as Marx, Lenin, and Mao, not to mention his own foster father. In reinventing his intellectual lineage, Liu Yingque is simultaneously reimagining his own patriline.

This reimagination of filial and paternal relationships, in turn, is alluded to in the narrator's observation, at the very beginning of the novel, that during Liven's summer blizzard, time itself had fallen "out of joint." The Chinese phrase in question, *shixu luan le gangchang le* 时序乱了纲常了, refers specifically to the "disorder" or "disjunction" (*luan*) of both the "temporal order" (*shixu*) and "relationships and virtues" (*gangchang*), with the latter phrase being short for Confucianism's "three foundational relationships and five constant virtues" (*sangang wuchang*)—which include the "relationship" between father and son as well as the "virtue" of filial piety. Just as Hamlet famously exclaims, on first encountering the ghost of his father, that "the time is out of joint," the remark on temporal dislocation at the beginning of *Lenin's Kisses* refers both to a moment of seasonal slippage marked by the summer blizzard, and to a tear in the political fabric of the nation, as symbolized by the uncanny fascination with Lenin's corpse together with Liven's own attempts to renegotiate its relationship to the rest of society.[10] It is, in other words, the untimely blizzard that sets in motion a sequence of events that underscores a set of ideological and temporal slippages on which the contemporary Chinese body politic is predicated.

"How May We Serve You?"

Jean-Paul Sartre, in his 1961 preface to Frantz Fanon's *The Wretched of the Earth*, notes that his presumptively European readers have traditionally perceived colonized natives as "dead souls" or "zombies" to whom the Europeans do not even deign to respond: "Their fathers, shadowy creatures, your creatures, were but dead souls; you it was who allowed them glimpses of light, to you only did they dare speak, and you did not bother to reply to such zombies." Sartre then proceeds to invert this critique by suggesting that the *next* generation of natives may come to treat the Europeans with the same disregard as the Europeans had treated them: "Their sons ignore you; a fire warms them and sheds light around them, and you have not lit it. Now, at a respectful distance, it is you who will feel furtive, nightbound and perished with cold. Turn and turn about; in these shadows from whence a new dawn will break, it is *you* who are the zombies."[11]

Sartre argues that Fanon's study illustrates a process wherein the power differential between colonizers and colonized undergoes a dialectical reversal accompanying a shift in perspective and enunciative agency. Whereas the tendency among European colonizers had been to view the colonized as subaltern others (which is to say, as zombies), Sartre points to the possibility that a new generation of colonized subjects will strategically reverse this perspective, refusing to acknowledge the colonizers as legitimate subjects and, in the process, transforming them into virtual zombies in their own right.

Lenin's Kisses may be viewed as an illustration of the very logic that Sartre describes. To the extent that the Liven villagers function as figurative zombies—paradigmatically subaltern figures who have been systematically marginalized by society—what we observe in the novel is a strategic inversion of this dehumanizing perspective, both in the village's attempts to regain its freedom and autonomy (and thereby reject the same social institutions that had historically marginalized the village itself) as well as in the villagers' enthusiasm for their "special skills" performances (wherein they effectively embrace the dehumanizing process of commodification to which they had been subjected).

Or, to switch metaphors, the villagers' abject status as figuratively "undead" figures may also be seen in view of what American linguist and political philosopher Noam Chomsky has recently called "unpeople." Just as Sartre uses undead zombies as a metaphor for the invisibility of the subaltern in the eyes of the developed world, Chomsky borrows George Orwell's neologism "unpeople," from the novel *1984*, to describe individuals whom the state has stripped of the right to live in an attempt to anchor its own claims to sovereignty. Noting that these unpeople are deemed "unfit to enter history," Chomsky suggests that they represent figurative fault lines within the historicity of the nation.[12] In *Lenin's Kisses*, the disabled residents of Liven similarly find themselves virtually forgotten by society, even as they struggle to be recognized within the new sociopolitical order. However, once they do manage to achieve some recognition (when they "enter society" in the 1950s), they discover that they are expected to sacrifice themselves for the greater good—either by giving away their final grain reserves during the post–Great Leap Forward famines, or by periodically sending token representatives to the commune to be "struggled against" during the Cultural Revolution. By this logic, Liu Yingque's demand that the villagers form a traveling performance troupe and put their disabilities on display may be seen as an extension of this pattern of self-sacrifice.

The twist, though, is that in the novel this latter process of self-commodification functions precisely to reaffirm the village's agency and autonomy. Just as the Cultural Revolution's iconoclastic tendencies are strategically redirected in Yan's *Serve the People!* against Maoist iconography itself, in *Lenin's Kisses* the necropolitical consequences of contemporary China's embrace of capitalist development are symbolically inverted when the Liven villagers embrace a strategy of collective self-commodification—and, by implication, self-sacrifice—in order to "serve the people" and invert the dehumanizing consequences of China's capitalist logic. Or, to paraphrase the tagline from Brugués's *Juan of the Dead*: "We sacrifice our loved ones. How may I serve you?"

Notes

1. Giorgio Agamben, *Homo Sacer: Sovereign Power and Bare Life* (Stanford, CA: Stanford University Press, 1998), p. 12.

2. Achille Mbembe, "Necropolitics," *Public Culture* 15, no. 1 (Winter 2003): 11–40; emphasis added.

3. Yan Lianke, *Shouhuo* (Shenyang: Chunfeng wenyi chubanshe), translated by Carlos Rojas as *Lenin's Kisses* (New York: Grove Atlantic Press, 2012); see p. 1 in both editions.

4. The opening chapter of the original Chinese edition of the novel specifies that the snowstorm takes place in the sixth lunar month of the *gengchen* Year of the Dragon, which corresponds to the summer of 2000. Based on the other dates provided in the manuscript, combined with the narrative's own internal chronology, however, it is clear that this should actually be the summer of the *wuyin* Year of the Tiger, or 1998. The English translation opens (with the author's approval) with the corrected date.

5. For a discussion of Yan Lianke's novel and Tao Yuanming's "Peach Blossom Spring" fable, see Liu Jianmei, "Joining the Commune or Withdrawing from the Commune: A Reading of Yan Lianke's *Shouhuo*," *Modern Chinese Literature and Culture* 19, no. 2 (Fall 2007): 1–33.

6. Yan, *Lenin's Kisses*, p. 360.

7. Julia Kristeva, *Powers of Horror: An Essay on Abjection*, trans. Leon S. Roudiez (New York: Columbia University Press, 1982).

8. Jacques Lacan, *Four Fundamental Concepts of Psychoanalysis* (New York: W. W. Norton, 1998), p. 112.

9. See, for instance, the selling of human skin in *Riguang liunian* 日光流年 (Time's passage) (Shenyang: Chunfeng wenyi chubanshe, 1998), and the selling of human blood in Yan Lianke, *Dingzhuang meng* 丁庄梦 (Taipei: Rye Field, 2006), translated by Cindy Carter as *Dream of Ding Village* (New York: Grove Atlantic Press, 2011).

10. Jacques Derrida famously uses this same phrase as a leitmotif in his analysis of the continued relevance of Marxian critique in today's nominally postsocialist world. Writing shortly after the collapse of the Soviet Union and Eastern Europe's other Communist governments, Derrida argues that Marxism is located within a similar temporal disjunction, in that even as the Communist regimes that Marx's work helped engender increasingly become a thing of the past and Marxism itself is increasingly regarded as "dead," the legacy of Marx and Marxism nevertheless continues to carry an anticipatory valence that looks forward to a future yet to come. In particular, Derrida contends that the spread of neoliberalism has contributed to an epidemic of "violence, inequality, exclusion, famine, and thus economic oppression" around the world, and argues that Marxian theory offers a productive response to these problems. See Jacques Derrida, *Specters of Marx: The State of the Debt, the Work of Mourning, and the New International*, trans. Peggy Kamuf (New York: Routledge, 1994).

11. Jean-Paul Sartre, preface to Frantz Fanon, *The Wretched of the Earth*, trans. Richard Philcox (New York: Grove Press, 1965), p. 13; emphasis added.

12. Noam Chomsky, "Recognizing the 'Unpeople,'" *Truthout*, January 7, 2011, at http://truth-out.org/opinion/item/5960:recognizing-the-unpeople (accessed October 5, 2015).

PART 5

Red Shadows

ELEVEN

MUSEUMS AND MEMORIALS OF THE MAO ERA

A Survey and Notes for Future Curators

Jie Li

In 1986, renowned writer Ba Jin 巴金 called for building a Cultural Revolution museum (*wenge bowuguan* 文革博物馆) to pass on to later generations memories of a "catastrophic era," so that "history would not repeat itself."[1] Although many intellectuals have since echoed the same wish, and although Mao-era memorabilia abounds in souvenir markets, there is nothing in China today like what Ba Jin originally envisioned: a museum where young people can learn about the causes and ramifications of the Mao era's tumultuous mass movements, about the passions, sufferings, and complicities of their parents and grandparents. The idea of a memorial museum retains its urgency and resonance, but there is also growing dissonance over its appropriate form and content, audience and message.[2] Instead of a concrete monument on Tiananmen Square, the idea of a Cultural Revolution museum has instead become a powerful discursive topos in which diverse memories and understandings of the Mao era crisscross.

This chapter attempts a genealogy of the Cultural Revolution museum in theory and in practice, analyzing existing physical sites in China invested with memories of the Mao era as well as providing a number of curatorial proposals. In surveying museums devoted to the "civilization" of Mao-era cultural artifacts as well as memorials devoted to the "cataclysms," or man-made catastrophes, I examine the agents behind the creation, maintenance, and neglect of sites over time; the form and media in which the past persists into the present; and the meanings these sites might convey to real or virtual visitors. Instead of a single museum to accommodate a nation's memories, I argue for a plurality of memory places to allow for the articulation of both trauma and nostalgia, for understanding the era's utopian ideals and reckoning with its human costs. Moreover, the public memory work of the Mao era could creatively inherit and transform some of the era's cultural practices from rituals of "speaking bitterness" to occasions for intergenerational dialogue, from "going among the masses" to "barefoot historians" collecting subaltern memories.

Envisioning a Cultural Revolution Museum

Perceiving the historical amnesia that set in less than a decade after the end of the Cultural Revolution, Ba Jin hoped that his own generation's evanescent memories could outlast their lifetimes to be transmitted to posterity. As he envisioned it, the Cultural Revolution museum would "exhibit concrete and real objects" as well as "reconstruct striking scenes." With the apocalyptic ring of Judgment Day, it was to remind visitors of both the panoramic historical "march of events" and "his or her behavior during that decade. . . . Masks will fall, each will search his or her conscience, the true face of each one will be revealed, large and small debts from the past will be paid." The museum's purpose was to reestablish moral clarity and humanistic values after a decade of violence, lies, and injustice, "when humiliation and inhuman tortures were inflicted on our compatriots, that great chaos in which truth and falsehood were reversed, white and black confounded, loyalty and treason mistaken for each other."[3]

As if to set an example, Ba Jin filled his essay collection *Reflections* (*Suixiang lu* 随想录) with reflections on his own participation in the persecution of friends and submission to rituals of self-humiliation. Some essays provide further clues for what should or should not be exhibited in the Cultural Revolution museum. For example, he wrote of the nightmares he had after hearing a neighbor sing tunes from the model operas (*yangbanxi* 样板戏) that dominated the mediascape of the Cultural Revolution. For him and many intellectuals and cadres once condemned as "ox-devils and snake spirits," model operas represented traumatic sights and sounds, since their persecutors had impersonated the operas' "heroes" and treated them as "enemies."[4] Ba Jin thus suggests that the period's cultural artifacts, if exhibited at all, should be exposed as oppressive propaganda tainted by a history of violence, not innocent works of art: "The flowers that bloom in human blood are bright and beautiful, but they are poisoned."[5] Thus Ba Jin repudiated the Cultural Revolution as an unmitigated disaster and conceived of no room for nostalgia.

In 1986 and 1987, Ba Jin's essay was reprinted in various newspapers and even broadcast on the radio. In 1988, Ye Yonglie 叶永烈, a reportage writer known for biographies of major historical figures, published a short story entitled "Ba Jin's Dream," in which Ye casts himself as "secretary" for the Shanghai Museum Society and establishes a committee to plan a Cultural Revolution museum. After issuing a call to the public for suggestions, the story goes, the committee receives nearly 30,000 letters in support of the motion from both older and younger generations, offering monetary donations, artifact collections, and imaginary blueprints. Most agreed on Tiananmen Square as the ideal location, whereas opinions were divided on the museum's color—red to suggest the era's passion, black to evoke catastrophe, or white, the color of mourning. An interesting proposal for the main entrance was to nail the sculpted heads of the sixteen ringleaders of the "Lin Biao and Jiang Qing counterrevolutionary cliques" on a pillar of eternal shame, whereas Ye's teacher suggested building a hell-like "museum of souls" underneath Tiananmen Square, since the Cultural Revolution was dubbed "a revolution that touched people's souls." After a long entrance corridor wallpapered with big-character posters, three exhibition halls were to be dedicated to three shapes of souls. "Square souls," like ink stones blackened a myriad times without losing their "squareness," were heroes and martyrs, such as Peng Dehuai 彭德怀 and Zhang Zhixin 张志新. "Triangle souls," like daggers that stab people in the back, were the Cultural Revolution's villains, like Lin Biao and Jiang Qing. Finally, "round souls," like cobblestones scraped smooth over time, were those who neither harmed others nor stood up to tyranny. The exit would display clubs, whips, denunciation letters, handcuffs, and various dunce caps: in the ominous glint of this "mirror," the visitor would reflect on the shape of his or her soul. To build such a museum, however, would have required fifty official seals of approval, and after describing the Kafkaesque journey to obtain just the first ten seals, Ye's short story ends with the planning committee's bitter laughter over its own pipe dream.[6]

Indeed, despite the widespread resonance of Ba Jin's appeal, building a Cultural Revolution museum in Tiananmen Square could have been only an absurdist fantasy when the CCP Central Propaganda Department issued explicit regulations that forbade the publication of works on the Cultural Revolution.[7] After 1989, the notion of a Cultural Revolution museum fell into hibernation, only to be transformed a few years later in the "Mao fever" of the early 1990s, when the market for Maoist memorabilia blossomed.[8] "Red collectors" spoke of their treasure troves of Mao badges, propaganda posters, and other "revolutionary" everyday artifacts as de facto Cultural Revolution museums.[9] Decorating their walls with old propaganda posters, staging Red Guard song-and-dance numbers, and serving dishes once consumed by sent-down youths, Cultural Revolution–theme restaurant owners also invoked Ba Jin and described their enterprises as mini-museums and public memorial spaces.[10] Tinged by playful nostalgia, such spaces are designed to bring back the "red old days" of people's youth rather than to warn against the recurrence of catastrophe. Instead of honoring heroes and indicting villains, instead of commemorating the traumatized bodies and souls of victims, these "museums" re-present the Cultural Revolution with the era's mass cultural artifacts, often turning erstwhile cult objects into commodity fetishes. Treating artifacts as objects of consumption rather than reflection, such spaces, as their critics have pointed out, may conflate propagandistic illusions with historical realities and thereby aid collective amnesia rather than collective memory of the Mao era.[11] In this sense, they have been considered less as implementations than as travesties of Ba Jin's original proposal.

Alongside private "red" artifact collections and themed spaces, however, many also began constructing Cultural Revolution museums in print and virtual media. In 1995, photography editor Yang Kelin 杨克林 published a large, two-volume work in Hong Kong titled *The Cultural Revolution Museum*, which presented a chronology of the decade with historical photographs and documents. Blessed with Ba Jin's calligraphy, this book is organized into twelve "exhibition halls" devoted to themes such as "origins," "deification," "factional warfare," "the arts," "reeducation," "economy," and so on.[12] Yang Kelin's book was just one among many other Cultural Revolution sourcebooks, historiographies, memoirs, and oral history collections that were published in the 1990s and 2000s—mostly in Hong Kong to evade mainland Chinese censors.[13]

In spring 1996, the first Virtual Museum of the Cultural Revolution was launched by the online Chinese periodical *Hua Xia Wen Zhai* 华夏文摘, or *China News Digest* (CND), based overseas and blocked in China. Calling for contributions from readers, by the summer of 2014 CND had published more than 700 special issues on the topic. Its contents, consisting almost exclusively of textual materials, are also catalogued under eight "exhibition halls," such as "Documents and Sources" and "Literary and Artistic Works."[14] Since the late 1990s, many other websites devoted to the Cultural Revolution have emerged in China and overseas.[15] Most of the sites still resemble databases and archives that *passively* store memories, rather than museums that *actively* memorialize, but they do encourage user contributions and participation through discussion forums. And although virtual exhibits are not as tangible as material artifacts, the multimedia presentation of images, sounds, and films can still create vivid and visceral encounters with the past. Indeed, among the most powerful "exhibits" in a virtual Cultural Revolution museum is a documentary film by Hu Jie 胡杰 about the death of Bian Zhongyun 卞仲耘, the first Beijing schoolteacher to be beaten to death by her own students, in August 1966. Based on photographs and other intimate relics collected by Bian's husband, the film has circulated widely on the Internet and constitutes the only audiovisual exhibit on the Chinese Holocaust Memorial website, founded in 2000 to commemorate victims of the Cultural Revolution.[16]

Proponents of a Cultural Revolution museum have often compared the period's violence to that of the Holocaust, a global symbol of human suffering in the hands of state-sponsored violence.[17] Even official Chinese museums have recently drawn on Holocaust museology in commemorating the Nanjing Massacre and other wartime atrocities.[18] Yet drawing any simple equivalence between the Holocaust and the Cultural Revolution reveals little about the *causes* of the suffering and may instead create taboos for topics of discussion or provoke unproductive debates about competing victimhoods—what Ian Buruma has called an "Olympics of Suffering."[19] As the editors of the volume *Some of Us: Chinese Women Growing Up in the Mao Era* wrote:

> Nowadays, it seems one of the easiest ways to arrive at a higher moral ground is to accuse someone of either being like Hitler or his mindless followers or even, curiously, his helpless victims. . . . Such accusations have often themselves become like those *gao mao zi* [high hats] that were readily forced onto the heads of the designated enemies during the Cultural Revolution. . . . To be sure, lessons of the Cultural Revolution have yet to be fully learned, but is it to be done only through a dichotomized framework of victims vs. victimizers, namely "helpless" (therefore good) Chinese vs. "evil" Chinese?[20]

The use of Nazi-related "high hats" obscures the power and appeal of Maoist utopian visions that mobilized mass participation, as well as the cycles of vigilante violence wherein victims of one campaign might have been victimizers in an earlier one. If a Cultural Revolution museum is to heed Ba Jin's call to examine complicities, sympathizing only with the victims while pointing a finger at the perpetrators would not be sufficient. Rather, a more productive international comparison would be to consider how nations of perpetrators and collaborators have come to terms with their difficult pasts. In this respect, Germany has done more than any other nation to memorialize the victims of the crimes it once perpetrated, to reflect on the complicities of its citizens, and to preserve the ruins of fascism and communism in its contemporary landscape. It is because of this layered and vibrant memorial culture that I will often turn to Germany in my notes for future curators.

Until his death in 2005, Ba Jin himself never took any substantial initiative to realize his vision. Instead, his proposal for a Cultural Revolution museum underwent multiple appropriations, revisions, and contestations. Ba Jin was criticized for having said nothing of Mao's place in his museum, and his memoirs never strayed far from the official 1981 Resolution on Party History. Singling out the Cultural Revolution decade as an unprecedented catastrophe, rather than tracing its historical roots, Ba Jin did not discuss earlier mass movements such as the 1957 Anti-Rightist Campaign or the Great Leap Famine from 1959 to 1961, which had a much higher death toll than the Cultural Revolution but attracted far less public attention because its victims were peasants rather than cadres and intellectuals. Privileging the suffering of the elite, Ba Jin's Cultural Revolution museum would not have accommodated the subjectivities of workers and peasants who might remember much of the

Mao era as a time of scarcity and deprivation when one knew the worth of things; a time of job security, free health care, and safe streets; a time of tight communities, selfless idealism, and simple virtues. For many, even the Cultural Revolution was a time of historical possibility rather than pure disaster, as it provided slivers of opportunity for the free expression of dissent and righteous protest against the status quo.[21] Born not just out of official indoctrination but also lived experiences, nostalgia for the Mao era may well serve as a resource for critiquing the postsocialist present. Such diverse memories of the Mao era, however, have only enhanced the idea of the Cultural Revolution museum as a powerful topos, not as a concrete monument in the nation's capital but as a place of discourse where contested memories of the Mao era intersect. Let us now explore the topography of Mao-era memories in the contemporary Chinese landscape.

Survey of Existing Memory Places

In recent years, China's patriotic education campaign and tourism development oversaw a museum boom driven as much by top-down political directives as by local economic initiatives.[22] Although official history museums in Beijing and Shanghai skim over the Mao era, often eliding the Cultural Revolution and other traumatic movements, some institutions began tapping into more sensitive layers of their local historical palimpsests.[23] The following survey consists of physical and publicly accessible sites in China that are invested with collective memories of the Mao era. I do not address private, interior, and domestic spaces unless the private memories are mediated and communicated to the public; nor do I focus on museums that exist only in print or virtual formats. Occupying actual space in the landscape, the memory places surveyed here bear imaginary and symbolic and also tangible connections to the past through their material remains. Meanwhile, they must also negotiate with postsocialist transformations. The agents who inscribe memory onto places include their original makers, natural and historical erosion or renewal, and those who inhabited or visited the site past and present, attributing to it their own meanings. I divide memory places between those primarily concerned with the *civilization* of cultural artifacts and others that focus on the *cataclysms*, or the human costs.

A MUSEUM FROM THE MAO ERA: THE DAYI LANDLORD'S MANOR

We begin in the small town of Anren 安仁 in Sichuan's Dayi 大邑 County, home to the most famous museum of "class struggle" in the Mao era and the site of China's largest private museum today. Formerly the residence of the local landlord Liu Wencai 刘文彩, the Dayi Landlord Manor Exhibition Hall (Dayi dizhu zhuangyuan chenlieguan 大邑地主庄园陈列馆) opened in 1959 and garnered nationwide fame in 1965 after the installation of the life-size clay sculpture series *The Rent Collection Courtyard* (*Shouzuyuan* 收租院). Sculpted by local museum staff with the help of professors and students at the Sichuan Art Academy, *The Rent Collection Courtyard* vividly portrays the suffering of peasants and the cruelty of the landlord and his lackeys. Reproduced in illustrations, posters, comic strips, and films, the work was upheld as an exemplar of Mao's revolutionary realism and served as a key precursor to the Cultural Revolution. "Using it as a grim reminder of the past," states a 1968 catalogue, "the Chinese people visit it so that they should never—from one generation to the next—forget class struggle."[24] In the 1960s and the 1970s, the manor-museum received tens of millions of visitors, but after the deemphasis of class struggle in the 1980s the number of museum visitors dwindled.[25] In recent years, however, the museum became a tourist destination again, its fame boosted by the work of contemporary artist Cai Guoqiang 蔡国强, who created a controversial new version of the *Rent Collection Courtyard* sculptures for the 1999 Venice Biennale.[26] Around the same time, popular revisionist historiography began to portray the evil landlord as a good philanthropist, and exposed old horrors—such as the "water dungeon" that imprisoned tenants who were in arrears—as Mao-era ideological fabrications.[27]

Bathed in waves of fame and notoriety, this local museum with a national reputation has made a successful transition into the post-socialist era. In the summers of 2009 and 2013, I visited the manor-museum amid hordes of tourists. Renamed the Liu Family Estate Museum (Liushi zhuangyuan bowuguan 刘氏庄园博物馆), its written and spoken scripts for those touring the museum emphasize Liu Wencai's specific biography and family lineage, instead of making him a demon of the feudal "Old Society." Liu's material possessions, his multiple wives, and his protection by the local militia are presented from the double perspective of the rich and the poor, as double-edged objects of desire and detestation. I overheard the whispers of my underwhelmed fellow tourists: "Is *this* all the luxury a landlord had?" In some ways, this museum has become just another mansion belonging to the rich gentry, the basis of the heritage tourism that has been springing up in small towns all over China since the 1990s. When explicating the tools of exploitation and *The Rent Collection Courtyard*, the tour guides on my visits tried to disentangle myths from facts, but for the most part they spoke of the sculpture series in terms of an art connoisseur. If class struggle was more ambiguous than previously assumed, it was at least possible to reclaim the sculptures' "artistic" value.

In the Liu Family Estate Museum, the tourist revisits two kinds of pasts: the prerevolutionary mythical past of class struggle and the more recent Mao era of myth making. Besides distinguishing between the "real" and the "fake" Liu Wencai, visitors learn how historical narratives served political ideologies, as well as how "testimonial museums" could serve propaganda purposes. Their melodramatic dichotomy of good and evil certainly inspired compassion for the oppressed and hatred of the oppressors, which in turn legitimated desires for justice and revenge. Thus the psychological origins of revolutionary violence may have less to do with insensitivity and malevolence than a misguided sense of righteousness. Future Mao-era museum curators might be forewarned against such Manichean representations in which Red Guards, rebel leaders, or local cadres are demonized in the place of capitalists and landlords. In addition to testifying to atrocities, a good memorial museum should also show how justice by the formerly oppressed could easily turn into injustice, as well as warn against the emotional manipulation of horror chambers.

RED ERA SERIES AT THE JIANCHUAN MUSEUM CLUSTER

A ten-minute pedicab ride connects Liu Wencai's manor with the giant Jianchuan Museum Cluster, founded in 2005 by Fan Jianchuan 樊建川, a real estate developer with a passion for collecting. My pedicab driver, a local who claimed that his grandfather used to be Liu Wencai's tenant farmer, was now Fan Jianchuan's employee and told me that the "new landlord in town" was "much richer than Liu Wencai." He added that "both are good" because they gave his family jobs and developed the town's economy. Whereas Liu Wencai collected only some gems and jewels, Fan Jianchuan amassed tens of millions of modern historical artifacts, bought thirty-three hectares of land in Anren, and built dozens of museums divided into four series, or themes—War of Resistance, Red Era, Folk Customs, and the Sichuan Earthquake—along with supporting facilities such as a Red Guard Inn, a People's Commune Restaurant, a revolutionary model-opera-theme teahouse, and various souvenir shops.[28] Outside the exhibitions, loudspeakers blast "red songs," consisting of hosannas to Chairman Mao and patriotic songs of resistance against the Japanese invasion from the 1930s. The museum staff uniforms were at once reminiscent of Red Army soldiers and Red Guards, visually conflating War of Resistance and Cultural Revolution themes and thereby using the former to legitimize the latter.

Fan Jianchuan claimed to have begun collecting Cultural Revolution artifacts twenty years before Ba Jin's call for a Cultural Revolution museum. Trying to understand why his cadre father was criticized and incarcerated in 1966, the nine-year-old Fan Jianchuan collected Mao badges, Red Guard armbands, and mimeographed pamphlets. He continued his hobby as a sent-down youth, soldier, student, and cadre, from the 1970s to the 1980s, though it was only in the 1990s, when all of China was moving house, that Cultural Revolution artifacts rolled out of private homes and into flea markets. Funding his collecting fever with his real estate fortune since the nineties, Fan Jianchuan has been receiving hundreds of containers of artifacts annually from his nationwide network of flea-market contacts. In his 6,000 square meters of warehouse space, there are thirty tons of handwritten materials, a million photographs, and more than a hundred thousand propaganda posters and LP records from the Mao era.[29]

To accommodate his collection, Fan Jianchuan decided to build museums, and he sought inspiration from museums around the world—his favorites being the Auschwitz-Birkenau State Museum and the Yasukuni Shrine Museum.[30] Still, he had a distinct curatorial vision of his own and considered his museum cluster a "supermarket" that supplied spiritual and cultural products according to people's everyday needs. Unlike history museums that follow a chronological order, he organized artifacts by material and function, so that the first four museums in the Red Era series, for example, are devoted to (1) porcelain, (2) daily necessities, (3) Mao badges, clocks, and seals, and (4) mirrors. The museum of Red Era Daily Necessities showcases items and furnishings from "typical" homes during the Cultural Revolution—those of a worker, a peasant, a soldier, and a cadre—as well as a library, a clinic, a broadcasting station, a photographer's studio, and a kindergarten. Two large halls display other everyday artifacts by category: matches, records, lantern slides, enamel cups, pencil boxes, musical instruments, and radios, all depersonalized to evoke collective memories and represent social types rather than individuals (plate 29).

The exhibitions show off the sheer quantity of the collection through an aesthetic of the mass ornament: arranging Mao badges into four giant Mao faces, turning seals into pavements, clocks into a catacomb-like wall display, and mirrors into labyrinths. Some installations are intent on conveying a message: "These seals," the tour guides explain, "once had power over people's life and death, so now we step on them to show our contempt."[31] The eerie ticking and chiming of 112 clocks from the Cultural Revolution period placed next to a rotunda displaying violent photographs from the time (fig. 11.1) are meant to serve as "alarm bells" (*jingzhong* 警钟) against history's repetition. The fifth and newest collection, the Red Era Museum on Sent-Down Youths, contains a central atrium filled with broken Cultural Revolution–era mirrors amid rusty farm tools, poignantly suggesting the disenchantment that accompanied the mass movement.

The word "mirror" is also a synonym of "history"—the past is to serve as a mirror for the present (*yi shi wei jian* 以史为鉴)—and Fan Jianchuan was especially proud of his Red Era Mirror Museum. Its white, hazy labyrinth has not only dazed and trapped many a tourist but also played hide-and-seek with the censors. After the original curated exhibit received official approval, Fan Jianchuan furnished a formerly empty room with "Wanted Circulars" (*tongji ling* 通缉令) from the Cultural Revolution and then waited for a good moment to fill another alcove with confessions and denunciations of neighbors and family members. He adopted the same guerrilla tactic for the alcove devoted to the film actor Feng Zhe 冯喆 in the Red Era Museum of Daily Necessities: Feng Zhe committed suicide in Anren in 1969, and Fan Jianchuan, an avowed fan, collected photos and documents from his surviving family members and created a small shrine to his memory after the museum's displays had passed the censors.

FIGURE 11.1. Rotunda displaying Cultural Revolution photographs (*left*) and clocks representing history's "alarm bells" (*right*) at the Jianchuan Museum Cluster. Photo by Jie Li.

Such unsanctioned exhibits could be ephemeral. In 2009, I saw an outdoor exhibition of photographs from the Great Leap Forward next to the People's Commune Canteen. The images of an agricultural utopia, clearly doctored and bearing their original captions, would appear ironic to anyone vaguely acquainted with the famine that had ensued.[32] In 2013, this exhibit disappeared. Instead, several of the Red Era museums added new vitrines that held politically sensitive documents: interrogation records, lists of counterrevolutionary slogans, reportage on economic crimes, inventories of objects confiscated by Red Guards. These guerrilla exhibits serve as placeholders for the museums Fan Jianchuan still wants to build. Pending official approval, his sixth Red Era museum will chronicle the three decades of the Mao era, year by year. He also envisions future museums centered on more taboo topics, such as the Great Leap Famine and the Cultural Revolution's home searches and factional warfare. Meanwhile, he keeps amending the exhibits in the open museums, replacing propaganda photographs with everyday photographs that are "more human and less idealized."[33]

In a 2005 essay, "From Cultural Industry to Mao Industry," Michael Dutton wrote about the Jianchuan Museum Cluster as it was still being planned: "What might at first appear as little more than a perverse and ironic parody of Ba Jin's solemn and heartrending vow to remember the victims proves to be the very best antidote to the infectious allure of the Sirens' song," that is, Mao's revolutionary politics. Dutton argues that both Ba Jin's call for a museum and Mao's posthumous hagiography continue to reify the "auratic" quality of the Chairman's politics. By contrast, "the commodified simulacrum of the Cultural Revolution Museum [in Anren] makes the past unthinkable as a horrendous event by remembering it nostalgically and by offering it to moderns as a light-hearted form of distraction. . . . In transforming events such as the Cultural Revolution and figures such as Mao Zedong into forms of consumer distraction and nostalgia, the commodity form robs them of their original transformative ability."[34]

Despite its relaxing and playful atmosphere, the Jianchuan Museum Cluster has turned out to be more than a commodified theme park. Less confrontational than Ba Jin's original vision, its exhibitions of Mao-era artifacts, with minimal textual explanations, nevertheless open up a space for public remembrance and plural interpretations. Visitors might find endearing artifacts of their childhood or reminisce about the "drab spiritual life in the ultra-leftist years."[35] Writing of a global "memory boom" in the 1980s, Andreas Huyssen points out that "there is no pure space outside of commodity culture, however much we may desire such a space," yet commodification does not simply equal forgetting, and the "memorializing drive has a more beneficial and generative dimension as well."[36] Similar to the Documentation Center of Everyday Life in East Germany in Eisenhüttenstadt, the Jianchuan Museum Red Era series exhibits create "a site of mourning" and a "stage for a requiem for communism."[37] Its catalogue speaks of "red collections" as picking up "foundlings" discarded by people who were weary of that era, so the museum could serve as their "tomb." It is also mindful of the political instrumentality of many everyday objects as means of social and psychological control—the exhibition of ration coupons, for example, was designed to testify to the "failure of the planned economy."[38]

Displaying the largest collection of "red artifacts" in China, the Jianchuan Museum Cluster is the most prominent example of the many red memorabilia exhibitions staged by "red collectors" throughout China, in their own shops, in red theme restaurants, and in other spaces open to visitors or consumers. In Shanghai alone, I came across various exhibits of Mao badges, Cultural Revolution propaganda posters, Mao-era films, and ration coupons, temporarily on display at the Shanghai Municipal History Museum in 2010. As Harriet Evans points out in Chapter 3, red memorabilia such as Cultural Revolution–era posters hold varied and ambiguous appeal for different generations of Chinese and Western consumers today, who may engage with the images through nostalgia and parody. And as Xiaobing Tang argues in Chapter 4, the reappropriation of Mao-era political images in contemporary Chinese art draws on the legacy of "socialist visual culture" to critique the present. Whatever their appeal, red memorabilia have become marketable commodities for contemporary artists and collectors, entrepreneurs, and even government officials, who have therefore created occasions and spaces for their exhibition and consumption in major cities and small towns. Turning its "red historical heritage" into a tourist asset, the "historic town" of Fengjing 枫泾 in Shanghai's suburbs developed the former site of its People's Commune headquarters and a bunker dug during the Cultural Revolution into tourist attractions. Similarly, Suiping 遂平 County in Henan Province proudly presents as its unique tourist resource China's very first People's Commune from the Great Leap Forward. Today, this "historical heritage site" hosts an exhibition of photographs and documents testifying to the locality's one-time glory, without any mention of the ensuing famine.[39] Leaving it to visitors' own historical memories to fill in the darker shadows of the Mao era, such museums of red memorabilia elide, for the most part, the revolution's human costs.

COMMEMORATING THE MAO ERA'S HUMAN COSTS

To reckon with the Mao era not only as a *civilization* but as a *cataclysm*, and to memorialize the lives sacrificed to Mao's utopian visions, one might turn to the ruins of banished and vanished communities. After all, political campaigns from the 1950s to the 1970s caused the involuntary migration of tens of millions of people, mostly from urban to rural areas, from the coast to the interior, from the center to the margins. Apart from the trauma of exile and family separations, the ghosts of many who died violent, unnatural deaths during the Mao era also haunt many places. There are indeed memorial sites that were once labor camps, collective farms, or cemeteries full of people who lost their lives in the Mao era—memory places where communities formed by Maoist policies either survived or perished. Among these are the Jiabiangou 夹边沟 labor reform (*laogai* 劳改) camp in Gansu, the Xianning May Seventh Cadre School (Xianning wuqi ganxiao 咸宁五七干校) in Hubei, the Red Guard Graveyard (Hongweibing muyuan 红卫兵墓园) in Chongqing, and the Pagoda Park Cultural Revolution Museum (Tayuan wenge bowuguan 塔园文革博物馆) in Guangdong. Given the right conditions, it has been possible to turn some of the ruined sites into memorials, mostly through the commemorative vigilance of survivors and the modest support of local officials.

Let us begin with Jiabiangou, once a labor reform camp located by a crumbling section of the Great Wall. In operation between 1957 and 1961, it held approximately 3,000 Rightists, about 2,500 of whom died during the Great Leap Famine. In 2002, a collection of stories based on interviews with Jiabiangou survivors was published to great acclaim, followed by a number of related memoirs as well as a 2007 documentary and a 2010 feature film by director Wang Bing 王兵.[40] In the literary and cultural sphere, the name Jiabiangou came to be associated with the traumas of the Anti-Rightist Movement, the Great Leap Famine, and the *laogai* labor camp system that incarcerated tens of millions for political reasons.[41]

No museum or memorial has yet been constructed at the actual site of Jiabiangou, today a tree farm; its history as a labor camp is visible only to the small number of people who seek to visit its ruins, several of whom have shared what they found there in texts or photos posted online.[42] The account that best allegorizes the memorialization of Mao-era victims at the camp comes from a woman named He Fengming 和凤鸣, a subject of Wang Bing's 2007 documentary. Fengming's first husband was labeled a Rightist and incarcerated in Jiabiangou. In 1961 she was allowed to visit him and bring extra food rations, but upon arrival, she was told that he had died a month before. Denied her request to see his grave, she had to postpone her work of mourning. As she wrote in her memoir: "For thirty years we never poured libation on his grave. Cruel politics forced us to cut off our kinship. I rarely spoke of him to our children, for if the children expressed sympathy for their father, they could hardly have a foothold in school or society."[43] It was not until 1991 that a friend finally helped Fengming locate Jiabiangou's burial ground.

Each grave was marked by a stone picked from the Gobi desert, on which the victim's name was written with paint and placed facing down to protect it against erosion. Nevertheless, after decades of ravaging weather, most names had faded and become undecipherable; Fengming turned over hundreds of stones but could not find her husband's grave. In fact, as she later learned, the local authorities had placed the stones with the names on them at the burial site only in 1979, almost two decades after the mass deaths, when the Rightists were formally rehabilitated. They took this measure in preparation for visits by bereaved family members, knowing that the names probably did not correspond to the human remains underneath.[44]

As metonymy and metaphor, Fengming's story resonates with the millions of dead from the Mao era who were never properly identified or mourned. The faded names on belated "gravestones" randomly placed on a mass grave poignantly illustrate that memorials in stone depend on the commemorative vigilance of individuals and communities, which in turn depends on political legitimation. "Without a people's intention to remember," James Young points out with respect to the former sites of concentration camps, "the ruins remain little more than inert pieces of the landscape, unsuffused with the meanings and significances created in our visits to them."[45] However belated, Fengming's remembrances in writing and on film, along with those of other Jiabiangou survivors, helped commence a commemorative vigilance that has since turned the ruins of the *laogai* camp into an unlabeled memorial. The tree farm continues to receive a trickle of visitors who leave traces of grave rites. For their sake, the local government took measures of preservation, surrounding the ruins with barbed wire and paving the path with cement slabs.[46]

Jiabiangou's evolution into a memory place exemplifies an emergent interest in revisiting sites of formerly banished and now vanished communities. Apart from the 10 million *laogai* prisoners, an estimated 17 million young people were "sent down" to the countryside between 1965 and 1979. In the later years of the Cultural Revolution, millions of cadres and intellectuals were sent to "May Seventh Cadre Schools."[47] The sites of banishment, in most cases, were collective farms that straddled organization and wilderness, discipline and freedom, cruelty and camaraderie. Most of those banished eventually returned home, but some did not, and many thought they would be forever uprooted, an assumption that imbued their memories of such places with various configurations of despair, pathos, and the sanctity of voluntary or involuntary sacrifice.

Such "tourism" to one's own past has also inspired the creation of more permanent forms of memory. As documented by the independent documentary filmmaker Hu Jie, the East Wind Farm in Mile County 弥勒东风农场, Yunnan Province, began as a *laogai* camp that hosted about 400 Rightists in the late 1950s and later also received large groups of sent-down youths in the late 1960s and early 1970s. The documentary creates a palimpsest of the site, beginning with "speaking bitterness" oral histories by former members of the farm, and concluding with the construction of a memorial statue in a socialist realist style that portrays Rightists and sent-down youths not as victims but as pioneers who turned wilderness into farmland.[48] A similar sublimation or conversion of bitter experiences from hapless victimhood to heroic sacrifice dominates the Heihe Sent-Down Youth Museum that opened in the fall of 2009 and other sent-down youth memorials, which tend to echo rather than critique the ideologies that sent them to the "Great Northern Wilderness."[49]

Turning victims into heroes and martyrs is not an uncommon way of memorializing the human costs of the Mao era. In the process, the meaning of suffering and death is turned 180 degrees, from waste to sacrifice, from negation to affirmation, from indictment to glorification, from delegitimation to sanctification. After the revolutionary ideology took away people's youth, or even their life, does it continue to usurp the meaning of their death? If people genuinely believed in Maoist ideals and wanted their sacrifices to wear the halo of a grander purpose, is it necessary to accuse such faith of being the result of brainwashing or false consciousness?

The art, politics, and ethics of turning the darker legacies of the past into a cultural resource or even symbolic capital for the present are perhaps best exemplified at the former site of the May Seventh Cadre School in Xianning, Hubei Province, which held more than six thousand cadres and intellectuals from Beijing's Ministry of Culture under austere conditions, from 1969 to 1974, among them the renowned writers Shen Congwen 沈从文 and Bing Xin 冰心. In the mid-1990s, Xianning's local official Li Chengwai 李城外 rediscovered this bit of local heritage from the prefectural gazetteer and decided to excavate what he saw as a "cultural gold mine" *wenhua jinkuang* 文化金矿. Since then, he has built up an impressive collection of books, documents, and oral histories of "cultural celebrities" who spent time there, convened a few conferences with former cadre school members and literary historians, and constructed a small museum at its former headquarters, exhibiting photographs and artifacts.[50] While publicizing its history through the mass media, Li Chengwai has also urged officials at higher levels of government to do more to protect and develop this "cultural resource" for future tourism.[51] Asking with some derision what there is to "harvest" on the "ruins of culture," critics accused the site's developers of "selling a shameful history" that would necessarily apply cosmetic lyricism to a cruel reality. Invoking Ba Jin's idea for a Cultural Revolution museum, Li Chengwai has fiercely defended his efforts as rescuing history from oblivion and reclaiming the resilient spirit of Chinese intellectuals.[52] To date, the memorialization of the May Seventh Cadre School in Xianning has not managed to secure much political or financial investment, but growing academic research and media publicity have contributed to its fame as a memory place of the Cultural Revolution.

Besides touring the former sites of banished communities, one can also reflect on the human costs of the Cultural Revolution by visiting the graves of those who perished in this period, be they famous individuals, such as Liu Shaoqi 刘少奇, Lao She 老舍, and Lin Zhao 林昭, or ordinary people like those buried in the mass graves of the Red Guard Graveyard tucked away in Chongqing's Shaping Park (plate 30). This is the last remaining cemetery filled with the graves of ordinary people killed during the factional violence of the Cultural Revolution. Chongqing ranked among the cities worst affected by the violence because of its concentration of munitions factories. Unlike the Jiabiangou mass grave, this cemetery holds not only hapless victims of state oppression but also those who actively participated in the violence. Their victimhood is comparable to the deaths of soldiers in a civil war without clearly "right" and "wrong" sides, for everyone died in the name of defending Chairman Mao. The tombstones are often obelisks built in the style of the Monument to the People's Heroes in Tiananmen Square, bearing grandiose inscriptions in Mao-style calligraphy that refer to the dead as "revolutionary martyrs." Yet four decades of neglect and erosion have turned even the most heroic monuments into decrepit ruins, rendering many inscriptions illegible. Such incongruities between form and content, between the site's state of dilapidation and the very miracle of its survival, make the cemetery a powerful memory place for family members who come to visit and others who chance upon it, some of whom have tried to identify the people buried there and document how they died.[53]

For the survival of this cemetery, one has to thank not only the commemorative vigilance of the visitors, but also Chongqing's Communist Party secretary in the 1980s, Liao Bokang 廖伯康, who suffered persecution during the Cultural Revolution. In 1985, faced with the decision to preserve or demolish the cemetery, Liao allocated funds to build a wall around it and ordered it closed to the public until the late 1990s.[54] As Everett Zhang shows in his extensive historical and ethnographic analysis, mourning activities at this graveyard underwent three historical phases. At the height of factional conflict in the late 1960s, the Red Guards and rebels who were buried there were glorified for their "revolutionary sacrifice." After the official negation of the Cultural Revolution in the post-Mao reform stigmatized Red Guards as wrongdoers, mourning them also became illegitimate and the Red Guards buried in the cemetery "died a second death." Since the 2000s, with the revival of Qingming grave-sweeping customs, relatives have returned for private mourning ceremonies, and the park administration has photographed every tomb and collected relevant historical records and oral histories for its archives, even securing for the graveyard the official designation of a protected cultural relic in 2009. This new designation legitimated a resurgence of mourners, whose open quarrels and graffiti at the site expressed their conflicting interpretations of the deaths and of the Cultural Revolution itself: some considered the Red Guards' young lives to have been wasted by their deluded belief in Mao and saw the graveyard in light of Ba Jin's warning not to let history repeat itself; others wished to reaffirm the Cultural Revolution as a critique of contemporary China's socioeconomic inequality and corruption. For fear of stirring up social unrest, the park administration has closed down the graveyard and now allows entry only to family members on Qingming festivals.[55]

In August 2013, I was able to visit the Red Guard Graveyard when a retired park manager, a childhood friend of a family acquaintance, briefly unlocked its gates. Amid overgrown weeds and mosquitoes, a few graves showed traces of recent mourners: fruits and flowers, liquor and cigarettes, incense and paper money, and red tracings over the faded inscriptions of names. While wandering through this impressive ruin, I could hear a choir of retirees singing Cultural Revolution songs just beyond the cemetery wall but could not tell if these were the sirens of memory or amnesia.[56]

As cemeteries are commonsensical public commemoration sites, it also makes sense that the first memorial site to adopt the name "Cultural Revolution Museum" originated as a burial ground of warring factions. In 1996 Peng Qi'an 彭啓安, retired deputy mayor of the city of Shantou in Guangdong Province, chanced upon dozens of disorderly graves by the Pagoda Mountain Scenic Spot (Tashan fengjingqu 塔山风景区) in the northern suburbs. Having learned that those buried there died as a result of factional violence during the Cultural Revolution, Peng conceived of a memorial park to commemorate that history and marshaled his old colleagues behind what he named the Pagoda Park (Tayuan 塔园) project. Over the next decade, Peng raised funds to build an array of outdoor memorials in traditional Chinese commemorative style, including a "corridor of history-inscribed steles" (*peilang mingshi* 碑廊铭史), a "pagoda of contemplation" (*si'an ta* 思安塔), and a "pavilion of the vigilant bell" (*jingzhong changming ting* 警钟长鸣亭) (fig. 11.2). In 2003 a friend gave him a copy of Yang Kelin's book *Cultural Revolution Museum*, and two years later Peng managed to transform this "museum on paper" into a "museum in stone." He commissioned a circular building that resembled Beijing's Temple of Heaven, enshrined Ba Jin's portrait and calligraphy at the entrance (fig. 11.3), and lined its inner walls with hundreds of gray granite slabs etched with pages from Yang's book, mostly photographs of mass rallies and graphic deaths. The museum also displayed in vitrines a few Red Guard armbands, Little Red Books, Mao busts, and badges, but these were removed after some artifacts disappeared in the absence of security guards.[57]

With the arrival of the fortieth anniversary of the start of the Cultural Revolution, the first Cultural Revolution museum to be named as such attracted a spate of attention from domestic and international media as well as from the central authorities. Peng Qi'an had hoped to turn his Pagoda Park into a "reflection education base" (*fansi jiaoyu jidi* 反思教育基地), similar to a "patriotic education base" (*aiguo jiaoyu jidi* 爱国教育基地), and he sought legitimacy for the site by asking the powerful figures who visited to leave behind a sample of their calligraphy.[58] Yet the authorities mostly avoided the site, discouraged media publicity, and excluded Pagoda Park from local tourist itineraries. Nevertheless,

FIGURE 11.2. Entrance to Shantou's Pagoda Park. Photo by Jie Li.

FIGURE 11.3. China's first private Cultural Revolution museum enshrines Ba Jin at its entrance. Photo by Jie Li.

FIGURE 11.4. The Rest in Peace Garden in Shantou's Pagoda Park. Photo by Jie Li.

since 2006 Peng and some younger volunteers have held an annual memorial service to mourn the "20 million lives claimed by the Cultural Revolution"—taking up a well-known estimate made by Marshal Ye Jianying in 1978 that scholars have discredited—and for this purpose they built a special Rest in Peace Garden (Anxi Yuan 安息园) with a statue of Liu Shaoqi at the center and the names of thousands of victims carved into the surrounding walls (fig. 11.4).[59]

A "victim's museum" rather than a "collector's museum," Shantou's Pagoda Park has thus far survived between the cracks of official censorship. Its stone inscriptions explicitly indict Mao Zedong for the Cultural Revolution and other catastrophic mass movements, but such bold statements may also ring hollow in the absence or paucity of an audience. The Pagoda Park newsletter claims that the site receives two hundred thousand to three hundred thousand visitors every year, though I encountered only two other tourists when visiting in the summer of 2013. The local villagers who managed the park compared this Cultural Revolution memorial complex to a child whose growth has been stunted but who has not yet been strangled to death by the authorities in power. Though assisted by a number of younger volunteers, its aging founder still needs to find an adequate successor with enough political and symbolic capital to help Pagoda Park thrive in the future. More than transmitting historical memories to a younger generation, the museum stakes out an injunction to remember and demonstrates the possibility of memorializing the human cost of the Mao era against state-sponsored amnesia.

The Memories of Others: Curatorial Proposals

STUMBLING STONES

Imagine that, for every unnatural death in the Mao era, the bereaved family could set a stone into the pavement at the site of the death or close to the former residence of the deceased, no bigger than the size of a foot, with the name, the person's birth and death dates, perhaps a photograph, and a line or two on the cause of death. The stone would be small enough to be ignored, but as there would be hundreds, perhaps thousands, of such stones laid in the remnant *hutongs* of Beijing, the new leisure districts of Shanghai, and the main streets of small towns and villages—as omnipresent as the various door gods, wealth gods, and earth gods that have reemerged in the landscape in recent years—then the unassuming presence of each might add up to a kind of rosary of vigilant memory. Perhaps it does not have to be stones; the markers could also be tiny temples; or perhaps they could appear only on the Qingming Festival of Mourning, flickers of light to show an awareness of the former lives of the dead, especially those who died unjust, violent deaths. The wronged ghosts could be enshrined as little gods of history.

I cultivated this fantasy as I "stumbled" over countless small Holocaust memorial plaques, called "stumbling stones," on the sidewalks of busy urban centers and sparsely populated towns in Germany. Each handmade by a single artist, Gunter Demnig, these stumbling stones begin with the words "Here lived," followed by the person's name, year of birth, and place and year of death. Modestly unassuming and yet like a fishbone that sticks in one's throat, these stones commemorate victims of National Socialism directly in front of their last voluntary place of residence. Demnig began the project in 1996 and by 2014 had laid more than 45,000 stones, not only in Germany, but also in nearby countries, from the Netherlands to Hungary. Sponsored privately for the most part, each stone cost around 100 Euros including installation. The donor must secure a permit from the local government. After being laid, the stones often rouse a deeper interest in those named, giving rise to further historical research, especially among school classes.[60]

More than any monumental obelisk or giant museum, I find the stumbling stones an inspiring paradigm for future memorials in China that seek to acknowledge past victimhood and injustice, since they mourn the loss of a life without turning it into an ideological instrument, and since each stone can inspire a deeper interest in those named, in their respective neighborhoods. Although contested interpretations of history may not achieve consensus at the national level, local authorities could have some autonomy in creating memory places for Mao-era victims, so long as they are not too conspicuous. After all, the larger cultural and geographic landscape of China can still tolerate many more voices and memories than Tiananmen Square. Moreover, since stumbling stones are so small and cost so little, just about anyone can start a memorial initiative without having to amass an enormous fund or to apply for approval from the central government. Hence my advocacy for the stumbling stone memorial paradigm has to do with its representational and interpretative plurality as well as its concrete situation in local communities, where historical facts are also much easier to ascertain than statistics about millions of people nationwide.

One might argue that such specific memorials—as opposed to monuments that subsume individual plights under a larger national tragedy—can potentially divide rather than unite communities. This is a valid objection that stopped the post–Cultural Revolution investigations into individual tragedies, whose fresh wounds could feed a dangerous thirst for vindictive justice, yet the passage of time and politic forms of mourning could also allow reconciliation without repression. There is of course good reason to believe that any physical memorial, plaque, or sign marking these victims in public spaces would be quickly removed. Yet if the Chongqing cemetery and the Shantou museum have come to stay, one might surmise that negotiations between official and unofficial memories are possible, depending on the content, form, location, and timing of the intended memorials. Finally, those who object to the deemphasis of peasants' and workers' suffering under feudalism or capitalism could also use the stumbling stone model to remind us of pre- or postrevolutionary cruelties. What makes this model work is precisely its inclusion of different types of victimhood.

REAPPROPRIATING MAOIST TRACES

Just as the Chongqing Red Guard Graveyard came under heritage protection, remnant traces of the Mao era in the form of faded slogans and paintings on walls could also be preserved and annotated, thereby enhancing historical consciousness by highlighting a place's archaeological layers. Taking into account the rediscovered tourist value of such Mao-era traces, architects or city planners might allow in the design of every new construction some fragment or historical trace on the palimpsest of its walls. Instead of perfect restorations, even the visible damage on cultural relics or the "Four Olds" destroyed in the Cultural Revolution can serve as poignant historical testimonies. Where new designs cannot accommodate old ruins, one might photograph the ruins before they are torn down and then exhibit the pictures at the original sites.

Contemporary Chinese artists and filmmakers have appropriated forgotten relics and ruins of the Mao era, turning them into mementos through remediation and recontextualization. In the series *Mao on the Wall*, Wang Tong 王彤 photographed hundreds of faded Mao portraits found in the Henan countryside. Filmmakers Wang Bing, Jia Zhangke 贾樟柯, and Zhang Meng 张猛 have captured the ruins of socialist industry before their final demolition in acclaimed films such as *West of the Tracks* (*Tiexi qu* 铁西区, 2003), *24 City* (*Ershisi cheng ji* 二十四城记, 2008), and *The Piano in a Factory* (*Gang de Qin* 钢的琴, 2011). In his installation *Waste Not*, artist Song Dong 宋东 moved the entire contents of his mother's home—where everything from old shoes to toothpaste holders was indiscriminately hoarded and where many of the everyday artifacts were remains from the Mao era—into the Museum of Modern Art in New York. To borrow Svetlana Boym's comment on Ilya Kabakov's recreations of Soviet everyday life in a Soho gallery, Song Dong's collection "resembles Noah's ark, only we are never sure whether the artist escaped from hell or from paradise."[61]

While Chinese artists have rendered visible collective and personal memories of the Mao era through various media, conspicuously absent from the Chinese avant-garde art scene is *public memorial art*, conceived as a performance of encounters between visitors and the past, where the work is not just the object itself but a set of relationships among art, space, time, and audience.[62] Unlike popular or mass art, contemporary public art "does not assume a preexistent generic audience to be entertained or instructed but sets out to forge a specific public by means of an aesthetic interaction."[63] The political sensitivity of public art—say, the 1989 work *Goddess of Democracy* constructed during the protests in Tiananmen Square—might account for such an absence, yet city planners, historians, artists, entrepreneurs, and educators might also collaborate on public memorial projects that would "haunt" an amnesiac landscape and help people work through existing memories.

Contemporary artists and curators have successfully secured enclaves for private art in galleries, theaters, and cinemas. In such spaces, exhibitions could be curated around a specific historical topic rather than around a group of artists. One could have, for example, an exhibition on steel, consisting of old propaganda posters, a backyard steel furnace relic or reconstruction with samples of the household iron that was collected and the "steel" produced, a section on the steel industry and the lives of the workers, and other historical information on steel production in China. Involving archival research, imagination, and entrepreneurial spirit, such a project, as well as more site-specific exhibitions, could potentially involve university students in association with private art galleries.

Beyond artistic and educational spaces, public memory work may also take place in commodified spaces like Mao-era memorabilia markets, red-theme restaurants, and selected red tourism destinations that refer to the Mao era rather than to pre-1949 revolutionary history. Instead of dismissing the red nostalgia and kitsch industry as a form of amnesia, more curators might consider combining its commercial potential and distractive capacity with some historical and educational content. If a site happens to attract visitors in search of their own past, one might set up a memory-sharing corner, where people could be encouraged to leave their memories in writing or photos. This would mean moving beyond presenting history from a historian's perspective to sharing the work of interpretation with visitors; for example, instead of depersonalizing the meanings of objects collected, an exhibit might couple every artifact with a memory note or oral history from the former owner. With new media technologies, one might also cheaply create audiovisual tours of neighborhoods and other places that incorporate local oral histories and evoke vanished communities.

BAREFOOT HISTORIANS: REINVENT MAO-ERA PRACTICES AND DIG WHERE YOU STAND

As Yunxiang Yan points out in his study of a village in northeast China, decollectivization in the early 1980s quickened the demise of political participation and socialization through meetings and party-sponsored organizations, collective labor and benefits from public infrastructure projects, and community-based social and cultural activities like village performance troupes and organized volunteer work to help the elderly. With the demolition of collective spaces, villagers spent most of their leisure time in their homes, in front of the TV or at mahjong tables, leading to a "decline of public life." Surely, participation in public life in the Mao era was not entirely voluntary, and "the kind of sociality generated in this social space inevitably bore the imprint of the official ideology of the party-state."[64] Yet those who had grown accustomed to such public life in both rural and urban areas came to miss it sorely in the 1990s and 2000s, as readily manifested in the omnipresent spectacles of middle-aged and elderly people singing red songs from the Mao era in parks throughout China—a sight and sound that would probably be nightmarish for Ba Jin and is often cited as a symptom of amnesia. Nevertheless, I would like to suggest the possibility of reinventing some of these Mao-era public cultural practices into "positive" legacies to curate public and communal memory work—among them, turning "speaking bitterness" into intergenerational dialogue, turning Mao's call to "go among the masses" into the encouragement of "barefoot historians," and turning mobile movie projection into localized and indigenous cinema.

Throughout the Mao era, Communists investigated and compiled local case histories of class struggle and provided stages for public articulations of private histories—always molded into formulaic narratives of preliberation bitterness followed by postliberation sweetness. "Speaking bitterness" was a practice first used to denounce landlords during land reform; by the mid-1960s it became a means to pass on class hatred to younger generations. After Mao's death, scar literature and oral history collections like *Ten Years of Madness* (*Yibai ge ren de shinian* 一百个人的十年) by Feng Jicai 冯骥才 also gave Cultural Revolution victims opportunities to "speak bitterness." With the development of digital video technology in the past decade, China's independent documentary filmmakers have made many oral-history-based films, while Chinese TV programs now competing for audiences in a market economy have given voice to many vivid testimonies of suffering and survival through the Mao era. More than the *content* of such oral histories, the *practice* of elder generations in passing on stories to younger generations might be one aspect of "speaking bitterness" worth inheriting. To encourage such intergenerational dialogue, teachers and the mass media could launch essay or video competitions for young people to record the stories of their parents and grandparents. While the publication or exhibition of "winning works" might be heavily (self-)censored, it could still provide an otherwise "amnesiac" younger generation with some historical consciousness.

Another Maoist legacy that could be creatively transformed would be to encourage amateurism and grassroots initiatives to promote memory work among communities. During the Great Leap Forward, the Socialist Education Campaign, and the Cultural Revolution, many ordinary people, including peasants, workers, and students, filled up public spaces with big-character posters, murals, performances, and other kinds of revolutionary propaganda, sometimes also staging exhibitions of class struggle using artifacts confiscated from "class enemies," like the aforementioned Landlord Manor in Anren. From the 1950s to the 1970s, tens of thousands of mobile projection teams brought films to the rural masses and complemented film programs with handmade slideshows on local heroes, accompanied by live oral storytelling. While such exhibitions and performances were often full of fabrications and could serve as catalysts for revolutionary violence, it would not be altogether unreasonable to revive grassroots participation in curating local histories, possibly drawing alternative inspiration from the Western European local history workshops that sprang up in the 1970s and 1980s under mottoes like "people's history" or "dig where you stand." At work were not only academic historians but also "barefoot historians" interested in recovering the histories of forgotten marginal groups like peasants and workers.

One emergent example of a "barefoot historian" project was initiated by independent documentary filmmaker Wu Wenguang 吴文光 in his Beijing studio. The Folk Memory Documentary Project has, since 2010, dispatched young filmmakers to family villages to ask elderly people about the Great Leap Famine. The films chronicle their journeys to retrieve and transmit dying memories. In *Luo Village: Me and Ren Dingqi* (*Luojia wu: Wo he Ren Dingqi* 罗家屋: 我和任定齐, 2011), Luo Bing 罗兵 searches for an elusive memoir by his neighbor Grandpa Ren, while contemplating the meaning of memory in voiceover. Grandpa Ren introduces him to other survivors of the famine, whose halting, inchoate testimonies are often interrupted shrilly by their adult children. In *Satiated Village* (*Chibao de cunzi* 吃饱的村子, 2011), Zou Xueping 邹雪平, despite fierce opposition from her family, summons the elderly and the children of her village to watch screenings of the video testimonies she has collected on the famine, and to discuss whether the films can be screened abroad. For her next film *Children's Village* (*Haizi de cunzi* 孩子的村子, 2012), Zou mobilizes the village children to raise funds and collect the names and backgrounds of the village's famine victims in order to erect a tombstone and memorial for them.[65] The Folk Memory Project is not merely an archive compiled for its own sake—in fact, its academic historical value may be dubious—but each young filmmaker or barefoot historian manages to initiate a (mostly therapeutic) discussion about a traumatic past within his or her village that otherwise would not have taken place.

Conclusion

At the 2006 Chinese People's Political Consultative Conference, forty-eight delegates submitted a proposal for building an official Cultural Revolution museum. Invoking Ba Jin and expressing concern over both the amnesia surrounding Cultural Revolution and its playful mythification, the proposal called for a loosening of censorship in research and publishing as well as for a nationwide infrastructure to collect materials for future museums. Not surprisingly, the proposal received no response.[66] Another decade has gone by, and there are still no prospects of building a monumental Cultural Revolution museum in Beijing, but state-imposed amnesia is neither ubiquitous nor omnipotent. Thanks to the efforts of entrepreneurs and collectors, enlightened local officials and various survivor groups, artists and intellectuals, collective remembrances of the Mao era do not have to be either determined by the current political authority or hidden away among fading private lives.

Indeed, much more effective than any central memorial museum are the grassroots initiatives among individuals seeking to educate themselves and their communities about the layers of their national, regional, and communal past. Instead of prescribing how the Mao era should be represented in museums, the best memorial museums should not claim authoritative truth about the past but encourage and enable people to discover their own histories in all of their complexity. Local history organizations could collaborate with local museums to research and mount exhibitions, collect oral histories, petition for historical preservation, create or commission public art or memorials, launch and run historical city tours, edit newsletters and magazines, and provide pedagogical resources for schoolteachers.

Memories of the Mao era have been fragmented within survivor groups and rarely transgress generational boundaries.[67] For this reason, existing memory places rarely foster dialogues among groups in order to integrate the personal traumas from the Mao era with a larger national identity. Apart from occasional labor protests or petitioning campaigns, the memories of workers and peasants are rarely articulated in public, whereas in memoirs and other media, intellectuals, party cadres, former Red Guards, and sent-down youths recount their own stories of suffering and disillusionment. Promoting sympathy for other people's suffering and repentance for one's own complicity require appropriate places and occasions. There is no Chinese counterpart to South Africa's Truth and Reconciliation Commission, but more modest alternative processes might be created by the civil society. The creation of more productive and tactful memory places would counteract the tendency for each to remember her or his own victimhood while singling out guilty individuals. Think of the popular attraction in Chinese temples and shrines of writing down prayers and hanging them on a "wish tree." Now imagine an "atonement tree" or "a garden of truth and reconciliation" at, say, the Chongqing Red Guard Graveyard, where those with a bad conscience could write anonymous notes of penance. To counteract the underrepresentation of "proletariat memories," intellectuals and former sent-down youths could try to include the experiences of peasant "others" in any memorial projects devoted to their own experiences.

Given the Communist Party's persistent reluctance to break the taboo on its traumatic past, it may seem quixotic to hope for a plurality of public memorial sites where different memories of the Mao era could be shared, acknowledged, and reconciled. Still, taking Ba Jin's testament a step further, memorials and museums should not simply offer an official representation of history, but should be the outcome of a *public process* of working through the past. Surely, as Susanne Weigelin-Schwiedrzik points out, "the struggle over whose memory of the Cultural Revolution can dominate the overall assessment" is "not about respect" but "about power."[68] To this one could add James Young's insight that "memory is never shaped in a vacuum; the motives for memory are never pure."[69] Granted that contemporary politics and economics have had a profound impact on the memory landscape, there are and can be more places in today's China for public and collective remembrances of officially repressed histories—places that seek to be more *politic* than *political*. In addition to historical facts that are open to interpretation, good memory places should be concerned with "faithfulness to what *ought* to be remembered, what can *legitimately* be forgotten, and what *might* be forgiven."[70]

Notes

1. Ba Jin, "'Wenge' bowuguan" "文革" 博物馆 (A Cultural Revolution museum), in *Suixiang lu* 随想录 (Reflections) (Hong Kong: Sanlian shudian, 1988), pp. 601–4. An English translation of this essay is available at http://www.cnd.org/cr/english/articles/bajin.htm (accessed June 11, 2014).

2. See Song Yongyi 宋永毅, ed., *Wenhua da geming: Lishi zhenxiang he jiti jiyi* 文化大革命: 历史真相和集体记忆 (The Cultural Revolution: Historical truth and collective memory) (Hong Kong: Tianyuan shuwu, 2007), esp. pp. 916–40, 1004–16.

3. Ba Jin, "'Wenge' bowuguan," pp. 601, 603.

4. Ba Jin, "Yangbanxi" 样板戏 (Model operas), in *Suixiang lu*, pp. 594–96.

5. Ba Jin, "'Wenge' bowuguan," p. 603.

6. Written in 1986, Ye Yonglie's short story was first published in a science fiction magazine in Sichuan in 1988; in later republications it was renamed "'Wenge' bowuguan zhi meng" "文革"博物馆之梦 (Dream of a Cultural Revolution museum). The full text is available in the inaugural issue of the Virtual Museum of the Cultural Revolution website, at http://www.cnd.org/CR/ZK96/zk77-2.hz8.html (accessed June 11, 2014).

7. CCP Central Propaganda Department and State Press and Publication Administration, "Guanyu chuban 'wenhua dageming' tushu wenti de ruogan guiding"

关于出版“文化大革命”图书问题的若干规定 (Regulations governing the publication of books about the "Great Cultural Revolution"), in *Zhonghua renmin gongheguo xianxing xinwen chuban fagui huibian (1949–1990)* 中华人民共和国现行新闻出版法规汇编 (1949–1990), ed. PRC State Press and Publication Administration, Policy Laws and Regulations Section (Beijing: Renmin chubanshe, 1991), pp. 231–32. For an English translation, see Michael Schoenhals, ed., *China's Cultural Revolution, 1966–1969: Not a Dinner Party* (Armonk, NY: M. E. Sharpe, 1996), pp. 310–12.

8. Geremie Barmé, *Shades of Mao: The Posthumous Cult of the Great Leader* (Armonk, NY: M. E. Sharpe, 1996), pp. 3–74.

9. Melissa Schrift, *Biography of a Chairman Mao Badge: The Creation and Mass Consumption of a Personality Cult* (New Brunswick, NJ: Rutgers University Press, 2001), pp. 169–200.

10. Jennifer Hubbert, "Revolution Is a Dinner Party: Cultural Revolution Restaurants in Contemporary China," *China Review: An Interdisciplinary Journal on Greater China* 5, no. 2 (2005): 123–48.

11. Xu Ben 徐贲, "Quanqiu chuanmei shidai de wenge jiyi: Jiedu sanzhong wenge jiyi" 全球传媒时代的文革记忆：解读三种文革记忆 (Cultural Revolution memories in the age of global media: Reading three types of Cultural Revolution memories), in Song Yongyi, ed., *Wenhua da geming: Lishi zhenxiang he jiti jiyi* (Hong Kong: Tianyuan shuwu, 2007), pp. 916–40.

12. Yang Kelin 杨克林, ed., *Wenhua da geming bowuguan* 文化大革命博物馆 (Cultural Revolution museum) (Hong Kong: Dongfang chubanshe, 1995).

13. For an overview of Cultural Revolution studies and publications in Chinese, see Xu Youyu 徐友漁, "Wenge yanjiu zhi yipie: Lishi, xianzhuang he fangfa" 文革研究之一瞥: 历史，现状与方法 (A glimpse of Cultural Revolution studies: History, state of the Field, and methodologies," in Song Yongyi, ed., *Wenhua da geming: Lishi zhenxiang he jiti jiyi*, pp. 2–32. For a discussion of how some of these memoirs and histories provided an alternative historiography of the period, see Susanne Weigelin-Schwiedrzik, "Coping with the Trauma: Official and Unofficial Histories of the Cultural Revolution," unpublished paper, 2005, at http://www.univie.ac.at/Sinologie/repository/seGG430_OfficialAndUnoffHistCultRev/culturalRevolutionTrauma.pdf (accessed June 11, 2014).

14. For the website's English homepage, see http://www.cnd.org/CR/english/ (accessed June 11, 2014).

15. For an overview of virtual museums, see Guobin Yang, "A Portrait of Martyr Jiang Qing: The Chinese Cultural Revolution on the Internet," in *Re-envisioning the Chinese Revolution: The Politics and Poetics of Collective Memories in Reform China*, ed. Ching-Kwan Lee and Guobin Yang (Stanford, CA: Stanford University Press, 2007), pp. 245–86.

16. Jie Li, "Virtual Museums of Forbidden Memories: Hu Jie's Documentary Films on the Cultural Revolution," *Public Culture* 21, no. 3 (2009): 538–50.

17. Vera Schwarcz, "The Burden of Memory: The Cultural Revolution and the Holocaust," *China Information* 11, no. 1 (1996): 1–13. Supporters of the comparison cite resemblances between the euphoric support of the Chinese and of the German masses

for a savior-dictator, between the Night of Broken Glass (*Kristallnacht*) and the campaign to Smash the Four Olds, between concentration camps and *laogai* camps.

18. Kirk Denton, *Exhibiting the Past: Historical Memory and the Politics of Museums in Postsocialist China* (Honolulu: University of Hawai'i Press, 2014), p. 138.

19. Ian Buruma, "The Joys and Perils of Victimhood," *New York Review of Books* 46 (1999): 4–8.

20. Zhong Xueping, Wang Zheng, and Bai Di, eds., *Some of Us: Women Growing Up Under Mao* (New Brunswick, NJ: Rutgers University Press, 2001), p. xviii.

21. Yiching Wu, *The Cultural Revolution at the Margins: Chinese Socialism in Crisis* (Cambridge, MA: Harvard University Press, 2014).

22. Denton, *Exhibiting the Past*, pp, 1–26.

23. Ibid., pp. 73, 92.

24. *Rent Collection Courtyard: Sculptures of Oppression and Revolt* (Beijing: Foreign Languages Press, 1968), p. 5.

25. Wu Jinzhong 吴金钟, *Dayi Liu Wencai dizhu zhuangyuan* 大邑刘文彩地主庄园 (The Liu Wencai landlord manor of Dayi County) (Beijing: Wenwu chubanshe, 1992), p. 1; Maureen Hynes, *Letters from China* (Toronto: Women's Education Press, 1981), p. 109.

26. Britta Erickson, "The *Rent Collection Courtyard,* Past and Present," in *Art in Turmoil: The Chinese Cultural Revolution, 1966–1976*, ed. Richard King (Vancouver: University of British Columbia Press, 2010), pp. 121–35.

27. Xiaoshu 笑蜀, *Liu Wencai zhenxiang* 刘文彩真相 (The truth about Liu Wencai) (Xi'an: Shaanxi shifan daxue chubanshe, 1999).

28. See the most updated information on the Jianchuan Museum Cluster website, at http://www.jc-museum.cn/ (accessed June 15, 2014).

29. Fan Jianchuan 樊建川, *Daguan nu: Fan Jianchuan de jiyi yu mengxiang* 大馆奴: 樊建川的记忆与梦象 (Slave of big museums: Fan Jianchuan's memories and dreams) (Beijing: Sanlian, 2013), pp. 108–11.

30. Interview with Fan Jianchuan, August 26, 2013.

31. Fan Jianchuan, *Jianchuan bowuguan jieshouci* 建川博物馆解说词 (Narratives of the Jianchuan Museum), independently printed book, 2007, pp. 108–17.

32. On the manipulation of press photographs during the Great Leap, see Jin Yongquan 晋永权, *Hongqi zhaoxiangguan: 1956–1959 nian Zhongguo sheying zhengbian* 红旗照相馆: 1956–1959 年中国摄影争辩 (Red Flag Studio: Debates on China's photography: 1956–1959) (Beijing: Jincheng chubanshe, 2009). If it had not been for state censorship, the images of the Great Leap Forward in the Jianchuan Museum could have been complemented by population statistics from 1958 to 1962, and by an exhibit of the food ration coupons and what people ate to survive in those years.

33. Interview with Fan Jianchuan.

34. Michael Dutton, "From Culture Industry to Mao Industry: A Greek Tragedy," *boundary 2* 32, no. 2 (2005): 165–66.

35. For a typical visitor comment, see http://blog.sina.com.cn/s/blog_53687c870100ft3j.html (accessed June 15, 2014).

36. Andreas Huyssen, *Present Pasts: Urban Palimpsests and the Politics of Memory* (Stanford, CA: Stanford University Press, 2003), pp. 19–21.

37. Charity Scribner, "Left Melancholy," in *Loss: The Politics of Mourning*, ed. David L. Eng (Berkeley: University of California Press, 2003), pp. 303–5.

38. *Zhongguo Anrenzhen Jianchuan bowuguan juluo* 中国安仁镇建川博物馆聚落 (China's Anren Town Jianchuan Museum Cluster), independently printed catalogue, 2009, pp. 78–130.

39. A blogger has posted recent photos of this former People's Commune transformed into a museum, at http://blog.sina.com.cn/s/blog_5fb0372e0101mhpe.html (accessed June 20, 2014).

40. See Yang Xianhui, *Woman from Shanghai: Tales of Survival from a Chinese Labor Camp* (New York: Pantheon Books, 2009); Gao Ertai, *In Search of My Homeland: A Memoir of a Chinese Labor Camp* (New York: Ecco Press, 2009).

41. Klaus Mühlhahn, *Criminal Justice in China: A History* (Cambridge, MA: Harvard University Press, 2009), p. 270.

42. The following blogs feature visitor "travelogues" about Jiabiangou, with photographs and texts (all accessed June 17, 2014), at http://blog.sina.com.cn/s/blog_47e34d690102e1hs.html (trip taken in 2003); http://jqgsy.blog.163.com/blog/static/1089263432009926519438o3/ (trip taken in 2003); http://tsrb.gansudaily.com.cn/system/2007/07/30/010426537.shtml (trip taken in 2007).

43. He Fengming, *Jingli: Wo de 1957 nian* 经历: 我的1957年 (Experiences: My 1957) (Lanzhou: Dunhuang wenyi chubanshe, 2001).

44. Fengming's story recalls one of the oldest stories about memory in Western tradition. The Greek poet Simonides, credited by Cicero as the "inventor of memory," was once invited to a banquet at a nobleman's palace. When Simonides stepped outside briefly, the ceiling of the palace suddenly collapsed and crushed the bodies of the victims inside such that their relatives could not identify them. However, Simonides, who survived, remembered where each one had been sitting at the table, so the relatives were able to bury their dead after all. See Frances Yates, *The Art of Memory* (Chicago: University of Chicago Press, 1966), pp. 1–2.

45. James Young, *The Texture of Memory* (New Haven, CT: Yale University Press, 1993), p. 119.

46. See the travel blogs cited earlier.

47. Frank N. Pieke and Hein Mallee, eds., *Internal and International Migration: Chinese Perspectives* (Richmond, Surrey, UK: Curzon, 1999), pp. 41–42.

48. Hu Jie, *Guoying dongfeng nongchang* 国营东风农场 (East Wind State Farm), documentary film, 2009.

49. A virtual tour of the museum in video format is available at http://www.tudou.com/programs/view/RslRcj8b5JI/?fr=rec1 (accessed June 17, 2014).

50. Li Chengwai was kind enough to give me a tour of the site and show me his collection in January 2013. See his blog for the most recent developments on the site, at http://blog.sina.com.cn/wcltzw (accessed June 15, 2014).

51. For a well-researched journalistic account of the former cadre school's history until 2009, see Zhong Gang 钟刚, "Xiangyanghu wuqi ganxiao manchang de kaifa zhilu" 向阳湖五七干校漫长的开发之路 (The long path of development for Xiang-

yanghu May Seventh Cadre School), *Nanfang dushibao*, April 26, 2009, at http://epaper.oeeee.com/C/html/2009-04/26/content_771431.htm (accessed June 15, 2014).

52. These controversies are collected in Li Chengwai, ed., *Xiangyanghu wenhua yanjiu* 向阳湖文化研究 (Studies of Xiangyanghu culture) (Wuhan: Wuhan chubanshe, 2010), pp. 338–78.

53. Philip Pan, *Out of Mao's Shadow: The Struggle for the Soul of a New China* (New York: Simon & Schuster, 2008), pp. 81–112.

54. Ibid., p. 110.

55. Everett Y. Zhang, "Grieving at Chongqing's Red Guard Graveyard: In the Name of Life Itself," *China Journal* 70 (2013): 24–47.

56. Also see Edward Wong, "Repackaging the Revolutionary Classics of China," *New York Times*, June 29, 2011.

57. Ke Peizhong 柯培忠, ed., *Shantou Denghai tayuan wenge bowuguan ziliaoji zhiyi* 汕头澄海塔园文革博物馆资料集之一 (Shantou Denghai Pagoda Park Cultural Revolution Museum sourcebook one), independently printed book, 2006, pp. 246–53. For a virtual tour of the Pagoda Park Museum in Shantou through a former visitor's blog, see http://stfmlx.blog.hexun.com/36508393_d.html (accessed June 20, 2014).

58. *Tayuan dongtai* 塔园动态 (Developments at Pagoda Park), independently printed book, 2012.

59. For various scholarly estimates of the Cultural Revolution's death toll, see Song Yongyi, "Chronology of Mass Killings during the Chinese Cultural Revolution (1966–1976)," *Online Encyclopedia of Mass Violence*, at http://www.massviolence.org/Chronology-of-Mass-Killings-during-the-Chinese-Cultural, August 25, 2011 (accessed June 28, 2014).

60. Monika Richarz, "Stumbling Stones: Marks of Holocaust Memory on German Streets," in *Mediating Modernity: Challenges and Trends in the Jewish Encounter with the Modern World*, ed. Lauren Strauss and Michael Brenner (Detroit: Wayne State University Press, 2008), pp. 325–38.

61. Svetlana Boym, *The Future of Nostalgia* (New York: Basic Books, 2001), p. 311.

62. Jiang Jiehong, ed., *Burden or Legacy: From the Chinese Cultural Revolution to Contemporary Art* (Hong Kong: Hong Kong University Press, 2007).

63. Hilde Hein, *Public Art: Thinking Museums Differently* (Lanham, MD: AltaMira Press, 2006), p. 49.

64. Yunxiang Yan, *Private Life under Socialism: Love, Intimacy, and Family Change in a Chinese Village* (Stanford, CA: Stanford University Press, 2003), pp. 232–35.

65. For an extensive account of the Folk Memory Project, see Jiayun Zhuang, "Remembering and Reenacting Hunger," *TDR: The Drama Review* 58, no. 1 (2014): T221.

66. Entitled "Fansi lishi, chuangzao tiaojian, choujian wenge bowuguan" 反思历史, 创造条件, 筹建文革博物馆 (Reflect on history, create conditions for the construction of a Cultural Revolution museum), at http://blog.sina.com.cn/s/blog_5408ee850100009ql.html (accessed June 14, 2014).

67. Susanne Weigelin-Schwiedrzik, "In Search of a Master Narrative for 20th-Century Chinese History," *China Quarterly* 188 (2006): 1089.

68. Ibid., p. 1091; also see Mobo Gao, "The Battle for China's Past: Mao and the Cultural Revolution," *China Quarterly* 195 (2008): 691–718.

69. Young, *The Texture of Memory*, p. 2.

70. This formulation is borrowed from Hayden White's review of Paul Ricoeur, *Memory, History, Forgetting*; see Hayden White, "Guilty of History? The *Longue Durée* of Paul Ricoeur," *History and Theory* 46 (May 2007): 238; emphasis in the original.

TWELVE

RED ALLURE AND THE CRIMSON BLINDFOLD

Geremie R. Barmé

This chapter discusses a few areas in which I believe we can find traces of the abiding, and beguiling, heritage of the Maoist era and state socialism in today's China.[1] In a number of interconnected spheres, a nuanced understanding of what have been called "red legacies" in China, as well as more broadly, can continue to enliven discussions of contemporary history, thought, culture, and politics. In the following I will focus on recent events before offering, in turn, some observations on history, the Maoist legacy, and academic engagement with the People's Republic.

Over the years, I have argued that the aura of High Maoism (1949–78) has continued to suffuse many aspects of thought, expression, and behavior in contemporary China.[2] This is not merely because the party-state of the People's Republic still formalistically cleaves to the panoply of Marxist-Leninist–Mao Zedong Thought (which it has elaborated upon through the addition of Deng Xiaoping Theory, Jiang Zemin's "Three Represents," and Hu Jintao's "Scientific Outlook on Development"). Just as High Maoism was very much part of global revolutionary discourse and thinking in the twentieth century, so in the post-Mao decades its complex legacies, be they linguistic, intellectual, charismatic, or systemic, continue to enjoy a purchase. Furthermore, having an understanding of Maoism in history and over time, both in terms of empirical reality and in the context of memory, as well as an appreciation of its lingering allure, remains crucial if we are to gain an appreciation of the "real existing socialism" in the People's Republic today.

The Red Patrimony

It is important to begin by situating the "red moment" within the context of an extended, and changing, historical narrative. While some recent work has noted the "long tail" of Maoist-era institutional practice, I would affirm earlier scholarship that locates the origins and evolution of what would become High Maoism from the 1950s in the cultural and political genealogies of the late Qing and Republican eras.[3] To this age of revolution we should also be mindful of adding a longer and overlapping age of reform, one that to all intents and purposes has enjoyed a longue durée: from the externally generated and autocratically imposed reforms, or self-strengthening, of the Tongzhi Restoration dating from 1860, through to the open-door and reform policies formally initiated by the Chinese Communist Party in late 1978.

When discussing China's historical legacy, we are usually invited by the Chinese party-state to accept a certain narrative arc and its particular official articulation.[4] It is the story not of Chinese greatness as much as the connected tale of the decline in power, economic might, and unity of the Chinese world from the eighteenth century through the century of humiliation (roughly 1840–1949) and the birth of New China and the two acts of liberation (1949 and 1978). This culminates in the present with the "great renaissance of the Chinese nation" (*Zhonghua minzu de weida fuxing* 中华民族的伟大复兴) formally announced by General Secretary Jiang Zemin more than a decade ago and repeatedly affirmed by General Secretary Hu Jintao on the occasion of the celebration of the sixtieth anniversary of the People's Republic, as well as when he marked the centenary of the 1911 Xinhai Revolution on October 9, 2011.[5] It is in this connected narrative that "The China Story" (*Zhongguo de gushi* 中国的故事), itself a relatively recent conceit, has been concocted.[6] It is a story that has been interwoven intimately with the grand romantic narrative of communism. This narrative speaks to the history of the party in the context of national revolution and independence, and it cleaves to Mao Zedong (and a panoply of lesser leaders) as well as to many aspects of his career, thought, and politics. Although the Communist Party–centric version of that narrative may appear to many to be politically bankrupt in all but name, the appeal of an overarching existential rationale for the power-holders, and indeed for people of various backgrounds who have been immersed in the carefully modulated party-state account of China's past, remains undiminished.

One of the most abiding legacies of the red era, and one particularly attractive for its advocates regardless of their present political persuasion, is the paradigm of the Cold War. In the eternal present of Cold War attitudes and rhetoric, the panoply of devices carefully cultivated during the era of class struggle is easily translated into the tensions between the People's Republic of China and its neighbors as well as other developed nations today. The rhetorical landscape in which the party-state and those in its thrall (from state think-tank apparatchiki and a swarm of left-leaning academics to semi-independent media writers) traverse comfortably also feeds the mimetic grandstanding of the other side in any given stoush.

Since 2009, rhetorical clashes of this kind have revolved around such issues as climate change, U.S. arms sales to Taiwan, the valuation of the renminbi, Internet freedom, territorial issues in the South China Sea, and ongoing disturbances in Tibet and Xinjiang.[7] These issues—and here I am concerned with Chinese rhetoric, not the substantive matters involving different national and economic interests—the default position of the Chinese party-state remains that of the early Maoist days when conspiracy theories, class struggle, and overblown rhetorical grandstanding formed the backdrop to any official stance.[8] Of course, any discussion of rhetorical opposition cannot detract from real clashes among national interests, worldviews, or political and economic systems.

The Maoist past continues to shape perceptions and discursive practices in the cultural-linguistic realm of China today. Elsewhere, I have noted that the language of "totalitarianism" (that is, holistic or totalizing systems in which the party-state—in particular its leaders and theorists—attempts to dominate and determine ideological visions and linguistic practices, as well as social, political, and economic policy), as it evolved over many years, came to operate according to rules and an internal logic that aid and abet a thought process conducive to its continued sway.[9] In the past, this attempt at *Gleichschaltung*—the coordination or "intermeshing" of the inner and outer individual, as well as the various arms and practices of governance—was part of the construction of the socialist enterprise and the "new socialist man." Today, the situation is far more complex, as elements of socialism are melded with neoliberalism, and the New China Newspeak of the party-state has been injected with the discursive practices of global managerialism.[10]

In the decades of its ascendancy, as well in the subsequent long years of tenacious reform, the totalitarian in China has exhibited an intriguing versatility, whereby it has continued to "commodify" or "domesticate" to its particular ends culture, ideas, and even oppositionist forces.[11]

We may well ask, however, has revolutionary politics, or even the potency of left-leaning ideas, been entirely evacuated from this story today? Has the neoliberal turn of Chinese statist politics of recent decades created less a story of revolutionary potential (or even leftist resistance) and more one that offers an account of self-interest constructed around a concocted "Chinese race," the main concern of which is a nationalistic rise on the world stage? Or do the various red legacies that date from the Republican era (Communist, socialist, or social-democratic) contribute something more than a turn of phrase, a glossy overlay of party culture, and a coherent (and now often glib) account of national decline and revival to China's political discourse and national mission? If so, then how does the leftist legacy distinguish itself from a failed Maoism? Or is Maoism and its panoply of language and practice the only viable source of resistance besides the discourses of universalism, as well as economic and human rights, in China today?

In discussing the past, it is of vital importance to appreciate motivating ideas and ideals; by the same token, we should be wary of those who would separate for their convenience theory from historical reality (even if the details of that reality may be contested). Some writers on contemporary China and its tangle of traditions find it enticing to engage in what could be called a "strategic disaggregation" of the ideological/theoretical from the historical/lived. Without a doubt, it is important for thoughtful academics to challenge the crude narratives related to modern Chinese history, whether they are authored by the Chinese party-state, by the international media, or indeed by a Cold War–inflected academic world. In the process, however, equally ham-fisted attempts to "recuperate" elements of Maoism or Chinese-inflected Marxism-Leninism in the context of the one-party state can too easily allow people to champion abstract ideas clear of the bloody and tragic realities of the past. Similarly, to privilege Maoism while overlooking the other leftist traditions, the "paths not taken" owing to the hegemony of the Chinese Communist Party, is to view the past with the same kind of ideological bias of which pro-Maoist writers accuse their liberal and neoliberal opponents.

In the following, I first touch briefly on recent events and their background, before going on to consider historical narrative, cultural phenomena, and intellectual careerism.

A Red Star Falls over China: Lessons from Chongqing

The red patrimony—and indeed it is mostly the construction of male thinkers, activists, and power-holders—contains within it a whole range of intellectual artifacts from various points in China's revolutionary theory and practice. The generation of "enemies" (*pace* Carl Schmitt and his contemporary acolytes) and the atmospherics of plots and conspiracies are still central to the way that the Chinese Communist Party channels and responds to the specters of the past. Although this formerly underground political party has recast itself as a legitimate government (*zhizhengdang* 执政党) with all the paraphernalia of state power, to this day its internal protocols and behavior recall all too frequently its long history as a covert, highly secretive, and faction-ridden organization. Even under Mao, some commentators called China a "mafia state." This aspect of the party-state was thrown into sharp relief in February 2012 when the former deputy mayor of Chongqing, Wang Lijun 王立军, a man famed for a time for having led the attack on that city's own "mafias," was ordered to undergo a euphemistically termed "extended period of therapeutic rest" (*xiujiashi zhiliao* 休假式治疗) following his appearance at, and subsequent disappearance from, the U.S. consulate in Chengdu, Sichuan Province (subsequently the "treatment" became detention and investigation). The next month, on March 15, his erstwhile local party leader, Bo Xilai 薄熙来, was dismissed from his various positions and put under investigation.

On March 14, 2012, a day before the sensational news of Bo Xilai's fall was announced, Premier Wen Jiabao, speaking at what would be his last press conference as the head of China's government, twice referred to the 1981 Communist Party decision on "Certain Questions in the History of Our Party."[12] That document is one of key importance for an understanding of post-Mao Chinese politics; it also provides the ideological rationale for China's post-1978 economic reforms. In that carefully worded text the socioeconomic policies that had underpinned the Mao era, including the Great Leap Forward and the Cultural Revolution, were formally negated. In March 2012, Wen referred to the 1981 decision in the following way:

> I want to say a few words at this point, since the founding of the People's Republic of China, under the leadership of the Party and the government, our country's modernization drive has made great achievements. Yet at the same time, we've also taken detours and have learnt hard lessons. Since the Third Plenum of the 11th CPC Central Committee [in December 1978], in particular since the central authorities took the decision on the correct handling of relevant historical issues, we have established the line of thinking that we should free our minds and seek truth from facts and we have formulated the basic guidelines of our Party. In particular, we've taken the major decision of conducting reform and opening up in China, a decision that's crucial for China's future and destiny. What has happened shows that any practice that we take must be based on the experience and lessons we've gained from history and it must serve the people's interests. The practice that we take must be able to stand the test of history and I believe the people fully recognize this point and I have full confidence in our future.[13]

More than a year before Bo Xilai was put under investigation for breaching party discipline, there were overt signs that ideological contestation and a concomitant power struggle were well under way. Since the last major public power struggle within the CCP more than two decades earlier, in 1989, it has become an accepted view of China's particular brand of one-party consensual authoritarianism that, prior to any leadership change, jostling for position within the top echelon of the hierarchy takes a number of forms. While it is all but impossible to track effectively the backroom dealings, power plays, and political feints involved in what is a byzantine process, the media still provide some indication of the nature of intraparty tussles—although Zhongnanhai-ology remains at best an imaginative art. Nonetheless, given the volubility of various critics of the party since 2009, by early 2011 observers were wondering what had happened to the usually outspoken organs of the party's Central Committee.

In late May 2011, the CCP did finally make itself heard over the din of fraught contestation. In an opinion piece published by the Central Discipline Commission on May 25, party members were warned to obey "political discipline" and to cease thenceforth from offering unsolicited and wayward views on China's political future. It declared that a "profound political struggle" presently was confronting the party; it was time to silence idle speculation, and furthermore it was necessary to reiterate General Secretary Hu Jintao's "Six Absolute Interdictions" (*liuge jue bu yunxu* 六个决不允许) for party members—basically, follow the party line and do not engage in public discussions or offer personal opinions; do not fabricate or spread political gossip; and do not leak state secrets or participate in illegal organizations.[14]

The document noted that there were those who were "pursuing their own agendas in regard to party policy and requirements, all the while making a show of being in step with the party; others had been taken in by various stories they pick up, indulge in idle speculation, and generate 'political rumors.'" Furthermore, it warned that dissenting party voices were leading to (disruptive) nonparty and international speculation about the Communist Party's leadership and its future. In other words, it could damage the national economy. In 2011–12, the issues of the Maoist legacy were not matters merely of academic interest; they directly impinged on the party-state's succession plans and more broadly on contending agendas for China's future direction both at home and internationally. One particular area of contention related to how the Maoist past could, and indeed should, contribute to China's future.

Metaphors of History: Rumors and Factions

More broadly, the events of Chongqing reveal a distinct political culture with its own specific history, one that reaches back into the High Maoist, Republican, and imperial eras. It is significant that Bo Xilai's own promotion of "red culture" included "red reading" that encouraged officials and citizens to "read the classics" covering thinkers and works from all of these periods. As rumors circulated—and were energetically denied or dismissed by the authorities—one was reminded of previous episodes in Communist Party history during which rumormongering, talk of corruption, and the crushing of dissent were rife. Of course, there is the earliest story, related to the writer Wang Shiwei. A critic of party privilege in the Yan'an period during the early 1940s, he was branded a Trotskyite and a traitor. Eventually he was beheaded.[15]

Political rumors (*zhengzhi yaoyan* 政治谣言) featured during various crucial periods in the People's Republic as well, in particular during the Maoist years. Given the party's control over the media and the secretive nature of its political processes, gossip and rumors have long been the stuff of informal comment on the issues of the day, and the means by which alternative accounts of party rule have circulated. For example, after the founding of the People's Republic, when Mao called on intellectuals and others to help the party "rectify its work style" in light of criticisms of party rule in the Eastern Bloc in 1956, many took advantage of the invitation to speak out against the secretive privileges and power of party cadres. They too were silenced. In 1966, when Red Guard rebels were first allowed to attack the party, they identified privilege, corruption, and abuse of power as the greatest enemies of the revolution. During this period of party civil war, word of mouth and big-character posters were the means commonly employed by individuals and groups to speculate and denounce. Again, around the time of Lin Biao's fall in 1971, there was a campaign against political hearsay involving Jiang Qing and her famous interviews with Roxane Witke. Following Deng Xiaoping's fall in April 1976, the "strange talk and odd ideas" (*qitan guailun* 奇谈怪论) of July to September 1975 were denounced by the official media. Then, shortly after Mao's death, when there was a period of relatively free criticism of the purged party leaders blamed for the mayhem of the Cultural Revolution, privilege and corruption were identified once more as the greatest threat. Another period of political speculation followed shortly thereafter, at the time of the Xidan Democracy Wall in 1978–79, and again in 1988–89 leading up to June Fourth, when rumors and speculation were rife. During the 1989 nationwide protests, some protesters released a detailed account of the connection between party bureaucrats, their children, and the new business ventures that had sprung up during the early stages of reform. (One of the party leaders named and blamed for the corrupt nexus between party power, private enterprise, and global capital was Zhao Ziyang, later ousted as general secretary.) Even from this cursory sketch, we notice that intensified political gossip and official attempts to silence it have been the hallmarks of ruptures in Chinese life for more than six decades. Thus it was no surprise that, shortly following the announcement of disciplinary and legal investigations into Bo Xilai and his wife, Gu Kailai, in April 2012, the authorities announced a new push to quell political rumormongering. On April 16, the *People's Daily* denied rumors of a coup and that military vehicles had been deployed in the capital.[16] In the days that followed, a series of denials and articles decrying the malign influence of rumormongering were published both in the national and local media.[17]

The political culture of historical inference—or, to borrow a formulation familiar from the period of High Maoism, "using the past to satirize the present" *jie gu feng jin* 借古讽今, or at least using the past to reflect on the present *yu jin* 喻今, is still familiar not only to writers who grew up in the days of Maoism and its official disavowal (1978–80s) but also to writers today. One could argue that historical metaphors are part of the fabric of Chinese social and cultural life that far predates the Mao era.[18] There is no doubt that finding esoteric meanings, clues to contemporary politics, messages for the masses, and so on in plays, novels, and movies, was a central feature of Mao-era politics and cultural life. During the post–Cultural Revolution disavowal of the politics of purges and mass campaigns, this use of history and culture was decried as being a "historiography by [political] inference" (*yingshe shixue* 影射史学).

Despite this, in the penumbra of politics a popular market for revelations about the inner workings of power continues to this day, something evident recently in the wave of microblog comments on the Chinese Internet surrounding Bo Xilai as well as his immediate and extended family. Rumors have a venerable history in modern China. At the end of the Qing dynasty, for example, rumors about court politics abounded. They filled accounts known as "wild" or "untamed histories" (*yeshi* 野史), and they provided an alternative to the formal records of the time. While the new Republican government appointed a bureau to oversee the writing of a formal Qing history (a controversial and flawed enterprise that produced a *Draft History of the Qing* 清史稿), unofficial or "wild histories" proliferated. As the historian Harold Kahn has noted: "Official history adjusted the record to suit the needs of the court; unofficial history embroidered it to meet the tastes of a broader, less discriminating public. And it is this embroidered record which has formed the stable of much of China's popular historical thought."[19] Shortly following the founding of the Republic of China in 1912, scabrous revelations about the inner workings of the defunct imperial court, as well as speculation regarding some of the most notorious incidents in the Qing dynasty, became the stuff of popular history writing and literature. There were, for example, stories about the rumored marriage between the empress dowager Xiaozhuang 孝庄 (d. 1688) and her brother-in-law Dorgon 多尔衮; details of the usurpation of the throne by imperial prince Yinzhen 胤祯 following the death of his father, the Kangxi 康熙 emperor; hearsay to do with the Yongzheng 雍正 emperor's sudden demise; discussions about the questionable relationship between the minister Hešen 和珅 and the Qianlong 乾隆 emperor; details related to the invasion of the Forbidden City during the Jiaqing 嘉庆 reign; lascivious accounts of the addictions (and afflictions) of the youthful Tongzhi 同治 emperor in the 1870s; talk about what went on between the Empress Dowager and the eunuch Li Lianying 李莲英; dark mutterings surrounding the mysterious demise of the Guangxu emperor (光绪), who predeceased the Empress Dowager by a day; and so on. What were elicit unofficial accounts in the past provided fodder for readers who had access to the booming publishing market and, with due consideration of the anti-Qing sentiment of the early Republic, were anxious to see fun made of the defunct imperial masters while at the same time indulging in patriotic entertainment.

After 1949, the modern tradition of employing fiction or unofficial histories to reveal and speculate on the inner workings of China's rulers (not only dynastic, but also Republican and eventually Communist) continued to flourish, but in Hong Kong. That is, until political relaxation and a commercial publishing boom from the late 1970s transformed the media landscape in both China and Taiwan. It is also perhaps hardly a coincidence that the first, albeit unsuccessful, cultural campaign of Maoist China was also one that involved historical verdicts and revelations of inner-court wrangling. This was the criticism that Mao Zedong launched, shortly after the founding of the People's Republic, of the Hong Kong film *The Secret History of the Qing Court* (*Qinggong mishi* 清宫秘史, 1948).[20]

The very culture of emperors, kings, ministers, and generals (*diwang jiangxiang* 帝王将相), as well as that of talented scholars and beauties (*caizi jiaren* 才子佳人), collectively excoriated in the early years of the People's Republic and then actively denounced as part of the prelude to the Cultural Revolution era, has since the 1980s become part of the mainstream once more. The production of Chinese historical costume dramas had previously been the province of television and film in Hong Kong and Taiwan. But in the 1990s, as a result of voracious TV audiences and a political environment that was more willing to accept the previously excoriated "feudal" past, numerous new accounts of the imperial era appeared in the form of "fanciful accounts" (*xishuo* 戏说) of emperors and empresses in their youth, at the height of their power, and in their dotage. One of the first of these was the 1991 Taiwan-mainland coproduction *A Fanciful Account of Qianlong* (*Xishuo Qianlong* 戏说乾隆), a forty-one-part TV series about the Qianlong emperor's Tours of the South, based on a fictional account of the ruler's supposed exploits during three of his provincial progresses.[21] The "fanciful account" genre would eventually become a version of historical narrative characterized by semi- or completely farcical recountings of historical incidents, figures, or even past fictions for the sake of popular entertainment. Films and TV shows in this semiparodic style would proliferate.

The recapturing of the past through such humorous and often lubricious fictions was liberating, and it appeared to challenge the historical schema formalized during the early decades of the People's Republic. However, the actual story may be somewhat more complex. The rehabilitation of traditional history and storytelling, in particular in the form of popular history, since the advent of policies to promote "spiritual civilization" first raised in 1979 and then pursued from the mid-1980s, serves well the political status quo. This is because the revival of the past is still, for the most part, expected to conform to the contours of national history as delineated in the Mao-era temporal landscape. This timescape was itself developed over many decades on the basis of debates about Chinese history, periodization, economic development, and social change, from the time of the New Culture Movement (roughly 1917–27).[22] Popular accounts of the imperial past aided the party's overarching efforts to reintegrate the history of dynastic China, and the country's greatness, into the modern record and the broad narrative of national revival.

The popular fictionalization of history, however, has hardly been limited to the dynastic past, nor has it simply accorded with official dictates. Film and fictional accounts of both Republican and Communist Party history accord with guidelines set down by party historians and propagandists. This policing of the past has been particularly prevalent since an incident in 2003 involving the multiepisode TV series *Toward the Republic* 走向共和. Produced to mark the 1911 Xinhai

Revolution and the founding of the Republic of China, the series was, at first glance, a relatively standard costume drama, mixing elements of theatricality with serious history. The writers of *Toward the Republic*, who included liberal Qing historians, offered a view of the 1911 Revolution that not only challenged the party's interpretation of the past but also was an indictment of its present autocratic behavior.

The sixty-part series has a finale in which the father of the nation, Sun Yat-sen, appears to be addressing the viewing audience directly. As he explains the symbolism of what we know as the Mao suit (*Zhongshan zhuang* 中山装), or Sun Yat-sen jacket, Sun describes each of the buttons and pockets of the garment as representing parts of his political program—economic progress, democratization, and the separation of powers. He then addresses the viewer:

> I have thought long and deep in recent times: how is it that so many feudalistic and autocratic things have appeared time and again in our new Republic? If this is not dealt with, it is inevitable that the autocracy will reign once more; the Republic will forever be but a mirage. The idea of a Republic is based on equality, freedom, and the love of humanity. But over the past six years we have been witness to how government bureaucrats at every level have treated the law like dirt; how the people have been enslaved.
>
> A Republic should be a place of freedom; freedom is the heaven-given right of the people. But over these six years we have witnessed the power-holders enjoying freedom. The more power you have, the more freedom you enjoy; the less power you have, the more circumscribed your freedom. The people have no power, so they have no freedom. . . .
>
> The Republic should be governed by the rule of law. But over the past six years we have seen administrative power used repeatedly to interfere with the operation of the law. If you are not obedient, I'll buy you off; if you fail to comply, I will arrest you, or have you killed. Lawmakers have been prostituted by the power-holders and they have their way at will.[23]

When the series was rebroadcast, this material had been removed. As a result of the controversy surrounding *Toward the Republic*, in 2004 the State Administration of Radio, Film, and Television established a new oversight group to police the production and censoring of all materials related not only to the revolution but to history overall.[24] It was this same government group that in early 2011, as rumors and power plays swelled in Beijing and elsewhere, placed a ban on films and TV shows that speculated either about the past or the future. As political rumor-mongering unsettled party equanimity, the possibility that people could contemplate alternative scenarios for China also seemed unsettling. In particular, shows featuring time travel (known as *chuanyue ju* 穿越剧) were interdicted because they "lack positive thoughts and meaning" and go "against Chinese heritage."[25]

As issues related to democracy and authoritarianism are debated today, we can also detect a nostalgia for a past in which a different kind of future was imagined, as opposed to a present in which the past is constantly being marshaled, trimmed, and massaged to legitimate the party. As film and TV accounts of the past proliferated through the 1990s and into the new millennium, a new category of revived culture appeared, that of the red classic (*hongse jingdian* 红色经典). First promoted as part of the patriotic education campaign instituted following the events of 1989 to teach both students and wider audiences about the history of the revolution and the dangers that had beset it and continued to do so, so-called red classics, or old propaganda movies, were rebroadcast nationwide. In more recent years as media offerings have proliferated, a new genre of culture has developed under the old rubric of the red classic. This category includes not only films and TV shows but also songs, novels, poems, and artworks. Collectively, they form a narrative of revolution that has been stripped of revolutionary politics but retains a highly romantic depiction of the past and its achievements, in which the glories of the party are intertwined with accounts of heroism, love, sacrifice, and noble aspiration.

Until the appearance of the "sing red" campaign championed by Chongqing party secretary Bo Xilai and his supporters in 2009, the red classic genre was easily derided as being of marginal interest and importance for understanding contemporary China and its worldview. I would ask, rather, a series of questions:

> Is the corpus of red classic works merely fodder for the avaricious maw of a media market that must work with the material available, and as such is it of little significance?
>
> Or is it part of the very skein of modern mainland Chinese culture that through repetition and adaptation has normalized the historical narrative of the modern party-state? And, if that is the case (even partially),

Does the depoliticized narrative of the revolution not cannily employ petit-bourgeois sentimentality as a means to disallow audiences from imagining significant social change?[26]

Is there some greater, more "progressive" potential in the repetition of familiar cultural "classics," so much so that in fact these works refamiliarize audiences with the revolution, its values and rhetoric, so that concepts of social justice, fairness, and freedom that were so important during the long years of struggle before 1949 find a new lease on life?

Or should these concerns be swept aside, as it is all just commercialized fun and a story about canny media players cynically taking advantage of party-state dictates to promote and produce uncontroversial material?

Is this yet another chapter in the degradation of the sublime (*chonggao* 崇高) that the novelist and former minister of culture Wang Meng 王蒙 decried in the 1990s?

Or, perhaps, can we detect in the remakings, spoofs, and recountings of High Maoist policies cultural styles and ways in which the impotent, powerless, and dispossessed can express opposition to the eternalizing presumption of a party-state, one that maintains its dominion over the mainstream historical narrative, national identity, and real political power?

Is this "resistance within" not also part of the red legacy—the opposition to the party's theory-led monopoly on discourse, ideas, and everyday politics?

Waving the Red Flag to Oppose the Red Flag: Red Heirs and Intellectuals

History, distorted accounts of the past, and the power of metaphor have all played a role in the unfolding of recent Chinese political dramas, just as they have engaged with the Maoist legacy in complex ways.

In April 1984, a group of students who had graduated from elite Beijing middle schools created an informal association to celebrate their camaraderie and their origins. They called themselves the Fellowship of the Children of New China (Xinhua Ernü Lianyihui 新华儿女联谊会).[27] At the time of the centenary of Mao Zedong's birth in 1993, the group renamed itself the Beijing Children of Yan'an Classmates Fellowship (Beijing Yan'an Ernü Xiaoyou Lianyihui 北京延安儿女校友联谊会). Its members were the descendants of men and women who had lived and worked in the Yan'an Communist base in Shaanxi Province from the 1930s to the 1940s, as well as the progeny of the party who were born and educated in Yan'an. From 1998, the group held annual gatherings to coincide with Spring Festival (Chinese New Year), as well as a range of other events organized around choral and dancing groups, Taijiquan classes, and painting and calligraphy activities. In 2001, they shortened their name to the Beijing Children of Yan'an Fellowship.

From 2002, the Beijing Children of Yan'an Fellowship was led by Hu Muying 胡木英, daughter of Hu Qiaomu 胡乔木, a party wordsmith par excellence and Mao Zedong's one-time political secretary. In 2008, the fellowship expanded its membership to include people with no specific link to the old Communist base and its revolutionary éclat. With a core membership of some one hundred people, the Children of Yan'an Fellowship not only boasted the leadership of Hu Muying but also key participation by Li Min 李敏, Mao Zedong's eldest daughter; Zhou Bingde 周秉德, Zhou Enlai's niece; Ren Yuanfang 任远芳, daughter of party elder Ren Bishi 任弼时; Lu Jian-jian 陆健健, son of former party propaganda chief Lu Dingyi 陆定一; and Chen Haosu 陈昊苏, son of Chen Yi 陈毅, the pre–Cultural Revolution mayor of Shanghai and later minister of foreign affairs. On February 13, 2011, the group held its annual Chinese New Year gathering in the auditorium of the August 1 Film Studio, an organization under the direct aegis of the People's Liberation Army.

On that occasion, apart from the Children of Yan'an Fellowship, a range of other interested groups, or what were dubbed "revolutionary mass organizations," were also present.[28] During the speechifying that day the various attendees were collectively represented by Chen Haosu, a former film and TV bureaucrat with a noble party lineage, as noted. The Children of Yan'an Fellowship was represented by Hu Muying and her deputy, Zhang Ya'nan 张亚南) formerly the political commissar of the PLA Logistics Department and previously secretary to Wei Guoqing 韦国清, a Cultural Revolution–era vice chairman of the Standing Committee of the People's Congress.

Following a series of platitudinous remarks and a brief recounting of the long years of struggle that their revolutionary forebears had gone through to found New China (an account that, not surprisingly, glossed over the bloody horrors of the first three decades of party rule from 1949 to 1978), Hu Muying said:

> The new explorations made possible by the Reform and Open-Door policies have, over the past three decades, resulted in remarkable economic results. At the same time, ideological confusion has reigned and the country has been awash in intellectual currents that negate Mao Zedong Thought and socialism. Corruption and the disparity between the wealthy and the poor are of increasingly serious concern; latent social contradictions are becoming more extreme.
>
> We absolutely reject the label of "Princelings" (*Taizi Dang* 太子党), nor are we "Second-Generation Bureaucrats" (*Guan Erdai* 官二代). We are the Red Successors, the Revolutionary Progeny, and as such we cannot but be concerned about the fate of our Party, our Nation and our People. We can no longer ignore the present crisis of the Party.[29]

Hu went on to say that through the activities of study groups, lecture series, and symposia, the Children of Yan'an Fellowship had formulated a document that, following broad-based consultation, would be presented to the Communist Party Central Committee. The document was entitled "Our Suggestions for the Eighteenth Party Congress" (*Women dui shibada de jianyi* 我们对十八大的建议).[30] Hu continued:

> We cannot be satisfied merely with reminiscences, nor can we wallow in nostalgia for the glories of the sufferings of our parents' generation. We must carry on in their heroic spirit, contemplate and forge ahead by asking ever-new questions that respond to the new situations with which we are confronted. We must attempt to address these questions and contribute to the healthy growth of our Party and help prevent our People once more from eating the bitterness of the capitalist past.[31]

For his part, Zhang Ya'nan declared that China's Communist Party, the Communist cause, and Marxism-Leninism itself were being directly challenged and indeed disparaged by the enemies of the revolutionary founding fathers. In particular, he despaired at the de-Maoification that continued to unfold in China. He reminded his audience that "Chairman Mao bequeathed us four things: one piece of software and three pieces of hardware. The hardware is the Chinese Communist Party, the Chinese People's Liberation Army, and the People's Republic of China. The software is Mao Zedong Thought." Zhang went on to praise the red culture campaign launched by Bo Xilai in Chongqing in 2008, the stance of Major-General Luo Yuan 罗援, and the writings of Zhang Tieshan 张

铁山. He then commended to his audience the document formulated for the Communist Party's Eighteenth Congress in late 2012. He declared that it was a manifesto that gave voice to their wish "to love the party, protect the flag, and to revitalize the as-yet-unfinished enterprise of our revolutionary forebears." He also suggested that the Children of Yan'an Fellowship should invite activists who were involved in the Mao Zedong Banner website (Mao Zedong qizhi wang 毛泽东旗帜网) and the Workers' Network (Gongren wang 工人网) to their next Spring Festival gathering, in January 2012.[32]

The Children of Yan'an site made no mention of the 2012 Spring Festival, which, in the event, was a low-key affair. After all, by then the "atmospherics" of Chinese politics had undergone a dramatic transformation. Not long after Spring Festival, Wang Lijun made his dramatic visit to the American Consulate in Chengdu. By mid-March, around the time of Bo Xilai's fall, key leftist or revivalist Maoist sites such as Utopia, Mao Zedong Banner (Mao Flag), and Red China had been suspended by the authorities; the Workers' Network, however, remained active.[33] One could summarize the views of this informal comradely coalition, which is based both in China and overseas, in the following terms: China's party-state system (from the party, army, and government bureaucracy through to the legal system and academia) has for the most part fallen under the control of agents who, in the long run, are working for foreign interests; the mainstream Chinese elite consists of pro-U.S. agents. In response to the incursions of global capital, it is necessary to renationalize all assets, abolish private enterprise and the nonstate private market, and reinstitute central planning. By and large, these groups reaffirm the importance of class analysis and class struggle in the nation's political life; some declare that it is once again necessary to obliterate "bourgeois elements taking the capitalist road" in all areas of government. Among other things, some call for a reform of China's legal system so that the death penalty can be extended to intellectual "traitors"; they obliged the authorities by compiling a list of writers, editors, and intellectuals who would be candidates for elimination.[34]

With their gaze fixed more on the past than the present, the drafters of "Our Suggestions for the Eighteenth Party Congress" reaffirmed the primacy of what is known as the "mass line" (*qunzhong luxian* 群众路线). First articulated by Mao as early as 1929, the mass line is regarded as one of the foundations of Mao Zedong Thought. It calls for the party to rely unwaveringly on the masses (a vague and ill-defined group at the best of times), to put faith in them, arouse them, go among them, honestly learn from them, and serve them.

The Children of Yan'an Fellowship declared that their reform proposals were a practical realization of the long-standing principle of the mass line, one that was enshrined in the party's constitution and that had in the past ensured the party's successes. Moreover, they declared that party leaders could ill afford to use social and political stability as an excuse for further delays to substantive reform of China's political system. The Children of Yan'an Fellowship declared that new political talent could be found among the masses, in particular among the enthusiastic party faithful. They claimed, for instance, that the Red Song Movement that originated in Chongqing and later spread nationwide had seen the appearance of just the kind of enthusiastic younger party members who would help ensure the continuation of the Communist enterprise far into the future. On the eve of the Cultural Revolution in 1966, Mao Zedong is said to have cautioned that after his demise people would inevitably "wave the red flag to oppose the red flag" (*da hongqi fan hongqi* 打红旗反红旗).[35] Now it would appear that the Children of Yan'an Fellowship was using its very own red flag to oppose the red flag of economic reform that, since 1978, had been employed to oppose the red flag of Maoism. This was one of the underpinnings of Zhang Musheng's 张木生 re-reading of the party's 1940s program related to "New Democracy" formulated by Mao Zedong and Liu Shaoqi, one that attempted to reconcile party traditionalists with the desire for political reforms in keeping with the original ethos of the Mao years.[36]

The revival of a patriotism-oriented Maoist red culture in Chongqing under Bo Xilai would for a time be affirmed (or was it really to be co-opted and marginalized?) by party leaders, in particular by Politburo Standing Committee member and head of the Central Political and Legal Affairs Committee Zhou Yongkang 周永康. Around the time that Bo Xilai led a delegation of "red songsters" to Beijing in mid-June 2011, Zhou called for the "forging of three million idealistic and disciplined souls who are ready to face all dangers with an unwavering faith." Of importance in the crucible of the engineers of human souls was what would now be called the "Five Reds": "Reading red books, studying red history, singing red songs, watching red movies, and taking the red path."[37]

Not only did the Children of Yan'an Fellowship formulate a manifesto and agitate for a form of political reform before the looming change of party leadership, but also it was said that in its pursuit of a new Maoist-style "mass line" they tried to engender tentative contacts with grassroots organizations and petitioner groups in and outside Beijing. For left-leaning figures in contemporary China to engage in such practical, and nonhierarchical, politics was highly significant, especially when considered in contrast to the academic New Left (Xin zuopai 新左派) that had arisen in the 1990s and 2000s.

For more than a decade the New Left intellectuals—a disparate group that, like their rhetorical opponents, the "liberals," was generally lumped together—had been variously celebrated and derided. In the late 1990s I wrote about the "confrontation of caricatures"—that between New Left and liberal—that was polarizing the Chinese intellectual world.[38] It is a topic that the intellectual historian Xu Jilin 许纪霖 has frequently addressed since then.[39] The critics of the New Left claimed that they were primarily "on-paper generals" (*zhishang tan bing* 纸上谈兵) who could talk up a storm (both in China and at the various international academic forums to which they are frequently invited). They may well profess to being intellectually committed to "recuperating" radical sociopolitical agendas, critiquing the capitalist turn in China, and thinking of how best to utilize the "resources" of Marxism-Maoism in the context of the reform era. To their critics, however, members of the New Left rarely seemed to demonstrate any practicable desire to deal with the deprived, marginalized, dispossessed, or repressed individuals in the society as a whole. Their critics also noted that when issues of free speech or intellectual freedom came up, this usually vociferous group was generally silent.[40] While elite members of this leftist claque formed meaty alliances with their global intellectual coevals, on the ground in China protests, resistance, and opposition to the oppressive practices of party capitalism remained the province of lone activists, nongovernmental organizations, liberal intellectuals, lawyers, and the woefully "undertheorized."

Not only was the revivalism of Chongqing appealing to the Children of Yan'an, it also attracted a range of left-leaning, or New Left, intellectuals both in and outside China. Bo Xilai and his circle actively cultivated this disparate group through targeted support for seminars, conferences, and other generously funded activities. As has been the case for intellectuals attracted, mothlike, to the flame of power in the past, many of these individuals, with their myopic attachment to theory, convinced themselves and others to overlook the evidence in front of them. However, the purblindness and reticence of members of the New Left is, perhaps, also understandable. Apart from the usual intellectual qualms about direct social engagement among those who are more comfortable dealing with academic jousting and refereed publications in prestigious journals, in China principled activism does exact a high price. After all, the engaged intellectual soon confronts a policed authoritarian environment that is infamously punitive, and the fate of such prominent naysayers as Liu Xiaobo 刘晓波 and Ai Weiwei 艾未未 would deter all but the most foolhardy. More disturbing yet is the cruel abuse of numerous (and often nameless) men and women of conscience who have been harried, detained, and persecuted by local power-holders and business interests, often for the most spurious reasons. One of the issues this chapter returns to in various guises is the question: Is a pro-Maoist rhetoric the only form of left-leaning critique available to Chinese thinkers and their international supporters? And if that is the case, are critiques of Mao and his bloody legacy always to be deemed orientalist, reactionary, or pro-neoliberal?

Arbitrage: The Global Trade in Red Rhetoric

In discussing red legacies it is necessary to be mindful of the long tradition whereby left-leaning causes, and discourse, in China (not to mention elsewhere) have been entwined with a nationalist or patriotic mission related to independence, economic growth, and identity politics. In the context of legacy-creation, the Chinese party-state has inherited and invested heavily in the Maoist heritage by transposing social class analysis and the three-world theory into the context of contemporary geopolitics. Thus, the People's Republic, despite its regnant economic strength and international heft, portrays itself as a proletarian-agrarian developing nation that is primarily in solidarity with the dispossessed and underdeveloped nations, against the bourgeois bullies of Euramerica. No matter what elements of truth this self-description may have, as a rhetorical device and canny transmogrification of High Maoist categories, it remains a powerful tool in global power politics and one area in which the Maoist legacy is particularly vital, and successful.

The transvaluation of Maoist categories into international relations discourse is only one of the ways in which the heritage persists into the present. Another is the way that rejigged elements of the Maoist canon are employed to bolster careers, align research projects, and guide personal trajectories. (I would observe that the same holds true even for those who use Maoist-style patriotism to pursue neoliberal goals, be they academic or mercantile.)

In the late 1990s, a disparate group that I think of as the interrogators of the intelligentsia set themselves apart from the restive throng of their educated fellows by claiming a unique purchase on critical inquiry. In their writings, they pursued a project of visualization toward a "China imaginary" that would cast all liberal (and I don't mean neoliberal) intellectuals as being of one cloth. As we consider the varied roles of participant-observers, theorizing nonactivists, and academic middlemen (among whose number I would, of course, include myself), a term current in the world of international finance suggests itself. It is "arbitrage," referring to "the purchase of securities in one market for resale in another." As André Aciman comments on the practice in terms of nostalgia and time:

> As soon as a profit is made, the cycle starts again, with subsequent purchases sometimes paid for with unrealized profit drawn from previous sales. In such transactions, one never really sells a commodity, much less takes delivery of anything. One merely speculates, and seldom does any of it have anything to do with the real world. Arbitrageurs may have seats on not one but two exchanges, the way the very wealthy have homes in not one but two time zones, or exiles two homes in the wrong places. One always longs for the other home, but home, as one learns soon enough, is a place where one imagines or remembers other homes.[41]

In the context of our own academic pursuits, while one can appreciate divergent agendas for intellectuals who practice their armchair activism in the relatively oblique language of the academy, an accounting for the past requires an approach that is mindful not only of frustrated political agendas and the failure of ideas in practice but also of the complex human dimension of ideas in social practice.

In his study and summation of Leszek Kołakowski's monumental work *Main Currents of Marxism*, Tony Judt in particular identifies the abiding attraction of that political philosophy: its "blend of Promethean Romantic illusion and uncompromising historical determinism."[42] Marxism thus, in this account, "offered an explanation of how the world works. . . . It proposed a way in which the world ought to work. . . .And it announced incontrovertible grounds for believing that things *will* work that way in the future, thanks to a set of assertions about historical necessity. . . . This combination of economic description, moral prescription, and political prediction proved intensely seductive—and serviceable."[43] We may well speak of the clever commercialization of China's red legacy, the canny ways in which elements of the Mao era are insinuated into contemporary political, social, and cultural discourse. Some writers and commentators are, even still, diverted by the tired uses of socialist irony in culture (art, film, essays, blogs, literature, and so on). Others may be beguiled by the latest in a long line of attempts to recuperate Marx or indeed Mao himself from "distortion," or by the academic subprime market devoted to holistic, globalizing interpretations of the Marx-Engels-Lenin-Stalin-Mao project. In terms of activism, one legacy of the revolutionary Mao era—that of direct political involvement, organized resistance, and struggle, however, seems to be less appealing.[44]

It is here, perhaps, that the post-Maoist, Marxist turn in China contributes to our understanding of the categories of the Maoist or red legacy in the new millennium. Needless to say, much can be made of the glib (and cynical) commercialization of red tourism, of the audio-video and digital wallpaper generated in various cultural forms that quote, revive, and cannibalize works of high-socialist culture. But has the continuation of one-party rule in China achieved something particular, not merely the party as a particular Chinese phenomenon, and therefore regarded as only being on a national mission of "prosperity and strength," but also something else? I would ask whether the language of the red legacy and its various manifestations offers merely a sly way of packaging Chinese materialism and worldliness, or is there more at stake and more inherent in it?

While thinkers labor to salvage Marxism from the egregious failures, and crimes, of communism (be they of the Soviet or the Maoist variety), the red legacy is no cutesy epiphenomenon worthy simply of a cultural studies or po-mo "reading"; rather, it constitutes a body of linguistic and intellectual practices that are profoundly ingrained in institutional behavior and the bricks and mortar of scholastic and cultural legitimization. The on-the-ground reality of the People's Republic is that topics couched in Marxist-Maoist terminology remain privileged within Chinese educational institutions and among publishers, think tanks, and funding agencies. It is a living legacy the specter of which continues to hover over Chinese intellectual life, for weal or for bane. And it is worth asking whether this particular red legacy does in fact leech out the power of other modes of left-leaning critique and independent thought, thus only aiding and abetting the party-state's pursuit of a neo-liberal economic agenda.

Fellowships and Factions

In 1044 CE, the Song-dynasty political figure and writer Ouyang Xiu 欧阳修 submitted a memorial to the throne entitled "On Factions" (*Pengdang lun* 朋党论). In it he argued against the long-standing taboo on coalitions in government. He suggested to the throne that political groupings of like-minded men working for the benefit of the court and its dynastic subjects were in fact a constructive development. Regarded as the most famous argument in favor of political alliances in Chinese history, "On Factions" has resonated through the ages. In his memorial Ouyang wrote:

> Thus, Your servant claims that petty men are without factions and that only superior men have them. Why is this so? Official salaries and gain are what petty men enjoy; wealth and goods are what petty men covet. When they seek mutual gain, they will temporarily form an affiliation [*dang*], but it is erroneous to consider them to be a faction [*peng*]. When they glimpse gain and contend to be first [to take it], or when the gains have been exhausted, and they squabble over what remains, then they will cruelly injure each other. Even if they are brothers or kinsmen, they will not be able to protect each other.
>
> 然臣谓小人无朋，惟君子有之。其故何哉？小人所好者利禄也，所贪者财货也; 当其同利之时，暂相党引以为朋者，伪也。及其见利而争先，或利尽而交疏，则反相贼害，虽其兄弟亲戚，不能相保。故臣谓小人无朋，其暂为朋者，伪也。
>
> [T]his is not so for superior men. The Way and righteousness are what they defend; loyalty and sincerity are what they practice; and reputation and

> integrity are what they value. Since they have cultivated themselves, their common Way [*tongdao*] is of mutual benefit. Since they serve the polity, their common hearts help each other, and they are always as one. Such are the affiliations of superior men.
>
> 君子则不然。所守者道义，所行者忠信，所惜者名节；以之修身，则同道而相益，以之事国，则同心而共济。终始如一。此君子之朋也。

Mao Zedong was notorious for construing those with political differences as being members of dangerous factions and alliances. He frequently warned against the dangers of "cliques" (*zongpai* 宗派); he demonized his perceived rivals as pursuing a political line invidious to the Chinese Revolution, and he was merciless first in toying with those whom he suspected of having formed alliances in opposition to him and then in obliterating them. Differences in policy, strategy, and even personality were depicted as "line struggles" (*luxian douzheng* 路线斗争), and for decades the history of modern China as accounted by the Communist Party was a record of such struggles.

In the landscape of authoritarian Chinese politics there has occasionally been an attempt to recognize, if not formalize, the role of a "loyal opposition" in government. In the history of the Chinese Communist Party, which celebrated it ninetieth anniversary on July 1, 2011, inner party factions were outlawed, often in the most violent manner. Although the Chinese Communist Party may well maintain that China in the twenty-first century is led by one party in coalition with other "democratic parties" (*minzhu dangpai* 民主党派) that contribute to the political process, the reality is that no quarter is given to formal oppositionist politics.

In the realm of media and the Internet, contentious discussion in China is more freewheeling in many regards than during other periods of party rule. Today, however, major differences in policy are papered over or suppressed under the guise of collective leadership. Line struggles are a Maoist relic; in their place there is talk of "party discipline" (*dangji* 党纪) and "state law" (*guofa* 国法). Whatever his disciplinary infractions or criminal misdeeds, Bo Xilai is seen by some as being the victim of a party line struggle that not only aimed at purging Bo and his associates but also gestured toward a Maoist-era form of egalitarianism. Ideological contestation has been occluded by a formalistic legal process.

The historian F. W. Mote offered the following observation on Ouyang Xiu's Song-dynasty memorial and the problems it highlighted for future generations. Mote's comment is relevant to a discussion of political contestation under authoritarian rule in China even today:

> The failure of Neo-Confucian thinkers and political activists to break through this formal barrier against concerted political action by groups of like-minded men, by disallowing any distinction between good and bad factions, severely limited Chinese political behavior thereafter, up to the end of the imperial era in the early twentieth century. . . . The attempt to redefine "factions" would arise again and again, up to the eighteenth century, but the state's definition always prevailed. Legitimate political parties could not take form, and any who expressed political disagreements were, by definition, morally deficient, hence insidious. "Loyal opposition" could not be acknowledged within a system of politics defined by ethical and personal rather than by operational and institutional norms. China still struggles with the heritage of this eleventh-century political failure.[45]

A Crimson Blindfold

During the "history wars" in Australia that stretched out for a decade from the mid-1990s, historians who brought to light through their research unpalatable truths about the ugly colonization of the country and the devastation of its indigenous population were condemned by government leaders, right-wing media commentators, and others claiming objectivity. The concerned historians were derided for promoting a "black armband" view of the past. Their historical perspective, one that by its very nature encouraged a heartfelt recognition of the complex history of settlement and a thoughtful reflection on its impact on the present, was seen as a threat to national cohesion and more uplifting narratives of progress and modernity. The power-holders and their media supporters were, in turn, chided for championing a "white blindfold" view of the national story. In China, the blindfold is of a crimson hue.

Cozy theorizing regarding a supposedly retrievable red legacy enjoyed a regional boost during the short-lived "red renaissance" championed by Bo Xilai and his supporters (political, military, and academic) until early 2012. His ouster does not mean, however, that red culture is defunct. Some of the motivating ideas, sentiments, and emotions of the

Chinese Revolution remain part of the fabric of life, and they find different levels of articulation and resonance in the society. To appreciate more cogently the valence of China's red-suffused heritage, the overlay and interplay of historical tropes, language, practices, and evocations are key to understanding the multifaceted commerce between past and present, traditions real and invented, and the evolution of contemporary ways of being, seeing, and speaking in China today.

Even in power, Mao Zedong frequently spoke about the dangers of bourgeois restoration and revisionism. He declared on a number of occasions that he would go back into the mountains to lead a guerrilla war against the power-holders—that rebellion would be justified. While many discuss the legacy of revolutionary politics in the cloistered security of academic forums, that spirit of rebellion, the active involvement with a politics of agitation, action, and danger, is one legacy that seems safe to contemplate only at a distance. Restive farmers and workers in China may cloak themselves in the language of defunct revolution, but evidence suggests that rather than the crude categories of class struggle and revolutionary vanguards, their metaphorical landscape is a complex mixture of traditional cultural tropes, revolutionary discourse, and an awareness of modern rights and ways to stretch social rules.

As we consider the steely determinism of the Marxist lesson, we can detect how that historical determinism and articulations of a Chinese "national mission"' dovetail today. The necessity of history remains at the heart of many attempts to find a more capacious meaning within the red legacy. Indeed, as we consider the long tail of Maoism both in and outside the People's Republic of China, we should be alert to the abiding allure, and uses, of the crimson blindfold. After all, it is because of its nature as a *belief system*—as a body of thought, practice, language, and cultural heritage—that it forms part of China's red legacy, a system that has proved serviceable in the past and remains seductive, and useful, today.

Notes

1. In this chapter I review some of my previously published work, which has appeared under various scholastic guises as well as in the virtual pages of the online journal *China Heritage Quarterly* (www.chinaheritagequarterly.org). For essays relevant to this topic, see: "Time's Arrows" (2001); "The Revolution of Resistance"

(2000, rev. 2004 and 2010); "I'm So Ronree" (2006); *The Forbidden City* (2008, 2009, 2012); "Beijing, a Garden of Violence" (2008); "China's Flat Earth" (2009); "Beijing Reoriented, an Olympic Undertaking" (2010); "For Truly Great Men, Look to This Age Alone: Was Mao Zedong a New Emperor?" (2010); and "The Children of Yan'an: New Words of Warning to a Prosperous Age 盛世新危言" (2011). For an early book devoted in part to the issues discussed in this chapter, see Geremie R. Barmé, *Shades of Mao: The Posthumous Career of the Great Leader* (Armonk, NY: M. E. Sharpe, 1996), and for a work that notes the abiding legacies of the Maoist era during the 1980s and in particular during the protest movement of 1989, see the narration for the feature-length documentary *The Gate of Heavenly Peace* (1995), of which I was the principal author, at www.tsquare.tv.

2. I divide Maoism into a pre-1949 form; High Maoism, when the complex body of thinking, policies, and personality cult held sway in China from 1949 until the end of 1978 (and the launch of the reform era); the 1978–89 decade of contestation; the 1989–99 decade of recalibration; and the era from 1999 forward, in which Maoist and Marxist legacies have found new champions both inside and outside of Chinese officialdom. Such a schema is but a crude convenience.

3. For an example of a recent work noting the "long tail" of Maoist-era institutional practice, see Sebastian Heilmann and Elizabeth J. Perry, eds., *Mao's Invisible Hand: The Political Foundations of Adaptive Governance in China* (Cambridge, MA: Harvard University Asia Center, 2011). Elizabeth Perry's later work on the miners of Anyuan offers a specific account of the domestication of revolution in China. See Elizabeth J. Perry, *Anyuan: Mining China's Revolutionary Tradition* (Berkeley: University of California Press, 2012).

4. See, e.g., William A. Callahan, *China: The Pessoptimist Nation* (Oxford: Oxford University Press, 2009).

5. See, e.g., such analyses as "'Sange daibiao' yu Zhonghua minzu weida de fuxing" 三个代表与中华民族伟大的复兴, February 8, 2002, at http://www.bjqx.org.cn/qxweb/n807c5.aspx, and "Zhengque lijie Zhonghua minzu de weida fuxing" 正确理解中华民族的伟大复兴, January 27, 2007, at http://www.bjqx.org.cn/qxweb/n7499c5.aspx (both accessed October 5, 2015). Hu Jintao used the expression "Chinese national revival" (*Zhonghua minzu fuxing* 中华民族复兴) twenty-three times during his Xinhai Revolution speech on October 9, 2011. See "Hu Jintao 23 ci ti Zhonghua minzu fuxing, minzu fuxing bixu zhaodao zhengque daolu" 胡锦涛23次提中华民族复兴, 民族复兴必须找到正确道路, *Nanfang ribao* 南方日报, October 10, 2011, at http://politics.people.com.cn/GB/1026/15842000.html (accessed October 5, 2015). For a recent comment on various aspects of this narrative as generated in China and internationally, see William A. Callahan, "Sino-speak: Chinese Exceptionalism and the Politics of History," *Journal of Asian Studies* 71, no.1 (February 2012): 1–23.

6. For more on this, see my analysis of the Opening Ceremony of the 2008 Beijing Olympics: Geremie Barmé, "China's Flat Earth: History and 8 August 2008," *China Quarterly* 197 (March 2009): 64–86, and "Telling Chinese Stories," which I presented at the University of Sydney, May 1, 2012, at http://www.thechinastory.org/yearbook/telling-chinese-stories/ (accessed October 5, 2015).

7. Although U.S.-based academic audiences will invariably see things through the particular (dare I say "distorting"?) prism of U.S.-China-specific relations, for those of us in the Antipodes the various kerfuffles in 2009 involving the Sino-Australian relationship over Chinalco, the aluminum corporation of China, and its investment plans; Stern Hu's arrest in Shanghai (and March 2010 trial); and the visit of the Ughyur activist Rebiya Kadeer to Melbourne, are more salient. For more on this, see *China Story Yearbook 2012: Red Rising, Red Eclipse*, (Canberra: Australian Centre on China in the World, Australian National University, 2012).

8. See, e.g., Qiang Zhai, "1959: Preventing Peaceful Evolution," *China Heritage Quarterly*, issue 18 (June 2009), at http://www.chinaheritagequarterly.org/features.php?searchterm=018_1959preventingpeace.inc&issue=018, and Geremie Barmé, "The Harmonious Evolution of Information in China," *China Heritage Quarterly*, issue 21 (March 2010), at http://www.chinaheritagequarterly.org/articles.php?searchterm=021_peacefulevolution.inc&issue=021 (both accessed October 5, 2015).

9. See Michael Schoenhals, *Doing Things with Words in Chinese Politics: Five Studies*, China Research Monograph (Berkeley: Institute of East Asian Studies, University of California, 1992), and Anne-Marie Brady, *Marketing Dictatorship: Propaganda and Thought Work in Contemporary China* (Boulder, CO: Rowman & Littlefield, 2008).

10. For an extended essay on New China Newspeak, see the China Heritage Glossary, *China Heritage Quarterly*, issue 29 (March 2012), at http://www.chinaheritagequarterly.org/glossary.php?searchterm=029_xinhua.inc&issue=029 (accessed October 5, 2015).

11. This is my particular focus in Geremie Barmé, *In the Red: On Contemporary Chinese Culture* (New York: Columbia University Press, 1999).

12. "Resolution on Certain Questions in the History of Our Party since the Founding of the People's Republic of China (Adopted by the Sixth Plenary Session of the Eleventh Central Committee of the Communist Party of China on June 27, 1981)," at http://www.marxists.org/subject/china/documents/cpc/history/01.htm (accessed October 5, 2015).

13. For a report on the press conference and Wen's remarks, see http://www.reuters.com/article/2012/03/14/china-npc-highlights-idUSL4E8EE11K20120314 (accessed October 5, 2015).

14. See "Jianjue weihu dang de zhengzhi jilü" 坚决维护党的政治纪律, at http://opinion.people.com.cn/GB/14727703.html; and the independent commentary at http://www.chinese.rfi.fr/中国/20110525-中纪委警告中共党员莫对重大政治问题"说三道四" (accessed October 5, 2015).

15. See Dai Qing 戴晴, "Wang Shiwei yu 'Yebaihe hua'" 王实味与'野百合花' (Wang Shiwei and 'Wild Lilies'), the full text of which is at https://www.marxists.org/chinese/reference-books/yanan1942/5-09.htm (accessed October 5, 2015); and Dai Qing, *Wang Shiwei and "Wild Lilies": Rectification and Purges in the Chinese Communist Party, 1942–1944*, ed. David E. Apter and Timothy Cheek, trans. Nancy Liu and Lawrence R. Sullivan. comp. Song Jinshou (Armonk, NY: M. E. Sharpe, 1994).

16. See "'Junche jin Jing' yaoyan jiyi yingxiang wending" "军车进京" 谣言极易

影响稳定, *Renmin ribao* 人民日报, April 16, 2012, at http://www.rbw.org.cn/article.aspx?ty=uuB&i=Bq9&ky=!YVc8kd7k17L2xV2T&pg=0&pgnum=15811 (accessed July 3, 2014).

17. See, e.g., Zhang He 张贺, "Renqing wangluo yaoyan de shehui weihai" 认清网络谣言的社会危害, *Renmin ribao* 人民日报, April 16, 2012, at http://paper.people.com.cn/rmrb/html/2012-04/16/nw.D110000renmrb_20120416_1-04.htm (accessed July 3, 2014).

18. This is a point made at length by Paul Cohen in *Speaking to History: The Story of King Goujian in Twentieth-Century China* (Berkeley: University of California Press, 2007).

19. Harold L. Kahn, *Monarchy in the Emperor's Eyes: Image and Reality in the Ch'ien-lung Reign* (Cambridge, MA: Harvard University Press, 1971), p. 51.

20. In December 2007 the film enjoyed a limited rerelease as part of a commemoration of the life and career of its female lead, Ruan Lingyu. For more on this, see my book *The Forbidden City* (Cambridge, MA: Harvard University Press, 2008), pp. xxxi and 100, and the notes at http://ciw.anu.edu.au/projects/theforbiddencity/notes.php?chapter=chapter5 (accessed October 5, 2015).

21. *Qianlong xia Jiangnan* 乾隆下江南. The TV series was a coproduction of the Beijing Film and TV Studio and Feiteng Film Company 北影电视部与飞腾电公司. See also Zhao Zhizhong 赵志忠, "Da Qing wangchao re jiedu" 大清王朝热解读, in *Cong Xingjing dao Shengjing: Nu'erhachi jueqi guiji tanyuan* 从兴京到盛京: 努尔哈赤崛起轨迹探源, ed. Fu Bo 傅波 (Shenyang: Liaoning minzu chubanshe, 2008), pp. 373–82. *A Fanciful Account of Qianlong* was soon followed by *A Fanciful Account of the Empress Dowager* (*Xishuo Cixi* 戏说慈禧).

22. See Q. Edward Wang, *Inventing China through History: The May Fourth Approach to Historiography* (Albany, NY: State University of New York Press, 2001).

23. For the scene, see http://v.youku.com/v_show/id_XMTY3Njk2MDA=.html (accessed July 3, 2014).

24. See Matthias Niedenführ, "Revising and Televising the Past in East Asia: 'History Soaps' in Mainland China," in *Contested Views of a Common Past*, ed. Steffi Richter (Frankfurt and New York: Campus Verlag, 2008), pp. 351–69 and 364–65.

25. See David Barboza, "Making TV Safer: Chinese Censors Crack Down on Time Travel," *New York Times*, April 12, 2011, at http://artsbeat.blogs.nytimes.com/2011/04/12/making-tv-safer-chinese-censors-crack-down-on-time-travel/ (accessed October 5, 2015); for the Chinese document, see http://www.sarft.gov.cn/articles/2011/03/31/20110331140820680073.html. See also http://travel.cnn.com/shanghai/life/china's-new-ban-time-travel-274122 (accessed November 15, 2015).

26. "Depoliticized politics" is a term grafted from the work of Wang Hui. See also Yang Jinhong 杨锦鸿, "Man tan 'hongse jingdian' gaibian" 漫谈"红色经典"改编, http://qkzz.net/article/f3ab77d9-5b11-4cfa-9b16-050c70ada9d7.htm (accessed October 5, 2015).

27. This overview is based on material available on the Children of Yan'an website, at http://www.yananernv.cn/geren.html (accessed November 15, 2015).

28. These groups included the New Fourth Route Army Research Group 新四军研究会, the Children of Jinggangshan 井冈山儿女联谊会, the October 1 Classmates

Society 十一同学会, the Children of Red Crag 红岩儿女联谊会, the Association of the Western Flower Pavilion 西花厅联谊会, the Beijing Eighth Route Army Shandong Anti-Japanese Base Research Society 北京八路军山东抗日根据地研究会, the Transmitters of the Taiyue Mountains Tradition Group 太岳精神传承会, the Children of the War of Resistance University 抗联儿女联谊会, the Mid-Hebei Research Group 冀中研究会, the Children of the West Route Army Group (preparatory committee) 西路军儿女联谊会筹备组, the Founding of the Nation Marshals Choral Society 开国元勋合唱团, Beijing October 1 Classmates Club 北京十一同学会, the 101 Middle School Club 101中同学会, the Yucai Middle School Club 育才同学会, the August 1 Classmates Club 八一同学会, the North China Primary School Club 华北小学同学会, and the Yuying School Club 育英学校同学会. All of the groups boast complex backgrounds, affiliations, and party-state-army connections.

29. For Hu's speech, see "Hu Muying huizhang 2 yue 13 ri zai Yan'an ernü lianyihui tuanbai dahui shang de zhici" 胡木英会长2月13日在延安儿女联谊会团拜大会上的致辞, at http://club.kdnet.net/dispbbs.asp?boardid=1&id=6859620 (accessed December 8, 2015).

30. For details, see http://www.oh100.com/a/201212/192148.html (accessed December 8, 2015).

31. "Hu Muying huizhang," http://club.kdnet.net/dispbbs.asp?boardid=1&id=6859620 (accessed December 8, 2015).

32. For Zhang Ya'nan's speech, see "Chunjie tuanbaihui zhuchici (zhailu) 春节团拜会主持词 (摘录), at http://club.kdnet.net/dispbbs.asp?boardid=1&id=9163727&read=1 (accessed July 3, 2014). The "de-Maoification" referred to by Zhang was actually a formal process launched by the Chinese Communist Party in the late 1970s. In recent years, however, more detailed critiques of Mao and his period of rule have been published by those with less sympathy for the Communist cause. One of the most recent appeared in April 2011, some two months after Zhang Ya'nan's hand-wringing. It was by the academic Mao Yushi 茅于轼: "Ba Mao Zedong huanyuan cheng ren: Du *Hongtaiyangde yunluo*" 把毛泽东还原成人:读《红太阳的陨落》 (Make Mao human once more: On reading *The Sun Also Falls*), http://china.dwnews.com/news/2011-04-26/57658778.html (accessed July 3, 2014).

33. See Robert Foyle Hunwick, "Utopia Website Shutdown: Interview with Fan Jinggang," April 14, 2012, Danwei, at http://www.danwei.com/interview-before-a-gagging-order-fan-jinggang-of-utopia/ (accessed July 3, 2014). See also http://maopai.net/.

34. On December 28, 2011, the Maoist revanchist site Utopia published the results of a year-end poll on China's top traitors 乌有之乡: 评选'十大文化汉奸'. The CIW-Danwei Online Archive project provided this news and the decoded list originally published at http://www.wyzxsx.com/Article/Class22/201112/284230.html, but now no longer available; see instead the Editor's Introduction to "A View of the Hero Yue Fei and the Traitor Qin Gui" 岳飛與秦檜, at http://www.chinaheritagequarterly.org/features.php?searchterm=028_yuefei.inc&issue=028 (accessed October 5, 2015). The nominees in infamy were: (1) economist Mao Yushi 茅于轼; (2) history teacher

Yuan Tengfei 袁腾飞; (3) "science cop" (anti-Chinese medicine, etc.) Fang Zhouzi 方舟子; (4) economist Wu Jinglian 吴敬琏; (5) diplomat Wu Jianmin 吴建民; (6) CCTV host Bai Yansong 白岩松; (7) military scholar, and Mao Zedong and Lin Biao biographer Xin Ziling 辛子陵; (8) retired government official/reformer Li Rui 李锐; (9) legal scholar/law professor He Weifang 贺卫方; (10) economist Stephen N. S. Cheung 张五常; (11) economist Zhang Weiying 张维迎; (12) economist Li Yining 厉以宁; (13) *Southern Weekly* deputy general editor Xiang Xi 向熹; (14) former *People's Daily* deputy editor-in-chief Huang Fuping 皇甫平; (15) writer and Nobel Prize–winning dissident Liu Xiaobo 刘晓波; (16) former Mao doctor and Mao biographer Li Zhisui 李志绥 (deceased); (17) Peking University journalism professor Jiao Guobiao 焦国标; and (18) former *People's Daily* editor-in-chief/director Hu Jiwei 胡绩伟.

35. A line from Mao's famous 1966 "Letter to Jiang Qing" Mao Zedong zhi Jiang Qing de yifeng xin 毛泽东致江青的一封信), officially dated July 8, although it is highly doubtful that the letter that was released following Lin Biao's demise in September 1971 was actually composed in 1966.

36. Here one is reminded of Wang Shuo's 1989 novel, *No Man's Land* (*Qianwan bie ba wo dang ren* 千万别把我当人). In one scene the protagonist falls in with a leftist underground study group that discusses official corruption, the need for workers' rights, and the need for another revolution. The group is broken up by the authorities, who declare that they are escapees from a mental asylum. As the latter-day Trotskyites are being dragged away, one shouts out: "What are you going to do when the [real] Communists come back?" See "The Apotheosis of a *Liumang*" in Barmé, *In the Red*, pp. 91–92.

37. For the *Chongqing Daily* online report, see "(Chongqing) Zhonghua honggehui longzhong kaimu" 重庆中华红歌会隆重开幕, at http://news.online.cq.cn/chongqing/2011/06/30/3350893.html (accessed October 5, 2015). For those interested in another form of realpolitik, it is perhaps also noteworthy that the "old friend of China," Henry Kissinger, attended the rally. Around the time of Bo Xilai's demise, the fate of his presumed Politburo patron, Zhou Yongkang, was also much discussed.

38. Geremie Barmé, "The Revolution of Resistance," in *Chinese Society: Change, Conflict and Resistance*, ed. Elizabeth J. Perry and Mark Selden, 3rd ed. (London: Routledge, 2010).

39. See, for instance, Xu Jilin, "Jin shinian lai Zhongguo guojiazhuyi sichao zhi pipan" 近十年来中国国家主义思潮之批判, July 6, 2011, at http://www.21ccom.net/articles/sxpl/sx/article_2011070638713.html (accessed October 5, 2015).

40. See phone and email interviews with Cui Weiping 崔卫平 published via Twitter, "Cui Weiping jiu Liu Xiaobo an fangtan Zhongguo zhishifenzi" 崔卫平就刘晓波案访谈中国知识分子, at http://xiangeliushui.blogspot.com.au/2009/12/cuiwenping-interview-about-liuxiaobo.html, and my comment in "China's Promise," *China Beat*, January 20, 2010, at http://www.thechinabeat.org/?p=1374 (both accessed October 5, 2015).

41. André Aciman, "Arbitrage," *New Yorker,* July 10, 2000, p. 36. This material on

arbitrage first appeared in my chapter "Time's Arrows: Imaginative Pasts and Nostalgic Futures," in *Voicing Concerns: Contemporary Chinese Critical Inquiry*, ed. Gloria Davies (Boulder, CO: Rowman & Littlefield, 2001).

42. Tony Judt, "Goodbye to All That? Leszek Kołakowski and the Marxist Legacy," in *Reappraisals: Reflections on the Forgotten Twentieth Century* (New York: Penguin Press, 2008), p. 133.

43. Ibid., pp. 133–34.

44. Perhaps we may recall Kołakowski's scathing observation of the pursuit of Marxism by Euramerican intellectuals and academics: "One of the causes of the popularity of Marxism among educated people was the fact that in its simple form it was very easy; . . . an instrument that made it possible to master all of history and economics without actually having to study either." Ibid., p. 135.

45. F. W. Mote, *Imperial China 900-1800* (Cambridge, MA: Harvard University Press, 1999), p. 137. See also Geremie Barmé, "The Children of Yan'an: New Words of Warning to a Prosperous Age 盛世新危言," *China Heritage Quarterly*, at http://www.chinaheritagequarterly.org/features.php?searchterm=026_yanan.inc&issue=026 (accessed October 5, 2015).

Contributors

Geremie R. Barmé is Professor of Chinese History and Founding Director of the Australian Centre on China in the World at the Australian National University. He is the author of, among other books, *In the Red: On Contemporary Chinese Culture, Shades of Mao: The Posthumous Career of the Great Leader, An Artistic Exile: A Life of Feng Zikai*, and *The Forbidden City.* He has co-written and co-directed documentary films including *The Gate of Heavenly* Peace and *Morning Sun*. He is also the editor of *China Story Journal* and *China Heritage Quarterly.*

Xiaomei Chen is Professor of Chinese Literature in the Department of East Asian Languages and Cultures at University of California, Davis. She is the author of *Occidentalism: A Theory of Counter-Discourse in Post-Mao China* and *Acting the Right Part: Political Theater and Popular Drama in Contemporary China*. She is also the editor of *Reading the Right Texts* and *The Columbia Anthology of Modern Chinese Drama*. Her latest book, *Staging Chinese Revolution: Theater, Film, and the Afterlives of Propaganda*, is forthcoming from Columbia University Press, 2016.

Harriet Evans is Professor of Chinese Cultural Studies and Director of the Contemporary China Centre at the University of Westminster. Her research interests include gender, sexuality, and women's lives in modern and contemporary China; memory, heritage, and the transformation of urban life since the mid-twentieth century; and visual culture of the

Mao era. She is currently finishing a book on an oral history of a poor neighborhood in central Beijing. She leads the Leverhulme Trust–funded "Conflicts in Cultural Value" project, which investigates local meanings and practices of heritage conservation in southwest China.

Denise Y. Ho is Assistant Professor in the Department of History at Yale University. She received her Ph.D. in Chinese history from Harvard University and taught previously at the University of Kentucky and the Chinese University of Hong Kong. Her research interests include the social and cultural history of twentieth-century China, with a focus on the Mao period. She is completing her first book, a history of museums and exhibitions entitled *Curating Revolution: Politics on Display in Mao's China*.

Haiyan Lee is Associate Professor of Chinese and Comparative Literature at Stanford University. She is the author of *The Stranger and the Chinese Moral Imagination* and *Revolution of the Heart: A Genealogy of Love in China, 1900–1950*, which was awarded the 2009 Joseph Levenson Prize from the Association for Asian Studies.

Jie Li is Assistant Professor of East Asian Languages and Civilizations at Harvard University, where she teaches Chinese film, media, and cultural studies. She is the author of *Shanghai Homes: Palimpsests of Private Life* and is completing a book manuscript titled *Utopian Ruins: A Memory Museum of the Mao Era*. She has also published essays on modern Chinese literature, cinema, and public culture in various journals and anthologies.

Jason McGrath is Associate Professor in the Department of Asian Languages and Literatures at the University of Minnesota, Twin Cities, where he also serves on the graduate faculty of Moving Image Studies. He is the author of *Postsocialist Modernity: Chinese Cinema, Literature, and Criticism in the Market Age*, and his essays on Chinese film have appeared in various journals and anthologies. His current projects include an anthology of Chinese writings on film and a book manuscript titled *Inscribing the Real: Realism and Convention in Chinese Cinema from the Silent Era to the Digital Age*.

Andy Rodekohr is Assistant Professor in the Department of East Asian Languages and Cultures at Wake Forest University, where he teaches Chinese literature, film, and culture. He is currently completing a book manuscript on the imagination, representation, and dissemination of crowds in modern China. His next project compares the emergence of the "new waves" of cinema in Hong Kong, Taiwan, and the PRC.

Carlos Rojas is Associate Professor of Chinese Cultural Studies, Women's Studies, and Arts of the Moving Image at Duke University. He is the author of *The Naked Gaze: Reflections on Chinese Modernity*, *The Great Wall: A Cultural History*, and *Homesickness: Culture, Contagion, and National Transformation in Modern China*. In addition, he is the co-editor of five volumes on Chinese literature and culture, and he has translated literary fiction by Yu Hua, Yan Lianke, and Ng Kim Chew.

Xiaobing Tang is Helmut F. Stern Professor of Modern Chinese Studies and Comparative Literature at the University of Michigan. His publications include *Visual Culture in Contemporary China: Paradigms and Shifts* and *Origins of the Chinese Avant-Garde: The Modern Woodcut Movement*. He is currently working on a study of wartime experiences in relation to forms of artistic creativity in 1930s–1940s China.

David Der-wei Wang is Edward C. Henderson Professor in Chinese Literature and Comparative Literature at Harvard University. His specialties are modern and contemporary Chinese and Sinophone Literature, late Qing fiction and drama, and comparative literary theory. Wang's recent publications include *Globalizing Chinese Literature* (co-edited with Jing Tsu) and *The Lyrical in Epic Time: Modern Chinese Intellectuals and Artists through the 1949 Crisis*. He is the editor of the forthcoming volume *A New Literary History of Modern China*, to be published by Harvard University Press.

Zhu Tao is Associate Professor and Deputy Head of the Department of Architecture at the University of Hong Kong. He practices in China and writes on contemporary Chinese architecture and urbanism. He has published essays in *AA Files, AD, a+u, Bauwelt, Domus*, and *Time + Architecture*. His book *Liang Sicheng and His Times* (Beijing: Imagist,

2014) examines Chinese architectural development in relation to Mao Zedong's sociopolitical campaigns of the 1950s. He received the Architectural Critics Award 2010 from the China Architecture Media Awards organized by China's mass media *Southern Metropolis Daily* in collaboration with eight major Chinese architectural magazines.

Index

Page numbers in *italic* refer to figures.

Harvard Contemporary China Series
(*out-of-print)

1. Jeffrey C. Kinkley, *After Mao: Chinese Literature and Society, 1978–1981*
2. Elizabeth J. Perry and Christine Wong, *The Political Economy of Reform in Post-Mao China*
3. Merle Goldman, Timothy Cheek, and Carol Lee Hamrin, *China's Intellectuals and the State: In Search of a New Relationship*
4. Joshua A. Fogel, *Ai Ssu-chi's Contributuion to the Development of Chinese Marxism*
5. Denis Fred Simon and Merle Goldman, *Science and Technology in Post-Mao China*
6. Roderick MacFarquhar, Eugene Wu, and Timothy Cheek, *The Secret Speeches of Chairman Mao: From the One Hundred Flowers to the Great Leap Forward*
7. Deborah Davis, *Chinese Society on the Eve of Tiananmen: The Impact of Reform*

*8. William A. Joseph, Christine P.W. Wong, and David Zweig (eds.), *New Perspectives on the Cultural Revolution*

9. Ellen Widmer and David Der-wei Wang, *From May Fourth to June Fourth: Fiction and Film in Twentieth-Century China*
10. Christina Gilmartin, Gail Hershatter, Lisa Rofel, and Tyrene White, *Engendering China: Women, Culture, and the State*
11. Andrew G. Walder, *Zouping in Transition: The Process of Reform in Rural North China*
12. Merle Goldman and Roderick MacFarquhar, *The Paradox of China's Post-Mao Reforms*
13. Merle Goldman and Elizabeth J. Perry, *Changing Meanings of Citizenship in Modern China*
14. Elizabeth J. Perry and Merle Goldman, *Grassroots Political Reform in Contemporary China*
15. Kevin J. O'Brien, *Popular Protest in China*
16. Martin King Whyte, *One Country, Two Societies: Rural-Urban Inequality in Contemporary China*
17. Sebastian Heilmann and Elizabeth J. Perry, *Mao's Invisible Hand: The Political Foundations of Adaptive Governance in China*
18. Jie Li and Enhua Zhang, *Red Legacies in China: Cultural Afterlives of the Communist Revolution*